91499

MUSLIM MINORITIES IN THE WEST

Visible and Invisible

EDITED BY
YVONNE YAZBECK HADDAD & JANE I. SMITH

ALTAMIRA PRESS
A Division of Rowman & Little
Walnut Creek • Lanham • I

ALTAMIRA
PRESS

D1376832

ALTAMIRA PRESS
A Division of Rowman & Littlefield Publishers, Inc.
1630 North Main Street, #367
Walnut Creek, CA 94596
www.altamirapress.com

Rowman & Littlefield Publishers, Inc.
4720 Boston Way
Lanham, MD 20706

12 Hid's Copse Road
Cumnor Hill, Oxford OX2 9JJ, England

British Library Cataloguing in Publication Information Available

Library of Congress Cataloging-in-Publication Data
Muslim minorites in the West : visible and invisible / edited by Yvonne Yazbeck Haddad, Jane I. Smith
    p. cm.
    Includes bibliographical references and index.
    ISBN 0-7591-0217-1 (cloth : alk. paper) — ISBN 0-7591-0218-X (pbk.: alk. paper)
    1. Muslims—Europe. 2. Europe—Ethnic relations. 3. Muslims—United States. 4. United States—Ethnic relations. I. Haddad, Yvonne Yazbeck, 1935– II. Smith, Jane I.

DI056.2.M87 M852 2002
305.6'97101821—dc21

                                                        2001045914

Printed in the United States of America

♾TM The paper used in this publication meets the minimum requirements of American National Standard for Information Sciences—Permanence of Paper for Printed Library Materials, ANSI/NISO Z39.48-1992.

CONTENTS

Introduction

THE PORTRAYAL OF MUSLIMS by the American media generally promotes the image of extremists who live and operate in strange and distant lands. The reality, however, is that Muslims are a permanent and growing element in the populations of nearly all Western nations, including those of North America, Western Europe, the Caribbean, South Africa, Australia, and New Zealand. As residents and citizens of these nations, they are our neighbors, our colleagues, and often our providers of goods and services. This significant demographic shift poses a major cultural challenge to the countries where Muslims are now citizens and to the governments and resident populations of those countries, who must find ways to meet that challenge. Although small numbers of Muslims found their way to Western lands over the course of the nineteenth century (and sometimes even earlier), it is only since the middle of the twentieth century that their presence has become so consistently visible.

Muslim immigration to the United States and Canada began in the late 1800s, when young men from the Middle East came to make their fortunes with the intention of returning home to marry and to rejoin their communities. Primarily laborers and peddlers, they moved across the continent, establishing small pockets of Muslim identity. Gradually they began to settle, giving up their dreams of returning home and beginning the process of "belonging" in America. In the 1920s, immigration was curtailed by laws that imposed quotas on certain nations and peoples, including Arabs. By the 1970s Muslims were arriving in the United States and Canada from countries well beyond the Middle East, including India and Pakistan, Eastern Europe, and the Soviet Union. Although many of the earlier immigrants had moved into both rural and urban areas, those coming after the war tended to come from urban backgrounds and made their homes in major cities like New York and Chicago. They were also more westernized and better educated than their predecessors.

The most recent wave of Muslim immigration began after 1965 with the repeal of the immigrant quota law. Although most Muslims chose to come to America for financial reasons or for a better education, others were fleeing political turmoil in their homelands. A number of specific events in various parts of the Islamic world—including ongoing strife in Israel and Palestine, the Lebanese civil war, the Iranian revolution, turmoil in

Afghanistan, Somalia, Bosnia, Chechnya and Kosovo, and civil wars in a number of African countries—brought immigrants and refugees to the West for escape and asylum. Of the approximately six million or more Muslims estimated to be resident in the United States today, more than a million are Pakistani and Indian, and a quarter million are originally from Shi'ite Iran. Increasing numbers are arriving from countries such as Indonesia and Malaysia.

America is unique among the nations of the world in the heterogeneity of its Muslim population. Some 30 to 35 percent of these Muslims are African American. Some evolved out of the original Nation of Islam established by Elijah Muhammad in the 1930s; others are new converts to one of a variety of Islamic movements, both mainline and sectarian. African-American Muslims claim a long heritage dating from the slave populations of West Africa that contained significant numbers of Muslims and are often referred to as "indigenous" Muslims. Many are Sunni Muslims, some have identified with the Muslim American Society of Imam Warith Deen Mohammed and others with other Sunni and Shi'i groups. A very small number of blacks—probably fewer than 50,000—are members of the Nation of Islam under the leadership of Louis Farrakhan. Canadian Muslims number somewhere around 500,000, while the various countries of Central and South America and the Caribbean are probably home to some two million Muslims.

As there is no accurate way of determining exactly how many Muslims reside in the United States, it is very difficult to assume the size of the Muslim population in Western Europe. Current estimates, however, place it at close to ten million. The largest concentrations are found in France (c. 3,000,000), the United Kingdom (c. 2,000,000), and Germany (c. 250,000), all former imperial powers. The composition of the European Muslim community is directly related to European expansion into Muslim lands in the nineteenth and twentieth centuries and to the political, economic, and cultural relationships that developed during the colonial period. The first Muslims to arrive in any numbers in Europe settled in France and were mainly North African and Senegalese mercenaries who had been recruited to fight in French colonial wars. Early settlers in Germany were Tartars and Bosnians who had served in the German army.

For the most part, however, Muslims came to Europe after the Second World War, recruited as "guestworkers" to help in the postwar efforts of economic reconstruction. Both Muslims and their European hosts expected that their stay would be limited and that they would return home. This did not typically occur, however, and, aided by government policies supporting unification of families, workers remained to become part of the permanent populations of nearly every European country. This has presented a variety of problems, some clearly economic, for host countries. For example, when the oil boycott that resulted from the Arab-Israeli war of 1973 led to economic depression and widespread unemployment, some European countries tried various forms of incentives to encourage Muslim workers to return to their home countries. Most declined, however, opting to settle permanently, and, as they were joined by family members from their home countries, added to the dramatically increasing number of Muslims in Europe. In the last decade of the twentieth century, asylum seekers and refugees from a number of troubled areas around the globe have joined long-term residents.

The majority of Muslim immigrants in Britain come from the Indian subcontinent, in large measure because the Commonwealth allowed citizens of its member nations to live in and become citizens of the British Isles. Most are lower-class laborers, with a small number of professionals and a few wealthy Gulf State Arabs. In France most of the growing Muslim population is from the North African countries of Tunisia, Algeria, and Morocco, former French colonial territories. A large number of guestworkers from Turkey make up the majority of the Muslim community in Germany, although they are increasingly being joined by Muslims from a variety of other countries. Muslim communities in the Netherlands and Belgium consist mainly of Turks and Moroccans. In Scandinavian countries, Muslim communities are composed of Turks and Slavs as well as Muslims from Morocco, Pakistan, and Egypt. Countries of Southern Europe, most notably Italy and Spain, received significant numbers of Muslims about a decade later, an immigration pattern related to the growth of their economies and the need for an enhanced labor force.

The patterns of Muslim immigration to the various countries of Europe and to North America naturally vary according to different historical and current conditions as well as to forms of government. They do share some commonalities, however, such as the relationship of immigration to economic factors and the thwarted expectation by both immigrants and hosts that those who came for employment would not remain. These commonalities also apply to the populations of two countries distant from Europe and America but still considered part of the West by virtue of Western settlement there, namely Australia and New Zealand. Populations are still very small (some 200,000 in Australia and probably not more than 20,000 in New Zealand), but the presence of these Muslims is increasingly being felt as they become more visible and learn to insist on the rights due to them as citizens of the land. The same, of course, is true of their counterparts in countries of the Western Hemisphere. Their struggles as minorities wanting to be recognized as functioning religious communities within their countries, while striving to combat the always-present reality of anti-Muslim prejudice in the resident population, have echoes in both Europe and America.

Muslim populations in South Africa, Latin America, and countries of the Caribbean have somewhat different histories, depending on the political and economic factors that have influenced their development. Percentages of Muslims in the overall population of these countries vary significantly, although in raw numbers they are never large. In Surinam, for example, some 35 percent (150,000) of the population is Muslim, and in Guyana the proportion is estimated at 15 percent (130,000). South Africa's Muslim population is somewhere in the vicinity of half a million. The best guess for the near future of countries in which there were notable Muslim populations in 2000, is that Muslim numbers will increase.

All of these Muslim populations share some issues and concerns, whereas others are distinctive and area specific. What they do have in common is the experience of a general movement from being unnoticed in their overall populations to moving into positions of greater visibility and more obvious public participation. This book offers an opportunity to look inside some of the Muslim minority communities found in different areas of the world, to trace the movement from invisibility to visibility, and to see what kinds of issues present themselves as Muslims assume their legitimate places in Western societies that may or may not be eager to acknowledge either their presence or their demands.

* * *

On "Cairo Street" at the Columbian Exhibition of 1893 in Chicago, visitors were intrigued by the Middle Eastern buildings and atmosphere, and fascinated by the belly dancer, but they were less generous in their assessment of Islamic religious practices, particularly the call to prayer. In chapter 6, Garbi Schmidt quotes newspaper reports that label the faithful "bedraggled Turks," and she cites an instance in which the audience ridicules the *muezzin* (the one calling the faithful to prayer) by likening his call to the noise of a dogfight.

Although not all citizens of countries in which immigrant Muslims now make their home may welcome their presence, Islam is no longer a "visiting exhibition" in the Americas, Europe, or the areas of former European settlement (referred to collectively as "the West"). The call to prayer, one of the most evident signs of Islamic presence, has moved, in the United States, from the world of make-believe a century ago to a visible, regular feature of the more than two thousand organized Muslim communities across the country. Until recently, the *muezzin* has called the Muslim faithful from large Islamic mosques and community centers to small urban storefront prayer halls, its volume by court decision not to exceed that of Christian church bells. On Friday, 8 December 2000, a new threshold was crossed in American recognition of the presence of Islam when the call to prayer rang out from the bell tower of Emory University in Atlanta and, for more than three minutes, was audible to the whole university and beyond. Encouraged by such public recognition, Muslims are hoping that other institutions will make similar gestures to acknowledge the presence of Islam in America.

In all of the areas of the world to which Muslims have immigrated and established residence in the last century, new dynamics have been created. Early arrivals to many cities of Europe found that invisibility was inevitable because they were forced to live on the periphery in ghettos set apart from the center of urban societies. Saphinaz-Amal Naguib refers to such ghettos in Oslo, Norway, as places of adaptation or transposition. It is usually not until they become more financially secure that immigrants are able to move into more central areas of cities. In some cases their physical isolation has been enforced by specific ordinances designed to exclude them from mainstream society.

Immigrant Muslims in the West have progressed differently but steadily from the realm of the "invisible"—newcomers to new lands with little public voice or recognition—to more visible modes of participation in the structures of the societies of which they are now a part. Increasingly aware of their constitutional rights as citizens of Western nations, they are establishing their own Islamic institutions and demanding the privileges guaranteed to religious minorities by various Western democracies. Their very visibility is serving to mount a challenge to the general notion of what it means to be a citizen of countries populated mainly by people raised in the West and dominated by a Western mentality that for many generations has simply assumed its superiority over the Third World. In Germany, for example, James Helicke notes that tension between liberal ideals of democracy and inclusion and the German notion of the exclusionary nature of citizenship has impeded the participation of immigrants from Turkey in the German political process.

The ways in which Muslims have moved from the margins of their adopted homelands toward a more apparent public presence have been determined both by the contexts from which they have come and by the new countries and cultures in which their emergence has taken place. In some cases, Muslims are welcomed because of the host country's need for their labor, although that welcome has had to be earned; in others, they are still, and sometimes even increasingly, looked on with suspicion, fear, and prejudice. The presence of Muslim minorities in the West has raised a variety of issues that are now part of public discourse. In the process, Muslims have become more visible. This visibility is due not merely to the growth in their numbers, but more importantly, to the dynamic of the choices they and the nations to which they have immigrated have had to make.

Issues of Integration and Assimilation

Migrant laborers in Western countries in the early and middle years of the twentieth century often came with the understanding that they would remain only so long as it was economically advantageous and then they would return home. As they began to realize that the dream of return was not to be fulfilled and that their futures were to be in the new country, most tried to integrate into their new society to whatever extent possible and to emphasize no more than necessary those things that would set them apart as different, such as religion. As is illustrated in these essays, large groups of Muslims in America, Europe, and areas of European settlement still hope for integration. Some have felt the need to assimilate into Western culture for their personal success so strongly that they have paid the price for their initiation by giving up their Muslim identity completely.

Others opt for a kind of median visibility somewhere between full identification with Islam or with their ethnic roots. In their essay on Muslims in the Detroit area, one of the most dense concentrations of Arabs and Muslims in the United States, Gary David and Kenneth Kahtan Ayouby discuss the "gray area" in which some Muslims find themselves as they seek a middle ground between identifying with their cultural heritage and trying to hide it. Muslim youth in Detroit confidently affirm their visibility as they "Arabize" or "Muslimize" cultural elements that appeal to young people in general, such as wearing tattoos using Muslim symbols or phrases or conspicuously posting signs of Islamic identification on their cars. Enhanced visibility itself may serve to foster the processes of integration, as illustrated in the case of the Emory call to prayer. John Voll describes the public commemoration in the Caribbean of the death of Imam Husayn, noting that, as a great variety of activities came to be associated with the event over the years and more local people began to participate, religion itself was downplayed in favor of cultural attraction. Muslim identity thus became contained within a cultural or ethnic association.

For African Americans in the earlier part of the twentieth century, attempts at assimilation into white society were common. The process of "passing," which Robert Dannin refers to as "invisible migration," was precisely an attempt to cover up one's true identity and assume another. Some accomplished it by saying they were of Semitic (thus dark-complexioned) heritage. Others found conversion to Islam to be a more viable alternative, although many of those who identified with the Nation of Islam, for example, emerged more visible than ever. A number of African Americans, as Dannin's article indicates, opted to establish isolated and contained communities in which strict Islam was practiced, where they were separated from the dominant culture and were free to define their identity, culture, and behavior. Examples of such communities include Dar al-Islam, Cleveland's University Islamic Brotherhood, and Ezaldeen Village in Philadelphia. Khalid Fattah Griggs in his essay talks about the hope of the Islamic Party of North America to establish a "Muslimtown" in Washington D.C.—a kind of replica of Chinatown, a separate Islamic community that is culturally distinctive. The relative isolation of such communities gives participants a sort of societal invisibility, on the one hand, and on the other, provides opportunities for these individuals to be more visible than is possible in white society. Such communities represented an Islam that expressed a faith of resistance and liberation and a rejection of Western domination and enslavement. Members were visibly separating themselves not only from the white context but also from the ghetto itself, as they sought liberation from the lives of despair, drugs, and dehumanization to which American culture had consigned them.

Today, in many parts of the world, Muslims who are members of minority communities are increasingly aware that when they congregate, become visible, they may invite various forms of retribution. Visibility may lead to identification as dangerously foreign, ominous, and threatening given the anti-Muslim atmosphere that currently permeates Western society. Many Muslims, therefore, conclude that by assimilating and remaining invisible they will not be seen as a threat to society and can live their lives without fear of harassment. Despite these concerns, however, growing numbers of immigrant Muslims in all areas of the Western world are now opting to be more visible. Until recently, many Muslims wanted to stay away from *kafir* (unbeliever) society; now they are organizing for public participation. In America, for example, the fact that Muslims are increasingly involved in politics—not simply voting, but forming political action committees and urging Muslims to run for public office—indicates, as Agha Saeed points out, that Muslims are buying more fully into the hope that political participation can help determine national policies that will serve their interests and their aspirations. As citizens of a society that promotes participatory democracy, they are affirming their right to argue their own perspectives and values.

Loosening the Ties that Bind

Influences from overseas, and connectedness with the Islamic countries from which immigrants have come, affect visibility in the new lands in several ways. Chain migration tends to retard the integration process. Those who have immigrated earlier often help new immigrants in negotiating living space, finding jobs, and adjusting to a new rhythm of life. At the same time, they, in turn, are influenced by the new immigrants who serve to deter assimilation by reminding the earlier immigrants of overseas values and cultural taboos and holding them accountable for maintaining those values and taboos in the new environment.

In certain instances the host country itself may contribute to a solidification of cultural particularity in which identity with the country of origin is affirmed. Anthony Johns and A. Saeed, for example, tell us that in Australia the assimilationist model that fosters invisibility has been replaced by government policies favoring multiculturalism. As a result, religious and ethnic communities are encouraged to speak with their own voices. Such cultural and ethnic identification can foster a visibility that subsequent generations might want to reject. First-generation Muslim immigrants are often reluctant to leave behind particularizing dress, or language, or religious practices that are essential to their own sense of identity. This reluctance sometimes frustrates their children who are in search either of greater invisible assimilation or of a more essential Islam, not colored by regional variations and practices.

International events almost inevitably increase the visibility of immigrant Muslims. At the time of the 1973 oil boycott, for example, general feelings of hostility among Westerners increased indiscriminately toward the Middle East, Arabs, and Muslims and were expressed in the press and other forms of the media. The oil boycott put Europe and America, seen by Muslims as perpetrators of colonial hegemony before and after World War II respectively, on notice that oil-producing countries are capable of independent action that might serve to threaten Western interests. Such concerns inevitably heightened the visibility of immigrants from these countries, as well as of Muslims in general, and tended to increase the stereotypical presentation of Arabs and Muslims in the Western media.

Another area of impact has been the growing association of Muslims with terrorism. Unfortunately, terrorist acts become associated with the whole community, rather than those individuals who perpetrate the acts; however, it is also true that there are certain interests that find it expedient to promote such ideas, especially as they relate to the foreign policy interests of some nations. Because of this, Muslims are depicted as enemies of what the West stands for, and Muslim residents become the scapegoats of right-wing and racist elements in Western society.

As they seek to determine the extent to which they want to be visible or invisible in a new culture, Muslim immigrants must think carefully about the nature of their ties with their homelands. Naguib argues that in Norway, for instance, discussion of such issues did not occur until recently. Now, some twenty-five years after Muslims began to establish themselves as a community in Norway, younger Muslims are heard talking about multiple cultural identities. It is not clear as yet, Naguib says, whether such conversations are moving Muslims toward more self-conscious Islamic identity (visibility) or toward increased secularization (invisibility).

Discrimination

It is the fate of immigrants to face a variety of forms of discrimination based on a great many factors: race and ethnicity, inability to speak the language of the land, dress, customs, and religion. For Muslims, this discrimination has been aggravated as a consequence of growing hostility towards Islam in the West, sometimes called "Islamophobia." Recently, the religion factor has been especially significant. The stereotyping that has come from media responses to international events usually has repercussions on Muslims living in minority communities in the West. They become the focus of attention and of scapegoating.

Islamophobia results from the religion being depicted as violent, and the attribute of violence then stigmatizes minority Muslims. The situation gets even worse when, as has been the case in Chicago and other U.S. cities, Muslims are accused of being connected to and financing radical Islamic groups in the Middle East; accusations that receive great attention from the local and national press as well as from government security agencies.

Efforts of the host country to demonize Islam or its citizens have served to pave the way toward common religious identity and an affirmation of common beliefs and practices as symbols of distinction. During periods of crisis, many Muslims have tried to seek invisibility by extreme measures such as dissimulation, passing as members of other ethnic groups or religious affiliations (as American blacks did after Reconstruction), or even using peroxide to lighten their skin, as was reported of some women during the Iranian Revolution. The learned response is that visibility at such times invites further discrimination. All the studies in this collection confirm that it is more the cultural and political affirmations being promoted by various groups in the name of Islam and less the religion of Islam that cause fear and concern.

However, Muslims in a number of countries are also coming to learn that affirming their rights as citizens in visible reaction and response to negative portrayals of Islam can be very effective. It not only consolidates the community in a visible way, but it serves as an effective counter to the continued propagation of negative images. The Council for American Islamic Relations in the United States, for example, has done a great deal to raise the visibility of American Muslims, both immigrant and African American, precisely through its efforts to identify and redress instances of discrimination against Muslims in the workplace, in schools, in hospitals, and in other public contexts. African American prison inmates have fought what they perceive to be prejudicial circumstances by using the legal system to gain recognition for Islam and to achieve the right to eat, fast, dress, and pray in an Islamic manner. The result has been a raising of consciousness about Islam, and even a growing appreciation for the faith, in ways that are unprecedented on the American scene.

Events overseas have also precipitated violent attacks on the Muslim community (such as mosque burning, bombing, and trashing), which have sometimes evoked a sympathetic and helpful response from many churches and synagogues. Religious institutions have worked cooperatively to repair and rebuild mosques and have helped foster a community image of a moderate and socially responsible Islam. Arguably, it is the very visibility of Islam that has made it the target of such attacks, particularly in times of international crisis. Ironically, perhaps, the more extreme such violence has been, the more it has served to enhance both the cohesion of the community and the community's willingness to be visible, as well as bring about the cooperation and recognition of other civic and religious groups. As both the visibility and clout of Muslims have increased, the Muslim community has become recognized as a legitimate part of various national identities.

It is also obvious to Muslims in many different minority situations that race plays a significant role in questions of religious discrimination, and that such discrimination also can work insidiously within the Muslim community itself. In South Africa, as Tamara Sonn points out, Muslims share the double invisibility, as well as the double discrimination, of being both colored and Muslim. African Americans experience the same thing. Issues of visibility and discrimination also arise within Muslim communities themselves. Sylviane Diouf's chapter shows how Sahelian Muslims in France are overlooked within the Muslim immigrant community because of prejudice among North Africans, Middle Easterners, and Turks against sub-Saharan Africans. In the United States some African Americans express frustration about what they see as the attitude of immigrant Muslims. Many blacks feel that they are the "original" Muslims of America, both because they are descendants of slaves, some of whom were Muslim, and because the Nation of Islam and other so-called Muslim groups have been present in the country since the 1930s. Nonetheless, they sometimes are treated by their immigrant Muslim brothers and sisters as if they are invisible.

Women in Immigrant Muslim Communities

Perhaps no topic relating to issues of visibility and invisibility for Muslims is more beguiling than that of women, particularly given Western perceptions of Muslim women as traditionally absent from any kind of public view. It is a fact that circumstances for Muslim women throughout the twentieth century in predominantly Islamic countries have changed over the years, at different paces and in different ways, depending on state policies, current ideologies, and the impact of war. This is reflected in the immigrant communities in the West. Many Muslim leaders argue that a primary task facing immigrant Islam is determining what kinds of visible roles women are to play. Increasingly, women themselves are active participants in that discussion.

There is no question that the presence of Muslim women as part of the immigration process has made the Muslim community as a whole more visible. While early immigrants were predominantly men, those who chose to settle generally married local women who often did not adhere to the cultural practices of the immigrant husbands. Sometimes the only women available for marriage were themselves from "invisible" parts of the society, as Sameena Yasmeen relates of Aboriginal women in Australia. In the process, the men became less visible because they accommodated to local culture. Rarely did any of these women adopt forms of Islamic dress. The situation of single men coming alone as immigrant workers to Western countries changed for a number of economic and social reasons. Families of workers were brought for reunification, and other workers immigrated as family units, so Muslim men no longer sought partners from the host culture. In most cases, however, the immigrant women chose to remain at home, finding their identity as wives and mothers rather than as public participants in the new society. Thus, they stayed publicly invisible while at the same time remaining very important internal players in the task of creating new parameters of identity for the immigrant community.

In more recent years, however, that situation too has changed. Many women have had to enter the workforce for economic reasons. In doing so, they have encountered a variety of difficulties, such as issues concerning the appropriateness of a particular job for Islamic women, problems with language, concerns about who will be responsible for children and aging parents left at home, and apprehension about tightened family budgets. Many who do work have clerical or sales jobs or are laborers, with few reaching high status as professionals. Nonetheless from the 1980s on, as Sonn observes in relation to South Africa, increased literacy and economic independence have given some women more autonomy and more public visibility. Women's organizations, networks, and forms of communication, both locally and internationally through the Internet and women's journals and publications, have helped create a sense of communal visibility, at least for the more educated of immigrant women in the West. Many immigrant women are now becoming literate and, in the process, are affirming their right to participate in the process of interpreting religious texts.

One of the most contentious issues for immigrant women in almost all countries to which Muslims have moved is, of course, that of Islamic dress and, specifically, the headscarf. Ironically, while Islamic dress (long skirts, long sleeves, and the scarf) renders most of the female figure invisible to the eyes of strangers, it also serves to dramatically raise the visibility of women who choose to wear it.

Conservative dress, of course, takes many forms. Labor migration from Turkey and North Africa, for example, has been predominantly from the rural areas where rural habits are maintained. Clothing, therefore, is traditional, and wearing the scarf continues to be the sign of modesty. Other women are choosing new forms of Islamic dress, often very modish at the same time that it is appropriately concealing. Many recent immigrants, particularly political refugees and asylum seekers, are from countries that have cracked down on religious practices and banned the veil from official public space. For these women, the West, at least theoretically, provides the freedom to be Muslim in the way that one chooses. For many women, wearing the scarf is now no longer an act of defiance against an unwilling government but a gesture of obedience to what is believed to be a divine commandment. Women who seek their identity in contemporary Islamist movements resonate with the ideology that insists on veiling as a guarantee of protection for those who fulfill their Islamic obligation to participate in the public sphere. Such visibility enhances the modern Islamic vision of a woman as the maintainer of culture and the repository of Islamic values. For other Muslim women, the headscarf serves to focus their creative and artistic abilities as they design acceptable, yet sometimes very contemporary and functional, dress for various kinds of activities.

Has the West in fact fulfilled the hope of many Muslim women that they will have the freedom to dress as they choose? Certainly not in all cases. In nearly all countries where Muslim minorities are growing and becoming more visible, there are clear instances of discrimination against the veil. In France, for example, women and girls are not allowed to veil in the public schools. Immigrant women in many countries report that they were not given a job because they wore the veil, or that, despite meritorious performance, they failed to be promoted. With every instance of discrimination in which women make public their complaint, especially if that complaint is publicized by Islamic groups or organizations seeking parity, the visibility of the Muslim community, and in particular that of Muslim women, in the West rises.

And yet, there is arguably a way in which the strength of Islamic movements in the West, the support given to the development of a more public Islam, and the reaffirmation of a distinctly Islamic community reinforced by instances of discrimination against Muslims also serve to make women more invisible. Rather than opting for a more culturally accepted role as simply another religious denomination in Europe, America, or elsewhere, many Muslims are insisting on creating a culturally different, specifically Islamic, community. From this perspective, the veil acts as a shield against the penetration of the other. But at the same time, it may ensure that women are symbolically relegated to less visible positions, especially in the mosque. When high minaret mosques are built as the established symbol of Islamic presence and visibility, they serve as a reminder to Muslims and to the societies in which they are erected that there is a specifically Islamic way of doing things. Because traditional mosques have no place for women, their inclusion at all is an accommodation to changing circumstances. But the space women occupy, which is apart from men and the imam—at the back of the mosque, in an upstairs balcony, or even in a separate room where they can only hear the prayer broadcast over television or a loudspeaker—ensures that they will be invisible to the men of the community, at least for the duration of the prayer service.

Support and Propagation of the Faith

The growing awareness of Islam as a notable component of the religious fabric of Western societies, and of Muslims as active players in the process of making the faith more visible, is undeniable. It is not only the growth of Islam in terms of demographics that has led to that visibility but the specific efforts of some Muslims in the West to encourage and support the presence of Islam, to facilitate its practice, and to participate in its propagation both within and without the community.

Just as veils, and the beards that are increasingly chosen by Muslim men in imitation of the practice of the Prophet Muhammad, are the most obvious personal symbols of Islam, so the mosque is the most striking public testimony to the growing presence of Islam in the West. As a number of contributors to this book report, beginning in the 1970s and 1980s, Islamic visibility forcibly burst in on the West. To a great extent, the physical manifestation of this new visibility was due to the sudden wealth of oil-producing Gulf States and their efforts to financially support Islamic communities in lands in which Islam was a minority religion. The subsequent growth in mosque construction was due not only to the growing size of the Muslim community and its need for places of congregation and worship but to the new availability of funds. Obviously, large mosques are not a feature of every minority Muslim community—many Muslims come together for prayer in storefront buildings, converted flats and houses, and any other structures available to them. Nonetheless, in most major cities of the West, large mosques and Islamic community centers are present and visible, acting as reminders to the rest of society that Islam is here to stay.

One of the most significant concerns of Muslim immigrant communities (as well as of African Americans) is the availability of appropriately trained leadership. At first, immigrants did not have imams. Instead, ill-prepared individuals would rotate in serving as leaders of the prayer. When Muslims began to grow in numbers and establish religious organizations, the situation began to change. Many minority Muslim communities have gained greater visibility through the financial support of Muslims abroad, particularly those in the Gulf States. Such assistance reached its zenith in the 1980s, when Muslims in non-Muslim countries were able not only to construct very visible mosques, Islamic centers, and private schools, but to acquire trained leadership from overseas. While such leadership has been warmly welcomed, it has also presented the immigrant communities with some immediate problems.

The imported imams, whether sent by foreign governments or independently recruited by mosque organizations to serve immigrant communities, by definition, tend to propagate the official policies of the sponsoring government or the ideologies to which they subscribe. Immigrant Muslims have had to think carefully about the price of accepting either financial or ideological support from overseas while they struggle to understand their new environments and negotiate a place for the community. In the process, some tend to create new forms of Islamic identity that are indigenous to their host cultures. Imported leadership has not always understood or appreciated some of these new accommodations. Many communities report that their imams are not fully conversant in the language of the host country, they are unfamiliar with and sometimes quite opposed to Western culture and society and therefore are not able to be fully relevant to their new circumstances, and, especially, they alienate the youth. The need is great in all immigrant communities for indigenous leadership, especially for second generation immigrants who are coming of age and whose parents refuse to have foreign ways and interpretations imposed on them.

Meanwhile, pressures continue to be exerted for connectedness among individuals, groups, and organizations within Islamic societies. Many authors in this collection report how important the establishment of Muslim organizations at the local and national levels is to the heightened visibility of the Muslim community. William Shepard notes that FIANZ (Federation of Islamic Associations of New Zealand) was formed to coordinate activities of local groups and to maintain contacts between Muslims in New Zealand and those overseas. Australia, during the 1980s, saw a rapid growth in organizational development, including a number of local—and one national—women's groups. The Islamic Council of Norway, created in 1992, serves as an umbrella group trying to represent the interests of all Norwegian Muslims. Such organizations are eligible to receive government funding, which would not be available to individual groups at the local level. Sometimes national organization efforts bring together groups that represent different cultures and national origins, as in Germany where Turks and non-Turks, in banding together to achieve legal recognition similar to the recognition accorded Christian churches, have located their central authority in the Islamic Council for the Federal Republic of Germany. South African Muslims began to gain visibility when they organized in the 1970s and 1980s into movements for social justice, not only for Muslims but for all victims of apartheid. These types of movements are even more public today.

For Muslims, propagation of the faith is a commandment from God explicitly articulated in the Qur'an. More than a century ago, Alexander Webb, an American convert to Islam, was preaching and publishing one of the first Islamic journals, *The Muslim World*, in the attempt to attract others to the faith. Today, religious Muslims, through a variety of means, are trying to tell non-Muslims about Islam and to call back to the fold cultural Muslims who are not publicly practicing the faith. Mosques, trained imams, and Muslim central organizations all serve this purpose, as do books, journals, films, and videotapes, as well as extremely creative and widespread use of electronic media and other forms of information dissemination, which Abdul Hamid Lotfi illustrates in the chapter on communicating Islam in America. Today Muslim electronic engineers and Web page builders have "colonized" cyberspace and constructed a kind of virtual Islam that not only seeks to maintain the faithful in the religion but also declares the truth of Islam to the whole world. At least in America, the community has acquired enough sophistication to be comfortable in demonstrating its different voices. Not everyone, however, shares that comfort. The visibility of the virtual community has invited attack and criticism from outside groups who do not like Islam and from Muslims with alternative views of how Islam should be packaged for American or world consumption.

A number of international Islamic organizations, such as the Tablighi Jamaat of India, work actively for the propagation of the faith, *da'wa*, in various countries of the world. Muslims who are involved in interfaith activities through dialogue or cooperative social action debate the extent to which such efforts should be the occasion for an extension of propagation. In America, university campuses and prisons are especially fertile fields for potential conversion; in the latter case, proselytization is pursued especially, but not exclusively, by African Americans. Efforts to create programs for training Muslim chaplains to work in schools, prisons, hospitals, and the military are growing rapidly.

Other elements of an increasingly visible presence of Islam in the West mark, for many, a kind of "coming of age" for Islam as a minority religion. In many countries efforts to provide Islamic education for children are resulting in afternoon and weekend programs at local mosques, more home schooling provided within the community, and the construction of Islamic parochial schools. Whether or not to send children to separate schools is a major issue for many Muslims, as they debate costs, quality of education, and the relative merits of separating their children from the local learning environment. Within the public schools, Muslims are vocal in their concerns that physical education and sex education be provided in acceptable ways. These concerns raise the visibility of both the children and of the community. Islamic holidays are being emphasized, with many parents helping their children understand that Christian observances may not be appropriate for Muslims, who have their own occasions for celebration. Greater visibility is given within the Muslim community to observances, such as fasting during the month of Ramadan, at the same time that Western media are providing fairer and more sympathetic coverage of the rituals and observances of the faith.

Among the benefits of increased visibility for Muslims are public recognition, inclusion, and representation, as well as the ability to help shape public policies. Visibility also provides a platform from which Muslims can demand minority rights, mainstream acceptance of practices that differ from the prevailing norm, and equal status for alternative values and different definitions of what is morally, ethically, or even legally responsible. From their position of increased visibility, Muslims in many Western societies are being vocal about their demands for appropriate facilities in which they can practice their faith, for proper burial grounds where the dead can be interred according to Islamic law and custom, for slaughterhouses in which animals can be butchered in the Islamic way, for release time from schools and businesses to observe religious festivals and holidays, and for fair and unbiased media coverage.

It is clear that Muslim communities in Western Europe, in America, and in areas of earlier European settlement are growing both in numbers and in public visibility. As this growth takes place, accommodation on the part of Muslims to their new environment and on the part of the host culture to its new citizens, must, out of necessity, take place. Many factors still serve to mitigate that accommodation: the different cultural associations and pressures within each community; the response of Muslims to what is often perceived as a prevailing culture of Western secularism; the influence of Islamist activities abroad and of Western attitudes toward Muslims as a result of those activities; the range of views as to appropriate roles for Muslim women; and the hope of defining Islam as part of, yet distinguishable from, Western society as a whole. Many decisions have yet to be made, and the Islamic community is still clearly in transition. The question now is not *whether* Islam is a visible religion of the West, but *how* and *in what ways* it will come to define itself.

THE AMERICAN EXPERIENCE I

Spreading the Word: Communicating Islam in America

I

ABDUL HAMID LOTFI

Introduction

THE SPECTACULAR GROWTH of the American Muslim community in the closing decades of the twentieth century has led to an equally impressive growth of that community's efforts to communicate about itself and its faith. This growing flow of information is disseminated through a variety of formal and informal channels. American Muslims now appreciate the need to communicate about Islam and about themselves if they are to play a significant role in shaping the lives of their children and in modifying the negative perceptions of Islam and the Muslims in America.[1]

The need for communication can be traced back to those African Muslim slaves who used their Arabic literacy to point to their religious identity[2] and has been important to the community ever since. Mohammad Alexander Russell Webb (1846–1916), one of the earliest American converts to Islam, founded the American Islamic Propagation Society and the Moslem World Publishing Company. He published a journal, an illustrated prayer manual, and three books on Islam to familiarize the American public with his new faith. The individual efforts of the early pioneers who relied on the printed word have given way to concerted group efforts to communicate about Islam and the Muslims. The bulk of this communication today is carried out by such influential organizations as the Islamic Society of North America (ISNA), the Islamic Circle of North America (ICNA), and the Muslim American Society (MAS) of Warith Deen Mohammed, as well as by major educational foundations such as IQRA' and publishing corporations such as Kazi in Chicago. Professional associations and individuals also continue to play an important role in the dissemination of information about Islam.[3]

Information sharing takes place through personal encounters wherever Muslims worship, study, trade, work, or relax. Publishers, booksellers, software providers, and nationwide or regional conventions also play a significant role in the production of materials and their dissemination among community members. Internet sites, Webradio, and WebTV also serve as forums for networking, information gathering, and information exchange. *Da'wa* (spreading the faith) activities are unique contexts where information about Islam is imparted to non-Muslims with the purpose of inviting them into the fold of Islam.

Therefore, the translation of Islamic texts plays a major role in the dissemination of Islamic scholarship among English speakers.

Print

Islamic periodical literature has been produced in the United States for more than a century, dating back to May 1893, when Webb started *The Muslim World*, "a sixteen-page publication with various articles expounding upon and defending Islam in American society."[4] But it was only in the early twentieth century that products of the Arabic press, including many Islamic publications, began to appear in earnest. Sulayman Nyang reports that "one hundred and two Arabic language newspapers and periodicals came into existence between 1898 and 1929."[5] For understandable reasons, the mortality rate for these publications was very high, and only a few survived and succeeded. *Kombi*, the first Albanian newspaper, came out in 1906, but quickly disappeared to be succeeded in 1918 by *The Albania*. Writing in 1926, M. M. Aijian mentions the existence of a Turkish paper, *Sedai Vatar* (The Fatherland) and two Arabic papers, *El-Beyan* (The News) and *Kawkab* (Star).[6] Arab publications such as *As-Sirat*, edited by Mohni in the early 1920s, circulated news about the Muslim world and about the Arab community in America. More popular among Muslim groups, however, were the mostly short-lived newsletters that announced community news and printed general features about the Muslim individuals and communities. It was only in the 1940s that the Cedar Rapids Muslim community began to publish a regular newsletter, and in the 1950s that the Bosnian-American Cultural Association sponsored the short-lived *Glasnick Muslimana*. *The Muslim Star* was irregularly published throughout the decade.

Publications by sects who claimed Islam as their religion began with *Moslem Sunrise*, created by the Ahmadi missionary Mufti Muhammad Sadiq. *The Moorish Guide* was launched in the late 1920s by the Moorish Science Temple of America, while the Nation of Islam published the short-lived *Final Call*, followed in 1961 by *Muhammad Speaks*.[7] Two decades later Louis Farrakhan reintroduced *The Final Call*. These publications carried information and features about Islam around the world and about the Muslims in America. Today, Islamic sects continue to issue a variety of publications promoting their organizations, movements, and belief systems.

Over the past two decades, American Muslims have produced an ever growing number of periodicals. The now-defunct *Al-Ittihad* played a major role in the dissemination of orthodoxy and news about the American Islamic community throughout the 1980s and well into the 1990s. The widely distributed *Newsletter* of the Muslim Student Association of North America also played a vital role in spreading news and information about Islam before it gave way to its successor, *Islamic Horizons*. Muslim periodical literature is represented by a variety of weekly, monthly, bimonthly, quarterly, and irregular publications. Some are put out by national organizations, but the majority are issued by Islamic centers for a local or regional audience. Institutional mosques, particularly those located in correctional facilities, produce an undetermined number of newsletters.[8]

Today, America has no hard copy Islamic daily; the closest thing to a daily newspaper is provided by the coverage of Islamic news found on the Internet site iviews.com. For more than two decades, the weekly press was limited to the Muslim American Society's

Muslim Journal[9] until a group of Muslim businessmen and intellectuals of South Asian origin began publishing *The Muslim Observer* in Livonia, Michigan, in 1998, one of the very few Islamic publications that can be accessed online without subscription.[10]

Islamic monthly and bimonthly publications include a growing number of titles published almost exclusively by national organizations. The most widely distributed are *Islamic Horizons*, the star publication of the Islamic Society of North America; *The Message*, an influential publication by the Islamic Circle of North America; *The Muslim Magazine*,[11] issued by the Islamic Supreme Council of America; *Al Jumuah*, the organ of the American Islamic Revival Association; and *The Minaret*,[12] a bimonthly published by the Islamic Center of Southern California. *The American Muslim*,[13] published by the Muslim American Society since January 2000, follows the line of Hassan al-Banna[14] and is accessible online.[15]

Sufi orders are also engaged in the business of communicating about Islam through their *da'wa* and educational programs and their dynamic publishing houses that provide translations of Arabic texts. One of the fastest growing Sufi orders in America, the Naqshbandi-Haqqani Order, led by the controversial[16] Shaykh Hisham Kabbani, is very active in the communications world. It publishes the women's journal *Kamilat* and the bimonthly journal *The Muslim Magazine*, launched in June 1998. In addition, it maintains five popular Internet sites[17] and organizes biannual international Islamic Unity conferences in America. The Naqshbandi Foundation for Islamic Education (NFIE) sponsors an annual celebration of the Mawlid an-Nabi, during which Sufis and scholars of various Sufi affiliations give presentations. It also publishes a scholarly journal, *Sufi Illuminations*.

Regional and local publications, many of which are or were issued on a regular basis, include *The Arab-American Message*, published in Detroit, and *Al-Jihadul Akbar* and *Al-Nathir*, organs of the now defunct Dar-ul-Islam Movement. On the Eastern Seaboard, *The Islamic Revolution* and *The New Muslim Outlook* are published, conveying a radical and fundamentalist message, as well as *Islam*, a publication of the Muslim Development Corporation of Alexandria, Virginia. The West Coast provides such publications as *the Al-Bayan Bulletin*, a monthly publication covering international news from a radical Muslim perspective; *The Muslim Business Development Forum*; *The Bulletin of the Islamic Center of Washington*; and *The Western Sunrise*, which promotes Sunni Islam to native-born Americans. Other West Coast publications include the quarterly *The Search*, *New Trends* (Jama'at al-Muslimoon), *Al-Raya* (Hizbal-Tahrir), the *Muslim Magazine* (Naqshbandiyya order), *The Orange Crescent* (Orange County, California), *Ad-Dunya*, *Al Basheer*, *Al Moghtarib*, *Al Nur*, *Al-Qalam*, *Al Talib*, the Arabic monthly *Al Zaitonah*, *Encounter with Islam*, *Hudaa Magazine*, *Iqraa*, *The Light*, *The Muslim Commentary*, *The Muslim Monitor*, *New Dawn*, *Siratul Mustaqeem: Islamic Journal*, and *The Thinker*. All of these publications carry articles and news about Islam in America. Children's and women's magazines include *Umm Magazine*, *The Muslim Family*, and *Mother's Sense*. Among Shi'a publications are *Islamic Affairs*, published by the Islamic Society of Georgia, *Islamic Review*, started in the 1970s by the Shi'a Association of North America, *The Message of Islam*, a bimonthly magazine, and *Husaini News*.

Muslim professional associations issue a number of quarterlies: *American Journal of Islamic Finance* (California), *American Journal of Islamic Social Sciences* (Virginia), *Journal of the International Institute of Islamic and Arabic Studies* (Indiana), *Journal of Islamic Law* (Maryland), *Journal of the Islamic Medical Association* (Georgia), and *The Muslim Teacher's College Journal* (Virginia).

But the most widely used means of communication within Muslim communities are the community newspapers and newsletters, published by the hundreds, that represent good sources of information about the Muslim community in America.

Despite its diversity and recent development, the Islamic press in America still suffers from the lack of stable human and financial resources and the thin distribution of Muslims across the country. These problems adversely affect the publications of major Islamic organizations like ISNA and, certainly, the journals of professional associations. Despite these problems, the Islamic press testifies to the vitality of the Muslim community in America and its desire to communicate its values, hopes, and concerns.

Radio and Television

Unlike other religious groups in America, Muslims in this country have made very little use of radio and television to disseminate their views. Their absence from this field has been due to a variety of reasons including financial and human resources. Warith Deen Mohammed's Muslim American Society has traditionally bought time on various local radio and television stations to broadcast its weekly programs,[18] but very few other Muslim organizations have done so. Their leaders and spokesmen are on the air only when invited by commercial or educational radio and television stations.

This situation has changed dramatically with the advent of Webradio and WebTV, and a number of computer-savvy South Asian Muslims have started broadcasting on the Internet. The use of free software to access audio and video clips has opened the way for Muslim broadcasting on the Internet. (It is noteworthy that, although broadcasting uses Arabic for Qur'anic recitation, English is the most widely used language in Islamic Webcasting.) The most dynamic Webradio stations include Radio Al-Islam, RadioIslam, Muslim Wavelength Radio, and IANA Radionet.

Radio Al-Islam[19] provides live broadcast programs on a number of channels dedicated to Hajj, science, religious debate, conferences, and education. It airs programs on such Islamic subjects as beliefs, social relations, economic and political systems, the *Qur'an* and the hadith, and Jesus and Prophet Muhammad.[20] Launched by The Sound Vision Foundation, a communications branch of the Islamic Circle of North America, RadioIslam[21] is one of the very few daily radio stations dedicated to communicating Islam on the Internet through programs focusing on the American Muslim community. It provides news, features, and entertainment, weekly talk shows on community and family issues, audio recordings of children's stories, and links to audio broadcasts in several languages.

Muslim Wavelength Radio,[22] begun by the Muslim Public Affairs Council, communicates on a number of social and political issues concerning American Muslims.[23] The majority of its programs involve intellectuals and religious leaders, such as Maher M. Hathout, Salam al-Marayati, and Aslam Abdullah. The *da'wa*-oriented ISNA in June 1999 began IANA Radionet,[24] providing two hours of live daily programs, as well as archived programs that include Islamic classes, *khutbas* (Friday sermons), news, stories and entertainment for children, and documentaries on Muslim issues and countries.

At present, television Webcasting is not as widespread as radio Webcasting because of the community's limited resources and the shortage of qualified volunteers. Television

Webcasting often relies on programs scanned from satellite television from Muslim countries, including NileTV, Al Jazira, Dubai, Jordan One, and Saudi One. These programs bring the Muslim community into immediate contact with the rest of the Muslim world.

Internet Sites

Created by Tim Berners-Lee in 1991, the Web is a very recent development in communications technology, and yet it has vastly transformed both the way we exchange information and the world in which we communicate.[25] The Web is open to a variety of sites that provide information about Islam, including official Web sites of Islamic organizations, university resource guides on Islam, and private, unofficial home pages.[26]

Although the Web is used primarily by corporations, Muslims have turned to the Internet to compensate for their modest presence on radio and television in America. Traditionally, Muslims have favored direct contact and the use of media such as pamphlets, books, audiotapes, and videos. Now they are increasingly turning to the Internet, where sites are relatively cheap to produce and operate and where information is easily accessible to an ever growing public. The World Wide Web has been extensively colonized by Islamic sites[27] of varying quality and life spans. The American Muslim community seems to have very quickly realized the importance of this new medium for promoting itself, and for reinforcing intercommunity ties.

Most Islamic Internet sites duplicate information available in print and offer lists of links to sites from which additional information and materials such as pamphlets, books, software, audiotapes, and videos can be obtained. Some sites, particularly those of Shi'a and Sufi groups, offer tours of their facilities and often provide coverage of religious events and speeches in real audio or real video. Islamic organizations and individuals use the Internet primarily to deliver information about themselves, promote their views, disseminate their messages cheaply, and generate revenues through the sale of books, tapes, and other Islamic paraphernalia. Webmasters hope to get people interested enough in Islam and the Muslims to make contact with a mosque or an Islamic center for further information. The Frequently Asked Questions (FAQs) appearing on key Islamic sites provide short answers for essential questions about Islam.

Mastering the Web

American Muslims are not only using the Web, they are also trying to adapt it to meet their specific needs. Thus, ISNA has organized a number of conferences and workshops, such as the "Muslims and the Information Superhighway Conference," hosted by Indiana University and Purdue University at Indianapolis in April 1998, under the chairmanship of Syed Imtiaz Ahmad.[28] The conference "met to assess the current state of Islam on the Internet from a global perspective, and the strategies needed to ensure that Islam is properly represented and expanded on the Internet."[29] Some of the chief preoccupations of Muslims are concern for the authentication and certification of Islamic content on the Internet, the development of search engines specifically designed for the exploration of Islamic data, and the development of a vocabulary, like HTML (Hyper Text Markup Language), called IDML (Islamic Data Markup Language) to standardize the storage of Islamic content on the Internet.

The second conference, organized by ISNA in May 1999, entitled "Media for the Next Millennium," aimed at bringing together interested Internet professionals, content producers, and users to investigate ways of improving the Islamic communication channels to reinforce community ties among Muslims in North America and worldwide. This conference dealt with knowledge presentation and acquisition, Muslim Web site development, evaluation of Islam on Web sites, formal courses and academic programs over the Internet, virtual schools and libraries, e-commerce for Islamic products, and the role of the Internet in the social and moral development of the young. Speakers included Muslim software development entrepreneurs such as Safi Qureyshe, President of Skyline Ventures; Atiq Raza, President of AMD; and Sohaib Abbasi, Senior Vice President of Oracle.[30]

Muslims on the Internet

It is impossible to keep count of Islamic sites on the Internet, as new ones are set up almost daily. Islamic organizations of all kinds have Internet sites from which they provide information about themselves. These organizations include various types of associations, mosques, da'wa programs, Sufi orders, and businesses. Some individuals post their home pages on the Net. The majority of these sites provide useful and comprehensive information about Islam, often providing a list of Islamic links, while some are concerned only with spreading their own message and promoting the activities of their organizations. Muslims celebrate themselves, chat, find spouses, trade, learn, make *zakat* (tithe), check prayer times, study, lay down plans for a better future, or buy a plot in a cemetery for Muslims. The Web is also used to provide Sufi guidance.[31]

A handful of sites operated by some of the largest Muslim organizations often provide the most comprehensive coverage of the Muslim scene in America. These popular sites are the Internet addresses of ISNA, the Muslim Student Association of North America, the MAS, under the leadership of Warith Deen Mohammed, the ICNA, and a handful of Sufi orders. Although the majority of Islamic Internet sites are set up by organizations, some are launched and maintained by individuals who bring a great deal of dedication and professional attention to their sites or home pages. Among these are three sites set up by Muslim women of various backgrounds: Islam in the United States by Anayat Durrani;[32] Aisha Bewley's Islamic Homepage;[33] and Mammalist.[34]

The architecture of these sites often includes a brief historical presentation of the organization, a description of its mission, its departments and their projects, a calendar of events, a FAQs (about Islamic matters) box, and a listing of related links. Most of these links refer to various directories of Islamic organizations and personal home pages. Below is a brief presentation of some of these Islamic Internet sites that include immigrant Sunni and Shi'a Muslims, African American, and Sufi sites.

ISLAMIC CIRCLE OF NORTH AMERICA   Designed and maintained by volunteers, ICNA's Web site[35] is probably the most comprehensive and the most frequently updated Islamic Internet site today. It serves as a platform for ICNA's multifaceted activities, and includes links to *The Message* newsletter, Book Service, ICNA Relief, Sound Vision, MSI Financial, Resources, Dawah, Directory, Web Guide, Young Muslim Organization, Sisters

Wing, Family Services, Forums, Quiz, and a Games and Feedback section. This site also features an electronic media monitoring network, Muslim Alert Network, launched in 1987 to denounce anti-Muslim discrimination and campaign against human rights violations.[36] ICNA Relief is active on the major fronts where Muslims suffer because of wars (the Balkans, Chechnya, Iraq, Kashmir, Palestine) or natural disasters leading to famine (Ethiopia, Mozambique, Pakistan). Although the Muslim poor are to be found mainly outside the United States, ICNA has also developed relief programs such as UMMAH (United Muslim Movement Against Homelessness) and Muslim Women's Help Services to assist people confronted with social problems arising from joblessness, financial crises, homelessness, feelings of isolation, or marital strife in America.

ICNA programs often provide programmed growth. For example, the Young Muslims Program[37] establishes programmed development goals for young Muslims in high school, college, and later, aimed at fostering group cohesion through the organization of study and group action activities, and promoting involvement in life in the school, the college, the workplace, and the community.

IVIEWS.COM   One of the major Islamic players on the Internet, and probably one of its most dynamic sites, iviews.com is an Internet news publication designed to provide an American Muslim perspective on world issues, focusing upon timely news and reporting and contributing insightful analysis and commentary on matters of importance to Muslims. This newcomer was set up in Santa Clara, California, on May 21, 1999.[38]

Iviews.com is concerned primarily with the presentation of news and current events from a Muslim perspective, seeking to better represent Islam and the Muslims to the larger society and improve their image. During the past year, this publication has provided expanded news coverage of the Muslim world and in-depth analysis of national and world issues, and has placed onto the American agenda issues and stories that usually receive only a cursory attention from typical media sources. Although the publication is written from an American Muslim perspective, its focus is not religious. Its various departments provide news analysis, columns, and features exploring issues or events in detail, and coverage of current news to offset the biases of other media filters. Iviews.com is probably the only Internet site of its kind, and a cursory analysis of the editorials and news stories of its first year indicates that its writers and editors meet high professional and intellectual standards.

MUSLIM AMERICAN SOCIETY   A site operated since September 1996 by the MAS[39] <http://www.worldforum.com/ministry> provides information about Islam and the Muslim world primarily for the African American Muslim community, only rarely covering immigrant Muslim activities in the United States. This site is divided into three main sections. The first deals with the ministry of Warith Deen Mohammed and includes a selection of articles about the leader of the movement and the difference between the MAS and the Nation of Islam. Feature stories about the MAS, relevant news, Islamic radio and TV broadcast schedules, postings of various regional or national conventions, and a donation center for pledging support, are also included in this section.

A "Community Resources" component provides Muslims with a virtual space where they can exchange information about daily life concerns and religious topics.

The second section provides information about Islam from a Sunni perspective. All the feature stories accessible on this site stress the orthodoxy of the Muslim American Society and promote the unity of all Muslims. A FAQs page provides testimonials and biographies of Clara Muhammad and Warith Deen Mohammed. A final section gives information about the *Muslim Journal*, the most important Muslim weekly newspaper in America, without providing access to its articles. Besides matters of a religious nature, this site devotes a great deal of attention to women and family matters and to the investment program sponsored by the MAS under the name of Collective Purchasing Center.

ISLAMIC SOCIETY OF NORTH AMERICA   A Web site operated by ISNA, an umbrella organization started by the Muslim Student Association of North America in 1983, <http://www.isna.net> seems to cater mainly to the needs of immigrant Muslims and Muslim students. In addition to the standard sections dealing with Islam, this major Internet site details the various services it provides to the American Muslims in practical matters such as finances, *zakat* and estate planning, last wills, and *halal* (permissible according to Islam) investment, addressing the concerns of a constituency made up of well-educated and prosperous Muslims. This site also includes a matrimonial services section that seems to be popular among parents, usually of South Asian background, seeking a husband for their daughters (and sometimes a bride for their sons), suggesting that this constituency still views a number of social relations from a traditional perspective. A *fatwa* section dealing with matters of doctrine and personal conduct answers questions submitted by Muslims seeking guidance. This site plays the role of a clearinghouse for the affiliates of ISNA, while attempting to provide services, some of which are of a very practical nature.

Scores of other Sunni sites are active on the Net. One is HADI (Human Assistance and Development International),[40] which claimed over three million visitors who made over twelve million requests in 1998–1999.[41]

ISLAMIC SHI'A SITES   Shi'a Internet sites,[42] like other Muslim sites, are concerned mainly with the promotion of Islam from their own perspective, but unlike their Sunni counterparts, they sometimes provide links to other Islamic sites. The architecture of these sites reveals a high level of professional communications skills and esthetics through the use of pastel colors and background calligraphy.

Shi'a sites have sections on the Qur'an, hadith, *Sirah, Tafsir,* and other Islamic sciences, and, understandably, devote a considerable coverage to *Ahl al-Bayt* and Shi'a imams. They dwell on the lives of the thirteen African companions of Prophet Muhammad, devoting much space to the life of Bilal Ibn Rabah and condemning other Muslims for denying him the rank of a full companion. The special attention given both to Prophet Muhammad's black companions and to the militant stance of Shi'a Muslims partly accounts for the spectacular development of Shi'a Islam among the African American community over the past decade.

SUFI ORDERS ON THE INTERNET   Practically all Muslim Sufi orders, of varying degrees of orthodoxy, maintain individual sites on the Web.[43] Information about hundreds of Sufi orders is available on a number of Internet sites maintained by such organizations as the Naqshbandiya Foundation for Islamic Education <http://www.nfie.com>; the Sufi Women Organization <http://www.ias.org/swo/>; the Naqshbandi Foundation <http://www.naqshbandi.net>; the Qur'an and Sunnah Foundation, <http://www .sunnah.org>; and the Al-Baz Publishing Company <http://www.al-baz.com,>. All of which provide the most comprehensive information concerning Shaykh Abdul Qader al-Jaylani and his writings.

A VIRTUAL COMMUNITY   The American Muslim community is rapidly forging a virtual Islamic community, one that can be accessed by anyone from the privacy of one's home. HADI has even developed IslamiCity in cyberspace, complete with virtual mosques and marketplaces![44] Some students of Islam in America are conjecturing that the rapid growth of conversion to Islam among American professionals is partly due to the Internet. What is obvious, however, is that never before in history have the Muslims made so much information available about themselves in English, which is rapidly becoming a second language to a very large number of educated Muslims around the world and particularly in America.

The emergence of the virtual Muslim community bespeaks an interesting future for American Muslims who are mastering this communications tool with great rapidity and efficiency and who are taking steps to harness it for the benefit of their communities. The Internet revolution is rapidly shaping the American Muslim community, creating a Muslim cyberspace where ideas are exchanged and tested, and where discourse ceases to be the exclusive domain of specialists and Muslim scholars.

Conclusion

Many American Muslims were among the original builders of the Internet network; they contributed as software engineers, programmers, and specialists in computer science information fields. They started mailing lists, newsgroups, chat lines, and Web pages about Islam, feeling that the Web was a "free" arena where they could propagate the message of Islam to the outside world and touch people who would otherwise never encounter Islam or would learn about it only through biased media coverage. These initial high hopes had to be toned down when they realized that this medium was neither as "free" nor as friendly as they had thought. But this initial shock has now been overcome, as can be seen from the growing maturity of some Islamic Internet sites, and the launching of such Internet sites as iviews.com, which prefigure the place of Islamic sites on the Web. Muslims have learned that the Web is just another arena where they have to struggle to defend their rights.[45]

Muslim chat rooms attract high school and college-age Muslims and constitute meeting places where they "talk" to other Muslims. Some Islamic sites display strong anti-Muslim sentiments in an awkward attempt to defend their faith and respond to anti-Muslim propaganda on the Internet, while others accuse one another of being narrow-minded and hypocritical, declaring their opponents to be non-Muslim; a few nurture old-world rivalries such as those between Bangladeshis, Pakistanis, and Indians. Some of the major Islamic sites provide authoritative guidance, thanks to their resident scholars or sheikhs, but the majority provide guidance and *fatwas* to non-Muslims and Muslims alike without the authority of adequate scholarly knowledge.

Publishers and Booksellers

Publishing houses and bookstores often represent the first gateway for accessing information about Islam and the Muslims. Publishers, particularly those of both books and software, provide important services to Islamic educational, religious, and *da'wa* institutions. The major bookstores, some of which are publishing arms of national organizations or educational foundations, provide a wide range of services. In addition to books, videos, and audiotapes they sell multi-language software.

There are hundreds of Islamic bookstores[46] across the country ranging from very small outfits carrying a variety of goods in addition to a limited selection of books and tapes to well-established institutions with impressive inventories and thousands of titles in stock. Thanks to these publishers and bookstores, the scarcity of adequate Islamic materials in English, Arabic, and other Islamic languages is a thing of the past. Some of the leading bookstores operating in the United States today were founded by Muslim organizations or individuals to fill a serious gap in the American book distribution industry. Today, in addition to the bookstores and publishers that are branches of major Islamic organizations, many are operated by individuals. During the 1990s, the continued development of adult books on Islam was accompanied by a rapid increase in the number and quality of books and games designed for the young. These pioneers have now been joined by a new generation of software developers and publishers who are producing a wide range of materials to be used by Muslim children. The main publishers and bookstores are communication branches of major Islamic organizations such as ISNA and ICNA; the sample discussed below gives an idea of their geographical distribution and the range of services and materials they provide.

American Trust Publications

Based in Plainfield, Indiana, American Trust Publications (ATP), originally set up by the Muslim Student Association in 1976 to "produce high quality Islamic literature for Muslim children, youth and adults and to provide non-Muslim youth and adults with accurate literature about Islam," has become a branch of ISNA. Its publications include textbooks, reference works, and a "cultural orientation" series, which consists of both fiction and nonfiction materials designed to encourage the Muslim child to appreciate Islamic culture. This series includes folktales and fantasy told within an Islamic framework, books on Prophet Muhammad and his companions, biographies of notable and heroic Muslims, and books of Islamic art and architecture. ATP literature for youth deals with areas relevant to a child's experience, viewed from a Muslim perspective, and with issues like violence, alcoholism, drugs, family, sex, and marriage, while attempting to relate the message of Islam to the contemporary American environment.

Kazi Publications

Founded in 1972, KAZI Publications, Inc.,[47] is one of the oldest important Islamic book-stores and publishers in America; it has published more than two hundred books on Islam and distributes more than two thousand more. Some of its works are translations or revisions of existing Islamic texts on topics not dealt with in English, while a growing number are schol-arly writings of American Muslims. KAZI also specializes in translations of Sufi writings.

Astrolabe Pictures

From Sterling, Virginia, Astrolabe Pictures[48] distributes videos, books, and software for the study of Islam and Arabic. It offers a large collection of materials designed specially for children and produced in a variety of formats including tapes, videos, CD-ROMs, and language instruction (English, Arabic, Urdu, and Malay). These materials include songs, puppets, and animated films as well as instructional materials for the teaching of Islam and Arabic. Software materials include a wide selection of interactive materials for children. One such collection is the *Arabic Playhouse*, which teaches every level of Arabic reading, be-ginning with practicing the Arabic alphabet and leading to reading the Qur'an, through a variety of entertaining ways, including games. *Da'wa* films, such as *Pathways to Islam, The Guest of God*, and *The Life of the Last Prophet*, include features about Islam and famous Muslims and Western converts to Islam. Among current best selling videos are *The Hajj*, based on the 1998 CNN live coverage of the Muslims' pilgrimage to Mecca; *The Message*, about the birth of Islam in Mecca; and *The Lion of the Desert*, which relates the epic struggle of Omar Mukhtar, leader of the Libyan resistance to Mussolini's army.

Halalco Books

Opened in 1982 in Falls Church, Virginia, The Halalco Books bookstore[49] is probably the best-stocked Islamic bookstore in America. Its August 1998 catalog lists over 4,500 titles of books, tapes, and software on Islam and the Muslim world, in addition to a broad se-lection of ethnic Muslim clothing, health, and beauty products.

As well as books in English, it carries Arabic, French, Hindi, Persian, and Urdu books on Islam and an impressive collection of translations of the Qur'an in English by Al-Mawdudi, Mohsin Khan, Marmaduke Pickthall, Yusuf Ali, and Shakir. Translations of the Qur'an are also available in the Baluchi, Bangla, Bosnian, Chinese, French, German, Gu-jarati, Hindi, Indonesian, Kannada, Kazakh, Korean, Malay, Persian, Pushtu, Urdu, Uigur, Russian, Sindhi, Somali, Spanish, Tamil, Telegu, and Turkish languages.

Subjects covered include *da'wa* literature, dream interpretation, hadith, health and medi-cine, life after death, *ibadah* (acts of worship including prayers, fasting, *hajj* and *umra* [lesser pil-grimage], *zakat*, etc.), language studies, Islam in the United States, the Muslim world, political science, science and Islam, *sira* (life of Prophet Muhammad), Qur'anic exegesis, and Sufism.[50]

IQRA' Book Center

IQRA' Book Center is the book distribution arm of the IQRA' Educational Foundation.[51] The foundation's curriculum guides for Islamic studies top the list of the materials they distribute. Their catalog is rich in titles written and produced primarily for young readers, including coloring storybooks, stories based on the life of Prophet Muhammad and his companions, stories with Muslim heroes, and Islam for children. Most of the titles are commissioned books written for Muslims living in the West, where special attention is paid to clarity and simplicity.

The subjects covered include traditional areas dealing with Qur'an and hadith studies, *'ibada* (religious observance), family life in Islam, life in the hereafter, economy, politics, comparative religion, modernity, ideology, and African American studies. Books dealing with "rights, roles and status of women in Islam" include a collection of Muslim and Western authors who have chosen to investigate the status and role of women in Islam and Islamic societies.[52] A collection of video, audio, and software titles completes this high-quality offering.

IslamicSoftware and Sakhr

Responding to the demand for interactive educational materials, a number of software companies such as IslamicSoftware,[53] founded in Houston, Texas, in 1986 by Muslim college students, and Sakhr[54] are providing Islamic literature on CD-ROM. IslamicSoftware developed *Alim* and *Arabic Playhouse*, an interactive Qur'anic and Arabic learning program. *Alim* accesses Islamic resources in English and includes the entire Qur'an in Arabic, as well as its rendering in English by Yusuf Ali and Marmaduke Pickthall. Collections of hadith by Bukhari and Muslim, the *Muwattaa* by Imam Malik, *Fiqh-us-Sunnah*, and biographies of sixty companions of the Prophet are usually included in the software. *Sakhr*, on the other hand, provides the world's premiere database with both Arabic and English search capabilities, including recitations by Hussary and Sudaysi, instruction on recitation, translations of the Qur'an in French, German, Turkish, and Malay, and the Arabic *Tafsir* of Ibn Khatir, Qurtubi, and Jalalayn. *Al-Bayan* provides a hadith collection searchable in English, Arabic, and Malay featuring the 1,700 agreed-upon hadith that appear in both Bukhari and Muslim's *Sahih* collections.

MeccaCentric

The Miami-based MeccaCentric Da'wah Group specializes in making available video and audio tapes of about twenty very popular American Muslim speakers such as Siraj Wahhaj, Abdullah Hakim Quick, Warith Deen Mohammed, Jamal Badawi, and Hamza Yusuf. These materials cover such topics as the foundations of Islam, the Muslims in America, Islamic perspectives on health and the environment, and family counseling.

Sound Vision

An ICNA branch, *Sound Vision*,[55] specializes in instructional materials for children produced on paper and in software format. The production of Islamic-content educational and recreational materials for children is based on ICNA's desire to help Muslim children achieve competence in English without exposing them to the non-Islamic values. Sound Vision pioneered the use of popular-culture characters inspired by the Muslim religious tradition and imagery and publishes the *Young Muslim*, a magazine designed for children and junior high school students. Its multimedia educational and learning series include the popular *Adam's World* and *Al-Qari*, while its documentaries, such as *Bosnia: The Untold Story*, *Islam a Closer Look, Choosing Islam* and *The Wonders of Islamic Science*, have been considered good enough to be shown on public television in America.

Major Sufi orders translate classical Sufi writings and disseminate information about Islam through several publishing houses: MTO Shahmaghsoudi Publications (Verdugo City, California); Zahra Publications (Blanco, Texas); Khaniqahi Nimatullahi (New York); Sufi Islamia/Prophecy Publications (San Francisco); Kazi Publications (Chicago); Inner Traditions (New York); Threshold Books (Putney, Vermont); Ansanri Publications (Napa, California); The University Press of America (Lanham, Maryland); and Omega Press (Santa Fe, New Mexico), as well as through their Internet sites.

Translating Islam

Three distinct groups, each with its own goals and traditions, concern themselves with translating Islamic texts into European languages. The first and oldest tradition is represented by the European Orientalists, the second by the various Muslim countries who launched translation programs designed to advance their own religious and political agendas, and the third, and most recent, by immigrant and convert Muslims living in England and America.

Arabic traditionally had been used as the main vehicle for the transmission of Islamic knowledge and for spreading the faith. Gradually, Islamic texts were translated into various other languages such as Persian, Turkish, Urdu, Malay, and Wolof, which themselves became accepted as Islamic languages. The major texts of Islam were first translated into European languages by Western Orientalists[56] in an attempt to build a body of knowledge about the Islamic world. Today, Muslims are using a number of languages in addition to Arabic to call to Islam and are themselves engaged in the translation of Islamic texts into English, which is the language increasingly used by diaspora Muslims and international Muslim organizations as a means of communication.[57]

English language translations of classical Islamic texts have also been carried out by private, public, national, and regional institutions, as well as by individual scholars in countries such as Egypt, the Sudan, India, Nigeria, Pakistan, and South Africa, where English is either an official or a widely used language. Even countries where English is little used, such as Morocco,[58] have commissioned English translations of classical Islamic literature. *Da'wa* literature in English has been published since the early 1970s, often sponsored by nations with major *da'wa* programs such as Libya, the Gulf States, Iran, or Saudi Arabia.

Muslims living in the United Kingdom and North America have begun to translate classical Islamic texts, including Qur'an and hadith, on a significant scale, and for the first time in centuries, translations from Islamic languages are being done by believers who are also the end users. Translations of classical Islamic textbooks are used to preserve, develop, and transmit an Islamic scholarly discourse. British and American Muslims have a marked advantage over the Orientalists, who often displayed little sympathy for their subject matter, or traditional Muslims, who often lacked understanding of the target culture of Muslims living in the West. In addition to their better understanding of both Islamic and Western cultures, and their natural sympathy with both, they translate texts for their own scholarly, spiritual, and cultural use. The translation of Islamic texts is part of a conscious attempt to rediscover and to reappropriate the Islamic scholarly heritage and discourse. Translations of this kind are based on the premise that English has already become an Islamic language and that "Islamicized" English[59] will play an important role in the Islamization of knowledge[60] called for by a number of Muslim intellectuals in America and around the world.

These translations are used as a means of transplanting a heritage into this country where Muslims are taking root, a means of acquiring the classical Islamic library that was available to all Muslims in its original Arabic. Some of the textbooks translated into English are considered by many as dated productions of specific sociocultural conditions, rather than original and indispensable Islamic texts, whose translation is essential for the continuity of Islamic thought. Some textbooks, such as *Al-Ajarrumiyya*, a fifteenth-century grammar textbook in verse, and *Ibn 'Ashir*, a versified version of Maliki Fiqh published in the eighteenth century, used by the Zaytuna Institute, fall within the category of books providing cultural and educational continuity for particular ethnic groups. Their usefulness in the transmission of essential Islamic knowledge is often marginal. These translations, or original productions, are mostly sponsored by some South Asian Muslims and serve to spread a more ethnic and more traditional Islamic outlook.

Some English-language translations available in the United States are imported from Muslim countries where English is widely used, but many translations are produced in America. Some are carried out within the framework of planned translation programs launched by educational institutions such as the International Institute of Islamic Thought or IQRA' foundation. Others are made by individual American Muslim converts who are actively translating their new heritage into English to make it available to the English-speaking community. All publishing houses sponsor English translations of classical Islamic texts, but Al-Baz Publishing Company, based in Florida, is almost wholly devoted to the translation and publication of Islamic texts. Prolific translators include Ahmad Thompson, Jamila Jones, Aiesha Bewley, and Ya-Sien Mohamed.[61] Other active translators include Abdal-Hakim Winter, who translated *Jaurahat at-Tauhid* by Ibrahim al-Laqqani, Shaykh Nuh Keller, who translated *'Umdat as-Salik*, a major Shafi'i text, and Muhtar Holland. Scholars engaged in the translation of Islamic texts include the Moroccan-born Laroui-Cornell, who has translated Abu 'Abd al-Rahman al-Sulami's (d. 1021) *Dhikr an-Niswat al-muta'abbidat as-sufiyyat*, under the title, *Early Sufi Women*, a work that challenges many notions about Muslim women. Laroui-Cornell's husband, Vincent Cornell, has recently published *The Way of Abu Madyan*, which includes a number of Arabic texts written by the Sufi Shaykh Abu Madyan (d. 1198) with their translations into English.

Some original translations are available both in hard copy and in downloadable versions on the Web[62]. They include translations of Maliki and Sufi texts produced by Aisha Bewley and her husband, Abdalhaqq Bewley, by Abdassamad Clarke, and by Shaykh Abdalqadir Al-Murabit.[63] Aisha Bewley has translated about a dozen classical Islamic texts including *Miftah al-falah* and *Hikams* by the Sufi Shaykh Ibn 'Ata' Allah al-Iskandari (d. 1309) and selections from the *Letters of Shaykh al-Darqawi*.

Despite the existence of numerous English language translations of the meanings of the Qur'an, such as those published by Yusuf Ali, Marmaduke Pickthal, T. B. Irving, and others, new English language translations of the Qur'an are constantly being attempted. Many translations of classical Islamic texts are "accredited" by religious scholars to ensure quality.

This massive translation program primarily works on classical Islamic texts, but also includes other literature such as children's stories. It is very likely that America will soon have enough literature to cover the needs of its Muslim population.[64]

Conventions and Seminars

National and regional conventions attended by large numbers of people are organized annually by many American Muslim organizations. These gatherings are often immense marketplaces where ideas, notions, goods, and services are exchanged, and where important decisions concerning the community are debated, made, or communicated. Reflection about community matters is carried out through a variety of informal and formal ways, including lectures and panels, and networking is reinforced through formal and informal contacts. These conventions also serve to build leadership by reinforcing the existing structure and favoring the emergence of a younger generation of student or youth leaders. Conventions mirror the communities and organizations that plan and attend them, and, therefore, they constitute interesting vantage points from which the American Muslim community can be observed.

All the major Islamic organizations in America hold annual conventions. In 2000, for example, ISNA, the Muslim Student Association, and the Muslim Youth of North America held their thirty-seventh conventions, ICNA and MAS, their twenty-fourth, respectively, and the North American Bangladeshi Islamic Council,[65] its nineteenth. Those of the MAS, ISNA, and ICNA are the most important in terms of attendance, participants, and media coverage.

Islamic Society of North America

In September 1998, the St. Louis Convention Center in Missouri welcomed the thirty-fifth ISNA annual convention as well as the national conventions of the Muslim Students of America and Canada (MSA) and the Muslim Youth of North America (MYNA).[66] These parallel conventions totaled over one hundred sessions, of which sixty were organized by ISNA.

In addition to the sessions, a bazaar with over a hundred stalls sold everything from Islamic educational materials in Arabic and English and da'wa literature in book, audio, video, and digitized form to ethnic clothing, perfumes, jewelry, and art. Some merchants promoted a variety of financial services. A limited number of stalls were managed by organizations concerned with da'wa, relief, and civil rights, and by advocacy groups such as the American Muslim Council and the Council on American-Islamic Relations. In one stall, a Muslim of Pakistani ancestry sold fresh California dates, probably harvested from palm trees planted by his ancestors in the 1920s.

Over fifteen thousand American Muslims from different ethnic backgrounds, as well as a handful of foreign speakers and visitors, attended the convention. Most of the participants, accompanied by spouses and children, were under forty. They were mainly of Asian extraction, with a sprinkling of Middle-Eastern and African American representatives. Delegates from international or national Muslim organizations such as the International Islamic Center for Information (U.K.), the International Council for Da'wah and Relief, the Muslim World Congress, the Organization of the Islamic Conference, and the World Assembly of Muslim Youth also attended this convention, along with various American Muslim professional associations and advocacy groups.

Although some sessions dealt with political situations in various Muslim countries such as Algeria, India, Iraq, Kashmir, Kosovo, and Palestine, most were on issues concerning the American Muslim community itself. Sessions dealt with topics related to building Muslim economic, educational, and religious institutions in America, ways and means of preserving and developing Muslim values, and achieving political and social involvement in the larger community.[67] Fundraising, estate planning, establishing Islam in the schools and the workplace, providing relief, *fiqh*, health issues and human dignity, and the future of Islam in America were also debated. The overall message was that American Muslims should concentrate on building their own communities, address issues concerning the larger society, and attend to the needs of the disadvantaged, regardless of their ethnic or religious background. The MYNA sessions included workshops dealing with *da'wa*, relief work, outreach and urban development, and career choices, as well as with intergenerational relationships.

ISNA also organizes regional conferences and a series of major meetings on specific themes. These are becoming annual events, during which specialists and field persons share ideas. These conferences try to analyze such issues as the impact of the rising number of conversions to Islam in American prisons, various concerns confronting American Muslims, and the potential of the Internet as a tool for effective presentation of knowledge on Islam and for the establishment of personal and organizational connections.

Muslim American Society

Every Labor Day weekend, the followers of Imam Warith Deen Mohammed hold an Islamic Convention, during which he delivers a State-of-the-Muslim-Community[68] address. This annual event always includes workshops, seminars, banquets, sports activities, and an outdoor carnival and is attended by thousands of African American Muslims from around the country, often straining the limited budgets of the different local mosques. Recognizing that national conventions put a heavy financial and organizational burden on the Muslim American Society and its membership, MAS leadership decided in 1998 to hold only regional conventions for the benefit of local and regional constituencies. Thus, Imam Mohammed's "State of the Muslims" address delivered in the California regional convention, held in the fall of 1999, was telecast live via satellite[69] to designated sites in Atlanta, Chicago, Dallas, New York, and Washington, D.C., where similar gatherings were taking place. In addition to these annual conventions, a number of regional conferences and local events are regularly organized; for example, on Memorial Day weekend in May 1999, the First Young Adult Conference was held in Chicago to discuss means and strategies for the preparation of today's youth to assume leadership roles in the educational, economic, cultural, and political arenas.

Islamic Circle of North America

Like ISNA, the ICNA[70] is an offshoot of the MSA, but unlike the majority of national Islamic organizations, it is a membership organization. ICNA attracts and keeps only highly motivated individuals, fully committed to active participation in its many social, educational, and *da'wa* programs.[71] The membership is made up mainly of Pakistani and Indian Muslim professionals (products of the so-called brain drain) and their educated children, who bring considerable talent and commitment to ICNA.[72]

Using the strategies of al-Mawdudi and the Jamaat-i-Islami[73] of Pakistan, ICNA tries to be an ethnically diverse movement with a special emphasis on spiritual development. At the same time, it is a growing professional organization with thousands of members scattered throughout the United States. ICNA's publishing division includes an English-language monthly magazine, *The Message* (formerly *Tahreek*), a quarterly Urdu magazine, an Islamic book service, a multimedia company that produces Islamic materials for children and adults, and a dynamic Internet site. ICNA also operates an international relief agency.

ICNA officers, members of the National Shura Council, and the Amir are selected by its governing body, the General Assembly. While the majority of the organization's membership is Indo-Pakistani, the organization has attempted to include various ethnic groups, and today there are two African Americans and a Moroccan[74] on the National Shura Council. ICNA's resources are generated by the membership and the organization has a policy of accepting no funding from foreign Muslim governments.

In addition to these national conventions organized annually by the major Islamic organizations, which draw thousands of participants, seminars organized by the Muslim professional associations, such as the Association of American Muslim Social Scientists, the Islamic Medical Association, and the Association of American Muslim Scientists and Engineers, are attended by small, select numbers of interested scholars and intellectuals. These seminars bring together people with a common interest in the development of knowledge by Muslims about Muslims; they constitute an arena where Muslim community issues are debated and where new research is communicated in pre-publication format.[75]

Conclusion

Several points about Islamic communication in America must be emphasized. First, it is a multiform and multivocal enterprise involving a large number of actors who speak with different voices about a shared faith and a common heritage. Despite variations in culture, ethnic identities, and ideological perspectives, commonalities unite all those involved in spreading the word. Second, Islamic communication in America is financed and carried out mostly by organized bodies and institutions established for the express purpose of serving and leading the community. These are Muslims who are concerned about the future of their communities and determined to promote Islamic contributions to American life. If Muslims are chagrined by American media bias, their own media do not dwell on this matter, and rather than squandering their limited resources to rebut sophisticated and well organized anti-Muslim movements, Islamic media concentrate on community-building activities.

Islamic communication has undergone very important changes through the 1990s and into the new century, thanks to the widespread use of the Internet and the use of English to communicate with other Muslims. For the first time in history, English is used to achieve an infusion of Islamic knowledge into today's world and among Western publics. Muslims are appropriating English and putting it to work in contexts where traditional Islamic languages such like Persian, Turkish, or Urdu are blocked by technological and software obstacles. The use of English and the growing sophistication of the Islamic media are helping Muslims overcome their invisibility and present themselves as productive and law-abiding citizens. There is a tendency for the Islamic media to over-represent solidarity issues as they deal with economic and political crises and with poverty in the Muslim world. Spreading the word seems to revolve around solidarity and community-building agendas. The Islamic media function both as identity markers and channels through which Muslims communicate among themselves and reach out for others; they point to the vitality of the Muslim community in America and its desire to communicate its values, hopes, and concerns. More than business or communication ventures, they are beacons of Islamic presence in America.

Muslims have embraced the World Wide Web, but they remain wary of its side effects. Insisting that Islam is a communal experience that requires proximity and direct contact, they do not want it to turn their religion into a "cultural resource" to be packaged for off-site consumption. But because these technologies are extensions of individualism, favoring and promoting mainly disembodied and abstract connections between persons, their effects on Islamic communities will almost certainly translate into new expressions of solidarity and identity. Despite the potentially negative influences of the Internet, Muslims are using this medium to reactivate their transnational networks, which had been seriously disrupted by colonialism and the rise of nation states, and strained by immigration. The emergence of the wired Muslim community in the new era of globalization bespeaks an interesting future for American Muslims, who are mastering this communications tool faster than their brethren around the world and who are taking steps to harness it for the benefit of their communities. Whether Muslims will succeed in taming a technology born out of a different culture is difficult to predict. What is certain is that their adoption of English and of Western methods already indicates that they are adapting to their new environment, and if we bear in mind the observations of Marshall McLuhan concerning the nature of the media,[76] we can already identify the ways in which these media are shaping Muslim relations to each other and with the rest of the world.

Notes

1. Research for this paper was carried out thanks to a Fulbright grant provided by the Moroccan American Educational and Exchange Commission. Special thanks go to various friends and colleagues at Mohammed V University, Rabat, Morocco; the Center for Middle Eastern Studies at the University of Texas at Austin; and the Center for Muslim-Christian Understanding at Georgetown University.

2. Such individuals include Ayyub ibn Sulayman (1702–1773), also known as Job ben Solomon; Bilali Muhammad (1760–1859?); Abderrahman (1762–1829); Omar ibn Said (1770–1864) and Lamen Kaba (1780–?). For more information see Philip Curtin, ed., *Africa*

Remembered: Narratives by West-African Slaves from the Era of the Slave Trade (Madison: University of Wisconsin Press, 1967); Allan Austin, *African Muslims in Antebellum America: A Sourcebook* (New York: Garland Publishing, 1984) and *African Muslims in Antebellum America: Transatlantic Stories and Spiritual Struggles* (New York: Routledge, 1997), and Sylviane Diouf, *Servants of Allah: African Muslims Enslaved in the Americas* (New York: New York University Press, 1998).

3. This chapter will not concern itself directly with the efforts of non-American Muslims to disseminate information about Islam in this country.

4. Sulayman Nyang, *Islam in the United States of America* (Chicago: ABC, 1999), 103.

5. Ibid., 104. More than twenty-six issues of this monthly magazine were published almost single-handedly by Webb, who was assisted for a while by Nefeesa M. T. Keep.

6. M. M. Aijian, "The Mohammedans in the United States," *The Moslem World* (1926): 31.

7. This weekly publication remains viable, changing its title to *Bilalian News* in 1975, *The American Muslim Journal* in 1985, and *Muslim Journal* thereafter, thus mirroring the changing positions of Warith Deen Mohammed on the issue of color.

8. See Keith Butler, "The Muslims Are No Longer an Unknown Quantity," *Corrections Magazine* (June 1978): 55–63 and Robert Dannin, "Island in a Sea of Ignorance: Dimensions of the Prison Mosque," in *Making Muslim Space*, ed. Barbara Metcalf (Berkeley: University of California Press, 1996), 131–146. The Islamic press in America has not yet been analyzed in any systematic or scholarly fashion, and Muslim inmate publications are the least well-known part of this press.

9. *Muslim Journal*, 929 W. 171st Street, Hazel Crest, IL. 60429. <Http://www.muslimjournal.com>.

10. *The Muslim Observer*, 20331 Farmington, Rd., Suite #, Livonia, MI 48152. <Http://www.Muslimobserver.com>.

11. *The Muslim Magazine* is sold in over five hundred locations across the United States and is available in some of the larger bookstore chains such as Barnes & Noble, Borders, and Hastings.

12. Its editor-in-chief, Dr. Aslam Abdullah, doubles as the editor-in-chief of *The Muslim Observer.*

13. <Http://www.AmericanMuslim.org>.

14. Al-Banna (1906–1949) was the founder of the Muslim Brotherhood in Egypt, the most influential Islamic revivalist movement, in 1928.

15. <Http://www.americanmuslim.net>.

16. Kabbani launches regular attacks on what he calls Wahhabi doctrines. For example, he made statements during a panel discussion forum at the State Department that drew unanimous condemnation from Muslim organizations and individuals in America.

17. <Http://naqshbandi.org>; <http://sunnah.org>; <http://naqshbandi.net>; <http://kamilat.org>; and <http://unityone.org>.

18. For example, the April 14, 2000, issue of *Muslim Journal* lists seventy-one radio stations located in twenty-three states where Islamic programs are broadcast once a week, usually on Saturdays or Sundays, except in Baltimore, MD, where WJRO broadcasts a daily program from Monday to Friday.

19. <Http://islam.org/radio/default.htm>.

20. See <http://islam.org/Radio/ch200.htm> for a sample of programs provided.

21. <Http://radioislam.com>.

22. <Http://islam.org/mpac>.

23. Check <http://islam.org/mpac/archive.shtm> for a sample of topics and issues discussed on this station.

24. <Http://ianaradionet.com>.

25. Jeff Zaleski, *The Soul of Cyberspace: How New Technology Is Changing Our Lives* (New York: HarperCollins, 1997).

26. The search engines of Yahoo, AltaVista, Gopher, AOL, and CompuServe, among others, list an ever increasing number of Islamic sites, or sites providing some kind of information about Islam.

27. Many of the sites claiming to provide information about Islam actually engage in a real virtual war on Islam. Some calling themselves Islamic organizations, such as the Bahai, the Ahmadiyya, and the Nation of Islam, to name only a few of the most visible ones, often use Arabic lettering and designs to claim an Islamic identity but are considered outside the pale by mainline Muslims.

28. Syed Imtiaz Ahmad, a former president of ISNA, and a former dean of the School of Engineering at the International Islamic University of Malaysia, is the current president of the Association of Muslim Scientists and Engineers.

29. Shahid N. Shah, "The Virtual Islamic Bond Expands," *Islamic Horizons* (March–April 1998):17.

30. Ashfaq Lodhi, "Muslim Internet Experts Meet in Silicon Valley," *Islamic Horizons* (July–August 1999):12.

31. The Shadiliyya Sufi School of Spiritual Healing <http://www.sufipath.org> provides guidance through e-mail.

32. <Http://suite101.com>.

33. <Http://www.ourworld.compuserve.com/homepages/Abewley>. (Accessed August 8, 1999.)

34. <Http://jannah.org>.

35. <Http://www.icna.org>.

36. See <http://www.icna.org/MAN/> for more.

37. See Young Muslims: Brothers and Sisters for Faith and Action, <http://www.youngmuslims.org>

38. <Http://www.iviews.com>, 3000 Scott Blvd., Santa Clara, CA 95054.

39. *Muslim Journal* (February 28, 1997): 4.

40. HADI, P. O. Box 4598, Culver City, CA 90230. <http://www.islam.org>.

41. <Http://www.islam.org>, August 8, 1999.

42. A good gate to Shi'a sites is <http://www.iua-net.org>. Also, very useful points of access are: <http://www.answering-islam.org> and <http://www.geocoties.com/>.

43. These include the following sites: <http://www.naqshbandi.org>; <http://www.sufipath.org>, <http://www.qadiri-rifai.org>; <http://www.chisti.com>; <http://www.tijaniyya.org>; <http://www.muridiyya.com>, and <http://www.murabitun.com>.

44. <Http://www.islam.org>.

45. Newsgroups dealing with Islam are often the vehicles of non-Muslims bent on attacking Muslims and slandering Islam, as well as of Muslim groups and individuals opposed across doctrinal lines. A number of mailing lists, including MSA-net, had to confront special interest groups working to shut them down.

46. Directories of Islamic bookstores and publishers can be accessed on the Muslim Student Association of North America Internet site, <http://www.msa-natl.org>.

47. 3023 W. Belmont Avenue, Chicago, IL 60618. <Http://www.kazi.org>.

48. 201 Davis Drive, Suite I, Sterling, VA 20164. <Http://www.astrolabepictures.com>. E-mail: info@astrolabepictures.com.

49. Falls Church, VA. <http:// www.halalco.com>; e-mail: halalco@halalco.com.

50. See *Books on Islam and the Muslim World: Catalog 1998-B.* Falls Church, VA.: Halalco Books (August 1998).

51. Established in Skokie, Illinois, as an Islamic *waqf* (religious endowment) in 1983, the IQRA' Foundation has produced and published, with the support of the Saudi-based IQRA' Charitable Society, over a hundred books designed to meet the needs of the Muslim community.

52. IQRA', *Books on Islam*, 1998–1999 Catalog. This section includes Huda al-Khattab, *Bent Rib: A Journey through Women's Issues in Islam*; Fatima Mernissi, *Beyond the Veil, The Forgotten Queens of Islam*; Muhammad Saeed Siddiqi, *Blessed Women of Islam*; Carol Anway, *Daughters of Another Path*; Mai Yamani, *Feminism and Islam: Legal and Literary Perspectives*; Jamal Badawi, *Gender Equity in Islam*; Annemarie Schimmel, *My Soul is a Woman: The Feminine in Islam*; D. A. Spellberg, *Politics, Gender and the Islamic Past: The Legacy of Aicha Bint Abi Bakr*; Yvonne Haddad, *Islam, Gender and Social Change*; and Laila Ahmad, *Women and Gender in Islam*.

53. <Http://www.islsoftware.com>; e-mail: sales@islsoftware.com.

54. Falls Church, VA. <Http://www.sakhr.com>; e-mail: sakhrus@erols.com.

55. Chicago, IL. <Http://www.soundvision.com>; e-mail: info@soundvision.com.

56. See Edward W. Said, *Orientalism* (New York: Pantheon Books, 1978).

57. Many International Muslim organizations use English as a working language to facilitate communication and information dissemination.

58. The Ministry of Waqf and Islamic Affairs has commissioned English-language translations of a number of Maliki texts.

59. See Isma'il al-Faruqi, *Toward Islamic English* (Herndon, VA.: International Institute of Islamic Thought, 1986).

60. Mohammad Mumtaz Ali, "Reconstruction of Islamic Thought and Civilization," *Islamic Quarterly* 43, no. 1 (1999): 21–36 and Muhammad Shafiq, *Growth of Islamic Thought in America: Focus on Isma'il Raji al-Faruqi* (Brentwood, Md.: Amana Publications, 1994).

61. See Ta-Ha Publishers' home page for a list of the books translated by these Muslim converts.

62. Aisha Bewley's Islamic home page at <http://ourworld.compuserve.com/homepages/Abewley> (Accessed August 8, 1999.)

63. A Scottish Shadili Shaykh, who, under the name of Ian Dallas, published *The Book of Strangers* (Albany: SUNY, 1989).

64. The level of dissemination and use of these materials among the various Muslim communities may merit further investigation. My impression is that these texts tend to circulate among a limited number of communities, each choosing to use a given selection of texts, often produced to meet that particular constituency's needs.

65. NABIC was formally founded by a number of Bangladeshi intellectuals at the University of Illinois, Urbana-Champaign, in March 1990. It is devoted to the promotion of dialogue between Bangladeshi Americans and their home country. See <http://www.nabic.org>.

66. This discussion is based on information gathered by the author during this convention.

67. See the convention programs for details.

68. An obvious comparison with the U.S. President's State of the Union address.

69. Sponsored by commercial advertisers, the telecast was carried out by BaitCal, a family-owned and operated Muslim communications company, which launched the *Muslim News Magazine* in 1991 and subsequently produced a number of programs about Warith Deen Mohammed, including "Tribute to Imam W. Deen Mohammed," "20 Years of Success," "Universal Respect and Acceptance," "The World Travels of W. D. Mohammed," and "W. Deen Mohammed & Guest."

70. ICNA started in 1971 as a *halaqa* (circle) founded by a group of Indo-Pakistani members of MSA who had been involved in Islamic movements in their home countries, particularly with Jama'at-i-Islami, to organize *da'wa* among the Urdu-speaking communities. As the *halaqa* membership increased, it established branches in several cities around the country, and in 1978 reorganized itself as the Islamic Circle of North America. Its headquarters are located at 116–26, 89th Avenue, Jamaica, NY, <http://www.icna.org>; e-mail info@icna.org.

71. Two levels of membership are available: general and general assembly memberships. The former is open to those who satisfy minimum requirements. Members are expected to study

the Qur'an daily, the hadith or *Sirah* at least once a week, and Islamic literature according to a set syllabus, spend at least four hours a month on *da'wa* work, invite at least two members a year to join ICNA, make minimum financial contributions to the central treasury, and invite at least one Muslim a week to start praying or attending congregational prayers. General assembly membership is open to those who show more commitment to ICNA's goals and work regularly to achieve them. See <http://www.icna.org/ICNA/organize.html> for more.

72. One of the very few "outsiders" in the regional leadership of ICNA is the Moroccan-born Mukhtar Maghraoui.

73. See Mumtaz Ahmad, "Islamic Fundamentalism in South Asia: The Jamaat-i-Islami and the Tablighi Jamaat" in *Fundamentalisms Observed,* ed. Martin E. Marty and R. Scott Appleby (Chicago: University of Chicago Press, 1991), 457–530.

74. The Moroccan-born Mukhtar Maghraoui is a popular speaker on the Islamic lecture circuit.

75. See the Conference Program of the Twenty-Ninth Annual Conference of the Association of Muslim Social Scientists, "Islam and Society in the Twenty-First Century," held at Georgetown University, Washington, D.C., October 13–15, 2000.

76. Marshall McLuhan, *Understanding Media: The Extension of Man* (Cambridge, Mass.: MIT Press, 1964, 1994).

The Politics of Transfiguration: Constitutive Aspects of the International Religious Freedom Act of 1998

2

KATHLEEN MOORE

I N RECENT YEARS, certain political and legal theorists who address the issues of citizenship have argued that liberal democracies should accommodate distinctive religious or cultural groups by granting them special rights or by offering some measure of autonomy in matters of self-governance. This is what Will Kymlicka means when he writes about "differentiated citizenship rights."[1] These accommodations would give religious or cultural minorities the option of maintaining their own normative universe (*nomos*) in which law and cultural narratives are inseparably related.[2] For the United States, however, the problem with this framework of pluralism is that it risks a certain level of *misrecognition* in politics. By this, I mean that certain stereotypes persist in what some have called identity politics and in pro-identity group policies. More importantly, the discourse of foreign relations, and how this discourse shapes how Americans perceive their national interests abroad, tends to befuddle the issues of equality and religious liberty for particular minority cultures at home. For instance, where public opinion is concerned, the questions "Whose Islam?" and "What Islam?" become significant when trying to separate the perceived threat of Islam as a destabilizing, global political force "out there" from the presence of Muslim citizens and residents in the United States. Conservative Christian leader Jerry Falwell explained his online statement to a religious Web site that "the Moslem faith teaches hate" by later telling the press that his comments were aimed at such Islamic countries as Iran and Iraq, not at American Muslims.[3] When addressing questions of diversity in society, especially regarding Americans' general openness to Islam in the United States, is mass opinion negatively influenced by images of Islamic terrorists in the Middle East?

A survey conducted in 2000 for the National Conference for Community and Justice shows that American Muslims remain unfamiliar to many people in the United States.[4] Moreover, the survey data show that Muslims are in limited contact with other Americans and, as a group, are among the most isolated in society and remote in people's feelings.[5] The problem, then, of misrecognition is not one simply of invisibility of Muslim Americans, but of a lack of intergroup and personal relations between Muslims and non-Muslims, and of the intersubjectivity that emerges from such relations.[6] A group can only make itself noticed in relation to others when it posits itself as uniquely situated in the world, with a particular contingent history. This claim requires that someone, some other, recognize the group; that recognition arises from situations in which the other generates normative behavioral expectations about the group in question. Does the group respond reflexively, and therefore become constituted by, generalized behavioral expectations?

Such questions of visibility become particularly challenging when large and increasing numbers of people live their lives across borders, giving rise to transnational forms of identities as partial outsiders, under circumstances in which they are simultaneously incorporated into the daily life of more than one nation.[7] These include not only permanent residents but "nonimmigrants" to the United States, such as "migrant laborers, emigrés who are awaiting return to their home countries (such as Iranians and Afghanis), a large number of students studying at American universities, businessmen, itinerant missionaries, and sizeable contingents of diplomats from forty-four Muslim nations to the United States and the United Nations."[8] Such persons have influence in varying degrees on questions of identity and marginality as they participate in their communities and institutions. Moving between these universes of experience, they are compelled to make constant choices and constantly learn quite new social languages.

Law in general, and "rights talk" in particular, are among these new social languages acquired by Muslim immigrants and their descendants now becoming visible in the United States. As Muslim groups organize themselves around "rights," they engage in a distinctive form of political action. The emergence of certain rights' advocacy groups, such as the Council on American-Islamic Relations (CAIR), the American Muslim Council, and various Muslim PACs, illustrates a particular kind of political consciousness that translates into a desire to achieve an emancipatory political recognition in the discourse of liberalism. The ideology of rights has long been part of the American experience, and when rights claims affect ways of thinking and acting collectively, they are said to be "constitutive."[9]

In this chapter I take up American Muslims' claims to rights under the liberal ethic of mutual recognition, how these claims are received, and what happens to the politicized identity of Muslims in the dialogic political processes of American pluralism. Specifically, I focus on the adoption by the U. S. Congress of the International Religious Freedom Act of 1998 (IRFA), a bill that attempts to redefine American foreign policy in the post–Cold War era, placing certain nations in diametric opposition to what many Americans believe about their own society and polity. The following section discusses religious freedom in the context of American liberalism. The remainder of the chapter turns to how Muslim Americans' rights become constituted in official discourses that profess a concern for religious freedom and how the creation of a social category, based on cultural determinism, in effect places institutional constraints on the practice of religious freedom domestically.

Religious Persecution Abroad

On October 27, 1998, after a lengthy campaign led by members of Congress who were upset by reports of increasing persecution of Christians in China, India, Russia, and a number of Muslim countries,[10] President Bill Clinton signed IRFA into law.[11] This law states in its preamble that its purpose is:

To express United States foreign policy with respect to, and to strengthen United States advocacy on behalf of, individuals persecuted in foreign countries on account of religion; to authorize United States actions in response to violations of religious freedom in foreign countries; to establish an Ambassador at Large for International Religious Freedom within the Department of State, a Commission on International Religious Freedom, and a Special Adviser on International Religious Freedom within the National Security Council; and for other purposes.[12]

Further on, IRFA defines a distinct political culture and commitment in the United States, premised on the religiously pluralistic nature of American society and the historical struggle to gain religious freedom. The statute reads:

The right to freedom of religion undergirds the very origin and existence of the United States. Many of our Nation's founders fled religious persecution abroad, cherishing in their hearts and minds the ideal of religious freedom. They established in law, as a fundamental right and as a pillar of our Nation, the right to freedom of religion. From its birth to this day, the United States has prized this legacy of religious freedom and honored this heritage by standing for religious freedom and offering refuge to those suffering religious persecution.[13]

The law, then, illuminates American national identity, and thereby justifies official action, by reference to freedom from religious persecution as fundamental. Though historically sited in the foundation of the independent nation, this value is maintained in the text of this law as a crucial and ageless symbol of American heritage.

On a practical level, the enactment of this new law requires the State Department to monitor and annually report the violations of religious liberty that occur worldwide, on a country-by-country basis. It also creates the position of U.S. Ambassador-at-Large for International Religious Freedom, and a supporting commission. The law authorizes the president to take appropriate measures to sanction an offending country when the State Department reports international violations of religious liberty. Measures include unilateral economic sanctions, tying improvements in religious tolerance to foreign aid, international loan approval, and preferential trade status.[14]

To explain why the United States would go so far as to monitor and take diplomatic action against religious repression in other nations, the text of the law reminds us that "the right to freedom of religion is under renewed and, in some cases, increasing assault in many countries around the world."[15] It asserts that more than one-half of the world's population "lives under regimes that severely restrict or prohibit the freedom of their citizens to study, believe, observe, and freely practice the religious faith of their choice. Religious believers and communities suffer both government-sponsored and government-tolerated violations of their rights to religious freedom."[16] Further,

State-sponsored slander campaigns, confiscations of property, surveillance by security police, including by special divisions of "religious police", severe prohibitions against construction and repair of places of worship, denial of the right to assemble and relegation of religious communities to illegal status through arbitrary registration laws, prohibitions against the pursuit of education or public office, and prohibitions against publishing, distributing, or possessing religious literature and materials.[17]

The list of religious abuses continues:

> Even more abhorrent, religious believers in many countries face such severe and violent forms of religious persecution as detention, torture, beatings, forced marriage, rape, imprisonment, enslavement, mass resettlement, and death merely for the peaceful belief in, change of, or practice of, their faith. In many countries, religious believers are forced to meet secretly, and religious leaders are targeted by national security forces and hostile mobs.[18]

The law also identifies—not specifically, but in a general fashion—the most common type of perpetrator of these abuses. It states, "though not confined to a particular region or regime, religious persecution is often particularly widespread, systematic, and heinous under totalitarian governments and in countries with militant, politicized religious majorities."[19] In resolutions adopted during the 104th Congress (the session preceding the one in which this law was proposed), the House and Senate each separately condemned the persecution of Christians worldwide, specifically in China, Russia, and Muslim countries, and expressed concern over the plight of the Bahai community in Iran. Congress acknowledged these concerns as a basis for congressional action, in the enactment of the law in 1998, by directing the executive branch "to use and implement appropriate tools in the United States foreign policy apparatus, including diplomatic, political, commercial, charitable, educational, and cultural channels, to promote respect for religious freedom by all governments and peoples."[20] Beyond condemning gross violators of religious freedom, this statute purports to "channel United States security and development assistance to governments *other than those found to be engaged in gross violations of the right to freedom of religion*."[21] In other words, U.S. funds, appropriated for foreign policy objectives, are to be used to reward allies and sanction enemies, where the term "allies" is limited to those countries that permit religious freedom.

Apart from the clear message that Congress has been busy carving up the map along a new axis in the post-Communist, post–Cold War era, critics of this legislation have argued that the unintended consequence may be to convince religious extremists around the world that the United States is attempting to serve its own particular religious preferences by standing for the liberty of Christians rather than the cause of religious freedom.[22] In the congressional debates leading up to the passage of this law, countries such as Pakistan, Saudi Arabia, Iran, Egypt, and the Sudan were indeed singled out for particular attention as consistent offenders.[23] In his testimony to the Senate Foreign Relations Committee in June 1997, Senator Joseph Lieberman (D-Conn.), the principal sponsor of the bill, reported that instances of persecution of Christians who refuse to convert to a "fanatical brand of Islam" are on the increase in Iran, Sudan, Saudi Arabia, and Egypt:

> In Saudi Arabia, more than 1,000 Christian expatriates have been arrested and imprisoned since 1990 for simply participating in private worship services . . . [we know also of] branding of Christian children in Sudan; driving Copts from their homes in Egypt; [and] beating and then murdering evangelical pastors and Baha'i in Iran—it is a call to action. [24]

Lieberman's characterization of this act of Congress as a "call to action" is a militant one, responding to what is apparently taken to be a serious threat to faith around the world. He is staking a claim to stand for (and defend) "something" in the wake of the collapse of world communism. Once nearly everyone around the world had abandoned planned economies, what was there left to struggle against? How do "we" differentiate ourselves as a superpower? The answer, this "call to action" suggests, lies in the realm of ethics.

In the House of Representatives, Rep. Lincoln Diaz-Balart (R-Fla.), in floor debates over the bill that was adopted as IRFA, provided the following defining duty, which is to stand for *something* in the post-Communist world:

> I often think about what we have witnessed in the last years and the fact that we are in a transitional moment. I often think about the fact, while doubtless, we saw an "evil empire," as President Reagan often called it, collapse, I wonder what it is that has won. What is it that has won? And what kind of a world is it that we are walking into at this stage in our history? In a certain sense that is what we are discussing. That is what will be discussed and debated with this particular legislation. We have to decide, ultimately, if what we accept and what we wish to embrace as a society and as a world, as an international community, is ethics as some sort of guide, some sort of factor in human conduct; or whether we are officially going to embrace the law of the jungle, if we are going to simply embrace the concept, as Dostoyevsky said when he pointed out that in his belief, those who say that God does not exist in effect are saying that anything is possible. In other words, if the concept of ethics will have no relevance whatsoever, then we might as well officially proclaim that in this era in which we are living.

Yet the sanctions supplied by IRFA, and the law itself, are gratuitous. Many of the violators of religious freedom are nations already sanctioned under U.S. law—for instance, Iran, Iraq, and Sudan. Others such as China have not been subject to sanctions because of some overriding interest of the United States, such as improved trade relations.[25] Finally, the law itself stands for freedom of religion, a value already expressed as fundamental law in the U.S. Constitution. The only difference is that this law would seek to extend American power beyond the nation's borders, to reach abuses under jurisdictions other than its own. For this unilateral extension of power, the United States has been criticized, and resisted, abroad. For instance, in March 2001 the U. S. Commission on International Religious Freedom (CIRF) visited Egypt, Israel, the Palestinian territories, and Saudi Arabia to monitor religious freedom. The Muslim Brotherhood condemned the delegation's visit as "provocative" and "an infringement of the jurisdiction and sovereignty" of these nation-states, interfering in their internal affairs.[26] In Egypt, a number of human rights organizations refused to meet with delegates from the commission because they viewed it as a unilateral organization, unauthorized by any bilateral or international agreement, designed to pursue American political intentions in Egypt.[27] Upon their arrival in Egypt, delegates met with Pope Shenuda III, the head of Egypt's minority Coptic Christian Orthodox community. Accounting for about 6 percent of Egypt's population, the Copts have complained of discrimination against them in education, state bureaucracy, the police, and the army. The Muslim Brotherhood, as well as some human rights organizations, see the American commission's decision to monitor the Copts' religious freedom as hegemonic and factional.

What are the implications of this renewed definition of foreign policy objectives, based on ethics, for the political formation of Muslim rights' advocacy groups as minority faith communities in the domestic context of American law and politics?

American Liberalism

Aside from the debates about the shape the post–Cold War world is taking, the reiteration of religious freedom as a crucial icon of national identity, and the search for some justification to continue the global expansion of American power, the adoption of IRFA is part of a larger regulatory framework with certain domestic implications that are well worth our attention. Whereas, once the American nation-state might have been said to have been a relatively minimalist, "night watchman" state, over the last half-century it has transformed itself into a heavily bureaucratized, highly interventionist "welfare-warfare state," a transformation caused by the imperatives of capital.[28] Feminist theorist Wendy Brown tells us that:

> [O]n the other side, the liberal subject is increasingly disinterred from substantive nation-state identification, not only by the individuating effects of liberal discourse itself but through the social effects of late-twentieth-century economic and political life: deterritorializing demographic flows; the disintegration from within and invasion from without of family and community as (relatively) autonomous sites of social production and identification; consumer capitalism's marketing discourse in which individual (and subindividual) desires are produced, commodified, and mobilized as identities; and disciplinary productions of a fantastic array of behavior-based identities ranging from recovering alcoholic professionals to unrepentant 'crack mothers.' These disciplinary productions work to conjure and regulate subjects through classificatory schemes, naming and normalizing social behaviors as social positions.[29]

As Congress formulates certain social categories of persons for purposes of regulation overseas—here on the basis of religious identification, in order to protect and defend the rights of the religiously oppressed—it is cutting across liberal-juridical identities (i.e., national identities) on the basis of an abstract right (religious freedom). Potentially, this produces political identity and alliance through these regulatory categories, destabilizing the power of sovereign nation-states to command the loyalty of their subject-citizens and creating a common identity based on the principle of freedom. Paradoxically, though, the effect of regulation can be the very antithesis of the meaning of freedom.

By this, I mean that the creation of any category of people makes it possible to generalize about their moral worth as a conceptually distinct group. Thus, in dialogue about the plight of the religiously oppressed—in other words, those people who are oppressed for their distinctive identities and for the strength of their convictions—we are likely to hear the message that *we* are normal, *they* are deviant and, furthermore, that *we* are innocent of contributing to their circumstances of oppression. Our feelings about this range from empathy to indifference to revulsion. Yet even in the most benign view, the religious minority that is oppressed is seen as different. Their differentness is a product of a single aspect of their lives, their religious identity and beliefs, and all other aspects are either ignored or seen through this particular lens. By creating this division and consequent category of people, we are able at once to distinguish *us* from *them* and to appropriate normalcy to our own lives and circumstances.[30] Thus, the law discussed here becomes a vehicle for the conventions of power and privilege that are constitutive of the late modern regulatory state, through which certain individuals and groups are cast as marginal while the powerful are normalized. Consequently, this law mandating religious freedom abroad among our allies can be understood as an expression of hegemonic power across juridical boundaries. It also rewards certain forms of religious behavior and has a different impact on members of dominant and subordinate religious and cultural communities.

A central aspiration of liberalism is to create a maximally tolerant and diverse society that provides ample social space for a wide array of religious and cultural groups.[31] Some have argued that the conferring of rights within that social space, for the historically disempowered and stigmatized, has been a powerful symbol of "all the denied aspects of their humanity: rights imply a respect that places one in the referential range of self and others, that elevates one's status from human body to social being."[32] And yet, the claim for rights on the basis of group identity (rights as Muslims) raises a central problem for liberal society, because, according to some theorists of political liberalism, respect for diversity does not require society to accommodate all forms of group life. In other words, there are some forms of religious and group life that are incompatible with the very idea of liberal society and thus cannot be tolerated in the name of respecting diversity.[33] In theory, then, groups that are hostile to liberal values (e.g., religious freedom, equality before the law) are not granted recognition. According to Seyla Benhabib, the "politics of fulfillment," or the notion that a future society might be able to realize the social and political promise that current society is unable to achieve, postpones the resolution of contradictory tensions underlying liberal democracy (for instance, promising religious freedom to the individual but refusing to recognize group-based rights).[34] The politics of fulfillment requires that a liberal civil society live up to the promises of its own rhetoric by offering the means to express demands for justice and rights.[35] Yet this begs the question, Who determines what forms of group life are tolerable? Who decides which groups profess illiberal values and traditions and thus are not afforded the protection of their interests from the decisions of a powerful cultural majority?

Much research has already been published on the perceived disparity in the treatment of Muslims in the United States and the prejudiced depictions of Muslims in popular culture and the news media. Yet this chapter is not about the mistreatment of Muslims domestically in the United States or the hypocrisy of American foreign policy, nor is it a critique of the domestic roots of foreign policy or the interest group politics of American pluralism. Rather, it is an attempt to explore the ways in which the institutional contexts of the regulatory state—i.e., the collection of structures, procedures, rules, and customs that define the legal and political processes of claiming "rights" and asserting interests— help to shape the aspirations of rights' advocacy and to channel its political strategies. Legal tools, beyond being instrumental in the pursuit of justice, actually shape forms of consciousness. It is about what cultural studies theorist Paul Gilroy calls a "politics of transfiguration," through which "qualitatively new desires, social relations and modes of association" within the subordinate community of interpretation and resistance emerge.[36]

What happens to the politicized identities of such persons as Muslims in the United States when there is a strong assertion of the preeminence of American hegemony on the global landscape? As Yvonne Haddad has noted, the fluctuation in American foreign policy during the last forty years or more "appears to have deeply troubled or even alienated the majority of Muslim citizens" of the United States. Haddad continues:

> As America's position of leadership in the world has increased during the last four decades, interaction between Muslims throughout the world and American society has accelerated dramatically. Yet the American establishment appears to continue to ignore Muslim sensibilities. . . . American foreign policy has been perceived as increasingly hostile to Islam and Muslims. This has been exacerbated by events such as the Israeli invasion of Lebanon, American bombing in Libya, the Salman Rushdie affair and the Iraqi invasion of Kuwait.[37]

IRFA can be added to a long list of U.S. foreign policies that drive the point home among Muslim American constituencies. That list makes problematic the kinds of political and cultural investments required for full participation in the liberal ethic of mutual recognition.

Representatives of several national Islamic organizations met recently with State Department officials to discuss issues related to American Muslim civil rights. The discussion focused on topics such as the use of secret evidence in INS deportation cases, allegations of FBI harassment by members of the Muslim community, and the lack of American Muslims at policy-making levels in government. Ambassador-at-Large for International Religious Freedom, Robert A. Seiple, who chaired the meeting, said, "If we don't get [religious freedom] right in this country, we have nothing to say to the rest of the world."[38] Muslim groups represented at the meeting included the Council on American-Islamic Relations (CAIR), American Muslim Council (AMC), Muslim Public Affairs Council (MPAC), the Islamic Institute, North American Council for Muslim Women (NACMW), and others.

Constitutive Effects of U.S. Law

The embodiment of cultural assumptions in case law occurs in two ways. Either judges state them explicitly ("Ours is a color-blind constitution."), or they implicitly incorporate such assumptions by making statements that invite the reader to supply them. In the following discussion of case law relating to workplace accommodation and gender, the outcomes can be understood as a function of prevailing cultural assumptions about Muslims, whether explicit or implied.

Appellate Court Decisions

1. NO-BEARD POLICIES IN EMPLOYMENT CHALLENGED.   In an appeals court case in New Jersey,[39] the court reviewed the First Amendment claims brought by two Newark police officers who are Muslim and wore beards in compliance with the requirements of Islam. Officers Faruq Abdul-Aziz and Shakoor Mustafa are both devout Sunni

Muslims who assert that they believe they are under a religious obligation to grow their beards. In spite of federal law mandating religion-based exemptions from workplace policies,[40] the police department penalized the officers for violating the department's no-beard policy. The officers argued that while the police department allowed exemptions from this policy for medical reasons, it did not grant exemptions for religious reasons, and this violated the First Amendment's guarantees of free expression and free exercise of religion. The appellate court ruled in favor of the Muslim police officers. More importantly, the appellate case record includes a Muslim cleric's testimony relating Islamic requirements for grooming. The decision reads, "according to the affidavit of an imam, it is an obligation for men who can grow a beard, to do so" and not to shave. The affidavit of the imam continues:

> The Quran commands the wearing of a beard implicitly. The Sunnah is the detailed explanation of the general injunctions contained in the Quran. The Sunnah says in too many verses to recount[:] "Grow the beard, trim the mustache. . . ." I teach as the Prophet Mohammed taught that the Sunnah must be followed as well as the Quran. This in the unequivocal teaching for the past 1,418 years, by the one billion living Sunni Muslims world wide. . . . The refusal by a Sunni Muslim male who can grow a beard, to wear one is a major sin. I teach based upon the way I was taught and it is understood in my faith that the non-wearing of a beard by the male who can, for any reason is as [serious] a sin as eating pork. . . . This is not a discretionary instruction; it is a commandment. A Sunni Muslim male will not be saved from this major sin because of an instruction of another, even an employer to shave his beard and the penalties will be meted out by Allah.[41]

The court relied on the expert testimony of one Muslim cleric to determine whether this was a matter of some external authority requiring facial hair. In effect, what the appellate decision attempted to do was to assess the strength and nature of the Muslim individual's obligation to grow a beard, and to couch this language in terms of institutionalized 'rights.' In other words, the court searched for an Islamic law that required men to grow beards, and, significantly, for any legitimate reasons why a man may be excused from this requirement. Since the Muslim cleric said there were no legitimate exemptions, that refusing to grow a beard was a major sin even if done at the instruction of an employer, the majority of the appellate bench concluded that the Muslim officers' request for a religious exemption from the police department's "no-beard" policy was valid.

In reaching this decision the court needed to represent Islam in a way that made it cognizable under the law. In other words, Islam was narrowed down to a set of obligations that set Muslims apart from everyone else. Once that was established, through the testimony of the Muslim cleric, the judicial task then became one of weighing the absoluteness of the Islamic requirement against the validity of the police department's policy. Through such a balancing test, the court recognized the police department's position that it had legitimate concerns about uniformity of appearance and a desire to convey the image of a "monolithic, highly disciplined force" and its contention that permitting beards for religious reasons would somehow "undermine the force's morale."[42] However, the court determined that these justifications for refusing to allow religious exemptions from the "no-beard" policy were not enough to outweigh the Muslim officers' interest in wearing beards in compliance with their religion. Thus the particular obligation of wearing a beard was given the status of a fundamental 'right' protected by the First Amendment.

My point here is that an issue that started out as a matter of belief and obedience to God's will became translated in the judicial process into terms that made sense in the eyes of the law. For example, Officers Abdul-Aziz and Mustafa contended in their appeal that since the Newark police department grants medical, but not religious, exemptions from its "no-beard" policy, the department "has unconstitutionally devalued their religious reasons for wearing beards by judging them to be of lesser importance than medical reasons."[43] In response, the department maintained that it gave medical exemptions in order to comply with a federal statute, the Americans with Disabilities Act (the ADA, adopted in 1994). In evaluating these claims, the court held them in tension. While it is true that the ADA requires employers to make "reasonable accommodations" for individuals with disabilities, the court noted, another federal statute, Title VII of the Civil Rights Act of 1964, also imposes the "reasonable accommodation" requirement on employers with respect to religion.[44] These parallel requirements in the law of reasonable accommodation reduce Islam to a series of rules. As an artifact of legal reasoning, Islam is not regarded as a transcendent belief system but as a set of ritual practices of traditional origin that applies to Muslims and not to others. As Michael King puts it, "Islam takes on an identity-in-law of 'legal religiosity,' offering to its adherents an absolute or limited right to engage in prayer and ritual . . . Muslims are accepted as different, but not so different that they cannot be brought within the ambit of the liberal state."[45] Once the transformation has been made, and Islam is reconstituted as a set of rules and rights, it can take its "place in a legal world where [its] particular demands and obligations may be related to, compared with and placed in rank order with all other rights, obligations and demands."[46]

Another dimension of the court's influence in defining the "essence" of Islam in this case—allowing just one cleric to provide testimony to the effect that men are required to wear beards—presents only one Muslim standpoint. This suggests that Islam is monolithic and provides a representation of Islam that fails to reflect the considerable degree of diversity in the socioeconomic backgrounds, gender, political orientations, and religious practices among those who profess Islam. Yet this reduction to one standpoint is necessary for the law to be able to "reconstruct religion" as a set of rights, such as the right to wear beards or headscarves, in ways that conform to certain religious obligations. If multiple versions of Islam were permitted to speak in court, a plurality of voices would clash over what Islam requires, and then courts would have to evaluate the relative merits of each claim in order to assess the "true" representation.

Following the appellate court decision in *Fraternal Order v. Newark*, a Muslim officer of the New York State Park Police filed a similar lawsuit against his employer, claiming that a police chief violated his civil rights by suspending him for refusing to shave his beard. Park Police officials denied his request for religious accommodation and requested him to surrender his gun and badge when he arrived for work.

More cases seeking to establish the right to workplace accommodation of religiously mandated beards have been litigated before the courts. For instance, in two cases, *Mamdouh M. Hussein v The Waldorf Astoria, Hotel, Restaurant and Club Employees and Bartenders Local #6 and Carlos Lopez* (184F. Supp. 2d 591; decided March 30, 2001) and *Mamdouh M. Hussein v Hotel, Restaurant and Club Employees and Bartenders Local #6 and Peter Ward* (108F. Supp. 2d 360; decided Aug. 11, 2000), the Muslim plaintiff, an occasional banquet waiter, sued various hotels and his union because he was not permitted to work as a food server while wearing a beard. In another example, the Equal Employment Opportunity Commission (EEOC) sued Delta Air Lines and its contractor ServiceMaster Company in late 1998 for refusing to accommodate Muslim workers who wore beards. In its lawsuit, the EEOC claimed six Muslim workers lost their jobs for refusing to shave their beards. The six men, employed by ServiceMaster at Hartsfield International Airport in Georgia, provided cleaning and other services under a contract with the airline. Delta officials insisted that the men comply with that company's policy forbidding beards. When the workers challenged this policy, they were terminated. Representatives of the EEOC and CAIR entered negotiations with the two named defendants in December 1998 to try to reach an out-of-court settlement.

2. MUSLIM HEADSCARF AND EMPLOYMENT   In an effort to resolve a complaint brought forward by the Council on American-Islamic Relations, the management of the Old Country Buffet restaurant chain admitted that it had failed to recognize its obligation to accommodate a job applicant's religious beliefs. One of its restaurants, located in Illinois, offered the Muslim complainant a new job interview and an apology after being denied a job because of her religiously mandated head scarf.

In a similar incident in Pennsylvania, a Muslim teenager received an apology, back pay, and a job offer after being denied a job at a Pathmark Stores supermarket because of the religiously mandated headscarf. The Muslim job applicant told CAIR that when she brought up the subject of the head scarf in her job interview, the interviewer stated: "Oh, they don't care, you aren't allowed to wear the 'head gear.'" According to the fall 1999 issue of the CAIR newsletter, a Pathmark Stores official responded to the advocacy group's letter of complaint by saying the company was "concerned with the insensitivity of [the interviewer's] remarks" and that the interviewer was "clearly uninformed about Pathmark's policies."

The U.S. Postal Service has also been contacted by CAIR, following a complaint by a female postal worker in New Jersey alleging that she was not allowed to wear the headscarf "in front of people." According to the 1999 newsletter of the advocacy group, the employee was allowed to wear her headscarf as a result of its intervention.

Conclusion

The growing demographic presence and activities of Muslim communities in the United States has led to a rise in the number of religious discrimination cases. How understandings about particular legal conventions and resources are mobilized within Muslim communities, and how this impinges on the development of Muslim Americans' legal consciousness, is not always obvious or direct, but represents a gradual shift in the ways people make sense of their environments. These have important consequences for the development of a uniquely "minoritarian" or "diasporic" legal culture.

The autonomy Muslims seek and experience in the politics of recognition is limited because it derives from a non-Muslim common law tradition and is vulnerable to state control. To the degree that a judge permits Islamic law to apply, Islamic law is authorized by her or him, and justice falls under the court's jurisdiction. It is drawn into the framework of official law and is dependent upon the courts' acknowledgment of the Islamic code as "law." On the other hand, the politics of recognition may show how an alternative legality, such as Islamic law offers, can supplement or subvert state law by constructing a cultural space more responsive to community norms—even if that alternative legality is phrased within the language and structure of state law itself.

Notes

1. Will Kymlicka, *Multicultural Citizenship* (Oxford and New York: Oxford University Press, 1995), 26–33. See also Will Kymlicka and Ian Shapiro, eds., *Ethnicity and Group Rights* (New York and London: New York University Press, 1997).

2. Robert Cover, "The Supreme Court 1982 Term, Forward: Nomos and Narrative," *Harvard Law Review* 94 (1983); Ayelet Shachar, "Should Church and State be Joined at the Altar? Women's Rights and the Multicultural Dilemma," in Will Kymlicka and Wayne Norman, eds., *Citizenship in Diverse Societies* (Oxford and New York: Oxford University Press, 2000), 199–223.

3. "Falwell Remark Sparks Outrage: Religious Leaders Renounce Views on Islamic Faith," *The Arizona Republic*, March 8, 2001, A7. Though Falwell's original comment may point out the relative *invisibility* of Muslims in the United States, his prompt qualifier, if not retraction, indicates the *visibility* of an American Muslim "public."

4. Tom W. Smith, "Taking America's Pulse II: A Survey of Intergroup Relations." Preliminary report prepared for the National Conference on Community and Justice; Survey conducted by Princeton Survey Research Associates, May 2000. On file with the author. The category of "Muslim" consistently received the highest "Don't know" responses throughout the survey. For instance, when asked "How close do you feel to Muslims?" 35 percent of respondents said "Don't know"; when asked "How much discrimination is there against Muslims?" 24 percent of respondents said "Don't know."

5. Other isolated groups identified in the survey are lesbians and gays, atheists, and American Indians.

6. Jurgen Habermas suggests that a network of interactions linguistically mediated through a process of socialization "makes" a certain identity (whether individual or group) where there wasn't one before. The creation of a distinct group with a core essence (such as Muslim Americans) is not carried out in isolation but in relation to an antecedent Other; it is a significant differentiation. See Noelle McAfee, *Habermas, Kristeva, and Citizenship* (Ithaca, N.Y.: Cornell University Press, 2000), 29ff.

7. This transnationalism accepts its construction as a supplement or complement to the universal "we" implied in the American motto, *E pluribus unum*. See forthcoming work by Kathleen M. Moore, *The Unfamiliar Abode: The Construction of a Diasporic Islamic Jurisprudence* (Ann Arbor: University of Michigan Press).

8. Yvonne Yazbeck Haddad, "The Challenge of Muslim 'Minorityness': The American Experience," in *The Integration of Islam and Hinduism in Western Europe*. W. A. R. Shadid and P. S. Koningsveld, eds. (Kampen, Netherlands: Kol,1991), 142.

9. John Brigham, *The Constitution of Interests: Beyond the Politics of Rights* (New York: New York University Press, 1996), 31.

10. Jim Lobe, "Rights: U.S. Chides China, Arab States on Religious Freedom," *Inter Press Service*, September 5, 2000.

11. *International Religious Freedom Act of 1998.* U.S. Public Law, 105–292. 105th Cong., 1st Sess., 10 October 1998. Signed by the President, October 27, 1998.

12. Ibid., 2787.

13. Ibid., 2787.

14. Ibid., Sec. 405a, 2086.

15. Ibid., 2789.

16. Ibid., 2789.

17. Ibid., 2789.

18. Ibid., 2789.

19. Ibid., 2789.

20. Ibid., 2790. The legislation was considerably softened over time. Provisions for automatic economic sanctions were replaced by more flexible legislative language that gives the President the power to waive sanctions for "national interests" or if the Administration deems that penalties might provoke a popular backlash against religious minorities.

21. Ibid., emphasis added.

22. In a press conference held by the Republican congressional leadership, announcing the bipartisan vote (98–0) to pass the bill in the Senate, a leading sponsor of the bill, Congressman Frank Wolf (R-Va.), made it clear that persecuted Christians were the focus of his concerns. He said, "This bill gives a voice to the voiceless. The Catholic priests who are in jail in China today will know that this bill has passed. The Protestant evangelical pastors that are in jail will know it's passed. The Coptic Christians in Egypt who are being persecuted today—the Egyptian newspapers will have to cover that this bill has passed. The Christians who are being persecuted in Pakistan will know that this bill has passed—the Catholics in East Timor in Indonesia and all over the world and all these others." Rep. Chris Smith (R-N.J.) in the same press conference referred to persecution of Christians and Tibetan Buddhist monks by China, and the persecution of Christians in the Sudan. See FDCH Political Transcripts, October 16, 1998, "Holds News Conference on the International Religious Freedom Act," Washington, D.C. However, U.S. Secretary of State Madeleine Albright professed a different concern. Taking a defensive posture when announcing the second annual report on religious persecution abroad, Albright stressed that the United States did not seek "to impose American values on the world or defend any particular religion, but, rather, to promote and defend the right of every individual on this planet to honor his or her own chosen beliefs." Citation from Jim Lobe, "U.S. Chides China," September 5, 2000.

23. See, for instance, Rep. Frank Wolf's (R-Va.) comment at the news conference following adoption of the religious persecution bill in the House of Representatives, where he states that the new law will allow "equal access to U.S. missions abroad for conducting religious activities in places where religious activity is otherwise prohibited. This will help American citizens abroad who desire to worship, but cannot worship safely in local churches and would otherwise have nowhere to go. In places like Saudi Arabia, this is a real problem." See Congressional Press Releases, "Congress Passes International Religious Freedom Act," October 13, 1998. See also testimony before the Senate Foreign Relations Committee provided by Bat Ye'or on second-class status of "dhimmism" in Islamic law (Prepared statement of Bat Ye'or, Senate Foreign Relations Committee Subcommittee on Near Eastern and South Asian Affairs, *Religious Persecution in the Middle East*, "Past Is Prologue: The Challenge of Islamism Today," May 1, 1997); Esmaeil Ebrahim (Testimony, Esmaeil Ebrahimi, Iranian Christian Refugee, Senate Foreign Relations Near Eastern and South Asian Affairs, *Religious Persecution in the Middle East*, June 10, 1997); Nina Shea (Nina Shea, Director, Puebla Program on Religious Freedom, Freedom House, Senate Foreign Relations Near Eastern and South Asian Affairs, *Religious Persecution in the Middle East*, May 1, 1997); and Rep. Frank R. Wolf, when he says that, although the predominant religion in the countries concerned is Islam, he does not intend to condemn Islam

or Muslims (Prepared testimony of Rep. Frank R. Wolf [R-Va.] Senate Committee on Foreign Relations Subcommittee on Near Eastern and South Asian Affairs, May 1, 1997).

24. Senator Joseph Lieberman (D-Conn.), prepared statement, June 10, 1997.

25. It is the President's prerogative whether or not to apply sanctions under the terms of
the International Religious Freedom Act of 1998.

26. "Muslim Brotherhood Statement Condemns U.S. Delegation's Visit," published by
Egyptian newspaper *Al-Wafd* on March 20, 2001, p. 1; reported in BBC Summary of World
Broadcasts, March 22, 2001, Part 4: The Middle East.

27. See <http://msanews.mynet.net/refusal-to-meet.doc> and <http://msanews.mynet.net.
CIRF.doc>. See also the Web site of Egyptian human rights organization, The Human Rights
Center for the Assistance of Prisoners, at <www.hrcap.8k.com>.

28. Wendy Brown, *States of Injury: Power and Freedom in Late Modernity* (Princeton, N. J.: Princeton University Press, 1995), 58.

29. Ibid.

30. Brown, *States of Injury.*

31. John Rawls, *Political Liberalism* (New York: Columbia University Press, 1993).

32. Patricia Williams, "Among Moses' Bridge-Builders: Conversations about 'Brown,'" in *The
Nation,* May 23, 1994, v. 258, n. 20, 694.

33. Rawls, *Political Liberalism.*

34. Seyla Benhabib, *Critique, Norm and Utopia* (New York: Columbia University Press, 1987).

35. See also Paul Gilroy's brief discussion of Benhabib's "Politics of Fulfillment" in *Small
Acts: Thoughts on the Politics of Black Cultures* (London: Serpent's Tail, 1993), 134f.

36. Gilroy, *Small Acts,* 134.

37. Haddad, "The Challenge of Muslim 'Minorityness,'"143.

38. See fall 1999 newsletter of CAIR.

39. *Fraternal Order of Police (FOP) Newark v City of Newark* (3rd Cir., No. 97–5542, decided
March 3, 1999).

40. For exemption jurisprudence, see *Sherbert v Verner,* 374 U.S. 398 (1963); *Wisconsin v Yoder,*
406 US 205 (1972); *Thomas v Review Bd. of Indiana Employment Div.,* 450 US 708 (1981); *Bowen
v Roy,* 476 US 693 (1986); and *Employment Div., Dept. of Human Resources of Oregon v Smith,* 494
US 872 (1990). The *Smith* decision changed the legal landscape dramatically because the majority of the Court refused to apply the "strict scrutiny" standard in a case of free exercise of
religion. ("The right to free exercise does not relieve an individual of the obligation to comply
with a valid and neutral law of general applicability on the ground that the law proscribes [or
prescribes] conduct that his religion prescribes [or proscribes]." *Smith,* 494 US at 879.) However, the *Smith* holding does not apply in this case because the Newark police department already makes a secular exemption from the "no-beard" policy for medical reasons. The appellate court concludes that the officers are entitled to a religious exemption because the
department already makes secular exemptions.

41. *Fraternal Order of Police (FOP) Newark v City of Newark* (3rd Cir., No. 97–5542, decided
March 3, 1999), 3–4.

42. Ibid., 24, 25.

43. Ibid., 19.

44. Ibid., 20.

45. Michael King, "The Muslim Identity in a Secular World," in *God's Law Versus State Law:
The Construction of an Islamic Identity in Western Europe,* ed. Michael King (London: Grey Seal, 1995),
111.

46. Ibid., 108.

The American Muslim Paradox

3

AGHA SAEED

It was the best of times, it was the worst of times, it was the age of wisdom, it was the age of foolishness, it was the epoch of belief, it was the epoch of incredulity, it was the season of Light, it was the season of Darkness, it was the spring of hope, it was the winter of despair, we had everything before us, we had nothing before us, we were all going direct to Heaven, we were all going direct the other way—in short, the period was so far like the present period, that some of its noisiest authorities insisted on its being received, for good or for evil, in the superlative degree of comparison only.

—Charles Dickens, *A Tale of Two Cities*

The Muslim Paradox

IN *THE FUTURE OF THE RACE*, Henry Louis Gates Jr. and Cornel West have observed that, for African Americans, there exists in the United State a paradox of triumphs and tragedies. Within this framework they explore "today's paradox of the largest black middle class in American history coexisting with one of the largest black underclasses."[1] At the beginning of the twenty-first century, there exists a similar Muslim paradox in the United States. It is characterized by extreme vilification on the one hand, and by a considerable degree of acceptance, even popularity, on the other. This paradox is further evidenced by contradictory images of Islam and Muslims as well as by ambivalent public and private, individual and corporate, attitudes towards American Muslims.

Obviously, this is not a logical, but an existential, paradox marking a moment of transition—roughly from 1996 onward—both in the public perception of Islam and in the collective life of American Muslims. This transition appears to have been set in motion by a number of interrelated factors and processes, including the growing numbers of Muslims and Arabs in America; changing attitudes on the part of immigrant Muslims; Muslim movement into public space; continued opposition by some groups to vilify Muslims and Islam; complex forms of intervention by mainstream American institutions; international events and developments; and prejudices of the learned coupled with the apprehensions of the uninformed.

Today, more and more Americans are becoming aware of Islam as a religion practiced by a large number of their fellow citizens, they are becoming aware of mosques on the urban landscape, and they are becoming aware of Islamic holidays, religious practices, social values, and symbols. At the same time, American Muslims are gaining a firsthand, meaningful, and practical understanding of America, its traditions, institutions, values, mores, ethos, social norms, and political practices. This two-way learning accounts for a complex transition of Muslims from outsiders to insiders. I have analyzed this paradox by looking at several aspects of public life: policy debates, laws, media, academia, interfaith relations, government institutions, and electoral politics.

The Post–Cold War Policy Framework

The end of the Cold War necessitated a major refocusing of American foreign policy and articulation of a new policy framework, which, for a complex set of reasons, led to a major focus on Islam, first internationally, and then domestically. This focus has been both negative and positive.

The first major proposal for a new policy framework was an article titled "The End of History?" by Francis Fukuyama, which presented a neutral view of Islam. Fukuyama's primary argument, derived from a complex reading of Hegel, postulated history as a process driven by competition among three ideologies: communism, fascism, and liberal democracy. Since communism and fascism have fallen and liberal democracy has won, Fukuyama sees no competition of ideas and, thus, no history in the Hegelian sense. He further argues that, while countries like Iran may be "local irritants," they lack both an ideology to attract non-Muslims and a state apparatus to project themselves globally. Thus, Fukuyama perceived a possibility of a long-term global peace.[2]

In response, Harvard government professor Samuel Huntington wrote that Fukuyama and others had missed "a crucial, indeed a central aspect, of what global politics is likely to be." In an often-cited 1993 article, "The Clash of Civilizations?"[3] Huntington observed that world history had gone through several phases of conflict, namely among princes, nation-states, and ideologies, and had now entered its fourth phase of conflict, that among civilizations. Therefore, history has not ended. Reflecting on a list of eight civilizations, including the Western, Confucian, Japanese, Islamic, Hindu, Slavic-Orthodox, Latin American, and African, Huntington concluded, "The most important conflicts of the future will occur along the cultural fault lines separating these civilizations from one another" and "a central focus for the conflict for the immediate future will be between the West and several Islamic-Confucian states."[4] Huntington argued that countries that cannot compete with the West form alliances of cooperation with non-Western countries, the most prominent of which is the Confucian-Islamic connection that challenges Western interests and values. Thus, he said, it is in the interest of the West to try to limit the military capacities of Confucian and Islamic states, to exploit the differences between those two civilizations, and to strengthen international institutions that support Western interests and values.[5] Clearly, this important policy proposal, with its strong anti-Muslim tone, had the effect of placing Muslim and Arab countries in the villainous role vacated by erstwhile communist countries.

The Clinton White House tried to take the middle path. In a major policy speech, "From Containment to Enlargement," Anthony Lake, the National Security Advisor in the first Clinton Administration, observed that, while democracy and market economics will only be accepted in the West and Asia, we have neither come to the end of history nor to a clash of civilizations, but to a great democratic and entrepreneurial opportunity. He urged that the United States remember the contributions of Islam and the bonds between Islam and Judeo-Christian beliefs: "We will extend every expression of friendship to those of the Islamic faith who abide in peace and tolerance. But we will provide every resistance to militants who distort Islamic doctrines and seek to expand their influence by force."[6]

In a nutshell, Lake was telling the world that, after the defeat of communism, there was nothing left to contain and that the goal should be the expansion of market democracies. Lake made a clear distinction between Islam and Muslims and between pro- and anti-Western Muslim countries by couching these distinctions in the vocabulary of law-abiding states and "backlash" states. Though, within a year, Lake had given up his initial policy framework of "Enlargement" and instead had come up with a policy of "Dual Containment" (meaning "dual, simultaneous and non-interdependent containment of Iran and Iraq"), he did not alter his primary assertion that there is no inherent conflict between Islam and the West.[7]

On January 24, 1997, Secretary of State Madeline Albright further substantiated this theory of "backlash states," a term mostly applied to Iraq, Iran, Syria, Libya, the Sudan, North Korea, and Cuba. She divided the international state system into four types of states: stable democracies that follow international law, evolving democracies that "obey the rules but may not have all the resources yet to fully participate in it," rogue states that try to disrupt the international system, and failed states.[8]

Lake and Albright thus shifted the criteria for conduct evaluation from culture to law and from religion to market economy. Overall, these policy disagreements have yielded two significantly different conceptions of Islam. The first, principally articulated by Huntington, views Islam as the enemy civilization and seeks to contain it. The second, expressed by Fukuyama, Lake, and Albright, does not see Islam as a rival ideology or civilization or Muslim states as a monolith. It calls for a pragmatic, country-by-country evaluation and determination of who is a friend or an adversary. Most of the fifty-six Muslim states, according to the second view, are classified either as friends or as "not enemies." During the second Clinton term, there was even some movement toward improving relations with some "adversaries" such as Syria and Iran.

Domestic Policies

In the early- to mid-1990s, anti-Islamic and anti-Muslim policy perspectives were supplemented with equally negative domestic policies. Three actions by the U.S. government, one each by the executive, legislative, and judiciary, had a seriously damaging impact on

Muslim and Arab civil rights in the United States, including the ability to participate in the American political system and American public debate.

First, on January 23, 1995, President Clinton signed Executive Order 12947 that prevented American citizens—in practical terms, American Muslims—from contributing to Palestinian charities that played a crucial role in sustaining Palestinian opposition to Israeli occupation. As a result, a number of legitimate Muslim human service organizations could no longer operate in the United States because they were accused (mostly on Israel's behest) of being "controlled" by other organizations that had already been classified as "terrorist" organizations by the Unites States.[9] This order had the immediate effect of stifling three separate networks: politico-military organizations in the occupied territory of Palestine, some of whom may have engaged in violent activities; charitable organizations like schools, hospitals, orphanages, libraries, women's organizations, and community centers that were providing much needed help to Palestinians suffering under occupation; and charitable Muslim organizations headquartered in the United States that collected funds from American Muslims. This Executive Order constituted the first curtailment of Muslim civil liberties and human rights in the United States.[10]

Second, Congress passed the Anti-Terrorism and Effective Death Penalty Act of 1995, signed by the president on April 24, 1996, that allowed law enforcement agencies to try non-citizens in a court of law without evidence being shown to the accused and his or her lawyer. According to this Act, the prosecution could "substitute a statement admitting relevant facts that the classified information would tend to prove,"[11] i.e., to accept claims without proof and to oblige the defense to do the same.[12] Gregory T. Nojaim, Legislative Council of the American Civil Liberties Union (ACLU), argued in a memorandum before Congress voted on the legislation that it "will allow the government to deport aliens, convicted of no crime at all, based on secret information." Although it was a clear violation of the due process clause of the Constitution, the Justice Department and certain lobbies were able to get the legislation passed.[13]

Third, in 1999 the Supreme Court validated the denial of first amendment rights to non-citizens who, in this case, happened to be Muslim and Christian Palestinians.[14]

Post–Cold War legislation, administrative action, and constitutional interpretation have resulted in a diminution of civil rights in America, though, so far, these legal limitations have been mostly applied against Muslims and Arabs, most specifically against Palestinians. Arabs and Muslims have also been affected by other laws, such as profiling at airports. Nonetheless, amid all these reversals and setbacks, there have been signs of considerable opposition to these reversals as well as slow and small changes in codification of institutional attitudes toward Islam and Muslims, at least toward American Muslims.

Efforts at balance and fairness in domestic policies achieved a focus when, on June 10, 1999, four Congressmen[15] introduced a bill to repeal the "secret evidence" clause of the Anti-Terrorism and Effective Death Penalty Act of 1996. This bill became nationally known for its aim to "ensure that no alien is removed, denied a benefit under the Immigration and Nationality Act, or otherwise deprived of liberty, based on evidence that is kept secret from the alien."[16] Since this bill affected a national constituency directly and many minority groups indirectly, it became both a rallying point for major Muslim and Arab organizations and an instrument of coalition formation with other communities.

The debate in the House Judiciary Committee brought Muslim and Arab-Americans in direct contact with members of Congress. Many senators and representatives expressed shock that a law like the Secret Evidence Act existed and was being used against the weakest populations in the United States.[17] The fight to repeal the Secret Evidence Act is far from over, but a nationwide multiethnic, multireligious coalition for fairness and balance has already come into existence. Many hope that the fact that John Ashcroft, Attorney General under President George W. Bush, during confirmation hearings, expressed his hope to work to protect the rights of citizens[18] signals the possibility of the repeal of such legislation.

Media

Most news about Islam and Muslims printed and broadcast in America is foreign news, skewed toward violent events and actions.[19] That sells newspapers and keeps listeners interested. But it can be argued that news about Muslims and Muslim countries is further skewed by such additional factors as Eurocentrism, the historical legacy of the Crusades, what is now seen as the North-South divide, perceived threats to American values and interests, and the continued occupation of Palestine by Israel. A disproportionately important role in framing the image of Islam and Muslims in America is played by what is called "the Israeli filter." No one has written more perceptively about the Israeli filter and how it nuances the vilification of Muslims and Islam than Edward Said in his November 8, 2000, column in *Al-Ahram*. Said writes, "The events of the past four weeks in Palestine have been a near-total triumph for Zionism in the United States for the first time since the modern reemergence of the Palestinian national movement in the late 1960s." Said continues, saying, "Political as well as public discourse has so definitively transformed Israel into the victim during the recent clashes, that even though 140 Palestinian lives were lost and close to 5,000 casualties have been reported, it is still something called 'Palestinian violence' that has disrupted the smooth and orderly flow of the 'peace process.'" Said goes on to cite the many ways in which support for Israel is elicited, such as affirmation of Barak's sincere offers of concessions, Arafat's weakness and cowardice, Palestinian violence, anti-Semitism, and ancient hatreds.[20]

The current method of news writing implies that to say anything critical of Israel is to threaten the peace process and, ultimately, the overall well being of the people of the Middle East. Such reporting makes no allowance for the impact of military occupation by Israel, economic hardships, social chaos, political instability, near-fatal fear psychosis, and increasing loss of hope in the lives of a significantly large number of Palestinians. As a consequence of this pattern of news coverage, the distinction between the oppressor and the oppressed gets blurred, victims become vilified, and Muslims in general are represented in exceedingly negative ways.

American Muslims are thus denied the right to speak for themselves. Frequently, though not always, it is the so-called expert—one who "knows"—who speaks for the Muslims. This denial of self-representation, which has left Muslims disempowered in the extreme, is rooted in the Manichaen metaphysics of American journalism that divides the world into two absolute categories of good and evil, rejecting any possibility of change, compromise, and redemption, and insisting on the exclusion of those considered evil from the public discourse. This metaphysics is incapable of handling the idea that something can be "relatively good" or "relatively bad."

As far as the metaphysics of American journalism is concerned, the image of Muslims and Islam is centrally tied to the image of an irrational person. This theme of irrationality and violence is continuously reinforced through a number of variations involving Iran, Iraq, the Sudan, Syria, Libya, Afghanistan, Palestine, and, occasionally, Pakistan. Any solidarity with Palestine is reverse-engineered into invalidation of the speaker's credibility on the charges of supporting extremism, violence, and terrorism. Since Islam is seen as a major source of Muslim solidarity with the people of Palestine, the religion itself is called into question and presented as an ideology that promotes violence and sheer degradation of the individual. This metaphysics ties anti-Muslim and anti-Islamic rhetoric to the discourse of American power, which is itself made contingent on its opposition to Islam. In subtle ways, then, being friendly or even fair toward, Islam, Muslims, and the Palestinians (regardless of the fact that a number of them are of Christian faith) is seen as an anti-American act.

The New Islam

At the same time, however, all this media attention has resulted in slow and even grudging recognition that the American Muslim community has become large enough to matter socially, sociologically, and politically; and that Muslims are here to stay and are making important contributions to American society. A new picture of the American Muslims—this time empirically drawn—is beginning to emerge. Neighbors, friends, acquaintances, fellow-workers, classmates, roommates, and others who have come in contact with the Americans of Muslim faith are beginning to form impressions that are significantly different than those presented by the media and a section of the academy.

Institutional observers (leaders of political parties, churches, PTAs, and other civic organizations) are beginning to realize that Muslim Americans are not homogeneous ethnically, economically, or ideologically. Most of their preferences, like those of any other large group, are distributed over a wide spectrum of choices. These observers are also beginning to realize that most Muslims are family-oriented and hold moderate-to-conservative positions on societal values at the same time as most of them strongly support policies for social justice, civil liberties, and human rights.

This cognitive dissonance between how the media reports about Muslims and how most Americans experience their interaction with Muslims has exerted subtle pressure on the media to bring at least some aspects of their coverage in line with the everyday experience of Americans. As a consequence, in the last few years, the American media has developed two different ways of talking about Islam: Islam in America and Islam outside America. The media narratives about Muslims in Palestine, Afghanistan, Kashmir, Iraq, Lebanon, Syria, and the Sudan continue to be mostly harsh, stereotypical, and bear a tone of damnation and disapproval. But on the domestic scene, the tone, the technique, the theme, and the texture of the media coverage are beginning to change. Articles are appearing about religious holidays and practices, about the unfairness of anti-Muslim discrimination, and about efforts to ensure equal opportunity in various public arenas. New themes are now echoing in the media all over the United States, often in religion, community, culture, lifestyle, and even food sections of local and national newspapers.

Academia

The complex web of linkages between various communities of discourse such as the academy, the media, the policy establishment, and political leaders plays a crucial role in the articulation of both the elite consensus and popular consent for such a consensus. Chief among the academics who have been and continue to be influential in the forming of public policy is Bernard Lewis, author of many books, including the *Jews of Islam*. Over the years, Lewis has grown increasingly more critical of Muslims and Islam and, in fact, posited the argument about the clash of civilization even before Huntington did. In 1992 Lewis wrote, "We are facing a mood and a movement far transcending the level of issues and policies and the governments that pursue them. This is no less than a clash of civilizations—the perhaps irrational but historic reaction of an ancient rival against our Judeo-Christian heritage, our secular present, and the worldwide expansion of both."[21]

Lewis sees the relationship between Islam and the West as consisting of five phases: rise of Islam (624–1683), colonization of Muslim countries by Europeans (1683–1947), revolt and subsequent decolonization (1947–1973), revival of Islamic belief and self-awareness (1979–1989), and rage against the West (1989 on). Calling the last phase a rage of impotence and backwardness, Lewis connects it with another phenomenon taking place in Europe. Reflecting that capital and labor have succeeded where Moorish and Turkish armies failed, he notes the rising numbers of Muslims now living in Western Europe, which he refers to as "the third Muslim invasion of Europe."[22] In documenting the history of relations among Muslims and Westerners, Lewis repeatedly frames the issue of Islam and the West in terms of "the menace of Islam . . . that threatened the souls as well as the bodies of Christian Europe" and the uncouth presence of Muslim "barbarians."[23] But what he essentially articulates is the prejudice of the learned, which is far more sinister and difficult to rectify than the prejudice of the ignorant.[24]

Some members of the pro-Israeli camp worry that a successful mainstreaming of Muslim Americans will end Zionist monopoly over American Middle East policy. This Eurocentric and Zionocentric conception of Muslim presence in the United States is perpetuated by writers like Lewis, *New York Times* correspondent Judith Miller, and independent scholar Daniel Pipes. Gary Rosenblatt, in an article, "Monitoring the Muslim Threat" (published in *The Jewish Week*), says, "Pipes is a soft-spoken academic, but the words he uses to describe the American Muslim threat to the Jewish community are chilling. 'It's a freight train coming down the track and headed for us,' says Pipes."[25]

Many American scholars view Lewis as a kind of neo-Orientalist whose pro-Israeli bias has contributed to the demonization of Palestinians, Arabs, and Muslims.[26] Among established scholars who reject Lewis's "invasion" theory are John Esposito, Nikki Keddie, Houston Smith, Thomas Clarey, Ralph Braibanti, Ross Dunn, Thedore Wright, Hamid Algar, Yvonne Haddad, John Woods, Laurence Michalak, and many others. Such scholars do not see American Muslims as a threat to America. Rather, many of them argue that

Muslims can play a major role in the moral revival of American society and that there are increasing opportunities for Muslims and Christians to form alliances around a number of important social issues. Houston Smith notes that while Islam is both geographically and ideologically closer to the West than other non-Western religions, it is the most difficult religion for the West to understand.[27] Those who reject Bernard Lewis, Daniel Pipes, and Judith Miller's brand of scholarship contend that if Islam is the most difficult religion for the West to understand, then the challenge for scholars is to create maps of intelligibility and understanding, not to cause conflict by inculcating fear, apprehension, and misunderstanding.

Do these Muslim immigrants bring any special baggage with them? Not necessarily, writes Ralph Braibanti: "The use of poison gas by the Buddhist Aum Shinrikyo, the Oklahoma City bombing by an American Christian, the long-standing terrorism by Northern Irish Catholics, the violence of Indian Hindus and Burmese Buddhists against Muslims, the vicious ethnic cleansing by Christian Orthodox Serbs in Bosnia and Kosovo, the violence of drug-related Catholic mobs in Latin America, and the terrorism of Hindu Tamils against the Sinhalese Buddhist government of Sri Lanka demonstrate the universality of terrorism and the cultural and religious diversity of its origins."[28]

Governmental Agencies and Institutions

In 1993, the U.S. Department of Defense commissioned (Imam) Abdul Rashid as its first Muslim Chaplain. All branches of the armed forces have been assigned Muslim chaplains, and a crescent symbolizing Muslims in now included in the Chaplaincy Corps's insignia. An article in the *Muslim Journal* (November 17, 2000), "Muslim Military Chaplains Gather for 1st Annual Professional Conference," tells the story of how Islam is becoming a part of the institutional framework of the United States. Today, not only are Muslim imams (chaplains) serving in the armed forces, but there are Muslim institutions that can educate and train these imams for their professional careers. The Graduate School of Islamic Social Sciences (GSISS), for example, serves as "an Endorsing Agent for Muslim chaplains who serve in active duty and reserve components of the U.S. Armed Forces."[29] Muslim institutions are acquiring more complexity, more heterogeneity, and more professional staff and skills. Many of these institutions are now actually training Muslim Americans to effectively participate in various aspects of public life.

A number of government institutions have also demonstrated openness and inclusiveness (though a few of them, such as the Department of Justice, are considered to have been particularly harsh to Muslims). During the second Clinton Administration, the White House, the State Department, and the Postal Service, among others, took important steps to provide access and inclusion to the Muslim community. The first-ever *iftar* (fast-breaking) dinner was organized in the Caucus Room of the Cannon Building during the month of Ramadan in 1992, and attended by a large number of congressional leaders. Thereafter, *iftar* parties have been held at the Departments of Defense and State.[30]

A number of Eid (Muslim day of celebration) parties were held at the Clinton White House; four were hosted by the First Lady, and the fifth by President Clinton in January 2001.[31]

Initiated by Robert Seiple, Ambassador-at-Large for Religious Freedom, the State Department has been holding regularly scheduled meetings—known as the Muslim Roundtable—with leaders of Muslim organizations since February 19, 1999. And on November 13, 2000, the U.S. Postal Service issued an Eid Stamp. A press release issued by the American Muslim Alliance included this statement: "A true multicultural society acknowledges the symbols and values of all its citizens. We really appreciate Postmaster General William Henderson's view that stamps like the Eid Stamp 'continue to bring history to life.'"[32]

Interfaith Relations

Over the last few years, more churches have come to accept Muslims as fellow-believers and are trying to create a common cause with them.[33] In most major cities, new interfaith groups have been set up, or existing ones have been expanded, to include Muslim groups and individuals. These interfaith groups have become a source for improvement of understanding among Muslims, Christians, and other religious communities. Christian-Muslim and Jewish-Muslim relations in the United States have gone through several stages, including dialogue aimed at better understanding, development of mutually agreed on codes-of-conduct to improve inter-community relations, exploration of a shared sense of spirituality and cross-pollination of spiritual ideas, and joint action on shared causes and common concerns.

A number of groups in California, for example, illustrate these new efforts. Since 1990, the United Muslims of America (UMA), a Fremont-based Muslim organization, has been involved in interfaith dialogue with various Christian groups, and since 1994, it has been devoting most of its organizational energies and resources to interfaith outreach and dialogue. Today, UMA is involved with Interfaith Groups for Homeless in San Francisco, the Interfaith Alliance of Northern California, and the United Religions Initiative.[34] United Religions, an ambitious project modeled on the United Nations, was initiated by Anglican Bishop William Sweeny. Headquartered in San Francisco, it currently has two Muslims on its board of directors.[35]

In Los Angeles, a number of Muslim and Jewish organizations are engaged in an ongoing dialogue and have so far produced such documents as a charter for the conduct of Muslim-Jewish relations. As reported by Jessica Garrison in the *Los Angeles Times* (December 6, 1999), "With slow, painstaking pen strokes, 20 Jewish and Muslim leaders put their signatures on a document they hope will help bring their two communities closer together. The code of ethics calls for Muslim and Jewish leaders to meet regularly to talk over important issues and to immediately and publicly repudiate any group or institution that appeals to prejudice, hate or violence."[36] "Here in L.A., Muslims and Jews are neighbors," said Rabbi Alice Dubinsky, the acting director of the Union of American Hebrew Congregations' Pacific Southwest Council. "We can no longer cling to fear and prejudices."[37] What is even more significant is the emergence of a shared sense of humanity and spirituality. It is not entirely new for a religious figure to speak in favor of an oppressed community, or to try to rehumanize those who have been demonized, but now more and more Christian priests and pastors, for example, are beginning to speak on behalf of the Palestinian people. The result is that more Americans are becoming aware of the fact that both Muslim and Christian Palestinians are oppressed, exploited, and subjected to physical and psychological violence by the occupying country.

At the institutional level, the Anglican Bishops have recently initiated a series of programs to develop better understanding of Islam and better relations with American Muslims. A press release issued on January 11, 2001, contains the following public commitments: "The Bishops of USA have decided to study Islam and jointly organize programs with the local Muslim communities in order to promote understanding between the two religious communities and build bridges of peace and cooperation between the believers in the Muslim and the Christians communities."[38] The decision came at the end of a three-day retreat organized by the Episcopal Diocese of San Francisco and attended by bishops representing each of the fifty states.

Imam Warith Deen Mohammed and other members of his Muslim American Society have been actively engaged in dialogue and collaboration with the Roman Catholic Church since the early 1990s. An extraordinary testimony to the profound impact of Catholic-Muslim dialogue is provided by Malik A. Sharif in a front-page article in the *Muslim Journal*, the semi-official organ of Imam Mohammed's organization: "I received an invitation later to be part of the delegation led by our leader, Imam W. Deen Muhammad, to travel to Rome in June, 1998 . . . [to] a Conference being held at Castel Gandolfo, Pope John Paul's summer residence. This experience was beyond words, and the inner transformation that I experienced will be indelibly etched in my heart."[39] If this cooperative effort is successful in achieving the desired goal of "Harmonious Living of the Human Family," it could bring about a moral integration of Muslims in the American mainstream and contribute to remaking America into an Judeo-Christian-Islamic society.

The leaders of the Islamic Society of North America (ISNA), the largest American Muslim organization, recently have been involved in "friendly discussion" with the Methodist Church as a result of expressed Methodist interests in building fellowship with Muslims as fellow believers.[40] Mormons and Christian Scientists have taken similar initiatives to develop close contacts with American Muslims. Muslim groups have established institutional liaison with the Mormons and have held initial "let us get to know each other" meetings with Christian Scientists.[41]

Three factors seem to account for a positive shift in the attitudes of faith-based communities: shared moral values, common social causes, and a pragmatic need for peaceful coexistence. As a consequence, a subtle and implicit awareness of a mutual moral obligation is evident, one which must be seen not in idealistic but in quasi-moral and quasi-pragmatic terms. Though there remains much to be desired about the quality of Christian-Muslim relations in the United States, and these relations cannot be totally separated from Christian-Muslim relations elsewhere in the world, the process has definitely progressed beyond tolerance and acceptance to fellowship and shared spiritual pursuits.

Islam and American Politics

During the 1990s, Muslims groups started to actively participate in mainstream politics and public affairs. They supported and contributed to both the Republican and the Democratic parties, with politicians increasingly aware of the importance of courting Muslim support. However, their right to full participation as equal citizens was called into question during the New York senatorial race of 2000 in which Democrat Hillary Rodham Clinton was competing against Republican candidate Rick Lazio. Fund-raising disclosures in the *New York Daily News* indicated that Mrs. Clinton had received contributions from a Muslim group critical of Israel. As the *New York Times* was to editorialize a few days later, "Israel is always going to be a sensitive and hotly debated issue in any New York contest."[42] The information about contributions from a Muslim organization triggered a controversy over the participation of Muslim groups in the Clinton campaign. Under attack from her opponent, Clinton announced that she would return the money raised by the Muslim group.[43] But Rick Lazio continued to attack Hillary Clinton for including Muslim groups in her campaign. His attacks became so sharp and his methods so devious that in an editorial on October 30, 2000, the *Times* rebuked him in unusually strong terms, describing his "attack politics" as "absurd," "extreme," "desperate," "unethical," and "misleading."[44]

At the same time Dean E. Murphy of the *Times* wrote a front-page article about the American Muslim Alliance and the American Muslim Council, in which he fairly and accurately presented the Muslim point of view.[45] A few days later, the *Times* published a lengthy personality profile ("A Lexus Republican, But No Friend of Lazio") about the president of the New York Chapter of the American Muslim Alliance.[46] The strongest denunciation of Lazio came from Richard Cohen of the *Washington Post* in a column titled "Lazio's Political Pornography," in which he denounced Lazio for pandering and inciting hate and hostility against Muslims and Arabs. "If political seasons were like years in the Chinese calendar," Cohen wrote, "then Rick Lazio could be said to have made this the Year of the Weasel."[47]

Lazio was soundly defeated by a 55–43 margin. He lost not only Muslim and Arab votes, but even failed to win a majority of Jewish support, and is said to have energized thousands of those who would not have voted at all to support Hillary Clinton. And, in perhaps the unkindest cut of all, Lazio, a Catholic, ended up losing to Clinton among Catholic voters as well. "Maybe they got tired," said one aide afterward, "of hearing about our campaign for the Knesset."[48] The Lazio/Clinton contest may be indicative of a maturing of sensibilities in America in which bigotry against any group is becoming more and more difficult to sell.

Internal Issues of Islam and Politics

In the late 1980s and early 1990s, the American Muslim community was faced with the basic issue of how to politically define and defend its identity, interests, and values. To that end, it confronted a number of crucial and consequential questions: (1) Should Muslims participate in the mainstream American politics? An affirmative answer would necessitate major changes in ways of conceptualizing self-interest, goals, and strategies, decision making, community development, resources mobilization, and value generalization. (2) Should Muslims ally with a single structure (that of the Democratic or Republican party) or should they, like many other ethnic and religious minorities, work through the dual structures of community-based organizations as well as the mainstream political parties? (3) Should Muslim politics be goal/issue oriented, party oriented, or candidate oriented? (4) What are Muslims trying to achieve by participating in mainstream American politics? (5) What kind of institutions should be built to define and protect Muslim interests?[49]

Such questions are being answered as much by pragmatic considerations and under the pressure of circumstances as by reflection, dialogue, and collective decision. A number of social, legal, and political factors have caused a continual reconsideration of the community's aims and interests. In 1992, the Muslim community was divided about participating in the American political system. In 1996, the major Muslim organizations were ready to move but lacked a clear definitions of goals, strategies, and mechanisms to coordinate their activities. In 2000, the primary goal was to get the community to vote, vote in high percentages, and vote for a specific agenda.

Since 1994, leaders of the American Muslim Alliance, a California-based organization with ninety-three chapters in thirty-four states, have argued that an optimal Muslim strategy has to be focused on the presidential elections because only there can seven million Muslims "combine their votes to achieve a common aim."[50] By 1996 there was a complete consensus over this approach. In 1996 Muslim Americans came close to endorsing Bob Dole. Dole did send a letter to the Muslim leadership acknowledging that America draws moral sustenance from 'its churches, synagogues, and mosques' and expressing his support for Muslim civil rights, a balanced and "even-handed" policy towards the Middle East and a "dialogue" with "all Muslim counties."[51] These efforts, however, did not bear fruit primarily for two reasons. First, the Dole campaign was not willing to publicize its pronouncement through a national press conference or during the presidential debates. Second, the main Muslim organizations were divided on whether or not to endorse a presidential candidate and, if so, which candidate to endorse.

The discussion among the Muslim organizations at that time was sporadic and inconclusive, lacking an institutional mechanism for mutual consultation and decision making. It was the realization of the need for such a mechanism that eventually led to the creation of the American Muslim Political Coordination Council (AMPCC), an umbrella organization representing the American Muslim Alliance (AMA), the American Muslim Council (AMC), the Council on American-Islamic Relations (CAIR), and the Muslim Public Affairs Council (MPAC). The AMPCC was based on two principles: unity of purpose and division of labor among its members. The Council for Good Government (CFGG), the semi-official political branch of the Muslim American Society led by Imam W. D. Muhammad, was involved with all major decisions pertaining to the formation of the Coordination Council but in the end decided to participate only as an observer.[52]

AMPCC's 2000 endorsement of George W. Bush for president was based on three factors: his accessibility as a candidate, his record on issues of importance to the community (especially support for the repeal of the Secret Evidence Act), and feedback from the community. The endorsement was preceded by a public commitment by the AMPCC leadership at the 37th Annual Convention of the Islamic Society of North America (ISNA) in Chicago, Illinois, on September 2, 2000. AMPCC leaders declared, "We are not fighting, we are united, and two weeks before the election, we will make up our collective mind, and issue an advisory for the presidential candidate." The moment was poignant and historic: while the audience of some ten thousand stood and cheered, American Muslim leaders held their clasped hands high and shouted, "We will make a difference."[53] On October 23, 2000, at a press conference held at the National Press Club in Washington, D. C., the AMPCC leadership did in fact announce its endorsement of Governor George W. Bush and Dick Cheney.[54]

Paul Findley, a former U.S. Congressman and author of the bestseller *They Dare To Speak Out*, has estimated that, because of the AMPCC endorsement, about 2.3 million Muslims voted for Bush.[55] Dalinda Haley, news editor for the *Washington Report on Middle East Affairs*, credits Marshall Witmann, a senior fellow at the conservative Hudson Institute as saying, "The underlying reality is that in the last week of this campaign, the Arab-American and Muslim communities are more important than the Jewish community in the presidential race. Jews are locked into their allegiance to the Democrats. The Arab-Americans and Muslims are a genuine swing vote that could go either way. That gives them a surprising last minute edge in the political leverage given the closeness in the presidential race."[56] The importance of the Muslim vote to his victory was recognized by Bush and the leaders of the Republican Party, some of whom have already held an important post-election meeting with Muslim leaders.

The Forty-Third President: A New Approach?

In his inaugural speech on January 20, 2001, President George W. Bush made explicit references to American Muslims in addition to Christians and Jews. This was a small but significant gesture of inclusiveness at the highest levels of the American administration. For the president to visualize America as a network of moral communities of which the Muslims are a significant part was gratifying to many among the Muslim community, and Muslim leaders expressed appreciation for President Bush having said that "[c]hurch and charity, synagogue and mosque lend our communities their humanity, and they will have an honored place in our plans and in our laws."[57]

On Monday, January 29, President Bush issued two executive orders to initiate faith-based and community-based programs in five areas: justice, housing and urban development, health and human services, labor, and education, in order to ease "regulations that inhibit religious charities and to promote grass-roots efforts." Again, he included Muslims in his list of invited guests as well as in his remarks: "First it is good to have so many groups represented here; religious and nonreligious, Catholic, Jewish, Protestant and Muslim, foundations and nonprofits. I want to thank you all for coming. This is the collection of some of the finest America has got to offer, people who lead with their hearts and, in turn, have changed the communities in which they live for the better."[58]

Conclusion

The conclusions of this essay are summarized in four parts dealing with 1) patterns and trends, 2) changing attitudes of the Muslim community and organizations, 3) changing attitudes of the mainstream communities and institutions, and 4) future possibilities.

Patterns and Trends

As Islam, and consequently American Muslims, has been placed under Western scrutiny, there has been a gradual shift in expression of hostility from Arabs to Muslims. Edward Said has correctly observed that "before the sudden OPEC price rises in early 1974, 'Islam' as such scarcely figured either in the culture or in the media."[59] But this shift in media and public focus from Arabs to Muslims served to transfer hateful stereotypes of Arabs onto Muslims. According to a survey conducted in 1981, "a large percentage of 600 people surveyed believed Arabs to be barbaric, cunning, anti-Christian, anti-Semitic, and bloodthirsty."[60] More recently, negative images of Arabs have been automatically generalized to all Muslims, and thus, common prejudices have been extended to an even larger number of people. Contributing to these prejudices are such factors as suspicion of strangers, lack of sympathy for foreigners, Eurocentric contempt for Arabs, Zionist racism against Palestinians, and a residual resentment against Muslims dating back to the Crusades.

Despite all the negative stereotypes, however, 152 Muslims were elected to various local, city, and state offices in November 2000.[61] Characterized by ambivalence and reactions to totally different kinds of stimuli, the American Muslim paradox, among other things, springs from conflicting expectations and contradictory experiences. This paradox bridges the gap between the corporate view of Islam, on the one hand, and interpersonal interaction among Muslims, Christians, and Jews, on the other.

Evolution of a New Organizational Culture

The 1990s were the decade of maturation of American Islam in terms of structural organization to which a number of factors contributed.

The law of unintended consequences has worked again. Penalties selectively imposed on Muslims and Arabs such as profiling, use of secret evidence, denial of first amendment rights, harassment by law enforcement agencies, and legal sanctions against humanitarian aid to the people of Palestine, have created a direct link between the Palestinian struggle for freedom and the Muslim struggle for civil rights in America. Interestingly, this has had the result of putting Palestine, or more precisely Jerusalem, at the center of American Muslim activism. Issues designed to create a wedge between Palestinian Muslims and other Muslims have turned the question of Jerusalem into a common cause for most, if not all, Muslims in America. This is clearly evidenced by the Charter of the American Muslim Political Coordination Council (AMPCC), which includes many organizations with substantial numbers of non-Arab Muslim members.[62] It is also clearly and forcefully expressed in the joint statement issued by the Council of Presidents of Arab-American Organizations and the American Muslim Political Coordination Council on January 20, 1999, identifying Jerusalem and the Secret Evidence Repeal Act as its two most important goals. [63]

The last decade has seen the emergence of multilevel relations and a "managed interdependence" among Muslim organizations.[64] These interorganizational relations are becoming knowledge driven and knowledge defined. Organizations producing knowledge about mainstream America are beginning to play an important role in reshaping the internal priorities and external modalities of a number of Muslim organizations. The infusion of new knowledge has brought about a reconceptualization of the purposes and priorities among these organizations. This reconceptualization, among other things, has led to changes in the definitions of the problems they are trying to solve. In the 1950s and 1960s, the main issue for the major (agenda-setting) Muslim organizations was the prevention of forced assimilation. By the 1990s, the problem to be solved became the removal of barriers lying between American Muslims and mainstream America. These barriers include stereotyping, vilification, discrimination, exclusion, prohibition, and double standards. Even partial removal of each of these barriers is beginning to bring about significant sociocultural and political changes. In the realm of perceptions, symbols are of great importance and can rapidly modify popular attitudes and opinions.[65]

The Muslim community is deep into the process of developing American roots. The American-born generation takes America as its hub in the universe and no longer looks toward ancestral lands. It is they who have visualized the need for culling out all the pieces of evidence of the Muslim presence in America and reconceptualizing them, at least as a frame of reference if not a lifestyle. In a carefully negotiated framework of continuity and change, of identity preservation and boundary negotiation, Muslim organizations are beginning to trace the history of Islam in America. The popularity of books about African Muslims in antebellum America, for example, testifies to an important shift in the institutional reckoning of Muslim history and identity.

This desire for discovery of Islamic roots in America is beginning to create new combinations of memory and imagination, value and interest, self and the other. The most powerful consequence—which had, until recently, remained removed from the community discourse—is acceptance of America as home by a vast majority of immigrant Muslims. Public recognition of the fact that America is home has changed many readings of history and has affected discernible changes in the agendas of major social and political organizations. Ever since Malcolm X's pilgrimage to Mecca, American Muslims have emphasized their religious values of racial equality and their historic legacy of racial harmony in America's interracial dialogues. Domestic issues—issues that spring from and can be reconciled within the boundaries of the United States—are being given increasingly greater importance. Even international issues such as Jerusalem/Palestine, Kashmir, Somalia, and Bosnia are being reconceptualized and reframed in domestic terms.

The question: "What is a Muslim issue?" is now getting answered in increasingly broader terms. "Every issue that deals with welfare of human beings, with the betterment of the society, with the improvement of environment, and with the preservation of resources is a Muslim issue. From this point of view affirmative action is a Muslim issue, environment is a Muslim issue, infrastructure development is a Muslim issue and so are crime, education and economy."[66] The fact that the American Muslims, like American Christians, are a multiracial and multiethnic community has only accelerated the process of collective interspersing with a number of ethnic groups and coalitions and within what Nathan Glazer has called "an American ethnic pattern."[67] American Muslims, it seems, participate in this pattern twice. First collectively, and then as members of specific ethnic groups, namely blacks, whites, Arabs, South Asians. This double participation is leading to double fusion and multidirectional acculturation.

Changes in the Mainstream Community and Institutions

A significant number of Americans have now come to recognize Islam as an American religion. This is evidenced by frequent references to churches, synagogues, and mosques, even by hard-line conservative leaders and thinkers. To the extent to which opposition to Islam still exists— and it is not insignificant—it can be characterized in two ways: (1) There is greater hostility toward Islam than toward Muslims. Most Americans find their interaction with Muslims in many different circumstance to be fair and even pleasant, or at least no different than with members of any other religious community. (2) There is a far greater acceptance of Islam in America than Islam outside America. Even when American Islam is vilified, it is by linking it to Islamic causes, movements, and social practices in the Middle East, South Asia, and Africa.

American Muslims face such challenges as acquiring detailed and comprehensive knowledge of their new homeland; fighting against the continued vilification of Islam and exclusion of Muslims; turning symbolic access into substantial access; and earning the right to coauthor America's vision of itself and its future. Many American Muslim leaders believe that the first decade of the twenty-first century is a time for Muslim initiative, creativity, and activism. It is a time for Muslims to build new models for community life that can handle the demands of modernity and postmodernity. They must accept the challenges of learning to work in open and democratic societies, of developing the art of policy debate in the public square, of accepting victory and defeat in accordance with the rules of the game, and of recognizing and acting on the need for coalition-building and compromise in a pluralistic polity.

Future Possibilities

New Internet technologies have brought forward multidimensional opportunities for communication, activism, intragroup cohesion, and diverse forms of participation in American conversations. More and more elected officials now hear from their Muslim constituents; many of them have met Muslim voters and supporters face to face, attended candidates' forums organized by Muslim groups, and given lectures and keynote addresses at conferences, seminars, and leadership training workshops organized by Muslims. A number of state legislatures including California, New Jersey, Wisconsin, and Texas have passed resolutions to applaud the American Muslim Alliance for its work in areas of civic education, voter mobilization, and leadership training. Likewise, resolutions have been entered into the permanent record of the U.S. Congress to appreciate the contribution of the American Muslim Council and the American Muslim Alliance.[68]

Now that Muslims are voting and running for public office and beginning to join political parties (not just Democratic and Republican but also other parties such as Green, Libertarian, and Peace and Justice), their participation in electoral politics is already an accomplished fact. Muslim leaders are now regularly invited for briefings and discussions at the State Department and the White House (at least, the Clinton White House) as well as for Eids and *iftar* parties. Muslim leaders have demonstrated considerable skill in developing greater clarity of purpose and agile structures of cooperation in their interaction with other groups and communities and greater flexibility and sophistication in conducting negotiations and building coalitions with their counterparts.

The American-born generation (those "who not only speak but also think without an accent"), has now become the second-tier leadership within the Muslim community. This leadership, born and raised in a democratic society, holds great promise of introducing Islam in a nonthreatening fashion as well as making American goals and ideals intelligible to their parents' generation. This generation of interpreters and bridge-builders is already playing an important role in reducing uncertainty on both sides, though presently more so within the Muslim community than in mainstream America.

This coming of age of a generation born and raised in the United States, instant and constant electronic communication with numerous communities of discourse, impressive achievements in the economic field, modest gains in politics—all of these factors have given American Muslims both the incentive and the confidence to start discussing an agenda for both internal reform and external negotiation. As articulated at the January 27, 2001, AMPCC meeting, the next goal is to transform symbolic into substantial access and to earn the right to participate in decision making, policy planning, and resource allocation.[69]

It appears that the time of confusion and ambivalence—Can we retain our identity in the American context?—is over.[70] (This ambivalence was the inner dimension of the Muslim paradox.) Today, most Muslim leaders recognize that it is their responsibility to take the first step to open a dialogue with mainstream groups, organizations, and institutions. Many of them seem eager to fulfill this responsibility, believing that it would help them turn the current paradox into a partnership for the collective good of America.[71]

Notes

1. Henry Louis Gates, Jr. and Cornel West, *The Future of the Race* (New York: Vintage Books, 1996), viii.

2. Francis Fukuyama, "The End of History?" *The National Interest* 16 (Summer 1989): 3–19. The article was later expanded into a full-length book, *The End of History and the Last Man* (New York: Free Press, 1992).

3. Samuel Huntington, "The Clash of Civilizations?" *Foreign Affairs* 72, no. 3 (Summer 1993): 22–26. Like Fukuyama, Huntington expanded this article into a book, *The Clash of Civilization and the Remaking of the World Order* (New York: Simon and Schuster, 1996).

4. Ibid., 25, 48.

5. Ibid., 45–49.

6. Anthony Lake, "Confronting Backlash States," *Foreign Affairs* 72, no. 2 (March–April 1994): 45–55.

7. Ibid.

8. Secretary of State Madeleine K. Albright, Press Conference at the Department of State, Washington, D. C., January 24, 1997 (Office of the Spokesman, Department of State).

9. Clause I (a) (iii) of Executive Order 12947.

10. President William J. Clinton. Executive Order 12947. (The White House, Office of the Press Secretary, 24 January 1995).

11. Clause I (A) (iii) of the Act.

12. U.S. Congress. Anti-terrorism and Effective Death Penalty Act of 1996. Also, "Omnibus Terrorism Act of 1995."

13. Gregory T. Nojaim, "Memorandum: Omnibus Terrorism Act of 1995," American Civil Liberties Union, March 2, 1995.

14. Reno v American-Arab Anti-Discrimination Comm., 525 U. S. 471 (1999).

15. David Bonior (D-Mich.), Tom Campbell (R-Calif.), John Conyers (D-Mich.) and Bob Barr (R-Ga.).

16. U.S. Congress. H. R. 2121. Introduced in the 1st Session of the 106th Congress by Congressman David Bonior (D-Mich.) on June 10, 1999.

17. Interviews with leaders of AMA, AMC, CAIR, MPAC, and members of Dr. Mazen Al-Najjar's defense team.

18. Senate Judiciary Committee. John Ashcroft Confirmation Hearings. January 16–21, 2001.

19. See Stephen Hess, "What Gets Covered and Where?" in *International News and Foreign Correspondents* (Washington, D. C.: Brookings Institution Press, 1996), 28–46.

20. Edward Said, "American Zionism," *Al-Ahram*, November 8, 2000. Cornel West has described Said as "the most distinguished cultural critic now writing in America." See the book jacket of Edward Said, *Culture and Imperialism* (New York: Alfred A. Knopf, 1993).

21. Bernard Lewis, "The Roots of Muslim Rage," *The Atlantic Monthly* 266 (September 1990): 47–60.

22. Bernard Lewis, *Islam and the West* (New York: Oxford University Press, 1993), 25, 42.

23. "The idea of the barbarian," Lewis reassuringly tells his readers, "comes directly from the Greek classics" (25).

24. Ibid., 25.

25. Gary Rosenblatt, "Monitoring the Muslim Threat," *The Jewish Week*, March 24, 2000, 7.

26. See, e.g., Dilnawaz A. Siddiqui, "Evolution of Bernard Lewis's Style of Covering Islam and Muslims." Paper presented at "Islam in America" Conference of the Islamic Society of North America, July 4, 1998.

27. Houston Smith, *The World's Religions* (San Francisco: Harper, 1991), 221.

28. Ralph Braibanti, *Islam and the West: Common Cause or Clash?* Occasional Paper Series, The Center for Muslim-Christian Understanding: History and International Affairs, Edmund J. Walsh School of Foreign Service, Georgetown University.

29. "Muslim Military Chaplains Gather for 1st Annual Professional Conference," *The Muslim Journal* (November 17, 2000).

30. Interview with Aly Ramadan Abuzakuk, Executive Director, American Muslim Council, February 15, 2001. Also, interviews with Tahir Ali, Chairman, American Muslim Alliance—Massachusetts; and Saleem Akhtar, Chairman, American Muslim Alliance—Midwest Executive Council on February 16, 2001.

31. Ibid.

32. American Muslim Alliance—Head Office, Press Release, November 13, 2000. (Available on the AMA Web site: <www.amaweb.org>.)

33. In Fresno, California, for example, the Islamic Society of East Bay and St. Paul United Methodist Church share a parking lot and other facilities.

34. Interview with Shafi Refai, President, United Muslims of America, February 12, 2001.

35. "The Bishops of U.S. Decide To Study Islam," Episcopal Diocese of San Francisco, press release, January 14, 2001.

36. Jessica Garrison, "Muslims, Jews Sign Agreement," *The Los Angeles Times*, December 6, 1999.

37. Ibid.

38. "Bishops Decide to Study Islam."

39. Malik A. Sharif, "All Roads Lead to Washington, D. C. for Faith Communities Together," *Muslim Journal* 26, no. 1, October 13, 2000, 1–3.

40. Interview with Dr. Sayyid Muhammad Sayeed, Secretary-General, Islamic Society of North America (ISNA), February 14, 2001.

41. Interview with Shabbir Mansouri, President, Center for Islamic Education, 27 January 2001.

42. Editorial: "A Report Card on Attack Politics," *The New York Times*, October 31, 2000.

43. Dean E. Murphy, "Mrs. Clinton Says She Will Return Money Raised By a Muslim Group," *The New York Times*, October 26, 2000.

44. Ibid.

45. Dean E. Murphy. "For Muslim Americans, Influence in Politics Still Hard to Come By," *The New York Times*, October 27, 2000.

46. Robin Finn, "A Lexus Republican, But No Friend of Lazio," *The New York Times*, November 3, 2000.

47. Richard Cohen, "Lazio's Political Pornography," *The Washington Post*, November 2, 2000.

48. Stephanie Saul and John Riley, "How Senate Race Was Won, Lost / Lazio's missteps aided Clinton's strategy." *Newsday*, November 12, 2000.

49. Taken from a series of interviews with leaders of the American Muslim Alliance (AMA), the American Muslim Council (AMC), Council on American-Islamic Relations (CAIR), the Council for Good Government (CGG), and the Muslim Public Affairs Council (MPAC) at various occasions during 1999 and 2000.

50. Minutes of AMA Meeting held in Sunnyvale, California, on October 1, 1994.

51. *Washington Report on Middle East Affairs* 15, np. 5 (October–November 1996): 42.

52. Interviews with leaders of the American Muslim Alliance (AMA), the American Muslim Council (AMC), Council on American-Islamic Relations (CAIR), the Council for Good Government (CGG), and the Muslim Public Affairs Council (MPAC) at various occasions during 1999 and 2000.

53. *Washington Report on Middle East Affairs* 19, no. 8 (October–November 2000): 21–22.

54. "American Muslim PAC Endorses George W. Bush for President," press release issued by The American Muslim Political Coordination Council (AMPCC) on October 23, 2000.

55. Findley reflected that Bush has Florida Muslims to thank for his victory as they discarded normal Democratic Party allegiance to vote as a bloc for a Republican. "The Muslim Bloc Vote," *Washington Report on Middle East Affairs*, 20, no. 1 (January–February 2001): 25.

56. "Historic Muslim- and Arab-American Bloc Vote a Coveted Political Prize," *Washington Report on Middle East Affairs* (December 2000): 6, 110.

57. President George W. Bush, *Inaugural Address*, <www.whitehouse.gov>.

58. Dana Milbank, "Bush Unveils 'Faith-Based' Initiative," *Washington Post*, January 30, 2001.

59. Edward W. Said, *Covering Islam: How the Media and the Experts Determine How We See the Rest of the World* (New York: Random House, 1996).

60. Belkeis Altareb, "Development of a Scale to Measure Attitudes Toward Muslims," in Phylis Lan Lin, ed., *Islam in American: Images and Challenges* (Indianapolis: University of Indiana Press, 1998), 55.

61. "152 American Muslims, Mostly AMA Members, Elected to Local and State Offices," American Muslim Alliance, Press Release, November 12, 2000. (Available on the AMA Web site <www.amaweb.org>)

62. *Charter of the American Muslim Political Coordination Committee* (AMPCC), May 5, 1998.

63. Text of a Joint Statement by Muslim-American and Arab-American Coordination Councils (July 5, 1999), *Washington Report on Middle East Affairs* 18, no. 6 (September 1999): 13.

64. This has been accomplished in several ways: projects shared by two or more organizations, unanimous positions and action through AMPCC, and randomized participation in larger coalitions involving dozens of local and regional organizations.

65. Interviews with leaders of the American Muslim Alliance (AMA), the American Muslim Council (AMC), Council on American-Islamic Relations (CAIR), the Council for Good

Government (CGG), and the Muslim Public Affairs Council (MPAC) at various occasions during 1999 and 2000.

66. Dr. Maher Hathout, "Contemplating Islam in the 21st Century America." Lecture delivered at the Fifth Annual Convention of the American Muslim Alliance held in Irvine, California, on September 30–October 1, 2000.

67. Nathan Glazer, "Emergence of an American Ethnic Pattern," in *From Different Shores: Perspectives on Race and Ethnicity in America*, ed. Ronald Takaki (New York: Oxford University Press), 13–25.

68. These resolutions/commendations were passed/signed on the following dates: 1) The State of Wisconsin, Office of the Governor, 14 October 1997; 2) The Commonwealth of Massachusetts, A Proclamation by His Excellency Governor William Weld, 14 September 1996; 3) State of New Jersey, The Senate and General Assembly, 22 June 1996; 4) State of California, The Senate and the Assembly, 14 February 1997; 5) U.S. Congress, Statement entered into the permanent record by Congressman Dennis Kucinich "In Honor of American Muslim Alliance on the Occasion of the 4th Annual AMA National Convention—Hon. Dennis J. Kucinich (D-Ohio), 21 September 1999.

69. Interviews with leaders of the AMA, AMC, CAIR, and MPAC, January 27, 2001.

70. Ibid.

71. Ibid.

The Greatest Migration? 4

ROBERT M. DANNIN

Hijra, Migration, and African American History

*H*IJRA IS REMEMBERED BY MUSLIMS WORLDWIDE as the event that marks the beginning of Islamic history. It designates the Prophet's migration from Mecca to Medina and the subsequent rise of Islamic civilization. As part of the divine law (Shari'a) it encourages believers to reenact the Prophet's migration as a sign of revival, purification, and strengthening of the faith. Usually, this occurs as a ritual celebration of the past in the form of scriptural recitation and prayers meant to consolidate Muslim communal identity. Such enduring practices maximize the impact of a distant event—revelation—upon the social and individual corpus. From a Westerner's perspective, this is also visibly codified in other aspects of Muslim culture, in theory reflecting the ways of life of seventh-century Arabia. One could say that *hijra* encapsulates Qur'anic scripture within a very specific temporal dimension and exercises its influence over competing notions of time and history (for example, the Gregorian calendar). Conversely, *hijra* represents for Muslims the continuous suppression of *jahiliyya* (Arab prehistory, called by Muslims "the period of ignorance, *jahl*") and the permanent guarantee of divine control over time. In the twenty-first century this culture is manifest throughout the vast *umma* (community), including North America where African Americans have emerged as a singularly identifiable group among the generally estimated four million practicing Muslims.[1]

By assuring the continuity of historical time, *hijra* simultaneously becomes a self-sustaining symbol of Islamic space. It demarcates territorial hegemony by defining a space where believers prevail socially over infidels. As a formula that constantly informs the Muslim imagination, *hijra* measures the equilibrium between the *dar al-Islam* (abode where Islam prevails) and the *dar al-harb* (abode of war, or non-Islamic space). At the same time, it envisions a gradual expansion of the former into the latter until the *umma,* or Islamic community, can be realized as the totality of humankind.

Jurists have traditionally interpreted *hijra* by examining the particular social conditions of believers from place to place and recommending appropriate action to safeguard and project Muslim identity. Relevant considerations pertain to the freedom to exercise Shari'a and, more generally, to the establishment of a legitimate Muslim voice in secular as well as religious affairs. Where Muslim power has waned and conditions for propagating the faith have deteriorated, jurists advise the faithful to consolidate themselves as a community of worship in order to protect the message of Qur'anic revelation from external sources of compromise. This can take many forms, such as a call for revival or, in the extreme, even *jihad* (so-called holy war). Muslims residing on the periphery of the *umma*, however, are usually summoned to migrate to the center.

Hijra is thus a globalizing force for organizing cultural meaning among the corpus of believers. It is an historically effective source for self-recognition and a defense against secularization. Through the optic of *hijra*, one can see easily how Islam has become a highly visible ideology of resistance, if not a revolutionary project, in a contemporary world dominated by neo-utilitarian values. In the course of studying religious conversion among minorities in North America, I have come to understand that Islam attracts African Americans because it addresses a similar need to constitute visible self-sustaining communities across time and space. Their conversion is facilitated by a recurrent allegory of spatial mobility, firmly rooted in African American experiences of social transplantation from the Middle Passage to slavery, the Underground Railroad to freedom, the Great Migration to the city, and the long march toward Civil Rights and racial equality.

To explain the Islamic movement in America, it is necessary to take into account popular African American religious symbols as well as the social movements and migrations they represent. Thus, a chronological description of African American history can be seen as a Biblical simile, personified by individuals like Harriet Tubman, whose code name was "Moses." Tubman guided slaves northward to freedom on the Underground Railroad, itself a network of religiously committed abolitionists willing to risk their lives for the sake of moral values. Another example is the image of Marcus Moziah Garvey exhorting members of the UNIA (United Negro Improvement Association) to invest in the Black Star Steamship Line. Such an investment was touted as the first step in a return to the African motherland, suggesting a redemptive Middle Passage in reverse. Particularly important to the twentieth century were the Great Migration (1916–1930), when one million blacks journeyed from the rural South seeking work and shelter in the industrial North, and the Civil Rights Movement (1954–1968), whose mass demonstrations and other actions led to the end of legalized racial segregation.

A form of migration more arcane although no less prominent in the black imagination was the practice of passing. Sometimes referred to as the "invisible migration," passing provided the opportunity for some African Americans to take advantage of New World "creolization" in order to assimilate into white society. In Louisiana—not the only region where miscegenation occurred—this practice resulted in a pseudoscientific movement called "bleaching" the race. "It is a fact," commented two early observers of identity politics, "that Louisiana quadroons have frequently found it convenient to imply that their lineage was Jewish."[2]

In the atmosphere of lynching and urban race riots (East St. Louis, 1917; Chicago, 1919) this single-file exodus could sometimes mean the difference between life or death. And if the migration worked in terms of religious identity, then one might also assume that even a dark complexion could be rendered invisible by reference to one's "Hamitic" or Semitic ancestry. Retold as family legends into the late twentieth century, these recitations of ancestral pedigree resonate even today among many African American Muslims who attest to the Semitic heritage of their parents and grandparents, affirming their Hebrew practices and Jewish affiliations.[3]

A singular problem encountered by participants in this process was the need to remain "invisible." If those who claimed Judaism wished to associate with Hebrew congregations (Moorish Zionists, Commandment Keepers, B'nai Zaken), then they risked the disapproval of the Ashkenazi immigrants from Europe, who monopolized claims of Jewish authenticity. Schism on the basis of these issues stood in the way of any significant judaization, despite the intriguing scriptural allegories that memorialize pasts in which both Jews and African Americans shared the terrible fate of slavery.[4] By contrast, conversion to Islam suggested a practical alternative because it permitted a similar degree of social latitude (by no means absolute) without the corresponding problems of authentication because "normative" Islam was demographically insignificant, and more or less invisible, until after 1965.

This absence of educated Muslim clerics represented some advantages as well as disadvantages for the convert. One the one hand, it allowed this invisible migration to flourish unobstructed by inquiries as to one's motivation in becoming Muslim. For example, the musician Dizzy Gillespie revealed that Islam caught on among his fellow beboppers when several realized that an Arabic name printed on their union ID cards entitled them to a better class of restaurants and hotels than those available under the "Jim Crow" system of racial apartheid.[5] During this period, conversion to Islam did not imply adherence to a single standard of worship and belief; competing doctrines ranged from orthodox Sunni Islam to Sufism, the Ahmadiyyat, and Black Nationalist forms of Islam.[6] Muslim nonconformists still abound, yet they may enter any mosque as long as their *salat* is proficient. In terms of self-selected leadership of Black Islam, there did not seem to be any doctrinal thresholds, exams, or litmus tests to prevent strong-willed, religiously inclined, and civic-minded men from becoming imams. Indeed, grassroots empowerment has been the hallmark of African American Islam, a process it shares with (and perhaps partially inherited from) the most effective elements of the Black Church.

When it comes to reckoning time and space, Muslims in America take several different approaches to *hijra*. Lacking the formal institutions (*madhahib*) to guide the application of Shari'a, the majority have interpreted the call to mean a figurative migration, conforming to the general pattern of spiritual revivalism found in mainstream American religions. The zealous integration of scripture into daily life characterizes many different fundamentalist sects. For some of the most devout worshippers, however, a willingness to abide by the civic pathways designated for achieving religious goals concedes too much. Rather than acknowledge these customary ways of struggle, they seek to uphold the tenets of their religion over and against the principles of the secular state. Some Muslims do this by participating in a religious retreat that is physically isolated from the rest of society. Others have tried to construct inner city colonies where individuals and families live in close proximity to their mosque; they attempt to find jobs or start businesses in the same neighborhood. Their goals usually include eventual ownership of a block or more of contiguous buildings, forming a kind of neighborhood where Islamic regulations are observed. In some cities, schools provide education from early childhood through high school, as well as adult-supervised recreational activities and sports facilities. This is the ideal of an enclosed *dar al-Islam*, a patch of "greenpeace" representing the faith that is encircled by the *dar al-harb* of the rest of the ghetto. Non-Muslims residing in these areas are sometimes informed that they will be subject to the same laws that prevail for the Muslims, including strict prohibition of vices, alcohol, narcotics, and sometimes even cigarettes. In this limited way, once a local community has attained a critical mass and a corresponding civic presence, it can seek to extend its morality over its entire neighborhood.

Examples of this interpretation of *hijra* exist in Cleveland's Universal Islamic Brotherhood, where the call to prayer (*adhan*) is broadcast for all to hear five times daily, beginning early in the morning for *fajr* prayer. This symbolizes the extension of *hijra* over inner-city space. Another such attempt to build an Islamic neighborhood occurred around Masjid At-Taqwa in the Bedford-Stuyvesant section of Brooklyn.[7] Historically, earlier attempts by the Dar ul-Islam Movement occurred also in Bedford-Stuyvesant as well as in adjacent Crown Heights, where the Chabbad Lubavatcher community of orthodox Jews served as an example for instituting autonomous religious authority inside an urban ghetto.[8] Two examples of these options will help to illustrate how the African American *hijra* is still being carried out. The following descriptions are based on original ethnographic field work conducted in the early 1990s in upstate New York and Cleveland, Ohio.

West Valley (*Jabul Arabiyya*)
Mohammedan Village Byproduct of Depression: Worshippers of Allah Carve Out Community in Hillsides of Cattargus County[9]

In 1938 the Buffalo chapter of the Adenu Allahe Universal Arabic Association (AAUAA) accepted the advice of their spiritual guide, Professor Muhammad Ezaldeen; they searched for a large parcel of land where they could build a Muslim village. Led by six fully employed steel workers, the group purchased one hundred acres on a hill above the small town of West Valley, New York. For several years they shuttled between their apartments in Buffalo, their jobs, and the building site. They dug wells and irrigation ditches and staked out individual plots for their homes where they excavated foundations and then erected wooden frames hewn from nearby timber that they harvested and sawed into boards. The first structure completed was a mosque meant to serve as the both civic and religious center for the settlement. With living quarters secured and winterized by 1941, they abandoned their city apartments and moved permanently to West Valley while continuing to work in factories, devoting all their spare time to the settlement. They purchased livestock and prepared gardens for planting. Matching their physical exertions with resolute determination, they acquired the necessary financial knowledge to negotiate loans and building supplies. They incorporated their community as "Jabul Arabiyya" (Arabian Hills), and quickly became known to local townsmen as the "Black Arabs."

Muslim women sawed wooden boards and hammered shingles alongside the men. They farmed and tended to their children during the daytime, prepared dinner when the men returned from work, and rejoined their labors until nightfall. Prayer services and Islamic instruction continued in the rudimentary mosque where children received daycare. By 1942, the village was permanently settled. The *muhajirun* (those who have emigrated) elected a leader (*emir*), appointed committees, and apportioned collective funds for further construction. Talib Sayyed, the first *emir*, built a duplex house to accommodate Professor Ezaldeen whenever he wanted to visit. Members of the Buffalo AAUAA who were unemployed were invited to emigrate with their families, their labor welcomed as sufficient collateral to acquire a residential plot and building materials. By 1945 twelve families formed a permanent core of villagers, not counting Professor Ezaldeen who made periodic visits between trips to other AAUAA "units" in Detroit, Syracuse, Philadelphia, and Newark. He would often bring members of these affiliated communities to observe the progress at West Valley, hoping to inspire their own plans for *hijra*.

Following this example, the Philadelphia unit acquired land across the Delaware River in southern New Jersey and soon established another settlement which they named Ezaldeen Village. The professor's blueprints outlined an internal constitution governed by Islamic law as well as the steps necessary to incorporate each settlement according to its respective state charter. But his dream of a national *hijra* composed of all AAUAA settlements floundered because many units were too poor to even purchase land. The Philadelphians insisted that West Valley continue to pay dues to AAUAA "headquarters," provoking resentment and poor relations between the two units. The latter, having leveraged all possible assets to pay for their homes, refused on the grounds that the notion of "headquarters" had no meaning in the Qur'anic interpretation of *hijra*.

West Valley's potential as a model Muslim community depended upon industrial wage labor. Farming produced some staples and seasonal crops, but the results were meager and neither the rocky soil nor deforested hills could guarantee anything resembling self-sufficiency. In fact, poor management of the timber harvest had left large patches of loose soil that gave way during seasonal rains inundating the village. Denuding the hillside also left the village without shade from the merciless summer sun. Several families could not cope and returned to Buffalo, but the six core pioneers persisted for years until, one by one, they retired to live out their dream of *hijra* on union pensions.

At ninety years of age, Sheik Daoud Ghani was the only surviving pioneer when I visited Jabul Arabiyya in 1992. He recounted the settlement's history not only in terms of *hijra* but also as the realization of his youthful dream of homesteading.[10] He focused on the legacy of a South Carolina farm that was deeded to his great-grandmother after the Civil War, but was seized as eminent domain by the U.S. Army just prior to World War I. As the son of Southern sharecroppers, Ghani learned this story directly from his grandmother. Ghani became a teenage deacon in the Baptist church and also joined the Prince Hall Masons. He began to nurture the hope of restoring the family's status of landownership. Motivated by this overriding desire, he sought out individuals with similar aims. He married a "free Ishi" woman (part Native American, part European, part black) and then cast his lot with thousands of others moving north in search of jobs during the Great Migration.

West Valley, New York, May 15, 1992—Sheik Daoud Ghani (d. 1995) the last surviving pioneer at Jabul Arabiyya, settled 1938. © 2000 Jolie Stahl.

After landing a steady job at the Republic Steel mill, Ghani resumed his quest. His first encounter with Islam was through the Ahmadiyya Movement, whose indigenous sheiks (recent converts themselves) proseltyzed in urban centers around the Great Lakes. After listening to the Ahmadiyyas for a few months, Ghani and his colleagues became disenchanted with their poor command of Islamic pedagogy. Someone had heard of Professor Ezaldeen through the grapevine and hopped freight trains to Philadelphia to recruit his assistance. Soon the professor arrived and immediately provoked intense debate with his ideas about converting to true Islam, changing one's name, and establishing an autonomous state according to the doctrine of *hijra*. "Ezaldeen said, 'I will teach you gentlemen how to love each other, how to help each other and how to put your money together and buy land.' And when he said that, it struck me and I hollered, Wow! Afterwards he asked why I had yelled. I said, 'Muhammad Ezaldeen, that's what I've been trying to do since I was fourteen!' and he replied, 'Well, you're the guy!'"

By 1992 Jabul Arabiyya had been in decline for several decades. Most of the original structures were abandoned and uninhabitable except for the mosque and three houses, including Ghani's. The permanent population had dwindled from fifty to fewer than twelve adults, most of whom relied upon occasional employment and public assistance. Some depended upon Ghani, now retired, for transportation into the neighboring village or to do even simple errands. Two pioneer children and one adult grandson remained there; having attended public high school in West Valley in the 1960s and performed military service, they had returned to assist their aging parents. Their siblings had long since departed for jobs and families outside the influence of the Shari'a. Two men were in their middle-to-late forties and spent their idle time carousing with non-Muslim friends from the area. One of them, Haaneyfan Rafeek, remorsefully explained his life growing up in Jabul Arabiyya as one long rebellion against the rigid code of law promulgated by Professor Ezaldeen. Rather than structuring an orderly religious community, the "little green rule book" became the source of intergenerational conflict and tremendous angst.[11] Eventually, the residents of Jabul Arabiyya suffered from the postindustrial recession and were unable to fully appreciate the virtues of the *hijra*, which gave them land but took away any chance of modern comforts.

Ghani voiced no bitterness about Haaneyfan's narrative, told in his presence. His own recollections furnished details of the pioneers who remained until the end as well as others who deserted the self-imposed hardships of rural homesteading in the name of Islam. He remembered vividly the reaction of his non-Muslim colleagues at Republic Steel who called him "crazy" for driving sixty miles back and forth in the icy snowbelt winters when he could have kept his five-room thirty-dollar per month flat on Peckham Street in Buffalo. "Okay, if I'm crazy, then I'm going to stay crazy!" he had replied defiantly.

One thing that Ezaldeen and the *muhajirun* had never anticipated was the prospect of taxes on the community. Although Jabul Arabiyya had been incorporated as a not-for-profit religious organization in 1938, its residents were still liable for local taxes to finance education and the regional infrastructure—road construction, maintenance, fire and police protection. As a consequence of its financial status, therefore, the settlement was constantly threatened by the specter of fiscal default. Over the years, outsiders came forward with rescue plans. A group of Arab immigrants had proposed building a chicken ranch but wanted to house immigrants coming down from Canada in exchange for their investment. This made Ghani, *emir* since the death of Talib Sayyed, suspicious and he declined to sign away the community's sovereignty. He similarly rejected another proposal to use Jabul Arabiyya as a halfway station for paroled Muslim inmates. Despite avowals of piety and promises of rehabilitation on their behalf, he continued to view crime as one of the reasons that pioneers had originally committed themselves to *hijra*. One resident reported that Louis Farrakhan once dispatched representatives to West Valley offering to pay the tax bill.[12] According to Rafeek, a "fundamentalist" sect had even tried to take over the village forcefully until Ghani called the state police to evict them.

Ghani was a quintessential pioneer like Nattie Bumpo, the plainsman depicted in James Fenimore Cooper's *The Prairie*. He retained his authority and garnered respect, admiration, and love from all the residents at Jabul Arabiyya, even those considered dropouts or apostates whom he refused to shun. *Hijra* was the vehicle by which he realized a lifelong dream of land ownership. Subsequent generations would need to learn the hard lessons for themselves, he once observed while watching a group of novice farmers toiling to renovate an old garden behind his house. By the time he died in 1995, stewardship of the community was shared between Shabburn Abdul-Naji, grandson of another pioneer, and an orthodox imam from Buffalo, Dawoud Adeyola. Muslims from this area seek to cultivate Jabul Arabiyya's symbolism yet understandably remain defensive about making it too visible for outsiders.

Cleveland's Universal Islamic Brotherhood

Approaching *hijra* from a different perspective, Imam Da'ud Abdul Malik (photograph 2) organized the Universal Islamic Brotherhood (UIB) amidst the abandoned buildings and ravaged postindustrial landscape of Cleveland's East Side. The community occupies several structures, including a large brick building that houses The Islamic School of the Oasis (TISO), an old parish hall renamed Masjid ul-Haqq, a three-story apartment building housing five Muslim families, and several dilapidated buildings and the empty lots that separate them along both sides of Hayden Avenue. Da'ud was a Civil Rights activist and a powerbroker, known throughout the city as "Diablo" before his conversion to Islam in the late 1970s. As a young grassroots insurgent, he commandeered an old Methodist Church and transformed it into "Black Unity House." This served as a center for militant nationalism, and it also provided community services including free breakfast and daycare after a model established by the Black Panther Party. Following his conversion to Islam, Da'ud assembled a group of former Muslim inmates from Ohio's Chilicothe Penitentiary and their families. Anchored by Black Unity House, which continued to collect some government funds, the community also attracted seekers from other parts of Ohio who became fascinated by Da'ud's plans to recreate a Muslim village in the middle of an American "hyperghetto."

Using his considerable experience and skills as an activist, Da'ud consolidated UIB's real estate through government rehabilitation grants, sweat equity programs, and the Project Headstart awards that continued to trickle into the Black Unity House, run

Cleveland, April 2, 1992—Students change classes at The Islamic School of the Oasis under the watchful eyes of Imam Da'ud Abdul Malik and Sister Hassinah Rance, seated at desk.
© 2000 Jolie Stahl

by his brother, Rusty Thomas. In the early 1990s, TISO became eligible for some state funding and then also obtained money through Cleveland's experimental school voucher program. Jameil Rahman, an early UIB stalwart who earned a master's degree in social work, successfully negotiated a half-million-dollar grant to establish a substance abuse prevention center. Da'ud also looks for resources during his frequent missions abroad.

While performing *hajj* in the late 1980s, Da'ud recruited a Ghanaian, Sheik Masoud Laryea, to become UIB's resident *'alim* or learned teacher. Sheik Masoud was being groomed for assignment elsewhere in Africa, but Da'ud persuaded him that American Muslims needed his Qur'anic knowledge desperately. Over the objections of the Masoud's Saudi sponsors, he helped him secure a visa to come to Cleveland. By that time, the school and adjacent mosque had displaced Unity House as UIB's center of gravity, completing the transition of a secular grassroots community into a Muslim community.

Some families do not live in the immediate area although their children attend TISO up to the ninth grade and the men show up to perform the prayer at Masjid ul-Haqq several times a day. Those who do not have outside employment are kept busy earning their rent in the community residence by working on Da'ud's many different projects. Parents pay a nominal tuition fee or render services in kind to the school. Under Sheik Masoud's direction, TISO's curriculum stresses Islam and Arabic along with typical elementary and middle school programs, which measure up to the local public school standards, based on standardized test results and the achievements of several TISO graduates. One was accepted to attend Massachusetts Institute of Technology, and another, Da'ud's own daughter, went to Case Western Reserve University. During fieldwork, sixty-five students were enrolled at TISO. All were Muslim with one exception, an eighth-grader expelled from public school as disciplinary nuisance. Da'ud seemed to be achieving results with a combination of strong discipline and sincere affection for this bright yet troubled young man. Though he was not Muslim, he had to follow Shari'a like everyone else. The school's success in this and similar cases were part of Da'ud's formula for proseltyzing Islam to other African American families on the East Side.

Girls are veiled and seated apart from boys in the classrooms, banter between members of the opposite sex is discouraged, and parents are advised to reinforce these rules at home. As children begin to mature, marriages are prearranged by parents with the imam's approval. Plans are made for the adolescent couples to live under adult supervision. I witnessed one of these teen marriages and was assured by Da'ud's wife, Hassinah that this system of betrothal conforms to Muslim tradition and solves the problems of premarital sex and unwanted teen pregnancy faced by many ghetto families.

The application of Shari'a and Islamic pedagogy at TISO illustrates what one contemporary anthropologist has termed "remythologizing inner city schooling" in the codification of a strict moral paradigm capable of preventing social pathology.[13] Sheik Masoud inculcates a system of Qur'anic virtue that breaks with the traditional Western distinction based on good-versus-bad behavior, implementing instead a framework for judging deeds according to degrees of advisability ranging from "obligatory" (*farz*) to "strictly forbidden" (*haram*). Situated in between are acts deemed merely permissible, unadvisable but lawful, recommended but not obligatory, etc. The boundaries of this alternative social discipline are policed throughout the community by leaders who are frank in discussing their willingness to apply corporal punishment to violators. In the absence of a physical separation (*hijra*) from *jahiliyya*, these sanctions are thought to be effective tools for the creation of a pious community like the one led by the Prophet Muhammad in Medina. If some observers would describe this form of social discipline as populist vigilantism, it nonetheless belongs to the complex practice of *hijra*.

These developments can also be seen in philosophical terms as the "negation of the negation": a unique ontology supplants a prior system that has failed its purpose. In the context of grinding poverty and relentless social exclusion, one can easily observe that the information superhighway may run through cities like Cleveland but does not exit anywhere near Hayden Avenue. If the negative consequences of educational inequality accumulate from one generation to the next, this increases the chances that oppositional strategies will emerge and eventually produce intellectual exponents who can articulate new social principles. In his enthusiasm to provide alternative conduits for spiritual as well as material success, Da'ud has opened links to parts of the Muslim and African world. If willing, TISO graduates can matriculate into Qur'anic academies in Senegal, the Sudan, Egypt, and Saudi Arabia.

Conclusion: A Virtual Migration

Prescriptive statements concerning the problem of *hijra* have been subject to constant debate within Islamic legal academies. But formulations derived from the time of the Caliphate seem inadequate in the instances illustrated above because they account for neither modern constitutional democracies guaranteeing freedom of assembly and worship nor postmodern transnational cultures linked by electronic communications and jet-age transportation. The problem of the African American *hijra* must be seen within the context of these historical developments and also in light of the current crisis in which the nation-state seems to be losing ground quickly to transnational corporations as symbols of wealth and statecraft. Very little attention has been paid to the evolution of the liberal nation-state. Does *hijra* mean migration only to a place where Muslims are clearly a majority? Must they control the government? Do constitutional guarantees allow sufficient freedom for the unrestrained practice of Islam? Is the United States a place where peaceful coexistence with other religions is possible?

From an Islamic point of view, there are many responses to these questions, some relying on fundamental points of belief and others straying toward the arcane. Each concerns the issue of Muslim identity and firmly depends upon how that identity is tracked relative to the original *hijra* of the Prophet Muhammad.

In terms of the Qur'an and the early Muslim communities, *hijra* was an obligation synonymous with faith. One either rallied to the forces led by Muhammad or became vulnerable to the forces of sin and unbelief. Allah exempted children, women, and the feeble from this obligation but made all other believers responsible for making a clean break with the past and participating in the struggle to propagate Islam. Historically, this suggested that "*hijra* was closely associated with *jihad*."[14] In other words there was no fence-straddling: either join the fray on the side of Allah or expose yourself to ignominious death as an infidel.

The terms of engagement changed after the consolidation of a vast Islamic empire stretching from the South China Sea to the Atlantic Ocean, from sub-Saharan Africa north to the Volga River. Between 900 and 1700 C.E. the Islamic Caliphate represented the greatest pluricultural fusion since the classical Roman Empire. Some legal scholars argued that *hijra* was no longer incumbent upon the believer since it referred specifically to the Prophet's migration from Mecca to Medina.[15] Others stressed more general interpretations, hinting that Muhammad's *hijra* to Medina was preceded by an earlier mission when he dispatched some of the persecuted believers from Mecca across the Red Sea to Abyssinia, a non-Muslim country whose ruler agreed to shelter them, although he never converted to Islam himself.[16]

Vacillation between these positions depended upon the political and economic fortunes of the Caliphate until its final collapse in the nineteenth century. In matters of international relations, on the one hand, the scholars of jurisprudence as well as the collectors of hadith issued formulations that reflected the relative posture of the Islamic regime in a world where diplomacy, commerce, warfare, and isolation were the acknowledged contingencies. On the other hand, rulings that applied to individual Muslims living outside the formally defined center, *dar al-Islam*, amounted to a definition of the periphery in eternal theological terms as opposed to the temporal reality of the nation-state. In times of heightened commercial or diplomatic activity, this might necessitate accommodating the status quo by downplaying the relevance of *hijra* in order to avoid complicating relations of coexistence with non-Muslim regimes. Conversely, *hijra* might become obligatory in times of hostility or isolation as a means of subverting the enemy. But "[t]he problem of the Muslim under non-Muslim rule hardly arose and, where it did, received only minor and fleeting attention."[17]

Other concerns about the obligatory nature of *hijra* went beyond the simple dichotomy between *dar al-Islam* and *dar al-harb* to include lands where Muslims might endure disease or financial insecurity, in which case the Maliki jurists allowed migration but did not make it obligatory.[18] Moreover, in cases where former Muslim lands came under colonial rule, such as in nineteenth century Nigeria, some jurists called for *jihad* while others "accepted British rule, arguing that so long as Muslims had freedom to practice their religious duties, the land continued to be dar al-Islam."[19] Here it is obvious that both *jihad* and *hijra* measure the same social and demographic potential. The strength of the local Muslim community must be taken into consideration if Islam is to prevail in alien territories. If treated as a collective obligation, *hijra*, like *jihad*, may be swayed by calculations of force.

But the United States has enjoyed a somewhat different relationship with Muslim nations in comparison to the pattern established by Old World nations. This distinction was formalized in 1826 when the State Department, under the administration of John Quincy Adams, instituted a specific section devoted to diplomacy in the Arab world.[20] While the Arabs and other Muslim nations have challenged the relationship of the United States with Israel, most notably during the 1973 oil embargo, they have generally remained allies. Operation Desert Storm in 1991 was organized by the

United States as the largest military campaign in modern history with the goal of defending the Persian Gulf emirates from the encroachment of a well-armed despot. To argue that the United States viewed Saddam Hussein's threat in terms of its national security prerogatives should not obscure the benefits of their striking victory for those in control of Islam's holy shrines.

In conjunction with constitutional guarantees of freedom, does this history suggest that America be recognized as neither the *dar al-harb* nor *dar al-Islam*, but be assigned, instead, to a category reserved for those societies with whom the Prophet made a treaty or peace pact? (Abyssinia is an example of a Christian nation that provided refuge for early *muhajirun*.) A deep sense of religious autonomy is pervasive in American culture, one that seems to thrive on mass revivals, spiritual awakenings, sectarian conflict, and cult activities. From Puritanism to New Age worship by way of experimental communities, sectarian movements, televangelism, and a plethora of cults, within the context of the American religious landscape, each religion sets its own goals and pursues them unconstrained by almost any rules.[21]

This raises a second difficulty in rendering *hijra* intelligible as a guiding principle for African American Muslims. In a time when globalization has deconstructed many national and ethnic boundaries, does migration serve any purpose that cannot be accomplished by information networks and long-distance travel?

In North America, opinion seems split between immigrants who find fewer obstacles to retaining their Muslim identity and African Americans who cope quite differently with issues of visibility and invisibility in the process of reckoning religious identity. The former have the advantage of permanent ties to their homelands and ancestral roots through language, family, and ethnic networks. This solidarity is reinforced and perhaps enhanced in the setting of large urban and suburban Islamic centers, which are made up of many cultural and ethnic groups and thus serve as viable representations of the *umma* as such. In these places, the immigrant Muslim can more or less adapt the American ideal of multiculturalism to the eternal image of the *umma*. The question of *hijra*, specifically migration, is superseded by evidence that Islam has become anchored in the New World and will continue to grow proportionately to the collective affluence of the immigrants.

The African American Muslim communities described above were excluded from a similar process of identity construction. In the case of West Valley, formed in reaction to the Great Migration, race was a determining, though negative, factor in religious identity. Since the time of slavery, religious identity had been a subaltern affiliation in the sense that an oppressed race could attain spiritual salvation only by means of the symbolic materials provided by their oppressors. Although this did not preclude the syncretic fusion of African cultural assemblages with Christian ritual, the Black Church limited the development of African American religion almost exclusively to ideals expounded in the teaching of Gospel. The Qur'an, by contrast, was largely unavailable to African Americans until the early twentieth century. As demonstrated equally by their more limited experience with Judaism, the advent of Islam provided a radical opportunity to redefine one's identity irrespective of race. By relating their worship to the central doctrines and institutions of Islam through Prof. Muhammad

Ezaldeen, the West Valley pioneers transformed themselves from tenants to independent property owners. The important key to this achievement was collective investment, which Sheik Daoud Ghani unsuccessfully sought in the church and the masonic temple and ultimately discovered in the Islamic concept of *hijra*. His migration was the expression of communal autonomy theretofore not exercised by African Americans but clearly visible at West Valley, both to the pioneers themselves and to their astonished neighbors, who could rationalize their presence only by creating the epithet "Black Arabs." Life within this new identity was not uncomplicated (dissension and attrition have always been the bane of utopian communes); nonetheless, the longevity of the settlement as a symbol of the *hijra* should probably be attributed as much to the pioneers' self-confidence as to their religious zeal.[22]

Nearly a half-century later, the Universal Islamic Brotherhood of Cleveland emerged from the combined forces of Civil Rights activism and Black (Power) nationalism. Both of these movements were powerful incubators for African American identity, but as they progressed toward their goals through democratic protest, legislation, and, occasionally, violence, considerations of race waned in comparison to those of class distinctions. Assimilation into middle-class American society became increasingly a strategy based upon education, dialect, employment, place of residence, and, sometimes, religious affiliation. This process bypassed African Americans who were unfavorably positioned to take immediate advantage of the opportunities created by school desegregation, affirmative action programs, and the equal opportunity agenda, depositing them into unsanitary, violent ghettos dominated by criminal syndicates and the criminal justice system.[23]

Unlike the West Valley pioneers, the individuals and families who migrated to the UIB are part of an underclass characterized by an intense anomie, splintered by perpetual cultural fragmentation, weakened by poor nutrition, and divorced from vital economic resources such as equity, credit, stable employment, and healthcare. Because of these deficiencies, their names are absent from the memory banks of global information networks; some do not even have telephones and may just as well be living in the bantustans, favellas, or bidonvilles of the underdeveloped Third World. Above all, their existence has been rendered virtually invisible as the result of the media's capacity to divert public attention away from issues of political urgency towards the demands of consumerism. Among the UIB residents, the single-parent families, recovering substance abusers, and parolees fighting for a second chance could never afford to invest their meager wages in building a rural commune, nor could they concentrate upon seemingly distant social and economic goals. Instead, their efforts focused upon survival—a more fundamental (and desperate) struggle to repair and defend an inhabitable space.

For Imam Da'ud Abdul Malik and other Eastsiders, the doctrine of *hijra* meant, literally, the conversion of ghetto real estate, formerly church property, into sacred Muslim space. He applied countercultural methods gleaned from the lessons of Civil Rights and Black Power—squatting, sweat equity, jawboning, grant-writing, etc.—to foster a relatively stable habitus that in turn gives adults and children the time and space to acquire well-defined roles and identities rooted in the patriarchal family order. By promulgating Shari'a codes and simultaneously broadcasting the severe penalties administered to violators, the community erected a set of visible boundaries that separates them from the rest of the ghetto.

To borrow a term, we are witness to a "remythologization" of inner-city existence.[24] Similarly oppressed communities around the world have "built their own 'welfare states' . . . on the basis of networks of solidarity and reciprocity" and likewise anchored their collective identity in religious movements.[25] Historically, this is a far cry from either Black Nationalism or the integrationist politics of the 1960s and more closely related, in the instance of UIB, to the rise of contemporary Islamic fundamentalism, which proceeds "not by returning to tradition, but by working on traditional materials in the formation of a new godly communal world, where deprived masses and disaffected intellectuals may reconstruct meaning as a global alternative to the exclusionary global order."[26]

By the same token, the *umma* is no longer the unitary symbol of internationalist Islam that attracted veterans of the Great Migration to reform their identities on the basis of a Hamitic pedigree, i.e., Muhammad Ezaldeen's Adenu Allahe Universal Arabic Association. The traditionalist vision that prompted the theory and practice of *hijra* is nearly defunct itself, having been replaced during the course of the tumultuous past century by a heterogeneous Muslim world divided among modernizers anxiously striving to reap the benefits of global development, fundamentalists promoting scripturalism, ethnic discontents who dispute Arab, Sunni, or Shi'a hegemony, and many others who profess a quietistic stance.

All these tendencies are amplified by modern communications and means of transportation, thereby attracting cultural entrepreneurs like Imam Da'ud to explore alternatives ranging from West African Sufism to Sudanese radicalism. Even his recruitment of a Ghanaian to serve as UIB's resident *'alim* reveals a decentralized, nuanced approach to *hijra* allowing local exigencies to redirect the priorities of higher echelons. Whereas Islamic order once implied the limits of a particular time and space, those conventions now seem malleable and uncertain. They dissolve as quickly as one can surf from one Internet address to another, blurring the process of Muslim self-identification in the same way that hip-hop recordings compress multiple musical genres and even random sounds, track layered upon simultaneous track, to create a richly textured "sample" of the African American urban experience.

My final point can only be provisional, due to the evolving nature of communities like Cleveland's UIB. What can be stated clearly is that the subjects of my inquiry are engaged in a process of reciprocal, indeed interactive, migration that can no longer be contained by traditional Muslim academies and judges, asynchronous as they are to either the time or space of the African American *hijra*. Future developments will depend upon the willingness of a critical mass of an intensely religious people to "sample" the free flow of information and knowledge emerging from the teachings of the Qur'an. For all intents and purposes, this suggests that the gates of knowledge and individual judgement (*ijtihad*) can no longer remain closed in a world of boundless information networks and that the new possibilities and surprises arising from Islam's westward expansion may yet prove its greatest migration ever.

Medina Kaolack, Senegal, August 17, 1991—Young American tablibs (students) surround their unofficial den mother Sister Tauhida Cisse, also an American, on the steps of their dormitory in the holy city of the Tijaniyya sufi brotherhood. The young men have come to the parched Sahel region, staying up to seven years, in order to become proficient hafis of the Qur'an.
© 2000 Jolie Stahl

Notes

1. Estimate based on recent demographic research in David B. Barrett, ed., *World Christian Encyclopedia* (New York: Oxford University Press, 2001).

2. Arna and Jack Conroy Bontemps, *They Seek a City*, (Garden City, N.Y.: Doubleday, Doran and Company, Inc., 1945), 104. Numerous Black Muslim eschatologies relate the story of Yakub, a black trickster who practiced a similar eugenics, intending to destroy the pure Black race. One can see in this myth's origins an oedipal backlash against such real practices. The "Yakub" myth quickly became part of the folklore of the Moorish Science Temple, Nation of Islam, and other "Black Muslim" spinoffs. Its anti-white sentiments were seemingly corroborated by references to the "guilty blue-eyed" who "shall bear a burden on the day of resurrection . . . when the trumpet shall be blown," found in a 1928 English translation of the Qur'an whose editions were disseminated in North American by Ahmadiyya missionaries (Muhammad Ali 1928), 322.

3. Audiotaped interviews by author with Hameeda Mansur (Cleveland, Ohio, April 1992; Heshaam Jabbar (Elizabeth, New Jersey, June 13, 1990); Yusef Shurney (Cleveland, Ohio, May 1, 1990); Umar Abdul-Jalil (New York, January 5, 1992).

4. A small Hebrew-Israelite movement still exists among African Americans, but its demographic expansion and intergenerational transmission remain obstructed by arbitrary regulations and even the preexisting schism between European (Ashkenazi) and Oriental (Sephardic) Jews who are themselves victims of racial stereotyping. This precluded migration (*aliyah*) to Israel except for the Abeta Israel, a small group from Chicago, who live as virtual pariahs in a single colony at Dimona. (See Hans A. Baer and Merrill Singer, *African American Religion in the Twentieth Century*, Knoxville, Tenn.: University of Tennessee Press, 1992; and Yvonne Chireau and Nathaniel Deutsch, eds. *Black Zion*, New York: Oxford University Press, 2000.) This example renders defunct the reality of this particular double-minority status.

5. Dizzie Gillespie and Al Fraser, *To BE, or not . . . to BOP* (New York: DaCapo Press, Inc., 1979), 293. In his autobiography, Gillespie expresses a certain ambivalence about Islamic conversion among his fellow musicians. He discusses both religious and social motivations, while also alluding to esthetic considerations. Generally, he describes conversion as the kind of social role-playing necessary to the life of a travelling musician.

> Man, if you join the Muslim faith, you ain't colored no more, you'll be "white," they'd say. "You get a new name and you don't have to be a nigger no more." . . . They had no idea of black consciousness; all they were trying to do was escape the stigma of being "colored." When these cats found out that Idrees Sulieman, who joined the Muslim faith about that time, could go into these white restaurants and bring out sandwiches to the other guys because he wasn't "colored"—and he looked like the inside of the chimney—they started enrolling in droves.
>
> Musicians started having it printed on their police cards where it said "race," "W" for white. Kenny Clarke has one and he showed it to me. He said, "See, nigger, I ain't no spook; I'm white, 'W.' . . ." Another cat . . . went into this restaurant, and they said they didn't serve colored in there. So he said, "I don't blame you. But I don't have to go under the rule of colored because my name is Mustafa Dalil." (Gillespie & Fraser 1979), 293.

6. The free flow of individuals between orthodoxy and the Ahmadiyya Movement documented between 1920 and 1950 is one example of this open-ended migration. It is impossible for those who regard the Ahmadi creed as heresy, which is the "orthodox" Muslim view because of Ahmadi doctrines regarding its founder Ghulam Ahmad, to deny that it played an important role in giving *da'wa* (the "call") to Americans.

7. Robert Dannin, "The 'Holy War' on Crack," in *The City Sun* (23 August 1988).

8. As early as 1937, Wali Akram of the First Cleveland Mosque began corresponding with the director of the U.S. Agriculture Department's Resettlement Division. He sought informa-

tion and financial assistance for five hundred families as part of The Muslim Ten Year Plan (Akram, Collected Papers, Box 7, Bundle 1, Folio RR.) These plans never materialized. The Moorish Science Temple of Islam acquired property and established a retreat in Prince George's County, Virginia.

Other examples of *hijra*: The Islamic Party of North America began as an inner-city commune in Washington, D.C., then decamped to a rural site in Georgia when its founder, Y. M. Hamid returned to start an Islamic movement to his native Dominica in the Caribbean. Also in the Caribbean, Imam Abu Bakr, a former policeman who lived briefly as a Muslim in Toronto, organized a Muslim jamaat on abandoned government property in Port of Spain. A bloody uprising ensued when officials threatened to repossess his turf. The Sufi al-Fukhra movement currently maintains a rural retreat in the Catskill region of New York state. Alternatively referred to as the Muslims of the Americas, the movement is led by Pakistani Sheik Gilani who operates the Quranic Open University. Orthodox rivals have accused Gilani of undermining Muslim solidarity by extolling the contemplative ideals of Sufism. Ironically, the FBI had depicted the same organization as "terrorists."

9. *Buffalo-Courier Express*, Sunday, June 1946, Photo essay. The attached caption reads: "Instead of selecting the desert sands as a site for their village, a group of Mohammedans is carving out a community in the wooded, windy hillsides of Cattaraugus County. With the steeples of New England-type churches in sight, they bow, upper right, in prayer to Allah, five times daily. Worshippers are, left to right, Haaneyfan Shareef, Ali Muhammad, and Abdullah Ashraf. In an effort to be self-sustaining, children are taught farming at an early age. In the center, Ibn Muhammad leads a calf home from the pasture. At right, Tahleeb Sayyed, early resident of the community, shown with his wife, examining a prayer rug. All residents are working on the temporary school and house of worship shown in the lower picture. Those in the front of it are, left to right, Elu Muhammad, Lafer Ahmad, Haanaayah Muhammad, Mrs. Zaharah Ahmed, and Abdullah Ahmed.

10. Audiotaped interview by author with Daoud Ghani (West Valley, New York, June 17, 1992).

11. Interview by author with Haaneyfan Rafeek (West Valley, New York, June 6, 1992).

12. Interview by author with Shabburn Abdul-Naji (West Valley, New York, June 18, 1992).

13. John Devine, *Maximum Security* (Chicago: University of Chicago Press, 1996), 199–221.

14. Muhammad Khalil Masud, "The obligation to migrate: the doctrine of *hijra* in Islam law." In Dale Eickelman and James Piscatori, eds., *Muslim Travellers* (Berkeley: University of California Press, 1990), 32.

15. Masud, 33.

16. This migration has even deeper meaning for our present considerations since it involves Africa as a refuge for Muslims.

17. Bernard Lewis, *Islam and the West* (New York: Oxford University Press, 1993), 48. Lewis's observations on the question of *hijra* regarding Muslims living as minority populations is worth quoting at length:

> In an age when the frontiers of Islam were continually expanding and when such losses of territory as occurred were tactical and temporary, it was hardly likely that the jurists would devote much attention to what was largely a hypothetical question. In the earliest juristic literature, the position of a Muslim permanently residing in a non-Muslim land is considered only in one contingency, that of an infidel in the land of the infidels who sees the light and embraces Islam. . . . The question they discuss is whether he may remain where he is or must leave his home and migrate to a Muslim country. The Shi'a jurists, more attuned to the idea of surviving in a hostile environment and under a hostile authority, allow him to stay and indeed see him as an outpost or beacon of Islam. The majority of Sunni jurists, accustomed to the association of religion and authority, insist that he must leave and remove himself to a Muslim land where he can live in accordance with the holy law of Islam.

18. Masud, 37.

19. Masud, 39.

20. Robert D. Kaplan, *The Arabists* (New York: The Free Press, 1993), 90.

21. The Mormons have gone the furthest by incorporating America into their founding mythology and apocryphal scriptures, thus establishing for themselves a New Holy Land. A recapitulation of the state of Utah's history might serve as an illustrative history here.

22. The rapid assimilation of the emigrants' children into the previously segregated public school system probably contributed to the obvious failures in relaying the ideals of *hijra* to the succeeding generations.

23. William Julius Wilson, *The Declining Significance of Race* (Chicago: University of Chicago Press, 1980).

24. Devine, 1966.

25. Manuel Castells, *The Power of Identity* (Malden, Mass.: Blackwell Publishers Inc., 1997), 62.

26. Ibid., 20.

Islamic Party in North America: A Quiet Storm of Political Activism   5

KHALID FATTAH GRIGGS

Prologue

FOR THE PARTICIPANTS IN THE INTENSE SPIRITUAL, EMOTIONAL, and social odyssey known as the Islamic Party in North America (IPNA), the tendency to speak in hyperbole when attempting to document the history of the organization is somewhat axiomatic. The group experienced a meteoric-like ascendancy across the social firmament of the United States and the Caribbean during the short span of just two decades—the 1970s and 1980s. In its wake, IPNA redefined da'wa, the techniques of inviting non-Muslims to Islam; IPNA developed a political assessment independent of Muslim nation states or their surrogate organizations in the West; and IPNA formulated and implemented an unparalleled training regiment for Islamic workers in the Western hemisphere, particularly among persons of African descent.

The Islamic Party owed its genesis to the confluence of several factors impacting the spread of Islam in America. The first factor evolved from immigration patterns that started during the last quarter of the nineteenth century. The initial wave of Muslim immigrants started to arrive in the United States from Greater Syria (Syria, Lebanon, and Palestine), and the Punjab region of the Indian subcontinent in 1875.

Around 1908, Kurds, Albanians, and Turks began a second wave of Muslims coming to the United States, primarily settling in the major metropolitan areas of the Midwest and Northeast. Following the conclusion of World War II, up to the decade of the 1960s, a third wave of Muslims from Yugoslavia, Egypt, and Lebanon immigrated to the United States. Yet, despite the presence of hundreds of thousands of immigrant Muslims clustered around urban centers across the country, African Americans, with few exceptions, remained oblivious to the "orthodox" call of Islam.

Numerous social dynamics contributed to this phenomenon, including the prevailing racial politics of the land, the immigrant's ignorance of the language and society, the fear of deportation, the preoccupation with trying to achieve economic prosperity, and the natural tendency of arriving immigrants to remain collectively introverted in an attempt to sustain their culture.

For whatever reasons, the fact remains that Muslim immigrants to the United States and the Caribbean failed, for the most part, to share the pristine message of submission to Allah with African Americans for approximately ten decades. The Islamic Party, in this regard, predicated its external program of propagation and internal training mechanism on the premise that a dedicated, properly trained core of Islamic workers was essential for bringing the liberating message of Islam to "struggling people of African descent." [1]

Said Ramadan, the Director of the Islamic Center in Geneva, Switzerland, queried Malik Shabazz (Malcolm X) in late 1964 about his embracing Islam after leaving the Nation of Islam and other issues. The seventh of nine written questions challenged Malcolm's continued emphasis on the liberation of Black people in light of Islam's confirmation of the oneness and equality of all races. Malcolm responded in part:

> Much to my dismay, until now the Muslim World has seemed to ignore the problem of the Black Americans. Most Muslims who come here from the Muslim World have concentrated more effort in trying to convert White Americans than Black Americans.
>
> There are two groups of Muslims in America: 1) those who were born in the Muslim World and migrated here, and were already Muslims when they arrived here. If these total over 200,000, they have not succeeded in converting 1,000 Americans to Islam; 2) American-born persons who have been converted to Islam are 98 percent Black Americans. Up to now, it has been only the Black American who has shown interest in Sunni Islam.
>
> If a student of agriculture has sense enough to concentrate his farming efforts on the most fertile area of his farm, I should think the Muslim World would realize that the most fertile area for Islam in the West is the Black American." [2]

The one notable exception to the unofficial maxim that immigrant Muslims refrain from giving Dawah (inviting to submission to Allah) to African Americans was the heterodox group known as the Ahmadiyya Movement in Islam. Founded in 1889 by Ghulam Ahmed of Qadian, India, the Ahmadiyyas based their doctrine on the belief that Ghulum Ahmed was a prophet. When Ahmed died in 1908, many of his followers dispersed throughout the world as missionaries, reaching the east and west coasts of Africa in 1916.

The Ahmadiyyas were prolific publishers of materials on Islam, such as prayer books, and are credited with widely distributing the first English translation of the Qur'an. When Mufti Muhammad Sadiq arrived in New York City around 1910, he quickly identified African Americans as a receptive audience for the Ahmadiyya message. Coming to the United States during a period of intense racial persecution, Sadiq correctly deduced that many African Americans were looking for a dignity-restoring way of life since American racists conveniently distorted Christianity to justify abominable acts against persons of color.

According to Tony Martin, perhaps the foremost authority on Marcus Garvey and the Universal Negro Improvement Association, Mufti Muhammad Sadiq helped to convert over forty members of Garvey's organization to the Ahmadiyya Movement prior to Sadiq's return to India around 1923. [3] In addition to socially conscious persons like members of the UNIA, African American jazz musicians similarly gravitated to the teachings of the Ahmadiyya Movement in the United States.

According to Daud Salahuddin, a Chicago-based musician and Secretary General of the Islamic Party for a brief period, jazz musicians were typically on the cutting edge of social and religious trends in the African American community. Salahuddin embraced Islam as a teenager during the 1950s under the tutelage of Hajj Talib Dawud, a trumpet player for the legendary Dizzy Gillepsie, and the husband of jazz singer Dakota Staton. Talib Dawud was an Ahmadi before becoming estranged from the movement. Like Daud Salahuddin, the Islamic Party's founder, Yusuf Muzaffaruddin Hamid, was mentored for a short time by Talib Dawud while the teenage Hamid sought a career as a musician.

In Daud Salahuddin's opinion, there was "only one process for an African American to become Muslim during the 1940s and 1950s; the Ahmadiyya Movement. If you were not an Ahmadiyya, you were nothing. There was not a Sunni presence to be found in our community (African American). If you were fortunate enough to be able to find a Muslim prayer book, you had better believe that it was produced by the Ahmadiyyas. There were very few books on Islam available in English at that time. Mostly, our Islamic literature consisted of mimeographed pages with blurry ink. English Qur'ans were few and far between, and were mostly found in the occult or spiritual shops."[4]

While Daud Salahuddin's observations were not intended to be all-encompassing, they do, nevertheless, capture the tenor of the time concerning the "Islamic" presence existing in close proximity to African Americans, and the dire need for a systematic presentation of Al-Islam to blacks in the United States.

The second factor germane to the establishment of the Islamic Party is the current of struggle that continuously flowed through the lives of Africans in the United States that started with their arrival en masse during the trans-Atlantic slave trade and reached its organizational zenith in the 1920s with Marcus Garvey's Universal Negro Improvement Association.

Included among the resisters to slavery were African Muslims who maintained their faith throughout their years as chattel slaves, with some even obtaining their freedom and returning to their ancestral homes in Africa. While the exact number of Muslims transported to America as slaves is impossible to determine, present research conservatively suggests that one out of every three slaves brought to the United States was a Muslim.

American slavers prized Muslim slaves for Deep South plantations in the United States, particularly those from the Senegambia region of West Africa, because of their knowledge of rice growing, strict moral discipline, abstinence from consuming spirituous drinks, and overall sense of responsibility. However, Muslim slaves were typically more resistant to "seasoning" (the practice of breaking the slaves' will to be free) than their non-Muslim counterparts. Yet, like Alex Haley's ancestor Kunta Kinte, whose story is chronicled in Haley's epic work *Roots*, Muslim slaves were often given positions of responsibility in the slave hierarchy.

In the aftermath of the United States government's complete dismantling of the legal and physical protections afforded African Americans in the South during the relatively short post-Civil War period known as Reconstruction, the physical well being of blacks was once again seriously jeopardized.

The Universal Negro Improvement Association, under the leadership of Jamaican-born Marcus Mosiah Garvey, provided, at the turn of the twentieth century, a global social change mechanism and instilled a sense of racial and cultural pride in African people in North and South America, the Caribbean, Europe, and throughout the African continent. While Mufti Muhammad Sadiq converted an appreciable number of American Garveyites to the Ahmadiyya philosophy, Marcus Garvey himself was profoundly influenced by an orthodox Muslim, Duse Muhammad Ali.

When Marcus Garvey arrived in London in 1912, he immediately became involved with politically active African students who were living there. This association led him to Duse Muhammad Ali, a prolific Pan-African writer and thinker. Born to an Egyptian father and a Sudanese mother, Duse was the editor of the journal *African Times and Orient Review*. Duse's influence on Garvey is attested to by his wife, Amy Jacques Garvey, and can be seen in the UNIA's motto of "One God, One Aim, One Destiny," and in various Islamically inspired anthems of the organization.

Garvey's appreciation of the religion of Islam and its global connection of Islamic peoples caused him to expose African people in the Western hemisphere to many of the tenets of Islam even though there is no evidence that he ever became Muslim himself. Although probably unintentional, Garvey, as a non-Muslim, exposed more socially conscious blacks to Islamic ideas than the tens of thousands of Muslim immigrants residing in the West at that time. The expansion of the Islamic Party into the Caribbean, and South and Central America reflected a Garvey-like vision of connecting African people throughout the hemisphere and, eventually, the world.

The Islamic movements of Egypt, Pakistan, Turkey, and Palestine during the 1960s profoundly affected the establishment and growth of the Islamic Party. Y. Muzaffaruddin Hamid traveled extensively throughout the Muslim Middle East and the Indian subcontinent for approximately five years during the 1960s. His contacts with Islamic movement leaders significantly shaped his understanding of Islamic ideology and organizational style.

"Between 1965 and 1969 I had the opportunity to spend a significant amount of time with individuals who had worked for years with renowned Islamic movements. For an example," Hamid explained in a 1987 interview with the journal *Vision*, "through the Ihkwanul Muslimeen (Egypt) and the Jamaati Islami (Pakistan), where I had an opportunity to be the house guest of Maulana Abul A'la Maududi (Pakistan), the Said Nursi movement in Turkey, and the Hizbul Tahria in Palestine, it was made clear to me by members of these groups that if Islam was to have any significance in the U.S., I would have to look at things nationally and internationally when I returned."[5]

The ideas of Jamaati Islami-Pakistan, particularly of Maulani Maududi, had more of an impact on the future structure, membership requirements, and program of propagation of the Islamic Party than any other group. Jamaati Islami-Pakistan widely distributed in the United States English translations of Maulana Maududi's works. Additionally, former members, associates, and admirers of Jamaati Islami-Pakistan residing in the United States, such as Kaukab Siddiqueand Omar bin Abdullah, were more than willing to translate selective Jamaat training materials from the original Urdu to English.

However, if Jamaati Islami-Pakistan provided the primary organizational model for the Islamic Party, it was the post-Nation of Islam ideas of Malcolm X (March 8, 1964–February 21, 1965, his conversion to Islam to his death) that most affected the ideological context of the organization.

In the 1960s, Malcolm X's ideological clarity and keen sociopolitical analysis elevated the critical dialogue about social change methodology from civil to human rights in the United States and the Caribbean. Malcolm's towering persona was a source of inspiration for Africans throughout the Diaspora, from the mean streets of Harlem, to the verdant pathways of Trinidad's countryside, to the tropical regions of Africa.

Malcolm's influence was not restricted by geographical boundaries, ethnic or racial background, political affiliation, or even religious persuasion. As Imam Yasin Abu Bakr, imam of the Port-o-Spain, Trinidad, Jamaatul Muslimeen, the first modern-day Afro-Trinidadian group to establish a *masjid* (mosque), reflected to this writer in January 1988 at a Hajj Conference in London, "Personally, Malcolm was the light of inspiration for all young black people in Trinidad and the Caribbean, especially since Malcolm had Caribbean roots [Malcolm's mother, Louise, was from Grenada]. As a Muslim, he represented the symbol of righteousness. Added to this is the fact of what we call in Trinidad 'rootical,' that is somebody who had come up from the grassroots level and was able to challenge and deal with anybody up to the level of the United Nations.

"I still feel that although he is dead, he is still alive as inspiration for all people, no matter where in the world people live, for the freedom-loving and the oppressed."

Malcolm, to many the consummate Muslim *mujahid* (struggler for truth) and epitome of righteous manhood, stepped on to the world stage through his extensive travels and contacts in the Middle East and Africa, and by the posthumous publication of *The Autobiography of Malcolm X*, as told to Alex Haley.[6] Africans in the Western Hemisphere, who heretofore were unaware of the religion of Islam, learned about the faith and the interrelated condition of their brethren overseas through the prism of Malcolm's experiences.

As the process of vicariously experiencing the evolution of Malcolm's ideas broadened, Africans in the West began to employ additional social change tactics, including exercising their right to armed self-defense from racist attacks, rather than nonviolent redemptive suffering. Members of the civil rights group Student Nonviolent Coordinating Committee (SNCC) like Kwame Toure (Stokely Carmichael) and Imam Jamil Abdullah Al-Amin (H. Rap Brown) acknowledged Malcolm as their ideological mentor.

Huey Newton and Bobby Seale, the founders of the Oakland-based Black Panther Party for Self-Defense (1966) also credit Malcolm X with providing them the ideological inspiration to organize the Panthers. Included in a group of prominent social activists who embraced Islam after being influenced by Malcolm are Imam Jamil Al-Amin (H. Rap Brown), Muhammad Ahmed (Max Stanford of the Revolutionary Action Movement, RAM), and Askia Muhammad Toure (revolutionary poet). For a brief period, Haki Madhubuti (Don L. Lee) and Amiri Baraka (Leroi Jones), both revolutionary poets, practiced Islam ostensibly because of Malcolm's influence.

The founders of the Islamic Party, including Y. Muzaffaruddin Hamid, were heavily influenced by the post-Nation of Islam life of Malik Shabazz. The Islamic Party in North America was known by various names throughout its organizational lifespan. But, regardless of its name at a particular time, the Islamic Party remained relatively true to its roots for its organizational life.

The American Muslim Universe of IPNA

Not since the organizational heyday in the 1920s of Marcus Garvey's Universal Negro Improvement Association (UNIA) had any group experienced the national grassroots identification in the African American community as the Nation of Islam enjoyed during the mid-1950s through the 1960s. Bolstered by the national media attention generated from the 1959 Mike Wallace–Louis Lomax television documentary, "The Hate That Produced Hate," the Nation of Islam further became the object of intense public interest after the 1961 publication of C. Eric Lincoln's ground-breaking book, *The Black Muslims in America.*[7]

In conjunction with media offerings on the Nation of Islam, the release of Malcolm X from prison in 1952, and his brilliant oratory while crisscrossing the country for twelve years, establishing temples for the Nation of Islam helped to define Islam in America's mind as being synonymous with that organization. The Nation's bold condemnation of white racism, particularly in the United States, and searing criticism of the social failings of the Christian church garnered supporters, if not members, especially among dispossessed African Americans.

Criticism of the heretical, un-Islamic theology of the Nation by African American orthodox Muslims appeared to have a relatively inconsequential effect on members of the black community during the 1950s and 1960s. To an African American audience, the Nation of Islam identified with, championed the cause of, and remained a fixture in the black community, rehabilitated the socially and morally downtrodden, promoted their ideas through a weekly national newspaper, encouraged self-help and entrepreneurial projects, and provided healthy food items through door-to-door distribution. It would be at least another decade before orthodox Muslims in the United States, indigenous or immigrant, matched the community efforts of the ("deviant") "Black Muslims." For most of the organization's pre-Caribbean experience, the Islamic Party in North America was an ideological gadfly to the Nation of Islam internationally, nationally, and on a grassroots community level.

The American Muslim universe that the Islamic Party in North America was born into included a few orthodox national Muslim groups, and other local groups that impacted the national agenda. One of the most significant pioneering organizational efforts among Muslims in the United States was the Dar-ul-Islam movement. Founded in 1962 by African American Muslims in Brooklyn, New York, the Dar would develop more mosques (*masjids*) in the United States than any other *masjid*-based group during the 1960s. The Dar-ul-Islam's paramilitary security unit, the *Rad* (Thunder), as well as the group's overall emphasis on physical/martial readiness and combat appearance posed somewhat of a deterrent to most physical reprisals considered against them by irate members of the Nation of Islam when the Dar verbally attacked their beliefs. The relationship between the Dar-ul-Islam movement and the Islamic Party in North America would remain somewhat tentative throughout the organizational life of the Islamic Party.

The formation of the Muslim Student Association of the United States and Canada (MSA) in 1963 was a pivotal development for immigrant Muslim students matriculating in North America. Linked together by a constitution and common goals, the MSA helped to facilitate a Muslim identity for foreign students heretofore prone to self-imposed public invisibility. The MSA's primary contact with African American Muslims came through its annual conventions, and its few on-campus African American members. Leading members of the Islamic Party, while acknowledging the positive work of MSA, viewed with a jaundiced eye the suspected unstated objectives of the organization: monitoring the activities of Muslim students by Muslim countries, the United States, and Canada, while the students studied outside of their home countries.

The North American orthodox Muslim landscape of the 1960s and 1970s also included other major players affecting the growth and development of Islam. The New York office of the Saudi Arabia-based Rabitat Islami (Muslim World League) distributed Islamic literature, sponsored Hajj trips, and otherwise attempted to influence the future ideological direction of the fledgling Islamic movement during this era. The Saudi-sponsored Islamic Center of Washington, D.C., a Middle Eastern-style architectural marvel at the time of its opening and dedication by President Dwight Eisenhower in 1958, was a focal point of Islamic activity in the nation's capital for the Muslim diplomatic corps, general immigrant Muslim community, and the minuscule number of African American Muslims. These groups and others maintained a symbiotic, and sometimes contentious, relationship with one another and with the Islamic Party after its formation.

IPNA's Birth and Early Life

The story of the conceptualization and formation of the Islamic Party in North America is arguably the account of the efforts of primarily one man: Yusuf Muzaffaruddin Hamid. Numerous others undoubtedly contributed to the organization's genesis, but it was Muzaffaruddin's experiences and vision that indelibly molded the birth and early life of the Islamic Party.

After graduating from high school in Atlanta, the eighteen-year old Muzaffaruddin moved to New York to pursue his ambition as a jazz trumpet player. The circle of potential mentors for his musical career was peopled by many Muslims who had been influenced by the Ahmadiyya movement, including Al Hajj Talib Dawud, who held an inveterate aversion for Elijah Muhammad and the Nation of Islam. Muzaffaruddin would not stay long in New York after embracing Islam.

Between 1965 and 1969 Muzaffaruddin had an extended stay in the Middle East, and traveled in Africa and Asia. His first stop was Saudi Arabia, where he enrolled in the University of Madinah, only to be arrested after a relatively short time for participating in a protest demonstration. He was subsequently expelled from the university. After extensive travel throughout the Middle East, Muzaffaruddin returned to the United States in early 1969 and started working at the Islamic Center in Washington, D.C. The Islamic Center, housed in a luxurious building on Washington's prestigious Embassy Row, was collectively financed by various Muslim governments, with Egyptians, notably the center's director, Muhammad Abdul-Rauf, holding the administrative posts. The facility was a tourist attraction and was open for only one congregational prayer daily—*Zuhr* (noon prayer). Muzaffaruddin would shortly leave his position in the bookstore/gift shop, frustrated over the center's apparent lack of interest in issues affecting African American Muslims and in communicating the message of Islam to the city's African American population.

Joining with Zayd Ahmed, Hakim Qawiyh, and Hassan Ali, Muzaffaruddin felt compelled to form a "community-based" mosque that would address the needs of the inner city. "The need was greater there (inner city) as opposed to the large foreign sector and the sectors of the society which were not directly affected by the basic problems of human rights, social justice, economic degradation, and, of course, racism" he later said. "Until this particular time," Muzaffaruddin said, "Washington, D.C. had no other mosque other than the Islamic Center, in those days the Islamic Culture Center Museum. So in order to facil-itate the ongoing interest of many indigenous Washingtonians and people in the United States who came to Washington seeking a knowledge of Islam and an understanding of the Islamic process, we founded the Community Mosque (Masjidul Ummah)."[8]

Hakim Qawiyh owned property at 101 S Street NW that he donated for use as the mosque. The property had formerly been used as a drinking and gambling house before being abandoned. Located about two-and-a-half blocks from Slowe Hall, one of Howard University's men's dormitories, and only a few additional blocks from the main campus, Masjidul Ummah, a three-story house, was nestled on a residential corner in a relatively quiet working-class section of the city. From the outset, Howard University students were frequent visitors to the mosque and constituted a significant portion of the group's initial congregation.

Masjidul Ummah (Community Mosque) was incorporated in 1969 with Yusuf Muzaffaruddin Hamid elected as the imam. Shortly after the establishment of the Com-munity Mosque, a "Declaration of the Islamic People of the Community Mosque" was issued. The document, with a few word changes, would be the basis for the "Declaration of the Federation of Muslim Communities," a working alliance of Muslim communities in Pittsburgh, Akron, Chicago, and Washington, D.C., established at the same meeting as the formation of the Islamic Party in December 1971. The membership of the Federa-tion of Muslim Communities would provide an immediate national membership for the Islamic Party once the Islamic Party was formed.

The Declaration of the Islamic People of the Community Mosque read:

1. We, the Islamic people of the Community Mosque, declare that there is nothing wor-thy of worship except Allah and that Prophet Muhammad is indeed Allah's final Prophet for mankind and our blessed leader;

2. We declare that we represent no sect nor division in Islam. Rather, we are Muslims fol-lowing only Islam as expressed in the Holy Qur'an and in the actions of the Prophet Muhammad. Also, we listen to and have great respect for all the good and correct con-tributions of all the great Imams, both past and present;

3. We declare that the only purpose of our community is to serve Allah and His religion and establish ourselves according to His Will;

4. We declare that we will guide our community by the Holy Qur'an and Sunnah of our Prophet, only;

5. We declare that for this community, all power of authority and law rests with Allah. In those areas of legislation where Allah allows us to use our reasoning, we will not insti-tute any laws that disagree with or contravene any of the dictates of the Holy Qur'an or Way of the Holy Prophet;

6. We declare that in order to help facilitate our coordination and unity, we will always elect one from among us who will be our Imam (leader or representative). An Imam will remain our representative as long as a majority of our adult Muslims agree that he should;

7. We declare that each and every adult Muslim of this community has the right to express himself on any aspect of the operation of his community.

As to the establishment of the Community Mosque before the Islamic Party, Muzaffaruddin would say, "It would be fair to say that when we started the Community Mosque, myself in particular, we felt there was a need for the Islamic Party. As I had learned from groups like Jamaati Islami, Hizbul Tahria, Maadsumi, the Ihkwanul Muslimeen, and other movements, to start a movement, you can't start off with a bang; sometimes you have to start with a pop. The Community Mosque was the pop phase of what was to be known as the Islamic Party.

> We were able to make contact with a significant number of Brothers and Sisters who were prepared to shoulder the responsibility of a fuller commitment for the Islamic work, not merely the coming to the mosque for prayer, but the organizing of Dawah programs, and the organizing of an internal discipline where their lives beyond the mosque could be accounted for. We wanted them to be prepared to face the larger society with the question of which way it wanted to go. It was when we realized that we did have contact with a significant number of Brothers and Sisters who were prepared to take some responsibility for this question that we began to organize the Islamic Party. . . . Therefore, the Community Mosque was founded as a necessary, but modest effort to indicate our interest in furthering the cause of Islam. [9]

Ahmed Abdullah recalled to this writer coming to the Community Mosque on a "warm, sunny day in April 1971" after moving back from New York City. "A friend of mine from high school invited me to come to Masjidul Ummah on Sunday for a two o'clock lecture and discussion series that was held each week. Although I missed the lecture, I was fascinated by the experience of being at the mosque. Hassan Ali was there that day, and he was very helpful in explaining things to me. I accepted Islam that very same day. After the deaths of Malcolm X and Martin Luther King, a lot of students were looking for direction. There was a lot of militancy in them that had to be channeled. Islam provided that outlet. Islam was growing by leaps and bounds at that time." [10]

Abdullah remembered how he and other single brothers committed to Islam were encouraged to live in a section of the mosque designated "the barracks" to facilitate the availability of a cadre of full-time workers for the mosque, thereby saving financial resources needed for the growth and development of the operation. "Those of us living in the mosque barracks didn't need a lot of money to live, so we pooled our resources and donated the bulk of our earnings to the mosque. Hassan Ali organized the brothers to make and sell jewelry, especially on the college campuses and on the streets of the Georgetown area of D.C. Muzaffaruddin was working with the Postal Service at the time. He eventually resigned from the Post Office, at Hassan's urging, and started to sell jewelry and other items with the rest of us. Saleem Mutakkabir, and Omar Barakat became very proficient in making jewelry. The work of the Community Mosque, and eventually the Islamic Party, could not have been accomplished without the availability of full-time workers. Our sacrifices for the Community Mosque prepared us for the sacrifices that we would later make for the Islamic Party. To see young people in their twenties doing so much together for the cause of Islam is still inspirational today. Allah allowed us to accomplish quite a lot in a short period of time."[11]

Along with Ahmed Abdullah, Kareem Abdul Ghani, at the time a medical student at Howard University, Najeeb Abdul Haqq, an accomplished golfer with professional aspirations, Khalil Abdul Karim (Faisal Khalili), a former member of the New York-based Latino activist group, the Young Lords, and many others received their initial Islamic movement indoctrination while bunking in the barracks at Masjidul Ummah prior to the establishment of the Islamic Party. These brothers and their eventual wives, Tahirah Abdullah (Ahmed), Samirah Abdul Ghani (Kareem), and Naimah Abdul Haqq (Najeeb) would form the leadership cadre of the Islamic Party once it was formed.

The official news organ of Masjidul Ummah was a bimonthly newsletter known as *Al-Ummah*. The objectives of *Al-Ummah* were: 1) To disseminate current news regarding the internal activities of this organization as well as the news of the Greater Washington (D.C.) area; 2) To give official expression to our attitudes and opinions on affairs that affect the lives of Muslim Americans; 3) To seek understanding, sympathy and communication among all Muslims; 4) To seek support for Islamic work.[12] The publication was distributed locally and nationally.

In addition to the externally distributed *Al-Ummah*, the Community Mosque produced an internal newsletter, *Masjidul Ummah Chronicle*. The *Chronicle* was produced quarterly to keep *masjid* members abreast of happenings and developments in the Community Mosque community. The *Issue Sheet* was periodically distributed locally by the Community Mosque to give Islamic expression to topical issues confronting the oppressed community in the United States generally, and African Americans in particular. Elements of the three publications would be included in the eventual official organ of the Islamic Party, *al-Islam*.

Muzaffaruddin and members of the Community Mosque were frequent visitors to MSA conventions and to other established Muslim communities nationwide. One such visit was to Bait ul-Quraysh in Newark, New Jersey in late August 1971. The ostensible purpose of the trip was to learn "some of the successful economic principles these brothers have employed in their enterprises. Among these is a fleet of motorized clothing store units and the acquisition of properties where Muslims and their families can live together. These are prime examples of self-help, since the brothers started with only a little money but devoted much work and cooperation to the cause."[13] The collective living and expense sharing of the Muslims of Baytul Quraysh would influence future economic enterprises within the Islamic Party.

Muzaffaruddin maintained communication with members of the global Islamic movement prior to the formation of the Islamic Party and transmitted this perspective to members of the Community Mosque. In October 1971, Malek Ben Nabi, a former president of the University of Algiers, and one of the foremost leaders of the Algerian Revolution against French colonialism, visited the mosque and delivered a dynamic address on the Algerian Revolution and the worldwide Islamic movement.

The Islamic Party in North America was officially organized during a meeting at Masjidul Ummah on the final weekend of December 1971. Its formation was declared on January 1, 1972. At the same meeting, the Declaration of the Federation of Muslim Communities was signed by Imam Yusuf Muzaffaruddin Hamid, Imam Daud ibn Ahmad Salahuddin, Al-Jamaat Al-Muslimoon (Chicago), and Amir Abdur Rahim Shaheed (Mutazzim), The Islamic Center of Pittsburgh. Muzaffaruddin appointed the latter two brothers, along with Ali Abdul Karim (Yamani), New York; Abdul Malik Zahir, Akron, Ohio; Kareem Abdul Ghani, Washington, D.C.; Najeeb Abdul Haqq, Washington, D.C.; and Khalil Abdul Karim (Faisal Khalili) to the Central Control Committee (CCC). The CCC members were official advisers to the amir of the Islamic Party and a steering committee for general party activities and party organizational development.[14] The CCC was the first official consultative body of the Islamic Party and preceded the Guidance Council, formed in 1974 after the establishment of the Islamic Party Constitution as the group's *Majlis ash Shura*. Amir Al-Islam (Chicago) would generally accompany Daud Salahuddin, the first and only secretary-general of the organization, to the Washington, D.C. meetings of the CCC. Tariq Abdul Hakim (Ishmaeli) likewise attended most sessions of the CCC with Abdur Rahim Shaheed (Mutazzim).

Like most of the initial members of the Islamic Party, Abdur Rahim Shaheed (Mutazzim) became interested in the organization through its charismatic leader. "I first met Muzaffaruddin at an MSA convention in Green Bay, Wisconsin. He was making critical statements about the lack of involvement of African Americans in the MSA and the MSA's apparent lack of concern in trying to involve African Americans in their work; particularly at any level resembling decision making. He was sharp, confident, and fired up," Abdur Rahim told this writer.[15] "Muzaffaruddin had the clearest vision of anyone I had met about the direction that the Islamic movement in North America should take. When I went back to Pittsburgh, I introduced the Islamic Party to the brothers. There were about fifty young brothers in Pittsburgh who eventually wanted to join."

Daud Salahuddin recalled Muzaffaruddin first broaching the subject of the Islamic Party with him. "Muzaffaruddin just sort of popped up in Chicago one day seeking me out to talk to me about this idea that he had about forming an organization that he wanted me to co-found. He impressed me with his intelligence and critical thinking. He had a special feel for analyzing the political implications of events. I arranged a meeting at my house with Muzaffaruddin and Ahmed Sakr, who was one of the foremost scholars/activists in the United States at that time (1971).

"When Muzaffaruddin told Ahmed Sakr of his intention to start an organization called the Islamic Party, Ahmed Sakr took exception to the proposed name by suggesting that the name would carry negative connotations like the Democratic and Republican Party in the U.S. Muzaffaruddin asked Ahmed Sakr to read, in Arabic, the verse in Qur'an calling for the success of an Islamic Party, Hezbullah, (Qur'an, 58:22). Muzaffaruddin then declared rhetorically, 'How can anything that Allah commands to come into existence have a negative connotation?' In my opinion, Ahmed Sakr was left without an explanation. Most Muslims, especially back then, would have been too intimidated by Ahmed Sakr's scholarship to challenge him in the way that Muzaffaruddin did. From that moment on, I was sold on the Islamic Party."

According to Abdur Rahim, "The Islamic Party definitely did not receive a warm reception from everybody, especially The Dar (Dar-ul-Islam movement). The Dar really had problems with the Islamic Party coming into being."[16] The primary point of contention between the ten-year old Dar-ul-Islam movement and the upstart Islamic Party was the Dar's insistence that Muzaffaruddin and his cohorts (smaller party) join the "bigger party" (Dar-ul-Islam movement). Muzaffaruddin steadfastly maintained that the Dar's position was based on their taking Qur'anic verses and hadith (narrations of the Prophet Muhammad) out of context. Muzaffaruddin further incensed the Brooklyn-based Dar membership by inviting the imam of the Dar-affiliated Masjid al Talib of Atlanta, Antar 'Abd-al-Khabir (Ibn Stanford), and two of his amirs to join the Islamic Party after they had traveled to Washington, D.C. in March 1972 to try to convince Muzaffaruddin of the errors of his position.

When Muzaffaruddin refused to relent to pressure to affiliate with the Dar-ul-Islam movement, Zayd Ahmed, one of the founders of Masjidul Ummah, and several other brothers left the *masjid* and formed Masjidul Muhajireen. Masjidul Muhajireen, located directly across the street from Howard University's main campus, approximately seven blocks from Masjidul Ummah, was the Washington, D.C. center for the Dar's activities.

A disagreement arose in June 1972 between the newly formed Islamic Party and the leadership of the Mosque of Islamic Brotherhood (MIB) in New York. MIB was founded in 1964 by former members of Malcolm X's Muslim Mosque, Inc., particularly the late Imam Ahmed Taufiq. The disagreement developed after a visit to the Community Mosque by members of the Baitul Quraysh in Newark. After returning to Newark, one member of the visiting delegation quoted Muzaffaruddin as having said that Imam Taufiq had secretly met with members of the Nation of Islam to form a pact. Although the misstatement was later retracted, tension remained just below the surface in relations between the two groups.

No stranger to controversy, Muzaffaruddin embarked on a mission to Libya in 1972 to convince Muammar Qaddafi not to give a reported four million dollars to the Nation of Islam because of the group's heterodox religious beliefs. The mission apparently delayed, but did not stop, the gift from Qaddafi to the Nation. From the earliest days of the Islamic Party to the death of Elijah Muhammad in 1975, the Islamic Party continually lambasted the Nation of Islam and Elijah Muhammad in its publications, lectures, and general conversations whenever persons asked about that organization.

While acknowledging the good works of other Muslim organizations, Muzaffaruddin felt that the Islamic Party was unique in its structure and mission. "There were others (Muslim organizations), but in terms of national aspirations, programs to address a national need for understanding and action from an Islamic perspective, it is our belief that the Islamic Party played a pivotal role in those days. . . . Now if you speak in terms of significant achievements, I would start with the fact that the Islamic Party was a constitutional organization. This is extremely significant in terms of the development of Islamic movements around the world. While the Islamic Party had its critics, I believe that the Islamic Party was the first national *jamaat*, to my recollection, that put forward a clear program in writing. It was a constitutional organization. Its organizational administrative head was voted by a one-man, one-vote principle. The officers of the Islamic Party were voted by one-man, one-vote. The duties, obligations, and responsibilities of the head of the Islamic Party, as well as the responsibilities of each member, were clearly defined in constitutional terms. We think that this constitutional organization put the Islamic work on a different footing.

"First of all," Muzaffaruddin said, "it took it out of the category of personality. Secondly, it brought into the picture what was expected of a worker when he joined the Party. I think it's fair to say that most Muslim mosques and movements are run similar to churches and for one reason or the other, agree on an implied set of beliefs without clearly defining those beliefs. There is generally a personality with whom you associate these beliefs, and that is the beginning and end of how things go. Whatever the imam or leader says basically is law. There are a few guidelines for determining how members of the *jamaat* relate to each other. That was not the case with the Islamic Party.

"There were no implications when we founded the Party that our leader was supposedly everybody's leader, or that he would speak for anyone other than members of the Islamic Party. He was elected for a five-year period and could be reelected if that were the desire of the membership. I think that when you probe this question of the constitutionality of the Party, it is at that point that you begin to realize that what was being sought was providing for longevity for an organization beyond specific people, beyond personalities.

"We never envisioned any short-term goals in terms of why we organized ourselves. It was not necessary to organize the Islamic Party just to publish a newspaper, for an example, which was, nevertheless, a very important part of the overall Dawah program. It was not necessary to organize an Islamic Party to teach people how to make *salaat* (prayer) and to practice the fundamentals of the religion. It was necessary to organize the Islamic Party in North America because we felt that many Muslims in this country were prepared to commit their lives to the establishment of an alternative society; the right society; the good society; the Islamic society. Now you must admit that is a noble goal, a high aspiration for children of ex-slaves."[17]

Ibrahim Hanif first came to Masjidul Ummah, the national headquarters of the Islamic Party, in the summer of 1972. Already a Muslim, Hanif was a medical student at Howard University. Hanif would quit his hospital job in 1973 to direct the organization's developing bakery, and become editor of the Islamic Party's journal, *Al-Islam*, a position he would hold until 1978. While impressed with the disciplined, systematic work of the organization, Hanif felt that the Islamic Party's chauvinistic attitude contributed to tensions with other Muslim groups.

"The official view espoused by the administration of the Islamic Party, the amir and Guidance Council, of which I was a part, always created tension with other organizations. We reflected a kind of arrogance that somehow we were 'The' Party of Allah, rather than simply people who were part of the Hezbullah. In a way, this was reflected in the journal's title, *Al-Islam, The Islamic Movement Journal*, rather than *Al-Islam, An Islamic Movement Journal*. Arrogance prevented us from cooperating with other organizations in a way that would have been mutually beneficial," Hanif told me in a telephone interview.[18] "To a great degree, that was a shortcoming that often prevented many of our members, on an individual level, from having cordial relationships with Muslims who were not a part of the Islamic Party; particularly African American Muslims who had similar goals. There were clearly people in our organization who knew people in other communities. We had an organizational policy, perhaps unwritten, but strictly understood, that we would not allow our women to marry brothers who were not members of the Islamic Party. We even got to the point that when anybody took *shahadah*, he was not only encouraged to join the Islamic Party, but was made to feel that if he didn't join, his covenant with Allah was in jeopardy."

Al-Islam, The Islamic Movement Journal, was launched as the official organ of the Islamic Party in January 1972. Published bimonthly, *Al-Islam*'s first editor was Sulayman S. Muffassir, a former Jehovah's Witness minister. Muffassir was a prolific writer and researcher whose articles appeared in Muslim publications worldwide. He was followed for a short time by Sayid Abu Bakr, a graduate student at Howard University. Ibrahim

Hanif remained the official editor of *Al-Islam* for most of the Islamic Party's period of operations in the United States.

Although accusations to the contrary abounded, Muzaffaruddin wrote relatively few articles for *Al-Islam*, even in the journal's earliest days of existence. Yasin Masjid, headquarters of the Dar-ul-Islam, sent a letter in 1972 to mosques around the country condemning Muzaffaruddin and *Al-Islam* for an editorial that called for the ouster of the director of the Islamic Center in Washington, D.C., Muhammad Abdul-Rauf, for stating that "700,000 Muslims of the world stand behind" Elijah Muhammad and the Nation of Islam. After receiving the letter, Jamaat ul-Muslimeen of Chicago wrote directly to the leadership of the Dar-ul-Islam. His letter reflected the general attitude of party members elsewhere: "Several brothers and sisters from our own *jamaat* here in Chicago have taken an active role in writing for, planning, distributing, and supporting the paper (*Al-Islam*) since it was started. We all feel very intimately that it is our paper, and is not the personal fief of anyone among us. In fact, very few articles in *Al-Islam* can be attributed to the Amir himself, when compared with the dozens of articles written by other brothers and sisters."

The printed word played a critical role in transmitting internal directives, organizational philosophy, and the Islamic Party's message to society. The party even bought its own printing press in 1975 to more cost-effectively produce its own brochures and pamphlets. A young nineteen-year old member of the organization, Muhsin Adbul Halim, was sent to a vocational program by the party to learn the printing trade. All publicly released written materials were meticulously scrutinized, edited, and proofread before reaching the public domain. From January 1972, when *Al-Islam* was first produced, until the end of the decade when the party shifted its organizational focus to the Caribbean, *Al-Islam* was the primary Dawah tool for the group's workers. From the earliest days of the organization, participation in the collective distribution of *al-Islam* was an important element in determining membership. Saturdays were designated as collective Dawah days with all members and applicants, with few exceptions, were required to spend about three hours canvassing neighborhoods and the downtown district introducing non-Muslims to Islam and selling *Al-Islam*.

In 1973, a full-time Dawah team of eight to ten brothers was established. Brothers spent eight hours a day, six days a week walking the streets of Washington, D.C., giving Dawah and selling the journal. The daily operations of the Dawah team were planned with almost military precision. Various areas were targeted and strategies devised to maximize their presence. Buses packed with commuters on their way to work in downtown D.C. were frequently preached to by a member of the Dawah team for the duration of the bus riders' inbound trip. Dawah tables were set up by the Dawah team, particularly in the downtown area, containing informational brochures, books, and other items on Islam. The propagation efforts of the Dawah team, as well as that of the collective membership of the Islamic Party, were enhanced by the wearing of uniform dress. The Class A dress uniform consisted of identical mid-thigh length green shirts, black kufis, black pants, and shoes. The Class B work uniform was identical matching green work shirts and pants, white kufis, and black shoes.

The overwhelming majority of the party's membership never challenged the significance of the journal as a Dawah tool nor their obligation to personally distribute it. Yet, in spite of its relatively extensive grassroots distribution, opinions differed among some leading members as to the effectiveness of the publication. Ibrahim Hanif, the former director of Islamic Party Publications and editor of *Al-Islam*, recalled that his personal view about the journal differed sharply from that of the amir of the party, Y. Muzaffaruddin Hamid. "I considered the significance of *Al-Islam* as a Dawah tool negligible. He (Muzaffaruddin) and I discussed this at length. We were trying to do too many things with *Al-Islam*. We tried to appeal to both a non-Muslim audience and a Muslim audience, and provide organizational policy and organizational philosophy, along with an understanding of Islam.

"The publication was used for too many conflicting purposes. At another point in the development of the organization, it became a revenue-generating source, which I definitely objected to. In my opinion, the most important Dawah of the Islamic Party was through personal contact. *Al-Islam* obviously exposed people to Islam, as I clearly remember non-Muslims reading it and giving me feedback, and visiting our organization as a result of that. Most of the people who actually became Muslim through the Islamic Party, did so, as I recall, through personal contact, not primarily because of something they read in *Al-Islam*."[19]

Muzaffaruddin viewed the significance of the Islamic Party's Dawah work, and *Al-Islam* in particular, in somewhat more global terms. "Many may want to forget that there have been great attacks on the integrity of Islam in this country. There has not always been a general consensus as to what Islam is and what Islam is not on fundamental questions of prophethood and the mission of Islam. . . . It is in that regard that the Islamic Party found itself being forced to defend the integrity of Islam against the onslaughts of misrepresentation, including the popular misrepresentations carried under the name of the Nation of Islam headed by Elijah Poole. I would even say most Muslims were either afraid, or were too ignorant of Islam themselves, to speak out on issues that were crucial to the Dawah, like Islam and the question of black people being gods in the "religious sense" that the Nation of Islam spoke of. It would be fair to say that the Islamic Party in North America took a very clear position on the Deen (religion), in terms of its integrity, when there were other popular voices corrupting the Deen. One of our greatest leaders (Malcolm X) gave his life over this controversy. The least we can do is say that we were there and that our voice was very clear on the questions."[20]

Every inch of the three floors of the house used as Masjidul Ummah and the national headquarters of the Islamic Party was utilized. The basement was renovated in early 1973, carpeted, and adorned with authentic Persian carpets that were donated to the Islamic Party by one of the local oriental rug dealers. The majestic-looking corner facility was painted light green and was a virtual beehive of activity in an otherwise laid-back neighborhood. An adjoining two-story property to the mosque, 1802 First Street NW, was rented for housing Islamic Party members' families. In addition to having leaders and committed members in close proximity to the *masjid*, the First Street house was the party's first collective/shared living arrangement, the predecessor experiment of a cornerstone shared living/resource saving project of the organization dubbed by Muzaffaruddin as Survival for Islamic Work. Kareem Abdul Ghani, the deputy amir of the party, Najeeb Abdul Haqq, Guidance Council member, chief of the organization's security, and confidante and constant companion of Muzaffaruddin, this writer, and their families were the occupants of the house.

Soon the attempt to house all of the organization's local operations in one building proved futile and a three-story row house around the corner from the *masjid* was rented. Called the Chancery, the facility, located at 225 Florida Avenue NW, initially housed the amir's office, two families, and the party's bakery operation. Other committed families established residences in the neighborhood of the *masjid*, thereby creating a physical Muslim community in the area. As the presence of Muslims around the *masjid* increased, Muzaffaruddin envisioned that that section of D.C. would eventually become known as Muslimtown; similar to Chinatown, the downtown Washington area known for its proliferation of Chinese residences and businesses.

The brotherhood of the party was subdivided into families. A family head for each unit was responsible for the oversight of the family and evaluation of each party applicant for membership. The family heads were appointed by and directly responsible to the amir. The families were organized to facilitate the further training of workers, act as security units for the organization, and carry out the work and program of the organization. In addition to consistently participating in Qur'anic study classes, mostly held immediately after *Fajr* (morning) prayer five to six days a week, and ideological training sessions, conducted at least twice weekly after *Maghrib* (sunset) prayer, family members were required to attend their individual family study circles. These sessions centered on ideological training and character building. As Abdur Rahim Shaheed (Mutazzim) of Pittsburgh pointed out, "Through its uniform ideological training, the party injected into Muslims in Pittsburgh and elsewhere a spirit of wanting to be a full-time Islamic worker. Our training laid the foundation for developing a realistic concept of the methodology to establish an Islamic society."[21] Abdur Rahim quit his job at Mobil Chemical after joining the Islamic Party to pursue "party business" (Islamic work) full-time. He supported his family by becoming a leather craftsman, tailor, and entrepreneur.

Muzaffaruddin also saw training of the Islamic Party's workers as a critical aspect of its existence. "I want to emphasize that while Dawah was a very important part of our program, the training, the discipline of the minds, spirits, and character of our members was of equal, if not greater, value. What we experienced was that the Islamic struggle was much larger than our imaginations. There is a principle that for every action there is a reaction. The Islamic Party received all types of reactions. Perhaps the most challenging reaction the Islamic Party received was the conspiratorial actions of the *munafiqun* (hypocrites) who had tied their destiny to the destiny of the various administrations in Washington, D.C., particularly the American government, and the administrations of the kingdoms of the Middle East, and the general Muslim governments there."[22]

Ibrahim Hanif observed, "Based on the resources that we were exposed to at that time, our training in the Islamic Party was excellent. It (training) helped us to see Islam as a dynamic system that looked at its social, political, and cultural environment, and then created a movement to establish the rule of Allah. The handbooks that we used clearly represented, at that time, the best thought of Islamic movement thinking. But, I think we had some shortcomings. Our ideological training was not adequately balanced with the development of the heart. The ideological training was excellent in helping us to be politically aware, politically astute, and understanding of the various forces that were acting on us and on people in general. It was good training as far as social analysis, and power relationships, but I think we were lacking in terms of developing that aspect of the Muslim character that deals with what we call 'the heart or the spirit'; a love of Allah that is reflected in our humility, and the way that we show affection toward other people. That is not to say that it was totally absent."[23]

After the Hajj 1973 in a Palestinian refugee camp in Lebanon, Kareem Abdul Ghani, Najeeb Abdul Haqq, and another Party member, came into contact with members of the Ihkwan ul Muslimeen as the Ihkwan members clandestinely distributed English translations of Sayid Qutb's illustrious work *Milestones*.[24] The brothers did not fully grasp the significance of the book until they returned to the States and were apprised of its importance by Muzaffaruddin. Islamic Party Publications subsequently mass-produced and distributed *Milestones* nationwide in an expanded *Al-Islam* format. This event marked the first time that English-speaking Muslims in the United States would have access to the book. *Milestones* was immediately incorporated into the ideological training offering of the collective and family study circles of the organization.

The Islamic Party's intense regimen of study and ideological indoctrination found a welcome reception with many college students, graduates, and persons given to contemplation and action. Consequently, party members were often derisively characterized by other local Muslims as "just a bunch of intellectuals." The academic and professional credentials of many of the Party's members, especially in the Washington, D.C. headquarters, did little to debunk the characterization. Included in its ranks were doctors, nurses, a nurse practitioner/midwife, lawyers, teachers, social workers, architects, accountants, and other professional or semi-professional brothers and sisters committed to the Islamic Party's program of action. Just as prominent in the ranks were the self-avowed "refugees" from the nationalist and activist community. Numerous former members of the Black Panther Party, or other more localized groups were Islamic Party members. One former Black Panther member, Tahirah Abdul Barr (Abdullah), had been a victim of the 1971 infamous police raid of the Philadelphia Black Panther office that resulted in Tahirah and other female and male Panthers being stripped and photographed naked outside their office on a cold wintry day.

A one-time influx of about five brothers in 1973 was noteworthy, though, even for an organization that was accustomed to constant replenishment of its ranks. Recent Vietnam War veterans had banded together in Washington, D.C. to form a bicycling group ingeniously called Gypsy Troop. The mostly fatigue-clad members of Gypsy Troop would be seen riding their multi-gear bicycles, thirty-five to fifty persons deep, down Pennsylvania Avenue, and anywhere else they chose to travel, whistles blowing, commandeering lanes of traffic, defying anyone or anything to impede their progress. The undisputed leader of this motley crew of war veterans, eventually known as Muhammad Yusuf, accepted Islam, joined the Islamic Party, and quickly became a very active and disciplined worker. In part due to Yusuf's influence, other members of Gypsy Troop, like Luqman Abdus Shakur, accepted Islam, joined the Islamic Party, and became life-long workers for the cause of Islam.

The women who constituted the Sisterhood of the Islamic Party were no less diverse, committed, and talented than their male counterparts. Many of the women attracted to the organization were impressed with the depth of expression of sisterly concern evidenced in the actions of Islamic Party women. Muneerah Afifa had been a member of the

Washington, D.C.-based Black Man's Development Center, a black nationalist organization heavily influenced by the Moorish Science teachings of Noble Drew Ali. In 1975, Muneerah accepted Islam after being more thoroughly introduced to the Islamic doctrine by Islamic Party member Khadijah Mahmud. "When I accepted Islam, my mother used to make a joke. She used to say, 'When you wake up, you go to the mosque. When you come in, you've been to the mosque. When you are at home, you talk about the mosque.' Everything was the mosque. The mosque was the focal point of our lives; the central place. I worked at the sewing factory making uniforms for the school, as well as taught in the school. I worked to help prepare dinners for sale. We had sisters classes twice a week, and attended *Jumahs* on Fridays. If we were not at the mosque seven days a week, we were there at least five. It was unheard of for us (sisters) not to see each other. The sister's involvement in the work of the Islamic Party was very prominent.

"The sisters wore uniform dress in public gatherings. In the summer and warm months, the sisters wore completely white outfits; including face veils. The white color gave the appearance of multiplying our presence at conferences or wherever we were together in a large gathering. In the winter, the uniform color was black. When we traveled to conventions, we moved in a caravan. We would actually take some of the conventions by storm because our presence was so strong with our uniform dress and message. At one gathering at the Islamic Center (Washington, D.C.), one party sister gave a speech, and at the end of the speech she started to recite the "Believers Pledge." All of the sisters stood up and recited the pledge with her. You can imagine that this display of unity created quite a stir with the other sisters," Muneerah remembered.[25]

Maryum Abdul Azeez (Funches) first became interested in Islam after seeing a poster proclaiming that "God Has No Sons or Daughters." while attending college in Mississippi. "Once I got to Howard University as a graduate student," Maryum recalled, "I saw this flier in the School of Social Work that said that the Islamic Party was feeding people at the mosque and giving away food to needy people during the month of Ramadan. That flier prompted me to want to find out about that organization. I contacted the Islamic Party through the number on the flier, and two brothers came to the dormitory to talk to me—Brother Kareem Abdul Ghani, and Brother Najeeb Abdul Haqq. They were very professional and polite, and assumed very good Islamic *adab* (etiquette). We talked downstairs in the lobby. After our conversation, they said that I would have the opportunity to talk to a Muslim sister. I eventually talked with Brother Kareem's wife, Samirah. All of my questions were basically answered. After tying up some loose ends, I took *shahadah* one day in October 1974.

"When I came into the party, they already had a very organized sisterhood. I was very impressed with it. Sister Tahirah Abdullah and Sister Samirah were in charge of the administrative affairs of the sisters. They appointed a sister to work with each new sister to help with *salat*, dress, hygiene, and things like that. They basically took care of us like we were a family. Sister Asma Hanif was a very dear sister to me. She provided me with the clothing that I needed, and helped me with my prayers. Asma was a sincere adviser to me. She became a nurse/midwife. The sisters got together to meet our social needs. We still did our plays and other forms of entertainment, but in an Islamic way. The sisters developed very strong relationships, and we really felt like we were sisters in the genuine sense of the word.

"The sisters believed and lived the hadith of the Prophet that 'you should want for your brother or sister what you want for yourself.' A sister who was getting married did not have to worry about who was making her dress, or who was going to provide or prepare the food for the feast. If any sister needed something in her house, other sisters would try to pitch in to satisfy that need. There was a very low divorce rate among party members; not even 10 percent. In some cases where divorces occurred, sisters or brothers may not have been ready for a truly Islamic lifestyle resulting in their leaving the practice of the Deen. Being in the *jamaat* offered a sense of security and belonging for all the sisters and brothers. The sisters were well protected by the brothers, and we did not feel oppressed. We did not have to go to the store or laundromat alone. If your husband was not available, or if you were single, all you had to do was to call the mosque and transportation would be arranged. It's so different today with sisters walking around in *nikab* (full face veil) with no brothers to offer protection for them. I have even seen veiled sisters trying to hitch rides at night after events at Islamic Centers."

Muneerah remembered what some may consider one of the ultimate expressions of Muslim sisterhood. "The sisters were so close in the party that some of us even breast-fed each other's babies. There was no such thing as a child disrupting the *khutbah* (Friday sermon) because the baby needed to be fed. If the mother could not immediately get to the child, the closest breast-feeding mother would nourish the baby. After you breast-fed your baby, if another baby was crying, you would breast-feed that baby also. Everyone helped each other."[26]

Creative and efficient use of space at the 101 S Street and 225 Florida Avenue NW locations only forestalled the Islamic Party's near inevitable move to a more space-friendly facility. Because of space constraints, attempting to operate a *masjid*, headquarters offices of the Islamic Party, including Islamic Party Publications and *Al-Islam*, a *halal* meat and grocery store, bakery, sewing factory, and public Dawah center in the two buildings proved after a while to be problematic. A three-story former church building located at the busy intersection of Sherman Avenue and Park Road NW (770 Park Road) was purchased by the Islamic Party in September 1974. The spacious building housed under one roof a *musallah* (prayer room) for several hundred persons, the Community Mosque Academy, a full-time kindergarten through twelfth-grade Muslim school, bakery, grocery store, administrative offices, single brothers barracks, and an auditorium/multi-purpose room. The facility presented its own set of challenges, not the least being the increased operating and maintenance expenses required by the larger building. Soon after settling into the new headquarters building, the Islamic Party leased a one-story row house next door on Park Road, and another two-story adjacent unattached house on the Sherman Avenue side. Departmental offices were placed in the Park Road house with a nursery for members' children in the Sherman Avenue site. Between the main building and the Sherman Avenue location towered a billboard that beckoned passersby to visit the Community Mosque.

Shortly after securing the headquarters property, the Islamic Party purchased seven new taxi cabs and registered them under the name of Imperial Cab Co., an already established local company. Each cab was driven practically twenty-four hours a day with two brothers sharing a vehicle for twelve-hour shifts, six days a week. The cabs were given service checks between shifts by Islamic Party mechanics. All of the money made from the cabs was turned in to the Islamic Party's treasury with minimum stipends given to the drivers. The revenue generated from the taxi cabs became the primary source of income for the Islamic Party, and many of its members throughout the group's organizational life in the United States.[27]

Within six months of establishing the cab operation, the Islamic Party opened the Nation Bookstore, a well-stocked, efficiently managed Islamic bookstore about six blocks north of Howard University's campus on Georgia Avenue NW. In addition to offering a comprehensive selection of Islamic books, the Nation Bookstore sold a wide array of health foods and other natural products. An adjoining row house was secured and used for a short time as a Culture Center where party members, Howard University students, and the general public were entertained by live jazz performances and poetry readings while sipping herbal tea and eating healthy sandwiches in a Middle Eastern ambiance. Islamic Party members, one a former performer with the critically acclaimed musician Pharaoh Sanders, mostly provided the entertainment.

Further north on Georgia Avenue, almost an equal distance from the party's headquarters, was the organization's twenty-four-hour-a-day restaurant, The Hunger Stopper. The Hunger Stopper's house specialty was the Curry Burger, a heavily spiced ground beef sandwich. Catering primarily to late-night cab drivers, the restaurant, as well as other Islamic Party business ventures, provided skills training and economic self-sufficiency for the group's members. Commenting on this organizational phenomenon, Ibrahim Hanif remarked, "There were opportunities in the Islamic Party for people, who had very limited skills, to acquire a greater sense of adulthood and responsibility. Not everybody in our organization was college educated. There were some people who did not have a high school education, or barely a high school education. The economic enterprises allowed some people who had little or no experience to develop some. For an example, some of the cab drivers received motivation that they ordinarily would not have received. Our taxi drivers had a sense of professionalism. I certainly would not have gone to the Department of Agriculture for graduate studies in editing had I not been given the assignment to be director of Islamic Party Publications."[28]

In the fall of 1973, Ahmed Abdullah and his wife Tahirah were assigned by the amir to go to Houston, Texas, to assist in developing the Islamic work in that region. The Sunni Muslim presence in the city was minuscule at that time. The Islamic Party, through Muzaffaruddin, had maintained contact with Ibrahim Yazdi, an activist Iranian Muslim in Houston, who in 1979 triumphantly returned to Iran with Ayatollah Khomeini as Minister of Revolution. *Al-Islam* printed two messages from Ayatollah Khomeini from Paris around 1973, and the auditorium/multi-purpose room of the Park Road headquarters of the Islamic Party was used as an overnight sleepover for hundreds of Iranian nationals protesting against the Shah of Iran.

Abdullah remembers that he and his wife were asked to go to Houston because "there were one or two brothers who wanted to build a community there and have a *masjid*. We gave Dawah on the campus of Texas Southern University, and spoke to people in the community about Islam. We tried to duplicate the Islamic Party program in Houston: the Sunday lecture, the teachings of the fundamentals of Islam, a Feed the Hungry Month program during the month of Ramadan, serving the poor and needy in the community, and periodic visitations to the prisons to visit inmates who showed an interest in Islam. After securing a nice facility for a *masjid*, the party made Houston its Southwest Regional headquarters.

"My family stayed in Houston for seven to eight months. When we returned to D.C. in 1974, most of the Houston brothers relocated. Only a small contingent stayed behind with the wazir of the party there, Ahmed Abdus Sabur. The main emphasis in the party then was to make the D.C. headquarters a magnet for the rest of the country to migrate to. A lot of families moved to the Washington area from about '74 to '77. We were still growing outwardly as our center was becoming stronger; the stronger the heart, the stronger the limbs. From '74 to '77, I was the imam of Masjidul Ummah. The amir wanted to separate the duties of Imam from that of amir of the party so he could concentrate more on launching a total program for the organization."[29]

Between 1974 and 1977, the Washington, D.C. headquarters of the organization attracted members from across the nation. Latino Muslims (primarily Puerto Rican) from New York migrated to the Party's headquarters. Prominent among them was Umar Abdur Rahim Ocasio, his wife Faiza, and Abdus Salaam Muhammad, self-named "The Latin from Manhattan." Although these Latino Muslims found spiritual and ideological compatriots in the Islamic Party, there existed, nevertheless, some cultural barriers that had to be transcended. Ocasio described the dilemma that he and other Latino Muslims faced during this era; even to a degree in the Islamic Party: "Latino Muslims encountered an interesting new world upon their conversion. Any lingering parochialism was shattered by the experience of suddenly being exposed to many different peoples and cultures in New York's varied Islamic tapestry. The indigenous American Muslim scene was dominated by thousands of newly converted African Americans who had established themselves in the mosques, primarily in the borough of Brooklyn.

"Yet curiously, it seemed Latinos believed it was essential to obliterate all vestiges of their ancestral heritage. Dressed in turbans and robes, they would even refrain from speaking Spanish in the *masjid*. . . ."[30]

"The Islamic Party was a little different," Ocasio explained to me. "But, still not all of the reservations to practice the elements of our culture that were consistent with Islamic teachings were removed when we migrated to D.C. Some party brothers were more receptive to our Latino identity than others. The 18th Street and Columbia Road NW area was fertile for Dawah for us due to the large numbers of Latinos. Mostly though, we sort of tried to blend in with everyone else."[31] Even though he was a frequent visitor to the headquarters, Yahya Figuero, the current director of Alianza Islamica, was a member of the Islamic Party who chose not to migrate to Washington. From Pittsburgh, Tariq Abdul Hakim (Ishmaeli), his wife Malaika, and Talib Ilm and his wife moved to Washington and became active workers for the organization, particularly in the areas of Dawah and education. Jamal Abdullah and his wife Sahar, and Khalil Ihsan Abdullah and his wife Amirah came from Syracuse, New York. Jamal would serve for a time as editorial assistant with *Al-Islam*, and director of physical training. Khalil was the manager of The Nation Bookstore, a family head, and unofficial drill sergeant for the organization.

The constitution of the Islamic Party in North America was officially ratified in 1974. Borrowing heavily from the constitution of Jamaati Islami-Pakistan, and influenced by the Ihkwan ul Muslimeen's guiding principles, the Islamic Party's constitution was first amended in January 1978. One change was to place the Believer's Pledge, learned by every party member and recited at the close of many organizational meetings, in the back of the Constitution. The Believer's Pledge became a mantra for party members. It read: "For me the Islamic movement is the very purpose of my life. My life is dedicated to it and my death should also be in pursuit of this purpose. Others may follow it or may not. In all circumstances this shall be my course and I will give my life for it. Even if not a single individual steps forward, I will yet do so, and if none accompanies me, I will walk alone. If the entire world unites to oppose me, I will contend with it single-handed, undaunted."

In 1975, Muzaffaruddin was the guest of the Libyan government at an international Muslim/Christian Dialogue. He was impressed by the material assistance and ideological leadership provided by Libya to liberation movements throughout the non-Muslim and Muslim world. Through extensive discussions with Qaddafi, Muzaffaruddin began to understand the necessity for the Islamic Party to translate its philosophical concern for social justice into a concrete methodology and program of action. Consequently, shortly after his return, the Islamic Party activated the Department of Oppressed Peoples Affairs (OPA). This department was constitutionally charged with "keeping abreast of the affairs that affect the lives of minorities, indigent, and oppressed people and recommending steps the Islamic Party can take to render assistance."[32] The OPA became the primary link of the Islamic Party to the non-Muslim oppressed and activist communities. Rather than employing preaching as the near-exclusive basis for interaction with non-Muslims, the Party suddenly cast itself, through OPA, as a significant player in the Washington, D.C. grassroots social activist arena.

The headquarters auditorium became a gathering place for such functions as symposiums on hunger, a meeting place for a local anti-rape group, Black Men Against Rape, and United Black Community, a grassroots advocacy, and empowerment coalition of nationalists, pan-Africans, socialists, and Muslims. The director of OPA eventually served as the convenor of United Black Community. An adjunct to the community orientation work of the Islamic Party was the establishment of the Community Mosque Southeast Center in 1975. The Southeast Center was located in a densely populated section of Washington, Anacostia, on the other side of town from the headquarters. The center's programs consisted of domestic and social counseling for non-Muslims, an odd job employment program for teenagers, recreational activities for youth, lectures on Islam, and other topics of interest, and the sale of Islamic books, paraphernalia, health foods, and other natural products.[33]

OPA organized the party's first outdoor rally in May 1976 in honor of Malik Shabazz, Malcolm X. Held in Stanton Park, a few blocks from the U.S. Capitol, the list of speakers included then City Councilman Marion Barry, controversial D.C. Judge Harry Toussaint Alexander, activist poet Askia Muhammad Toure, and Yusuf Muzaffaruddin Hamid as the keynote speaker. In July 1976, Muzaffaruddin, Kareem Abdul Ghani, and the director of OPA, this writer, attended an International Zionism/Racism Conference in Tripoli, Libya. The conference provided the opportunity for Muzaffaruddin to negotiate with Qaddafi to have interest removed from a $100,000 loan extended to the Islamic Party by the Libyan government. The stated purpose of the loan was to pay off the mortgage balance on the party's Park Road complex and to use the excess for program development. Although a considerable amount was applied to the mortgage, the total debt was not erased because of monies used for the purchase of organizational supplies/equipment and the social welfare of its members.

Also at the conference, the Libyan/Moroccan-financed English language version of the movie *Muhammad Messenger of God (The Message)* was publicly premiered for the delegates. The movie's director, Mustapha Akad, offered Muzaffaruddin the opportunity for the Islamic Party to be the exclusive U.S. distributor of the movie, an offer later turned down because of the party's lack of experience in the area of film distribution. Shortly after returning to the United States, plans to organize an OPA-sponsored National Zionism/Racism Conference in the organization's headquarters auditorium began. Within about six months of the international conference, numerous presenters at the Tripoli event participated in the Washington, D.C. conference.

In late 1976 after a swing through southeastern United States by Muzaffaruddin and some members of the Guidance Council, the amir proposed to the general membership in Washington, D.C. that the headquarters of the party shift to the Atlanta, Georgia, area. He argued that the national and international development of the party was being stifled by the preoccupation of the national department heads with local and area Muslim affairs.[34] Muzaffaruddin would explain the shift of headquarters in these terms: "The society was rapidly changing from a period of high idealism of the late '60s and early '70s. Now people were becoming more concerned about their daily bread. They naturally began to think less with their minds and more with their stomachs. We felt that it was time, if the Islamic Party was to survive according to its constitutional calling, that it must align itself physically with a set of circumstances which could lend itself towards an earlier realization of the Deen. My first action was to resign as the Imam of the Community Mosque and to focus my attention on my duties as the Amir of the Islamic Party. The Community Mosque was a thriving local mosque and I felt that I was not motivated to be the head of a local congregation at the expense of the national and international work.

"Since the international politics around the Islamic struggle were becoming chaotic, and the conspiracy was actively mushrooming, we decided to withdraw our headquarters from Washington. Now I want to emphasize the point that the Islamic Party had several years of experience behind it at this particular point. We realized that the quality and character of our leadership were going to be the key to the continuity of our work more than anything else. So, I sought to establish a leadership environment where the leadership would not be subject to the constraints of local politics and local situations. There were about a dozen brothers and sisters who at that time comprised the central leadership of the Party. We agreed to withdraw our presence from Washington and to move to a village in Georgia so that we could concentrate on the national work of the organization. I guess you could say that in the late '70s, we decided to go underground so that the work of the Islamic Party could survive. The leadership of the organization chose not to be a voice in the wilderness like John the Baptist, so to speak. We decided to be a part of a growing development that could, Allah willing, broaden our experience with the Islamic movement."[35]

As early as February 1977, houses were purchased for the party's new headquarters and residences for its senior workers in the sleepy Wishing Wells community in the village of Conley, Georgia, approximately twenty miles west of Atlanta. The transition of four-teen families from Washington, D.C., to Conley and surrounding communities was any-thing but smooth as moving dates were constantly changed from later to earlier time frames. The shift of the headquarters operations and personnel appeared to many within the organization to be uncharacteristically haphazard. The temporary destabilization of the lives of the senior workers of the group significantly impaired, in the relatively short term, the Islamic Party's ability to go on with organizational "business as usual." By July of 1977, the transfer of the headquarters to Conley was complete. In addition to the houses in the Wishing Wells community, the party's most significant acquisition during this period was arguably the purchase of a cluster of apartment units by individual mem-bers of the party's Atlanta work unit. The apartments, known as The Pines, were used as an information office and training center, as well as domiciles for Islamic Party members.

Of the fourteen families assigned to the headquarters operation in Conley, nine sen-ior workers, department heads, and their families resigned from the organization within eighteen months of their arrival. While the reasons for resignations were varied, a com-monly uttered refrain was that the organization was rapidly diffusing its focus by starting too many new initiatives simultaneously. One of those initiatives was the founding of the International Islamic Educational Institute (IIEI) in Lahore, Pakistan, in November 1977. During an eleven-week tour of Pakistan, Muzaffaruddin lectured to student groups, trade union leaders, politicians, and religious leaders. The tour was sponsored by Jamaati Islami-Pakistan and the Pakistan National Alliance. The IIEI was a cooperative venture between the Islamic Party and Jamaati Islami in which one purpose of the Institute was for Party members to be able to study in Pakistan under the guidance of renowned Islamic schol-ars. According to the official brochure of the Institute, other main aims were:

1. To make available books on Islam in the English language and to provide them to the non-Muslims and those who have recently embraced Islam;
2. Translation and publication of important Islamic books from Urdu and Arabic into English;
3. To prepare and educate preachers according to a prescribed syllabus.

The project was short-lived due to a shortage of operating income.

However, it was the Islamic Party's Trinidad initiative that started a process that would eventually change the identity of the organization forever. According to Kwesi Atiba, a thoughtful, skilled organizer in Trinidad, representatives of the Islamic Party first showed up on the island without any apparent local invitation. "The Islamic Party in North America first appeared in Trinidad and Tobago in February 1977 when Muzaffaruddin Hamid and Dr. Kareem Abdul Ghani came on an exploratory mission. The visit was en-dorsed by the Anjuman Sunnatul Jamaat Association (then the largest Muslim organiza-tion in the nation). There does not seem to have been any specific invitation, but infor-mation that was carried in the journal (*Al-Islam*) may have shown Trinidad and Tobago as ripe for the kind of expansion that was thought possible.

"Over a two-week period, two lectures were hosted while several meetings and discus-sions were held with interested parties. At the end, a number of persons were convinced that they should work within the framework of the IPNA. Of this group, some came from existing organizations, mainly Dar-ul-Islam Caribbean and the Islamic Trust, the two leading Islamic movement entities, both with a number of vibrant young workers. There were other brothers who were unorganized," Atiba explained to this writer.[36]

Lut Abdul Azeez (Williams), a tireless Islamic Party *Da'ee* (caller to Islam), was requested by the amir to go to Trinidad shortly after the amir's return to the United States. Abdul Azeez recalled that the amir went through a selection process of matching a brother with adequate organizational skills and work/family situation with the mission to establish a branch of the Islamic Party in Trinidad and Tobago. "The brothers, particularly the Afro-Muslims, were interested in an Islamic movement, an Islamic organization that had some very specific goals, a disciplined membership, and an ideological focus that was consistent with what they were interested in. Sociopolitical events on the island had conditioned the brothers not to be docile or inactive like many in the U.S.," Abdul Azeez recalled in a telephone interview.[37]

"Trinidad has a unique Islamic history in that there are a number of mosques on the island that East Indians built since arriving, primarily as indentured servants, over the last hundred plus years. Reportedly, there are over 127 mosques. I saw several of them, but most of them were abandoned except for on Eids. They were not even full on Jumahs. Whatever Islamic work that was being done was being initiated and paid for by funds from the Muslim World League. The Muslim World League had maintained offices in Trinidad that were primarily run by East Indians, or Lebanese Arabs. It was a situation where the Afro-Trinidadians were accepting Islam, but the only Islam that they were seeing practiced was coming from the Muslim World League. That is what led them to be more interested in a more aggressive and dynamic implementation of Islam. The presence of the Islamic Party in Trinidad served notice on the Muslim World League that they (Muslim World League) were not the only game in town."

Abdul Azeez recalled that at the end of Muzaffaruddin's trip to Trinidad one brother (Muhammad Sayyid) reportedly said in the midst of conversation, "Why don't we just join the Islamic Party?"

"Because he said that," Abdul Azeez said, "Muhammad Sayyid became the pivot person for the start of a branch in Trinidad. He was the first wazir of the branch in Trinidad. He was a young, active brother in his twenties. He was one of a group of brothers that stepped forward in a leadership position. Some of the others were Kwesi Atiba; Ahmed As-Siddique; Kibwe Atiba, Kwesi's brother; and Farid Scoon. There was a group of about seven brothers who formed the nucleus of the Branch Consultative Committee. But, from the time I stepped off the plane until I met him two weeks later, Bilal Abdullah was the brother that all the brothers said that I needed to recruit into the party. He commanded the respect of everybody. At the time of my arrival, Bilal had a prior commitment with the Darul Islam Caribbean. When I finally did meet Bilal, I understood why he commanded so much respect. After about three weeks of my meeting him, Bilal joined the Islamic Party."

Although the Islamic Party never officially designated Trinidad as its Caribbean headquarters, some of the organization's most significant work was achieved there. Kwesi Atiba explained, "The major thrusts of the Islamic Party were in the areas of training and

Dawah. The IPNA set up training programs for its workers who spent many hours study-ing the Qur'an, hadith, and Islamic Movement material in order to look at the implemen-tation of Islam in a Western environment. Taking the message to the people was priority, and two activities were set up for this: 1) Saturday afternoon lectures, and 2) weekly street Dawah.

"These activities were certainly new to the society, and helped to attract a number of people to the fold of Islam. The organization set up its own *masjid* headquarters (Com-munity Mosque Complex), started a school (Community Mosque Academy), and tried some economic projects. There were also cultural programs and social counseling sessions. The main challenges faced by the party were in delivering a relevant message to the peo-ple and living up to that message in the existing conditions, socially and economically. The Islamic Party was successful in permanently changing the approach to the Dawah in the Caribbean, and it took its effort to other islands and Guyana in South America. Within its membership, a certain self-confidence was engendered. It also clarified for its workers the things in Islam which were required, as opposed to those that were merely cultural ap-pendages of the Arabs, or any of our brothers and sisters in the East.

"The party was the first Muslim group to give support to the revolution in Iran, and the first non-state agency to send workers to Dominica after Hurricane David. We never established any ties with the politicians, although contacts were made, but time never al-lowed for the necessary follow up."

After years of work in Trinidad, the Islamic Party branch eventually broke up after the group had expanded its operation throughout the Caribbean. "The breakup of the or-ganization in Trinidad is still a bit of a mystery, and Farid Scoon, by then the wazir of the branch, may have more insight, if not all the answers," Atiba observed. "The break up took place while Y. M. Hamid was in Dominica trying to set up the New Madinah project. The project was a strain on most of the workers in Trinidad, ideologically and otherwise. Good workers from Trinidad and Tobago had gone to Dominica to support the project, and it affected the work being done locally. There was also a lack of openness with respect to what was taking place with some of our members in the U.S. One such situation related to Ahmed Abdullah, who had been injured in a mysterious fire. What Y. M. Hamid ex-pected of the brothers and sisters, I have no idea. However, he claimed that he was not get-ting the necessary support, and his sentiment was that he no longer wanted to be the amir of the brothers and sisters any longer. That message was brought to the community by Farid.

"Some members decided to go ahead and form a successor organization while a few opted to stick with IP, which was by then called the Islamic Peoples Movement. The break-up stunned most of the members, and the feelings of hurt and disappointment were very much present. For many of us, though, the original spirit of the Islamic Party still lives. The clear call of the Messenger of Allah has been cluttered by many things, social, cul-tural, political, etc., and the IP was able to view these things in context and clarify what belonged in the body of the Deen and what needed to be left out. Many people in Trinidad who benefited from the impact of the IP do not know of that phase, and some who know try to play down the impact. There are others who believe that the IP should not have set up its organization in Trinidad and Tobago. The brothers and sisters trained by the IP have found themselves in the leadership of most of the movement-oriented organizations of Trinidad and Tobago today."

When Abdul Azeez returned to the United States from Trinidad, he was asked by Muzaffaruddin to return to the area to organize another branch, this time in Guyana, South America. "One of the brothers from Washington wrote me in Trinidad telling me that he thought that it was necessary for me to be in D.C. to help resolve some of the issues that were going on there. While I was out of the country, Washington had become sort of a surrogate headquarters. A significant number of working brothers in Washington were contributing to financing the operation of the national headquarters. This was seriously draining the funds of the local work. There was also concern about the organization's apparent lack of focus and the emphasis on giving priority to serving the national headquarters even to the detriment of the local work. The Washington brothers stressed to me that I should not go to Guyana so that we could try to get the local work on a better footing.

"There was concern among some of the brothers that the party should not move to the islands; that the move to the islands was a move away from the core things that the organization was set up to do. Some felt that Muzaffaruddin was looking for greener pastures where the people would be more receptive to doing the things that he wanted to do. Muzaffaruddin had expressed a strategy to move the Islamic Party headquarters to the islands. In 1978, Muzaffaruddin flew to D.C. and asked me if I were going to Guyana. I told him that I needed to stay in the country to try to help resolve some of the issues of the D.C. brothers. Over the next six months, there was a breakdown of communications and organizational direction between the headquarters and the D.C. branch. Muzaffaruddin made a decision to clear out the Park Road building in Washington and move headquarters people in to take over the building. This move of taking over the building was a final straw that made it clear that the differences that existed could not be resolved within the confines of the organization. It was at this point that almost the entire membership of the Washington branch resigned from the Islamic Party. The building was eventually sold to a local nationalist group, The Nation, that was affiliated with Chicago-based poet/publisher Haki Madhabuti."[38]

By 1980, the Islamic Party had shut down its operations in the United States and shifted to the Caribbean. A base of operations was established on the island of St. Croix, U.S. Virgin Islands. Kareem Abdul Ghani, the deputy amir of the Islamic Party, Khalil Ihsan, Muhsin Abdul Halim, Muhammad Amin, Rafiq Tariq, and their families were among those setting up residences on the island. The island of St. Croix proved to be conducive for generating monies to finance the organizational work on the tiny island of Dominica,where Muzaffaruddin and other brothers from the United States established residences. The relative closeness and ease of travel between the islands facilitated the spread of Islamic Party doctrine across the Caribbean. One island where the organization spread was the tiny island of Grenada.

Muhammad Siddique, a social activist before embracing Islam, was first introduced to Islam while studying at the University of the West Indies in Trinidad. "A student at the University gave me a copy of *Towards Understanding Islam* by Maulana Abul A'la Maududi. After reading the book, I basically understood the concept of Islam. I decided that this was the way of life that I and the people of the Caribbean needed. At the time that I took *shahadah*, I was a part of the Rastafarian movement, dreadlocks and all. Many of us (who became Muslim) had become disenchanted with the various movements because they were not able to present themselves as a complete way of life, especially any kind of spiritual dimension. We started a group in the Caribbean called Darul Islam. At the time, it was not affiliated with the group in the United States, because none of us had knowledge of the U.S. organization. We traveled throughout the various territories that we came from, bringing the concept of Islam to our friends.

"Shortly after we started our work, the Islamic Party made contact with the brothers in Trinidad. By that time, I had moved back to Grenada. Members in the Darul Islam in Trinidad had the first contact with the Islamic Party. They came to us and presented the party's program of action. After thoroughly examining the Islamic Party, we felt that it had the structure, and the potential to bring about the kind of movement that we needed. We felt that black people needed to have the linkage, not just with North America, but with Africa, and wherever black people lived in large numbers. The party held the promise of being that vehicle to provide guidance for our people. I was the first amir of the Islamic Party in Grenada."[39] The training and program of action in Grenada was similar throughout the Caribbean.

The New Madinah project in Dominica involved the purchase of about two hundred acres of land. Monies and manpower from the other Caribbean branches were severely taxed to finance the ambitious project. The Islamic Peoples Movement (Islamic Party) became the publisher of a newspaper, *The Drum*, that competed with the island's only other newspaper, a government-run publication. Muzaffaruddin became a well-known outspoken advocate for the downtrodden in Dominica. Soon, the organization's welcome in Dominica was challenged as members were deported back to the United States. Muzaffaruddin was arrested and jailed for a short time before being deported on charges of bigamy. Consequently, the Islamic Party's land was confiscated by the Dominican government. Muzaffaruddin believed that the country's prime minister, Eugenia Charles, appealed to President Ronald Reagan for assistance in dealing with the perceived threat to her government that the presence of the Islamic Peoples Movement presented. Yusuf Muzaffaruddin Hamid "unwillingly" returned to the United States in 1984 where, with the assistance of Masud Abdul Khabir, purchased about sixty acres of mountain resort property in Tate, Georgia. The second New Madinah was seventy miles north of Atlanta. Soon the wooded land was partially cleared and graded and housing was established. At least one member of the Islamic Party from Trinidad moved to the New Madinah property in Georgia. A two-story Mountain Community Mosque was built on the property that housed a full-time school for Muslim youth. The mosque was perched atop a hillside with a breathtaking view of the mountainous landscape.

Muzaffaruddin summoned the Islamic Party members in St. Croix to join him in Tate. Not having been informed of Muzaffaruddin's move back to the United States, the brothers chose to remain in St. Croix. Sometime in the mid-1980s most of the brothers and sisters in the Islamic Party living in St. Croix became Shias. About eighteen months after establishing the second New Madinah, Muzaffaruddin, Najeeb Abdul Haqq, along with other party members and their families moved to the Central American nation of Belize and purchased another two hundred acres of land. The stay there was somewhat short and problematic as the land had been inadvertently purchased with a lien on the property. After losing the land, the organization moved to Honduras. In Honduras, land was again purchased and a sewing factory established. The sewing factory employed approximately thirty indigenous Hondurans who produced crowns (caps), ties, and kente cloths, all made from African print fabric. The goods were marketed primarily in the United States.

When asked about the break up of the Islamic Party, Muzaffaruddin responded in 1987, "I was asked by an ardent reader of *Al-Islam*, 'What happened to the Islamic Party?' I asked him if he knew anything about the Party, and if he was aware that each member of the Party made a pledge which started with, 'For me the Islamic Movement is the very purpose of my life'. . . and ends with 'if no one else steps forward, I will yet do so . . . undaunted.' I wanted to tell him that the Party, first of all, started in the hearts of believers, and if you are looking for the Party, first of all, look at the hearts of people who may have been at one time or the other closely aligned with the development of the organization. If you examine their hearts, and if you can look closely at their personal life and commitments, you may begin to determine where the Islamic Party is. The Islamic Party is alive because I am presently in collaboration and in communication with individuals who are interested in further organizational, re-organizational aspects of the Party in order that this program could become more known today than it was in the past.

"It is interesting to point out that in the Constitution of the Islamic Party, there is not one chapter that provides for its dissolution. The reason is obvious. The Party is an ideological movement out to establish a goal on this earth, or to die trying. Until this mission is accomplished, the Jamaat, the movement, the organization can never constitutionally be disbanded. . . . A genuine Islamic movement is determined by the continuity of its existence, despite public acknowledgment, public acceptance, and public support. The Islamic Party has been and continues to be a young Islamic Movement with a tremendous obligation as far as its perspective and what it seeks to accomplish. Yes, the Islamic Party has metamorphosed as a result of developments in the late '70s. But, it has never ceased its work by virtue of the explanation I just gave.[40]

In the home of Dawud Salahuddin in Chicago in August 1989, only months before his death, Muzaffaruddin was taped during an informal, intimate discussion with a small group of brothers. The discussion was punctuated with items Muzaffaruddin felt were of vital importance for the future of Islam in North America. He underscored one point by saying, "I want brothers to start thinking more about establishing the Deen in their lives and the lives of their families, and separate that from establishing the law. In the Islamic Party Constitution, we made a distinction between Deen and Shariah. We established the Party to establish the Deen, the government of Allah, the Islamic society. That is an important distinction. Deen is heart. Shariah is shell. The Deen has to be right. The heart has to be straight. The Shariah will develop around your society. That's why you have different schools of law."

Sometime in 1988, while living in Honduras, Muzaffaruddin was diagnosed with an acute form of leukemia. After undergoing three separate rounds of chemotherapy in an Atlanta hospital, Yusuf Muzaffaruddin Hamid succumbed on September 15, 1991. At his *janazah* (funeral) prayers, presided over by his oldest son Idris, current and past members of the Islamic Party somberly gathered to bid farewell to one of the most dynamic, skilled, indigenous, Islamic Movement organizers produced on North American soil during the last half of the twentieth century. Muzaffaruddin is buried next door to the Mountain Community Mosque in New Madinah (Tate, Georgia), one of many *masjids* he helped to establish in the Western hemisphere.

Notes

1. Islamic Party in North America, Introducing the Islamic Party in North America.
2. Malcolm X, "Nine Questions Answered," February 20, 1965.
3. Tony Martin, *Race First* (Westport, Conn.: Greenwodd, 1976), 73–76.
4. Daud Slahuddin, telephone interview, January 23, 2000.
5. Yusuf Muzaffuruddin Hamid, "History as a Weapon," *Vision* 6, no. 2 (1987).
6. Alex Haley, *The Autobiography of Malcolm X* (New York: Ballantine, 1964).
7. C. Eric Lincoln, *The Black Mulims in America* (Boston: Beacon, 1961).
8. *Vision* 3, no. 2.
9. *Vision* 6, no. 2.
10. Ahmed Abdullah, telephone interview, August 9, 2000.
11. Ibid.
12. *Al-Ummah* 1, no. 4 (October 1971).
13. Ibid.
14. Letter from Amir to members of applicants of IPNA, January 21, 1972.
15. Abdur Rahim Shaheed (Mutazzim), telephone interview, December 12, 1999.
16. Ibid.
17. *Vision* 6, no. 2.
18. Ibrahim Hanif, telephone interview, July 19, 2000.
19. Ibid.
20. *Vision* 6, no. 2.
21. Shaheed, December 12, 1999.
22. *Vision* 6, no. 2.
23. Hanif, July 19, 2000.
24. Sayid Qutb, *Milestones* (Islamic Party Publications, 1974).
25. Muneerah Afifah, telephone interview, August 15, 2000.
26. Ibid.
27. *Vision* 4, no. 2.
28. Hanif, July 19, 2000.
29. Ahmed Abdullah, telephone interview, September 24, 2000.
30. *The Message*, August 1997.
31. Umar Ocasio, telephone interview, August 1998.
32. *Vision* 4, no. 2.
33. Ibid.
34. *Vision* 5, no. 1.
35. *Vision* 6, no. 1.
36. Kwesi Atiba, telephone interview, December 14, 1999.
37. Lut Abdul Azeez (Williams), telephone interview, February 25, 2000.
38. Ibid.
39. Muhammad Siddique, telephone interview, February 6, 2000.
40. *Vision* 6, no. 2.

The Complexity of Belonging: Sunni Muslim Immigrants in Chicago

6

GARBI SCHMIDT

I HAD AGREED TO MEET MY INTERVIEWEE, the appointed president of the local mosque, at his workplace in one of Chicago's southwestern suburbs. We decided to find a suitable place for our interview and walked across the busy street to a small diner. As we walked down the pavement, my companion started talking about issues that he obviously thought relevant for our further discussion. "You know," he said, "I love this country. I am happy that I am an American citizen; I care about America. As I see it, this is the best country in the world to practice Islam."[1]

It is clear that for this active participant in the American Muslim community to be American and to be Muslim is in no way contradictory. His statement, in fact, reflects a confidence that he has found a place where he can practice his religion freely and to which he therefore owes his engagement and loyalty. Though this viewpoint by no means is shared by all Sunni Muslim immigrants in Chicago, it illustrates a late stage in the move from a status as transient to one of settlement that this religious community has undergone during the last hundred years. This transition will be the focus of this chapter.

The initial major Muslim encounter with the city came during the Columbian Exposition of 1893 and the subsequent settlement of Muslim immigrants from 1900 to 1938. Next came the twenty-year period after World War II (1948–1965), during which the status, ambitions, and sentiments of belonging changed among Muslims in Chicago, concurrent with shifts in American governmental policies towards non-European immigrants. Today, at the turn of the millennium, the Muslim community in Chicago has grown significantly in size and influence. In what ways do Muslims presently engage in the city around them, and how is their presence and engagement met by their non-Muslim co-citizens? How is the community affected by the fact that it no longer consists solely of immigrants, but now contains the children of immigrants, for whom American citizenship is not the consequence of choice and struggle, but a birthright? (A major component of the Muslim community in Chicago today is also African American, a subject that is beyond the scope of this essay.)

The Columbian Exposition: The Visitor

Four hundred years after Columbus set foot on the shores of the continent that we now know as North America, the members of another expedition anchored at the harbor of New York. They brought with them a mystique that made them quite spectacular in their day. The press reported excitedly about a female belly dancer who, when reaching Ellis Island, introduced the dance tradition of her home country to a breathless audience. Described as tall and graceful, with every muscle moving sensuously, she was said to have presented her art until a medical inspector demanded her to stop, fearing that she would "dislocate every joint" in her body.[2]

New York was the first stop on a journey that led her and her group—and with them many others—to the Columbian Exposition in Chicago. That city had been chosen for the historical celebration of Columbus's discovery of North America, since it was considered "a typical American city with a population from every quarter of the globe."[3] How many Muslims lived in the city at that time is difficult to determine, and the Exposition may actually have been the starting point for a considerable Muslim immigration to the city.[4]

At the Midway Plaisance in the southern part of Chicago, several countries had created streets, raised buildings, and filled them with beautiful artifacts characteristic of their culture and craftsmanship. All participating countries had sent representatives—men, women, and children—to give life to this creation of a world become one. Seven nations with Muslim majority were represented at the Exposition. Of these, the Egyptian "Cairo Street" became a favorite among the visitors. The house facades painted in yellow, red, and green were described as utterly realistic and gave substance to the audience's cravings for the exotic, the "oriental."[5] In Cairo Street you met the magician, the snake charmer, the fortune-teller, and the lemonade seller. In Cairo Street you could ride camels and donkeys and, each day, watch a traditional Egyptian wedding procession. You could see the whirling Sufis, publicly known as "torture dancers" because, in their ecstasy, they ate cactus leaves and pierced their skin with skewers,[6] and you could watch the "revolting" and highly controversial belly dance.[7]

At the Chicago Exposition you could also acquaint yourself with the faith of the East: Islam. In the early hours of the morning, Egyptian boys gathered in the *kuttab*, memorizing the scripture from copies of the Qur'an resting on bamboo stands. Five times daily, the air over the Plaisance was pierced by the call to prayer that the Muezzin Mohammad Abdullah gave from the mosque and minaret that stood as a central building in Cairo Street. Major Muslim holidays, such as Mawlid al-Nabi (the birthday of the Prophet Muhammad) and Eid al-Fitr ending Ramadan, the month of fasting, were celebrated in this mosque. A similar spectacle could also be found at the Exposition's impressive mosque erected at the demand of the Turkish Sultan, Abdul Hamid II.[8]

Though the audience found the Middle Eastern buildings and atmosphere enchanting, their reaction toward the newly visible Islamic practices was less tolerant. As one reporter described in *The Chicago Tribune*, "Up in the minaret—the muezzin mast, as one facetious be-fezed man dubbed it—a priest in flowing robes called the faithful to prayer, while crowds of curious people looked on and said sarcastic things to the bedraggled Turks, who in answer to the summons cast themselves upon their knees and turned their faces toward Mecca."[9] Another reporter and humorist reflected the general lack of appreciation of the

Muslim prayer: "You can't tell whether they're praying or in a dog fight," he wrote, "but I suppose it's all the same in Arabia."[10]

Stronger reactions against Islam came with the Parliament of the World's Religions, an event affiliated with the Exposition. When Muhammad Alexander Webb, an American convert to Islam, gave two lectures to the learned audience at the Parliament about his understanding of the faith that he had chosen, he met with strong negative reactions both in Chicago and abroad. Reverend George E. Post, at that time stationed in Beirut, challenged Webb's description of Islam as tolerant and peaceful. Appealing to the American intellect, Post quoted verses in the Qur'an that deal with the "killing of infidels" and the acceptance of polygamy. Muhammad was described as a lustful, manipulative person, and his claimed revelations as the means to fulfill his sexual cravings.[11]

In those years, the subject of polygamy in particular was raised as a way to "prove," conceptually, that Islam was incompatible with American morals and to make sure, demographically, that Muslims stayed outside the American borders. As earlier research has demonstrated, in an immigration statute enacted in the spring of 1891, polygamists were added to a list of persons guilty of criminal "moral turpitude" and, accordingly, denied admission into the United States.[12] Muhammad Sadiq, the Ahmadi mufti who was one of the first immigrants to preach a version of Islam in the Chicago context, was confined for two months after his arrival in the United States until immigration authorities were convinced that he would not preach polygamy as a part of his mission.[13] Muslims and Middle Easterners who participated in the Columbian Exposition were also severely restricted in terms of movement. Unlike the European participants, they were not allowed free access to the surrounding city. Those Muslims who eventually got the chance to see Chicago immediately became objects of curiosity, provocation, and ridicule.[14] To the American audience, the participating Muslims were a "race" to be studied, discussed, and observed, but they were to be kept temporally limited and spatially confined. At that time, few suspected that Muslims and Islam one day would be a permanent component of the booming Chicago metropolis.

The Sojourner

How many Muslims succeeded in staying in Chicago or other parts of the United States after the Columbian Exposition is difficult to determine. There is evidence that some participants appeared again at the Saint Louis Fair in 1904.[15] Other sources suggest that enclaves stayed and settled in Chicago.[16] In any case, it is clear that others followed the first sojourners within less than a decade; their number soon was so considerable that they became the subjects of both communal and research interest. That a Muslim presence in Chicago was on the rise can be illustrated by the fact that a Christian mission center was established on South Dearborn Street around 1920 "to give the Bread of Life to our unfortunate neighbors, the Mohammadans in this country."[17] Muslim Palestinians increasingly put their mark on certain neighborhoods. In the first Master thesis dissertation describing immigration from the Middle East to Chicago, Edith Stein, a social service student at the University of Chicago, writes that "Most of the Syrians in Chicago are from Lebanon, although there are also a number from Palestine. However, the last are said to be mainly Muhammedans. The two groups are quite separate, the first living around Ogden Avenue along about 2600 West, while the second group lives in the vicinity of 18th Street and State."[18]

Muslim immigrants coming in the period between the early and middle parts of the twentieth century were mainly male peasants from the Beitunya-Ramallah area in Palestine.[19] The majority spoke no English when they arrived in the United States and, therefore, took jobs in sectors where the linguistic barrier was not a hindrance in earning enough money to secure their existence and even to save a little. Of these jobs, peddling became the most prominent. One immigrant described his experiences as follows:

> I came to Chicago in 1912 with my brother. At that time we already had an uncle and a cousin here. They got us a furnished room on 18th Street and the very next day after our arrival, we started to work. In those days the Arabs had a couple of wholesale dry goods stores on 18th Street where us peddlers used to get our stock. We carried a suitcase in which there was linen tablecloths, napkins, small rugs, handkerchiefs and stuff like that. On the first day when my uncle handed me a suitcase and told me what I had to do, I got scared out of my wits. I couldn't speak a word of English, so how could I go door to door and sell that stuff? My uncle told me not to worry and so we took the streetcar over to the West Side and started ringing doorbells. I stood by shaking my head up and down and smiling but not understanding a word. . . . About four or five months later after I had learned a little English, I decided to go out for myself. My uncle and I would start at one end of a street, he would take all the houses on one side and I all the houses on the other. One day I made $13.00 while he hardly sold anything at all. In those days we saved every penny we had in order that we could open a store. We finally opened a dry goods store on 18th Street in 1923."[20]

This quotation illustrates facets of the life of this period's immigrants that seem typical. First, most were part of a chain migration and already had relatives living in the city when they arrived. Second, immigrants generally lived in furnished, low-rent rooms and apartments in the downtown area (the neighborhood of 18th Street and Michigan Avenue). Third, the initial goal for most of them was to buy a store, from which they could supply both their peddling countrymen and the inhabitants of the low-income, mainly black, neighborhoods.

Muslim Middle Eastern immigrants in those years, many of whom had left wives and children behind in the old country, were vocal about their wish to return back to the homeland as soon as possible.[21] Some stayed in Chicago for a period of ten years or so before returning home; they then remained in Palestine with their families for five or six years before returning to Chicago to work for another period of time.[22] Some found this kind of arrangement too difficult to put up with and either initiated liaisons with or married non-Muslim women in the new country. Such practices, together with a choice of not adhering strictly to Islamic requirements such as fasting, praying, and abstaining from the use of alcohol, were met with a high level of criticism among the small community's elders as well as in the growing Arab-American press.[23] This created a sense of anxiety among many immigrants that increased their desire to return home as soon and as fast as possible. As another immigrant stated,

Believe me, my friend, when I tell you I cannot remain here one day longer. I think my poor wife is waiting for me to come back to Beitunia while I am here in Chicago living the life of a *kafir* (unbeliever). If they ever find out I didn't fast this Ramadan in Beitunia, they will tell me I am not Muslim and to go and live with the Christians. It is very hard for a good man in this bad land where you can't keep the religion. . . . If I had closed my store and fasted during Ramadan, I would have had to go out of business and instead of bringing back money to Palestine, I would have had to borrow money to get my passage back."[24]

Even though immigrants in that period did not forget their religion entirely, other aspects of life seemed of higher priority to them. Doing well economically meant more than mere daily survival. It was a means of gaining recognition back home, of proving one's manhood, excellence, and authority. Those who did well in Chicago could, when they returned, claim a higher position in their villages in Palestine.

Among these first immigrants, the bonds of loyalty remained entirely with the old country, and assimilation to the surrounding society was an undesirable option. When not engaged in work, they preferred to keep to themselves at home or in the restaurants and coffeehouses they founded in downtown Chicago.[25] These places came to function as community centers where people could speak their own language without intrusion, and share news and letters from family and relatives. Once a month, an Arabic movie was shown in one of the downtown halls.[26] The organizations that Muslim Palestinian immigrants founded in that period were mainly concerned with activities that would contribute to the betterment of the situation in the homeland. For example, the Children of Beituniya Society, established around 1924, donated money for the building of a highway and a secondary school in the village.[27] Even though it is very likely that people met for prayers in private homes or in the back quarters of their shops, no mosque was planned for or built in that period. This, in itself, is indicative of the way the community in America was considered to be temporary. The mosque as a symbol of community and belonging was not seen as appropriate on U.S. soil, and to channel money into such projects would be wasteful and without purpose. Muslims were to stay in the United States for a short time and Islam was to stay a stranger to these shores.[28]

The Citizen

It is, I believe, impossible to describe the transition from Muslims as sojourners to Muslims as United States citizens without highlighting certain effects of the globalization that intensified after World War II. Though Islam as a world religion has always had a transnational aspect, the implications of this universalism have been stretched to the fullest in the second half of this century. As some researchers have noted, it is partially due to the availability of effective communication systems that Islam for the first time has been able to claim a universal status.[29] The idea of the *umma*, the community of believers, has become a unifying motive around which Muslims in both East and West coalesce and according to which they defend the applicability of their faith to a modern world. The image of the *umma* is used when Muslims want to carve out their own spaces of identity against Western ideologies, the legacy of colonialism, national fragmentation, and ethnic minority statuses.[30]

Besides the effects of an easily accessible and fast means of communication, another element of globalization influencing the ways in which Muslims perceive the borderlines of their community is the relative ease of travelling. Not only has travelling become a kind of commodity accessible to an increasing number of people all over the globe, but this commodification has been followed by a cognitive shift in frameworks of belonging, in the understanding of what places can be called home. For those who have the money, the education, or simply the desire, settlement in other parts of the world is a possible (though not a naturally given) option. Citizenship for many has changed from something that belongs naturally to an individual into a status that is chosen, fought for, and eventually granted. While citizenship in particular nations may provide certain privileges, for a growing number of people displaced by war and civil strife, it is sought because of particular and urgent needs, as is the case for the waves of refugees that the world ceaselessly witnesses.[31] As citizenship and national adherence, increasingly for some, have become concepts in continuous flux, the fact of this flux has affected peoples' understanding of the relationship between their identity as experienced and as rooted in a particular religious construction and a particular ethnicity or geographical area. The consequences have more than one form,[32] among them one in which the person may seek to stress the nature of the religious community as being a gathering of ethnicities under the supervision of a common set of absolute moral values. The consequences of globalization have had a noticeable effect on the Muslim immigrant community in Chicago.

Unlike earlier immigrants to America, those arriving in the period after World War II and, in particular, after the 1965 Immigration Act, generally came with the intention to make the new country their home. Many of those who had been in this country for some years now made the decision to stay.[33] The choice of permanent settlement is perhaps most clearly shown by the intensive establishment of religious institutions in this period. Between 1964 and 1994, at least thirty-two mosques were established in the greater Chicago area.[34] The majority of these mosques were set up in already existing buildings, but some were built specifically for the purpose of Muslim community service and worship.

The major mosques built during this period all follow a prototypical, easily recognizable, architectural form with a dome and often a minaret. This choice can be said to have been made in an attempt at authenticity, based on the conviction that mosques are supposed to look a certain way, unaffected by their geographical environment.[35] But what is of greater interest to this present study is that such mosque architecture demands attention; it is eye-catching and recognizable for non-Muslims as well as for Muslims. Although a prototypical mosque structure may easily be interpreted as rejecting the environment of the "other" in which Muslims find themselves, in this case it can be understood as a way of arguing persuasively for inclusion. By specifying certain spaces in Chicago as recognizably Muslim through the construction of such Islamic structures, Muslims not only perpetuate a specific architectural tradition but also strive to indigenize Islam. By making it an American tradition, they look for recognition of authenticity and distinction similar to that granted to churches and synagogues for decades and centuries.

Muslims have also established other institutions in Chicago. Prominent among these are what Larry Poston has called "paramosques": organizations that emphasize individual spirituality and activism and carry out their activities independent of mosques.[36] Community activism and propagation of the faith are done in the context of involvement with American society and the conditions in which Muslims find themselves. Paramosque participants are dedicated to the goal of having non-Muslim Americans accept Muslims as valid co-citizens, demonstrating that the Islamic faith is in accord with the moral standards on which the United States claims to be based. A number of national paramosque organizations, claiming to reach a widespread audience consisting mainly of non-Muslims, have offices in Chicago. Some of these organizations, such as the Islamic Information Center of America (located in Des Plaines) and the Institute for Islamic Information and Education (on North Elston Avenue), concentrate their activities on *da'wa* (proselytizing) among Muslims, claiming it to be both a way to disseminate information about Islam and a means to convert Americans to the true faith.[37] The desired outcome of *da'wa* is understood to be conversion, but it also serves as a means of asserting Islamic values over those of the "other" (i.e. American secular values). It provides a way to demonstrate that Muslim-ness and American national identity are not in conflict or competition and that Islam can take root in American hearts and homes.

Still other Muslim institutions illustrate the domestication of Islam in the Chicago context. In less than two decades, Muslims have founded two colleges and five full-time private schools in the metropolitan area of Chicago. In these institutions, children and young grown-ups enjoy a Muslim environment (accommodating prayers, dietary rules, specific dress-codes, and separation of space according to gender) at the same time that they learn a state-required curriculum. Teaching takes place in English, and by the end of their education, students are rewarded with high school diplomas or bachelor of arts degrees. Even the most secluded Muslim school in the area, a *hafiz* (Qur'an recitation) school in the suburb of Elgin, illustrates the integration of American and Islamic symbols. During the few hours of the day when the boys are not engaged in memorizing the Qur'an, they usually can be seen playing basketball in front of the school buildings.

While Muslim schools and colleges have been developed because of the concern of parents and communities that their children might lose their religious heritage in a non-Muslim environment, such institutions should not be seen as expressing resentment against Muslim settlement in America. Rather, their existence underscores the fact that parents are aware that their children will stay and live in North America, that it is their home. Accordingly, Muslim institutions of learning attempt to integrate the Islamic and American heritages and perceptions of truth, trying to guarantee that second and third generation Muslim Americans will be able to live successfully with a hybrid identity.

The Younger Generation

The use of the terms "second generation" and "third generation" immigrants is in many ways misleading and potentially discriminatory. Quantitatively framing a group of people whose parents made the choice of resettlement (or were forced to do so) one, two, three, or more generations back may be reasonable, but at the same time we may ask whether the qualitative implications of the terms are equally justifiable. Should someone be referred to as an immigrant, years after his or her parents or grandparents arrived in the United States?

Is the category "immigrant" appropriate at all for someone who has always lived in the same country? The relevance of such questions becomes clear in dealing with the younger generations of Muslims in Chicago, where a move away from the ethnic identity of their parents is often intentional and articulated. Whereas members of the immigrant generation speak in nostalgic tones about the country they left behind, their children may speak of the ethnic home of their parents with some disappointment and even resentment. Among those active in Muslim youth organizations such as the MSA (Muslim Student Association), such disappointment is often formulated in religious terms. As a college student in her early twenties expressed it,

> Me and my sister we don't go that often [back to India]. . . . The weird thing is that India, even though there are so many mosques, there are so many people who consider themselves to be educated in Islam, the majority of the people aren't very Islamic. Among my cousins there is only one family that has the same Islamic knowledge that I do. And I consider myself to have a very low level of Islamic knowledge. . . . And that really hurt me, because I expected them to know much more. Because they have the language, they know Urdu, and there are so many books on Islamic knowledge. But they are so materialistic too. And the only thing they want to do is to come to America, because America is the window to the world, or whatever it is. America or Saudi Arabia. . . . The only way that I think that I can help them is by praying to Allah *subhanahu wa ta'ala* (May He be glorified) for them.[38]

Statements such as this illustrate an obvious disappointment with an ethnic past. What is interesting is that a desirable alternative is presented not in other ethnic terms, but in religious terms. The young woman does not portray North America as fulfilling the social and moral expectations that she believes are righteous. Rather, she makes a connection between the "wrongful" preferences of her relatives in India and the value system of the United States. The dream of immigrating to America, in her eyes, exposes their preference of a materialistic lifestyle over a spiritual one.

There may be two possible explanations for this kind of portrayal of the country from which one's parents came and the arguments employed in the process. First, the underscoring of contrast between the interviewee and—in this case—India, represented by her cousins and relatives living there, shows her discomfort with being associated with her home country, as well as her sense of not belonging, of not wanting to be identified with what is "back there." The student's sad description of her Indian relatives' dream about travelling to the West even marks a break with the immigration experience, with an element of her parents' life history. She is not an immigrant, she is not an Indian, and she is not entirely an American either. What she is, is a Muslim. This leads us to the second level of argumentation, that dealing with a hybrid identity. Young Muslims, born and/or raised in America, are exposed, through their upbringing, to two variable sets of normative behavior: that of the culture of North America and that of the culture of their parents. To some groups, not described in this article, the answer may be to stress one of these alternatives at the cost of the other. To others, the answer may be a third alternative that, on the ideological and moral level, is seen to encompass and supercede both ethnic preferences, i.e. the Islamic alternative. In Weberian terms it may be described as a movement from *gesellshaft* (solidarity with a society or a nation) to *gemeinshaft* (solidarity with a community).[39] Geographical boundaries become of limited importance, and morality becomes the ultimate standard according to which humans are judged, included, or excluded. Exemplifying this change are the young Muslims who argue that their parents' practice of Islam is cultural and implicitly "wrong" because, in these youngsters' eyes, it fragments the Muslim community and mixes the absolute message of God with the fantasy of human weakness and vice. Some youngsters even state that they feel forced to teach their parents about real Islam.

To this group of young Muslims, Islam is an absolute, exemplifying the right way of living and the ultimate utopian society. This is not to say that they isolate themselves from the society around them or deny their American citizenship. In conversations I had with them in Chicago, many mentioned that North America, as such, has facilitated their awareness about the message of Islam and strengthened its appeal. Since Muslims have come from different corners of the world and been exposed to their internal differences and similarities, these young people feel that in America they might be able to see the essence of Islam more clearly and better understand the timeless appeal of its message. The strong conviction that Islam provides the ideal constitution for a human community has made many of the activist young Muslims, particularly those engaged in chapters of the MSA, become deeply involved in Muslim voluntary organizations that seek to improve Chicago's inner-city neighborhoods.

One such organization is IMAN, (Inner-city Muslim Action Network), initiated around 1994 by Muslim students at De Paul University. Since the beginning, the organization has used the facilities of one of Chicago's major Arab centers for its activities. In the afternoon, when school is out, thirty to forty children gather in the spacious main room of the center. Here, a group of volunteers recruited from local MSA chapters, along with a couple of employed staff members, assist the children in doing their homework before they are allowed more pleasant activities such as arts and crafts or swimming.

One objective of IMAN is to give the children the means eventually to rise out of poverty. Since most parents speak poor or no English, they cannot help their children do their homework, and others have to take over. A second objective is to prevent the boys from joining local gangs. But the third and main objective of IMAN—one that frames every activity of the organization—is to keep the children within the boundaries of Islam: to teach them how to pray, about the Qur'an, that alcohol and drugs are against the word of Allah, and that they are all brothers and sisters of the global community of believers. In the word of a staff member, IMAN is supposed to convey an image of Islam as "a utopia, an idea of equality between the nations."

In the attempt to portray Islam as all-inclusive, IMAN fosters engagement with the surrounding neighborhood. One of the most remarkable of these was the festival "Taking It to the Streets," celebrated in the summer of 1997. Though the idea of the festival was the consequence of a gang-related shooting episode in which two Muslim youths were killed, the preparations for the festival became more and more centered on the issue of multiculturalism, under the umbrella of Islam. The festival's subtitle, "Nurturing Unity, Revitalization and Success," articulated an intent both to create unity among Muslims and to present Islam as a social movement, transcending borders of ethnicity, violence, and poverty for those who live in the surrounding neighborhoods. On a Saturday morning at the end of June, tents and game booths were raised in the local park, and speeches and even rap-songs generated the message from a central stage. *Zabiha*-burgers (made from ritually slaughtered animals) were sold from a large barbecue grill and *da'wa* material was distributed to those who were interested. In the early afternoon, when it was time to pray, one of IMAN's leading staff members took the stage, introducing the ritual. "Islam," he said, "encompasses many cultures. That is what we celebrate and mark here. In a moment when you see us pray together, you will see African Americans, Latinos, Arabs, and Indo-Pakistanis standing side by side." The moment of prayer became the vehicle for communicating the basic intent of the festival, which was to show Islam as an ideology uniting people regardless of race, and as the solution to the issues of social and racial inequality prominent in many American inner-city neighborhoods.

The example of IMAN illustrates that young activist Muslims in Chicago move from ethnic to transethnic definitions of identity. It could be argued that U.S. citizenship in this connection is of minor importance since it does not directly relate to the utopian vision that these youngsters seek to actualize. On the other hand, it is clear that such a vision takes concrete form within a specific social context, in an effort to alter and improve those prevailing social conditions deemed wrong by the members. In their utopian vision of Islam, young Muslims do not dismiss their identity as citizens of America; rather, they seek to contribute to it and improve it, proving the applicability of a righteous Islam to the social conditions of the country and ultimately of the world.

The Reception

So far, my focus on Muslim settlement in Chicago has centered on Muslim activities and ideologies. Very little attention, except in presenting some of the early history of the community, has been devoted to how non-Muslims in the city have approached, worked with, or, in some cases, worked against Muslims.

Muslims in Chicago have gained the attention of their non-Muslim fellow citizens due to their growing presence in certain neighborhoods, because of events on the international political scene, or as a result of national governmental legislation. Reactions have been negative as well as positive. Negative responses have escalated primarily in periods where Islam and Muslims have been portrayed as anti-American and violent, as was the case in the aftermath of the Iranian revolution and during the Gulf War. Two illustrations stand out in that respect. In 1979 members of the Muslim Community Center (MCC), then located at North Kedzie Avenue, wanted to build a new mosque at North Pulaski. The initiative was blocked by local residents who feared the consequences of having Muslims as a permanent part of their neighborhood.[40] When the MCC two years later purchased a school building in Morton Grove, they experienced a similar level of resistance when a group of residents sought to cancel the sale. In the end, a school district poll was needed to close the deal, and the Muslim Education Center was able to open its doors in 1990.[41]

Though the two cases obviously illustrate a negative response to Muslims and a wish to keep them from becoming a part of the local environment, they actually became occasions for the development of fruitful Muslim and non-Muslim interaction and support.

The Muslim school in Morton Grove, for example, was supported by a group of residents (Citizens Advocating Responsible Education) who found the opposition to the institution unjustifiable.[42] The school now serves as a balloting place during local and national elections, illustrating its ultimate inclusion and acceptance in the neighborhood. Similarly, even though the Muslim Community Center was denied permission to establish a mosque on Pulaski, they later established one at North Elston Avenue. As a result of the good will that they created prior to establishing the mosque, they now exist without resentment on the part of their neighbors. Contact with the surrounding neighborhood has been enhanced through annual friendship dinners.

Relations with non-Muslims have also improved through Muslim involvement in organizations such as the Council for the Parliament of the World's Religions (CPWR), based in Chicago. In 1997, five of the fifty-four members of the Council's board of trustees were Muslims.[43] As such, interfaith work has become a considerable asset in the presentation of Islam and of Muslims as members of Chicago's religious tapestry. Besides involvement in the CPWR, Muslims have gained acceptance from other religious denominations through shared events such as Thanksgiving services and 'Eid dinners.[44] A Muslim chaplain for the U.S. Navy has recently been trained through a program coordinated by the American Islamic College and the Lutheran School of Theology in Chicago. In January 1998, a Roman Catholic Archbishop, Francis George, broke fast at the mosque in Northbrook, the first of his vocation to do so.[45] Such events are often covered in the local press, supplemented with commentary on the Chicago Muslim community, such as that which said it is increasingly "step[ping] out in the larger society."[46]

The importance of the media in creating an image of Muslims as included or excluded in American society has not escaped the attention of Chicago Muslims. A media committee has been formed under the directions of the Council of Islamic Organizations in Greater Chicago (established 1992). This committee seeks to increase the amount of positive coverage that Muslim religious holidays and events such as Ramadan and 'Eid receive in the city's major newspapers. The primary spokespersons of the council, an Indian journalist and an African American professor of Islamic studies, often take the roles of news analysts and interpreters of local, national, and international events involving Muslims.[47] Similarly, Chicago Muslims seek entrance into the political life of the city and the nation, and representatives from political parties frequently visit mosques in the area, underscoring the fact that the Muslim community has gained a social position and power worth consideration.

One group of Muslims currently receiving a considerable amount of support and positive media coverage are the Bosnian refugees who have come to the city during and in the aftermath of the civil war in Yugoslavia. Chicago currently hosts between seven thousand and twelve thousand Bosnian refugees, more than any other city in the United States.[48] On several occasions Bosnian refugees in the city have received help from private agencies.[49] The University of Loyola's New Beginnings Program, a program seeking to help refugee immigrants to get acquainted with the American political and educational system, for example, chose the Bosnians as their first target group.[50]

Though Muslims in Chicago have gained considerable good will and access to opinion-forming agencies, they often portray themselves as victimized and misunderstood. Many have observed the ways in which media presentations or government decisions from one day to the next can change the perception and treatment of Muslims by neighbors, co-students, or co-workers. A common experience was the negative reaction they encountered in the days after the Oklahoma City bombing (19 April 1995). To Muslims in Chicago such experiences underscore that no matter how much they try to live up to the ideal of law-abiding, American citizens, they are often not perceived as such.

The ways in which Muslims are perceived and treated is sometimes the consequence of federal investigations. One group in the Chicago area that has come under such investigation is the Arab/Palestinian Muslim community. Arab Muslim immigrants primarily live on the Southwest side of the city, where they have founded one of Chicago's major Islamic centers and two full-time Muslim schools. Since the Gulf War, the community has come under federal investigation on at least three occasions. In January 1991, the FBI contacted thirteen prominent Arab-Americans in the city, asking them about their political viewpoints and knowledge about future Arab terrorist activity in the United States.[51] Although the American Civil Liberties Union of Illinois later filed and won a petition against the Bureau, claiming a violation of the U.S. Constitution's First Amendment,[52] investigation of Arab Muslims in Chicago proceeded a couple of years later. When four Muslim Arab-American citizens of Chicago in the years between 1993 and 1995 were held by the Israeli government, charged with supporting the militant Islamist groups Hamas and Islamic Jihad, the FBI once again questioned leaders of the Chicago community.[53] Interrogations also took place in 1997 and 1998. In the summer and fall of 1998, accusations against Chicago Muslim support of radical groups in the Middle East escalated to new heights when one resident had his home and assets seized by the FBI who accused him of being a high-ranking military operative of Hamas.[54] A local Muslim non-profit organization, the Qur'anic Literacy Institute, came under federal investigations on similar charges and was among others accused of channeling money through housing development projects in Chicago's western and southwestern suburbs.[55]

The claim that some Chicago Muslims are connected to and help fund radical Islamist groups in the Middle East has gained a high level of attention recently from both local and national press and from governmental agencies. The accusation is often made that individuals and organizations in the Chicago area are connected to a larger militant Muslim network in America, supporting militant groups and even organizing training camps for Middle Eastern terrorists on American soil.[56] Much of the recent investigation is defended as legal, according to the Omnibus Counter-Terrorist Act that was put into action by the U.S. House of Representatives in February of 1995.[57]

In Chicago such charges and investigations have left many Muslims enraged, and demonstrations have taken place on several occasions. To them, it only proves that Islam and Muslims are perceived wrongfully as evil and anti-American. A law such as the Omnibus Counter-Terrorist Act is seen by Muslims as intending to exclude Muslims from the United States by any available means. The weapon against this situation for some Muslims is to seek greater involvement in local and national social and political affairs. A new agency, Muslim Americans for Civil Rights and Legal Defense, was recently formed for this purpose. For other Muslims, the answer is isolation from and demonization of the

American nation, defending themselves with stereotypes that are just as unfair and uncompromising as the ones with which they believe they are encumbered.

What Now?

In this chapter I have tried to offer a concise overview of the move from the temporal, detached journey of the Muslim immigrant to the fixed, attached settlement of the Muslim immigrant-citizen in Chicago. Certain concepts must be highlighted in this respect.

One such concept is that of loyalty. Loyalty not only determines the gap between the national preferences of the sojourner and the settler, it also determines the way that the migrant, as such, is perceived by the host city or host country. Interestingly as well as disturbingly, the expectations of Muslim-American citizens are highly complex and subject to a kind of weary resignation. While Muslims on the one hand administratively are included and trusted on the same level as any other American citizen, and while they work, study, and live on equal terms with other Americans, distressing situations of crisis arise that often lead others to challenge their loyalty. The troublesome establishment of the MCC mosque and school and the FBI interrogations of members of the Arab-Muslim community in the name of the Omnibus Counter-Terrorism Act exemplify this attitude.

At a certain level, such reactions can be seen as consequences of widespread fear of and prejudice against (non-European) immigrants in general. But Muslim Americans are further burdened by a long Orientalist heritage, as well as reaction to more recent political events where the interests of the United States have been determined by the federal government to be counter to those of Muslim groups or nations. At the same time, Muslims in America have become increasingly visible and claim space (be it through mosque architecture or Islamic dress) in American cities and American life. This entrance into public life, the search not only for recognition but also for representation, is by no means easy or easily accepted. It not only demands that the immigrant community rethink its sense of identity, it also calls for a similar rethinking on the part of the majority, with implications for giving up power, truth, and tradition. In that sense Islam becomes a viable rival to what is, presently, considered "American."

Active entry into public spaces is usually engaged in by second- and third-generation Muslim Americans. Whereas the parental generation still express a longing for the country or geographical area they have left behind, the younger generation employ other concepts and images when expressing their place of belonging. As we saw, among young active Muslims, it is common to tone down the implications of nationality and replace them with a transnational, Islamically defended, formulation of identity. Such formulations can be seen as a way to cope with being hybrid, but it is also worth asking whether, at least partially, it is also a means to deal with a questioned definition of loyalty. Because the Muslim community, in spite of its fairly long history in the United States, is still not fully included and trusted as a part of American mainstream, Muslims are faced with several possible responses. They may formulate their religious identity as against this nation, they may fight harder for inclusion, or, as a third possibility, they may formulate their religious identity in terms of something that is above national loyalty altogether. That this third option is particularly favored among the young once again highlights the "split" condition of their identity: they can neither identify fully with the geographical origin of their parents, nor are they fully identified (by an "other") as "naturalized" Americans. Transnationalist religious formulations are means to fight cognitive dissonance, social isolation, and impotence. According to transnational and utopian formulations, young Muslims can, optimistically, engage in American social issues at the same time that they stay "beyond" and loyal to what they see as the essential (though culturally formulated) heritage of their fathers and mothers, i.e. Islam.

The concepts of transnationalism and transethnicity lead to the question of how Muslims in Chicago will, in the future, formulate their (religious) sense of belonging. There is no question that barriers between ethnic groups representing the community are slowly breaking down, to some extent because of generational changes but also because of the increasing awareness that such barriers weaken the community. Whether Chicago's Muslims will lean more toward isolationism or integrationism will depend to a great degree on the responses and actions of powerful American opinion-forming agencies such as the press, the government, and major religious denominations. As has been illustrated, much points to a more tolerant approach to Muslim immigrants, their families, and offspring, to a willingness to see them as Muslim Americans rather than simply as Muslims in America. Though some federal legislation and some popular imagery seem to promote an aggressive stand against Muslim American citizens, it is far from clear that such actions and their motives can prevail in the future. Not only does this kind of attitude bring into question the moral heritage and civil rights upon which the country claims to be built, but it fails to recognize that the Muslim community represents a growing asset for America that will not go away under pressure, but is here to stay.

Notes

1. A considerable part of the following chapter is based on the author's fieldwork among Chicago Muslims in 1995–1996, 1995–1997, and a visit to the city in the winter of 1998.

2. Adele L. Younis, *The Coming of the Arabic-Speaking People of the United States* (New York: Center for Migration Studies, 1995), 154.

3. Ibid., 150.

4. Immigration statistics shows that Muslim migration to Chicago in the period before 1890 was limited. By 1860, for example, we find no more than two immigrants from the Ottoman Empire, increasing to fourteen in 1880, 180 in 1900, and 2,224 in 1910. Emigration from India, another country with a considerable Muslim population, was limited until the middle of the twentieth century. By 1860 only fourteen people had migrated to Chicago from India, increasing to no more than 70 in 1890 and 126 in 1930. See *The People of Chicago: Who We Are and Who We Have Been: Census Data on Foreign Stock and Race: 1837–1970* (Chicago: City of Chicago, Department of Development and Planning, 1976).

5. Gertrude M. Scott, *Village Performances: Villages at the Chicago World's Columbian Exposition.* Ph.D. Dissertation, University of Chicago, 1991, pp. 143ff; Younis, 155.

6. Scott, 161.

7. The belly dance, or "dance du ventre," as it also was called, highly provoked some members of the Victorian audience. One committee involved in the Exposition, the Board of Lady Managers, demanded at one point that the "wild" dance should be entirely excluded from the fair. According to one source, the Chicago newspapers responded to this demand in a "semi-serious manner that made it quite evident that the consensus of the local opinion was in favor

of continuing the dance." *Oriental and Occidental, Northern and Southern Portrait Types at the Midway Plaisance* (St. Louis: N.D. Thompson Publishing Company, 1894). Still, as a consequence of the complaint the dance was "modified" until the last month of the Exposition. See also *Library of Congress: Information Bulletin,* 1991.

8. Interestingly, the Jewish holiday of Yom Kippur was celebrated in the mosque on September 19, 1893.

9. "Shriners Dedicate the Temple," *Chicago Tribune,* April 1893.

10. Cited in Richard B. Turner, *Islam in the African-American Experience* (Indianapolis: Indiana University Press, 1997), 64.

11. Walter R. Houghton, ed., *Neely's History of the Parliament of the World's Religions* (Chicago: F.T. Neely, 1983), 613–615.

12. Kathleen Moore, *Al-Mughtaribun, American Law and the Transformation of Muslim Life in the United States* (Albany: State University of New York Press, 1995), 38.

13. Turner, 117–118. Dr. Sadiq established the headquarters of the Ahmediyya mission in Chicago in 1922. The mission is still active in the city.

14. Scott, 166.

15. Younis, 158.

16. For example, a newsletter that circulated in Chicago in the late 1930s cited the settlement of Syrians in the city: "We usually associate Syrians with house to house vendors of oriental laces and rugs . . . . After the Exposition they settled around 18th Street and State Street." "Syrians in Chicago," *Tour Topics* no. 36 (9–15 January, 1938).

17. M. M. Aijian, "The Mohammedans in the United States." *Muslim World* 10 (1920): 35.

18. Edith M. Stein, *Some Near Eastern Immigrant Groups in Chicago.* M.A. Thesis, University of Chicago, 1922, 77–78.

19. Lawrence Oschinsky, *Islam in Chicago: Being a Study of the Acculturation of a Muslim-Palestinian Community in that City.* M.A. Thesis, University of Chicago, 1947, 23; Abdul-Jadil al-Tahir, *The Arab Community in the Chicago Area: A Comparative Study of the Christian-Syrians and the Muslim-Palestinians,* Ph.D. Dissertation, University of Chicago, 1952, 59.

20. Oschinsky, 24.

21. Unfortunately, almost no material exists on Muslim immigrants in Chicago other than Middle Easterners before 1950. Still, Muslims from other geographical areas also lived in the city in that period. The Bosnian community, for example, already had established a Muslim organization, the Khaivat Ummah, in 1906. See Harold Vogelaar and Asad Husain, "Activities of the Immigrant Muslim Communities in Chicago," in *Muslim Communities in North America,* eds. Yvonne Y. Haddad and Jane I. Smith (Albany: State University of New York Press, 1994).

22. Oschinsky, 24.

23. See, for example, Abdul-Jadid al-Tahir, *The Arab Community in the Chicago Area: The Muslim Palestinian Community.* M.A. Thesis, University of Chicago, 95. For a comprehensive description of the Arab press in the United States, see Ajami.

24. Oschinsky, 34.

25. All restaurants were established in the neighborhood of 18th Street and Michigan Avenue. *Al-Tahir,* 1952, 95.

26. Ibid., 104.

27. Ibid., 105.

28. It is worth some thought whether this emphasis on segregation had bases other than the ethnic-nostalgic. Religious ideas also may have promoted a wish for segregation, particularly among the immigrants who came to America before the dissolution of the Ottoman Empire (1921). In that period, following the claims of governments and titulations, it was still possible to speak about an abode of Islam (*dar al-islam*) and an abode of war (*dar al-harb*). A Muslim was supposed to stay within the *dar al-islam,* unless necessity forced him to seek his fortune

elsewhere. Still, a Muslim's travelling to non-Muslim lands should only be temporal, and could be validated if he was granted the right to manifest the signs of Islam in the country of visitation. See Bernard Lewis, "Legal and Historical Reflections on the Position of Muslim Populations under Non-Muslim Rule," in *Islamic Britain: Religion, Politics and Identity among British Muslims*, ed. Bernard Lewis and Dominique Schnapper (London: I.B. Tauris, 1994). The question of Muslim settlement in non-Muslim lands has become acute in the second half of this century where many Muslims have migrated to countries in Western Europe as well as the United States. Muslim scholars have presented diverse interpretations of the implications of such settlements. Some have seen this as a means of *da'wa* and have raised the immigrant to the status of missionary; other scholars have encouraged Muslim immigrants to isolate themselves from the host society or leave the West in order to same their souls. See Larry Posten, *Islamic Da'wa in the West. Muslim Missionary Activity and the Dynamics of Conversion to Islam* (New York: Oxford University Press, 1992).

29. Bryan S. Turner, *Orientalism, Postmodernism & Globalism* (London: Routledge, 1994).

30. Dale E. Eickelman and James Piscatori, *Muslim Politics* (Princeton: Princeton University Press, 1996).

31. The importance of asylum as a reason for migration and application for citizenship may be illustrated by the increase in legislative attempts on behalf of refugees introduced in the United States in his period. The Displaced Persons Act of 1948 and the Refugee Act of 1980 stand out in this respect. The acceptance of refugees is often coupled with the expectation of loyalty. For example, the 1980s continued to see a bias against refugees from Communist countries such as the Soviet Union, or anti-American countries such as Iran. See Alejandro Portes and Ruben G. Rimbaut, *Immigrant America: A Portrait* (Berkeley: University of California Press, 1996).

32. Peter Beyer, *Religion and Globalization* (London: Sage Publications, 1994).

33. The situation is somewhat complex when it comes to the Palestinian community. The hope to return to the lost country of Palestine has become a tradition that is shared not only by the elders, but also transmitted to the children born in the United States. See Louise Caincar, "Immigrant Palestinian Women Evaluate their Lives," in *Family & Gender Among America Muslims: Issues Facing Middle Eastern Immigrants and Their Descendants*, ed. Barbara C. Aswad and Barbara Bilge (Philadelphia: Temple University Press, 1996). The signing of the Oslo Accords seems to have modified this notion somewhat. Community activists told me that the struggle for a return to the homeland was slowly being replaced by an Islamic, "Ummatic" one. Accordingly, the question of a geographical belonging became less important.

34. *Islam in North America. Muslim Community Center: Accomplishments and Aspirations.* MCC 25th Anniversary Commemoration (Chicago: Muslim Community Center, 1995). The first Sunni mosque established in the area was the Bosnian American Cultural Association's mosque, then located on North Halsted Avenue. The mosque was founded in 1954. See Vogelaar and Husain, 240.

35. See also Gulzar Haider, "Muslim Space and the Practice of Architecture: A Personal Odyssey," in *Making Muslim Space in North America and Europe*, ed. Barbara D. Metcalf. (Berkeley: University of California Press, 1996).

36. Poston, 94.

37. See Poston, 99–101; Garbi Schmidt, *American Medina: A Study of the Sunni Muslim Immigrant Communities in Chicago.* Lund Series in the Study of Religions, Vol. 8 (Stockholm: Almqvist & Wiksell International, 1998).

38. Interview, taped by author, 29 February 1996.

39. See also Beyer.

40. MCC 25th Anniversary Video.

41. Eric Zorn, "Morton Grove Tells School Board to Get Off Muslim Neighbor's Back," *Chicago Tribune*, 8 November 1990.

42. MCC 25th Anniversary Video.

43. List of CPWR Trustees, obtained at the 1997 Parliament dinner, 1 June 1997.

44. Michael Ko, "Thanksgiving Service Unites Diverse Faiths in Harmony," *Chicago Tribune*, 26 November 1998.

45. Diego Bunuel, "Archbishop Breaks Fast at Mosque," *Chicago Tribune*, 18 November 1998.

46. Steve Kloehn, "U.S. Muslims an Emerging Force; Far From a Minority; Islam is the Fastest-Growing Religion in the Nation and in Metropolitan Chicago, Second Only to Christianity," *Chicago Tribune*, 28 August 1998.

47. See, for example, John H. White, "Muslims Invite All Faiths to Visit as Hold Period Ends," *Chicago Sunday Times*, 20 February 1996.

48. Merita Ilo, "So Many Were Killed, I Just Cannot Forget," *Chicago Tribune*, 27 July 1997.

49. Ana Mendieta, "Bosnian Refugees Thank Chicagoans Who Helped," *Chicago Sun-Times*, 11 October 1998.

50. Jeffrey Bils, "Bosnian College Gets City Branch," *Chicago Tribune*, 18 November 1998.

51. Jahan Hanna, "FBI Questioning Irks Some Arabs in the US," *Chicago Tribune*, 10 January 1991.

52. Charles F. Williams, "FBI Overstepped Consent Decree, ACLU Charges," *Chicago Daily Law Bulletin*, 14 June 1994.

53. See, e.g. *Chicago Tribune*, 1993.

54. See Matt O'Connor, "Hamas Laundering Charges Denied," *Chicago Tribune*, 13 June 1998; Holly Sullivan, "Arabs Battle Bias," *Daily Southtown*, 21 June 1998.

55. The Qur'anic Literacy Institute was founded with the intent to prepare an English translation of the Qur'an and to "bridge the spiritual breach between Muslims in the English-speaking West and the Koran." The leader of the institute is a former president of ISNA (the major Muslim organization in the United States). He has studied at al-Azhar in Egypt and has received a Ph.D. from the University of Chicago. See William Gaines and Andrew Martin, "Terror-funding Touches Suburban Group: The FBI is Investigating an Oak Lawn Organization Suspected of Investing in Real Estate to Launder Money for Hamas," *Chicago Tribune*, 8 September 1998, 56.

56. See, for example, Art Golab, "Chicagoan Hits Israeli Charges against Salah," *Chicago Sun-Times*, 24 October 1993.

57. U.S. House of Representatives, H.R. 17/0, February 1995. The Omnibus Counter-Terrorist Act has been criticized by Muslim American citizens as well as civil rights organizations as violating constitutional rights. The Act gives the President the ability to investigate or deport aliens without disclosing its evidence to the alien being tried.

Being Arab and Becoming Americanized: Forms of Mediated Assimilation in Metropolitan Detroit

7

GARY DAVID AND KENNETH K. AYOUBY

METROPOLITAN DETROIT is home to what is perhaps the largest Arab community outside of the Arab world. In many ways, the Detroit area community resembles a typical ethnic enclave inhabited by immigrants and their descendants. Aspects of the Arab world can be seen everywhere: in the signs decorating the windows of Arabic groceries and restaurants, in the minarets and calls to prayer of a variety of mosques, in the churches that bear the names of Eastern saints, in the clothing of elderly men and women who have yet to acclimatize to American culture, and in the daily rituals and habits that reveal the distinctive flow and flavor of Arab life and culture.

Although the different neighborhoods of the Metropolitan Detroit Arab community share many cultural traits, however, they do not constitute a singular and unified entity. One primary distinction lies in national origins. Of the twenty-two countries belonging to the "Arab World," as defined by membership to the League of Arab States, seven (Lebanon, Palestine, Syria, Iraq, Egypt, Jordan, and Yemen) are prominently represented by immigrants in Metropolitan Detroit. Figure 7.I illustrates the different primary countries from which Arabs have immigrated to the Detroit area.

The Metropolitan Detroit Arab American community is also diverse in regard to its religious representation.[1] The religions of Islam and Christianity in their Middle East versions are represented by a variety of sects, denominations, and groupings, including Chaldean, Coptic, Druze, Greek Orthodox, Maronite, Melkite, Shi'a, Sunni, and Syrian Orthodox. It is difficult to estimate exactly what percent of the total Arab American community is represented by each religious group. The large and growing number of religious institutions and organizations, however, makes it clear that the groups have been successful in maintaining a distinctive sizeable presence in their own right, impacting the formation of religious enclaves in terms of identification. While the various religious institutions of the city serve to maintain cohesion within their respective groupings,[2] these same institutions are often responsible for reinforcing separation between the groups by emphasizing the religious differences.[3] In Metropolitan Detroit the combination of religious and national distinctions has resulted in the formation of subcommunities, or enclaves, within the general Middle Eastern community.

Perhaps the most visible component of the Metropolitan Detroit Arab community is the Arab Muslim sector, located primarily in the region's West Side. The city of Dearborn in this area (and the immediate area surrounding it) is home to perhaps the highest concentration of Arab Muslims outside of the Arab World itself. Originally, most of the Arab inhabitants of Dearborn were Lebanese. While Christian immigrants from present-day Lebanon settled in the eastern sectors of the city, Lebanese Shi'a Muslims lived in Dearborn close to their employer, the Ford Motor Company. Arabs began coming in the 1920s, with their numbers increasing greatly in the second half of the twentieth century.

Following close behind the Lebanese were Yemeni Sunni Muslims who also sought employment in the growing automobile industry. The Yemeni immigration was largely a male movement, with women and children staying behind as men came to work and send remittances back home. Next to arrive were Palestinians and Jordanians, primarily Orthodox Christians, but also Sunni Muslims. They are considerably fewer in number than the Lebanese and the Yemenis, but their presence clearly is felt in their community activism and social organizations. Finally, large numbers of Iraqi Shi'a immigrants and refugees have come to Dearborn. They chose to emigrate not for economic but political reasons. Most are refugees expelled from Iraq after failed attempts to oppose Saddam Hussein at the end of the Gulf War.

Dearborn's main thoroughfares—Warren Avenue, Michigan Avenue, Ford Road, and Schaeffer Road—all bear the evidence of this large Arab community (see Figure 7.2). Interspersed with the many Arabic restaurants featuring "Middle Eastern" cuisine are shops that cater directly to the Muslim community. In many instances, abandoned storefronts

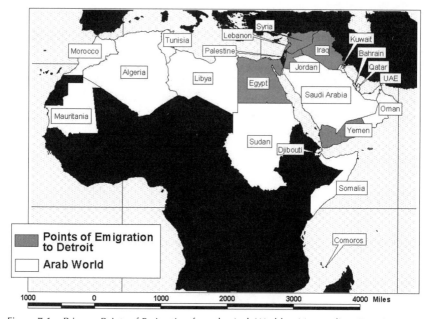

Figure 7.1   Primary Points of Emigration from the Arab World to Metropolitan Detroit

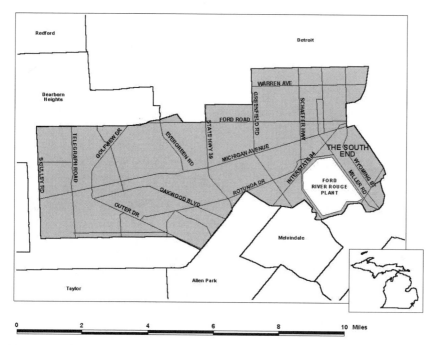

Figure 7.2   The City of Dearborn

have been transformed into community mosques, religious libraries and book stores, shops carrying religious merchandise (prayer rugs, veils, and other clothing), butcher shops proclaiming that their meat is *halal*, and other services that cater specifically to the area's Muslim community.

In Dearborn, the South End holds special importance as a kind of enclave within an enclave, where the cultural concentration is especially intense.[4] The South End has long been home to Arab immigrants due to its proximity to the Ford Motor Company's River Rouge automotive plant. The industrial monolith historically has employed immigrants from a number of cultural backgrounds, including many groups from Eastern Europe. Today, the area is primarily Arab and Muslim. The call to prayer rings out five times a day from the mosque located in the neighborhood. Children can be seen walking to the local elementary school whose student population is 99 percent Arab. A large park with a swimming pool is located in the community as well, where young boys and girls congregate daily, some wearing shorts and t-shirts, some with the *hijab* (head-covering). Arabic is spoken freely, and, for the majority, it is the preferred language of casual conversation. There is a large community organization whose chief clientele is from the Arab community. On any given day, the halls and offices of the organization are filled with Arab residents trying to process their immigration and naturalization papers, while in another area children get tutoring in such subjects as math, English, and American history.

It would be misleading, however, to give the impression that the entire Arab American community of Detroit is like the one described here. There is a great deal of variance between groups of Arab Americans, and this can be seen in the life styles and habits of the community members. While some parts of the community are in many respects indistinguishable from the Arab World, other areas are likewise indistinguishable from the American world. The latter form what might be called the *invisible* community, largely unnoticed because of its lack of obvious identifiable features. Even though this community is not an enclave in the same respects as the South End, it is part of the greater Muslim community by virtue of the fact that their ancestors at one time shared the same soil.

Somewhere between the ethnic enclaves and the "assimilated" Arabs is a kind of gray area where more and more community members are finding themselves. This is composed mainly of the young sons and daughters of immigrants who either came to the United States when they were young or were born there. Many view this as the battleground where Arab and American cultures are coming into conflict, each vying for cultural supremacy. The parents of these youth try to imbue them with Arab culture so that the cultural lineage will not end. Simultaneously, these youth are part of American society, are raised with American influences, listen to American music, watch MTV, and receive cultural messages that are distinct from those of their parents. This mix is evident in many ways. Youth use telecommunications technology like beepers and cell phones to maintain contact with their secret boyfriends and girlfriends while affirming beliefs in their parents' messages of morality. Boys drive their Mustangs and Jeep Grand Cherokees that bear slogans like "Chaldean Pride" and display Lebanese flags. Youth will speak Arabic in front of their American classmates, but speak English with their Arab parents. This is the third Arab American community, symbolically situated between East and West, but with the dynamism and fluidity to function within either. In essence, it is a new whole in the same way a child bears a resemblance to both of its parents.

The greater Arab American community is also home to over ninety community organizations,[5] at least twenty-seven of which are located in the area of Dearborn. Covering a wide range of community life, these organizations bear evidence that the Dearborn community is strong, broad, vibrant, and firmly established. The changing nature of organizational activity in Dearborn and in greater Detroit reveals how these organizations are operating as agents of mediation and are attempting to create the Arab American cultural hybrid.

Changes in Cultural Identity and Organizational Activity

Ethnic organizations are noted for their ability to provide support to their members and as contexts in which individuals can connect with others of similar backgrounds and interests. They strengthen the group's identity by raising consciousness from the individual to the communal level.[6] They also serve as intermediaries between the ethnic community and mainstream society, promoting the interests of the group to the society at large. They serve, in effect, as cultural buffers. In Metropolitan Detroit ethnic organizations are starting to serve a new function. Arab and Muslim organizations are playing a role as agents of mediation, where the organizations are attempting to act as cultural filters, removing American cultural "impurities" while retaining those American cultural traits that are considered positive. Through their structures and the nature of their activities, Arab and Muslim ethnic organizations in Metropolitan Detroit are attempting to incorporate aspects of both American and Arab culture. This hybridization is promoting a kind of assimilation and acculturation that encourages the incorporation of positive Arab, Muslim, and American cultural characteristics. Most often this is seen by members of the community as the desire for youth to become American, but not become Americanized. It is also characterized in the nature of the organizations themselves, shifting and evolving as their members undergo a cultural metamorphosis.

The organizational structure of the Metropolitan Detroit Arab community is as diverse and extensive as the communities served. Because of the numbers of Arabs in the area, it is very difficult to get an accurate sense of how many organizations exist and the exact nature of their activities. Furthermore, the organizational life of the community is so dynamic that any such list is out of date as soon as it is printed, as organizations are constantly coming into existence. The best source of organizations in the community is the *1998 Middle Eastern Community Directory of Organizations*,[7] which lists eighty-four Arab associations in Metropolitan Detroit. Subsequent to the directory's publication, five more organizations were identified. However, even the total number of eighty-nine is probably not exact, as there is evidence that the community is much more active organizationally.

Figure 7.3 lists the various organizations and places them in general categories based upon their primary organizational activities and the impetus for their creation. This does not necessarily mean that these are the only activities of the organizations. In fact, many of these groups have expanded into areas that go beyond the scope of their original activities. Furthermore, typologies of ethnic organizations generally "are arbitrary in the sense that any number of types can be produced according to the (organization's) general area of concern (i.e., religious, educational, political, recreational, fraternal, etc.)."[8] One advantage of these categories is that they help to give a general idea of the types of organizations that exist and provide a general picture of organizational activity in the community.

All the organizations play an important role in the community, often beyond the organizational niche that they occupy. Religious groupings, often the first to be formed by immigrants, are vital to the maintenance of networks and solidarity in any ethnic community.[9] Rather than simply meeting the spiritual needs of the ethnic community, they serve as places where community members can congregate on a regular basis and reaffirm their ethnic and cultural ties. All the village and family associations likewise have as a primary goal keeping alive a sense of connectedness with the ancestral land and of "blood" ties, especially with youth. Toward this end, these organizations often sponsor events where youth can meet and become engaged in the group's culture within a controlled environment created by the organization members. Organizations thus position themselves as key components in the cultural socialization of youth.

One set of distinctions among the Arab organizations in Metropolitan Detroit has to do with whether their membership is composed of the descendants of early immigrants or of those who have arrived more recently. Part of the division lies in what it means to be an ethnic group member. First (and sometimes second) generation Arabs retain certain things in common, most obviously having lived in the Arab World at some point in their lives and the continued use of the Arabic language. For third or fourth generation descendents of earlier immigrants, however, these elements generally no longer pertain. Many in this group no longer have the ability to speak Arabic outside of a few phrases such as *insha-allah* (if God wills it), *hamdillah* (praise be to God), *keef hallak* (how are you?), and *ahlan wa sahlan* (welcome), which means that there is often a division between those who can speak and those who cannot. Many of these Arabs have never visited the Arab world—what they know of their ancestral homelands has been learned through stories passed down or looking at pictures hanging in their homes as reminders of places they have never been.

Figure 7.3   Metropolitan Detroit Middle Eastern Organizations by Organizational Category

Religious 23	Village/Family 17	Cultural/ Education 15	Human Service 11
American Druze Society	American Federation Ramallah, Palestine	ADC-University of Michigan	ADC-Greater Detroit
American Moslem Society	Barachit Club	American Lebanese University Graduates	Arab-American and Chaldean Council
American Muslim Bekaa Center	Beit Hanina Social Club	Arab American Council	Arab Community Center for Economic and Social Services
Eparchy of Saint Thomas the Apostle Chaldean Diocese	Bint Jebail Cultural Center	Arab Theater and Actors Guild	
Foundation of Islamic Heritage	Bir Zeit Society	Chaldean America Student Association-University of Michigan Dearborn	Chaldean American Ladies of Charity
Islamic Center of America	Karoun Village Society		International Institute of Metropolitan Detroit
Islamic House of Wisdom	Kfarhouna Lebanese Club of America	Chaldean Federation of America	Islamic Health and Human Services
Islamic Institute of Knowledge	Mackie-Turfe Family Union	Chaldean Iraqi Association of Michigan	Palestine Aid Society of Ann Arbor
Islamic Mosque of America	Madaba Society	International Muslimah Artists Net	Syrian-Lebanese Ladies of Charity
Karbalaa Islamic Education Center	Mashgara Village Society	Jordan Club of Michigan	Yemeni American Benevolent Association
Mar-Addai Chaldean Church	Nineveh Club	Lebanese American Club of Michigan	Yemeni American Association
Our Lady of Chaldeans Cathedral	St. Michael's of Serhel Society	Lebanese American Heritage Club	Yemeni American Cultural Center
Our Lady of Redemption Melkite Catholic Church	Syrian Women's Ferouzi Club of Detroit	Sands Club of Detroit	
Sacred Heart Chaldean Church	Tirze Society	Syrian Arab Cultural Association	
St. George Syrian Orthodox Church	United Hasroun Men's and St. Laba Ladies Charity Societies	Thought and Education Club	
St. Joseph Chaldean Catholic Church	United Kesrawan Society	Ukadh Art Gallery	
St. Mark Coptic Church	United North Lebanon Society		
St. Maron Maronite Church			
St. Mary Antiochan Orthodox Church			
St. Mary Assyrian Catholic Church			
St. Mary Orthodox Church			
St. Sharbel Maronite Church			
Sts. Peter and Paul Syrian Orthodox Church			

Figure 7.3   Metropolitan Detroit Middle Eastern Organizations by Organizational Category (continued)

Mass Media 11	Professional 9	Political 3
Al-Muntada magazine	American Arab of Chamber of Commerce	Arab American Political Action Committee
Arab American Message		
	Arab American Bar	Arab American Voter
Arab American Journal	Association	Registration and Education Committee
Arab American News	Associated Food Dealers	
		Iraqi Democratic Union
Arab Network of America	Chaldean Bar Association	
Arabic Time Television	Metro Detroit Service Stations	
Chaldean Detroit Times		
	Michigan Food and	
Chaldean Voice	Beverage Association	
Harp Magazine	National Arab American Medical Association	
TV Orient		
	National Association of Arab and Chaldean Business Women	
United TV Network		
	Warren Avenue Business Association	

An even deeper division may well be found in the different understandings of Arab identity. Descendants of early immigrants tend to relate their ethnicity to symbolic elements[10] that define for them what it means to be a member of the group. These primarily include food (e.g. *hummus*, *tabbouli*, and *kibbi*), dancing (or *dabke*), and cultural artifacts like images of cedar trees, *argilles*, and antique coffeepots. Beyond these symbols, there is little else that is linked to ethnicity. This is not to say that the identity of these people is weak. In fact, members of this group can feel very strong in their identification and proudly state that they are *ibn 'Arab* or *bint 'Arab* (son or daughter of an Arab). However, how they view their ethnicity and what it means to be a part of that ethnic group is rooted in symbolic aspects of the culture that have been maintained during the hundred years that this group has been in the United States.

In contrast, one finds a marked difference in recent immigrants, who generally have a more politicized identity. Many have experienced civil wars and internal conflicts while living in the Arab world, such as the Civil War in Lebanon in 1975 and later in the 1980s, which determine to a great extent how they see themselves. Lebanese Maronites who recently immigrated to Metropolitan Detroit do not necessarily consider themselves to be "Arab," as do descendants of the earlier arrivals. Rather, they identify with the label "Lebanese," referring to themselves as "Lebanese Americans" rather than "Arab Americans."

Immigrants from the early years are usually satisfied with meeting and enacting their ethnicity in a ritualistic fashion by eating Arabic food, perhaps listening to Arabic music, and even speaking Arabic to their limited ability. More recent arrivals, however, are concerned about "doing something." They wish to use the ethnic organization as a means to an end, and not as an end by itself. The responsibility recent immigrants generally feel toward their homelands fosters their desire to use ethnic organizations in Metropolitan Detroit to assist their compatriots "back home." Commonly this takes the form of sending remittances to the "homeland." This practice has in fact been going on since the community was first formed and still continues today. There is no difficulty so long as the money is used to support one's ancestral or native village, to help build a mosque or a church, or to develop a civil infrastructure. The problem comes when the community organization is used as a political vehicle for motivating action directed at some "back home" issue.

Divergent perspectives over an organization's scope of activity can in fact become very contentious. In one religious organization, a longstanding member of the community said of new arrivals that "[t]hese people come over here and try to take everything over!" Another discussed how "we have to show them how we do things here." This was in the context of instructing fellow church members who were recent immigrants on how to receive communion during a church service. Recent immigrants, who do not understand how those "American Arab" community members can refuse to carry their organizational activism further, have voiced similar displeasure. In fact, in one instance, the split actually helped to lead to the formation of an entirely new organization. The new association's leader told how she belonged to an Arab professional organization in the area that had a membership of both Americans of Arab ancestry and Arab immigrants. At numerous meetings, she would try to rouse the membership to take action on a variety of issues, including the Gulf War, sanctions against Iraq, and other political topics of the day dealing with the Arab world. In fact, to her, the "meetings" amounted to little more than social hours where members would eat Arabic food, do professional networking, and talk about idle matters. Generally, her efforts to give more substance to the organization were rebuffed. She found to her frustration that other established Arab immigrant organizations were unwilling to tackle such issues as women's rights in divorce, abuse, and other gender-based topics. As a result, she created a new organization devoted to both the development of Arab women in the United States and to addressing political issues in the Arab world.

It is common for both the early and the later immigrant groups to find the other to be too Arab or too American. The early group tries to stem the political influence of the later group by keeping organizational work centered either on life in America or on social activities meant to symbolically keep the ethnicity alive. The later group, on the other hand, wishes to maintain a stronger presence in the affairs of their native land, an activism that extends beyond sending remittances back home. This is not to say that members of the early immigrant group are not concerned at all with affairs in the Arab world. On the contrary, they express their own displeasure with such matters as the previous travel ban to Lebanon, the double standard of American foreign policy toward Israel, and the sufferings of the citizens of Iraq. In general, however, they are willing to settle for moral indignation without any pointed activism. Recent Arab immigrants in these organizations, on the other hand, fear that future generations will become "too American" and "lost" to their Arab culture.

Similar issues arise in organizations whose membership comprises primarily recent immigrants, namely in Shi'a mosques within the city of Dearborn. It is here that one sees the impact of American culture on traditional structures of power and authority within the Shi'a religious sect. This is symptomatic of a larger movement toward a hybrid culture most often recognized in the behavior of the youth. The fact is that aspects of American culture and values are seeping in and mixing with the Arab culture, which many see not so much as capitulation as a kind of natural hybridization through the intermixing of two cultural forces.

The Creation of "Presbyterian Islam" and the Separation of Mosque and State

When the earliest Muslim immigrants (most of whom were Shi'i) arrived in Detroit, there were no mosques to support their religious needs. Today, many Muslim organizations and institutions are located in the area of Dearborn, each trying to assist in the observance of Islam and its constituent practices. Five mosques are located in and around Dearborn, each serving its own constituency. At least another eight organizations work to assist area Muslims in other respects, such as access to reading materials, religious supplies, health and human services, and religious education. In general, the main purpose of them all is to meet the religious needs and obligations of the area's Muslim residents.

Their work, however, has now gone beyond this primary task of religious adherence. Increasingly, the mosques and other religious organizations in the area are trying to help area residents become a part of American society. A consequence of this activity, one that was perhaps unanticipated, is an increasing interest on the part of area residents in keeping religion out of secular matters.

Separation of church and state in the United States means for the Muslims that they are left to their own devices to develop their religious institutions free of governmental as well as religious control. In this sense, one can begin to see the emergence of a specific form of American or "Dearborn" Islam that is highly grass-roots supported and, to the extent tradition and theology permit, very autonomous in its self-definition. One can discern in these mosques an overt conflict between religious clerics who wish to import the homeland model to America and members of the congregation who do not. This change in the way in which the Muslim religious institutions are structured in terms of control and decision making suggests a move toward "secularization."

Traditionally, Muslim organizations overseas, due to historical processes, are very much linked to the state governments under which they operate. That model, which made the state a funding source for religious activities, cannot exist in the United States. The overseas model of Islam also positions the imam, a state employee, as the final authority in the mosque. In Dearborn, governance of the mosque's activities is typically shared between the imam and the organization's governing board, whose members are very reluctant to give final authority to the imam. At times, this arrangement can produce a tumultuous situation, with the two arms at odds with each other. Indeed, one of the oldest Islamic organizations in Dearborn fired several imams for attempting to apply the overseas model. Even this organization's founding imam, during his tenure of several decades, "ruled" by consensus, conceding much to the lay leaders in his congregation. He had the air of authority born of sophisticated scholarship, yet all accounts of him depict a deep sensitivity to grass-roots needs and a fundamentally new vision for operating a Muslim religious institution in the American context. It is no wonder that, several years after his death, he remains a "patron saint" of this organization, one whose passing is lamented as a loss for the community and the cause of Islam in America.

Yet, while most people in his congregation highly valued the enlightened and "democratic" leadership of the late imam, they have also said that they want to see more power in the hands of the governing board and other governing organs of this institution. This desire has only increased, as evidenced by a history of clashes with the imams that succeeded in this mosque. Eventually, the mosque rewrote its bylaws to reflect, even more, the wish for board control of the center. More than just a power issue, the situation reflects an earnest grassroots effort at redefining the relationship between the community and the mosque as symbol of authority. In fact, elections to the board, which are very democratic and highly contested, show a commitment to the institution as well as the seriousness of the process and the importance attached to the politicization (or secularization) of the mosque. The need to fund these organizations independent of any religious or governmental authorities presents the opportunity for community members to get together at the grassroots level and, as a result, control the purse strings of the clerical leadership and resources of the organization. Those who are elected to the board act as its guardians, both in the religious and secular sense. In other words, able community men who serve on the boards of these institutions have become "elders" of the mosques, and of Islam. They are the ones who decide the direction or trajectory of Islam, at least in Dearborn.

Where the congregation is more traditional, its members often newly arrived, the imam has a stronger hold on the structure of the mosque. Such is the case in another of the area's mosques, which under the leadership of its imam has grown into a major socioreligious installation in Dearborn. But even this organization could not function without a viable board—at least politically speaking. In other words, even where the idea of a "one-man show" is desired, it cannot be achieved for fear of being too much behind the times! This reveals a new, but very real, need for organization that is borrowed from the secular (the more civic and political) experience of the members. Thus, even when traditionalism is determined to be the model and ideology, the American context changes it enough to make a new, but viable, hybrid.

The case of this mosque is interesting for its attempts to create a school whose aim is not only to teach Islam and those elements of Arab culture that are deemed necessary for ethnic preservation but also the state-approved curriculum. The state of Michigan has recently agreed to open "charter" or specialized schools that receive both private and public funding. To keep state funding, they have to adhere to curriculum standards set by the state, combining their specialities with traditional school subjects. Thus, the school must teach secular topics as well as religious ones. The presence of charter schools run through religious (in this case, Islamic) organizations highlights the role that communication organizations play in the socialization process of the community's youth.

Thus, by running programs and serving as the cultural and social centers of community life, these organizations are in a position to determine the cultural influences that children are exposed to, especially when it comes to the ethnic culture of the community. In the case of the Arab American community, these organizations, by and large, can determine what is acceptable Arab and/or Muslim culture, what is acceptable American culture, and how they should be mixed. The vision of Arab culture and community as expressed in organizational activity is also being portrayed in programs geared toward youth. The following section focuses on how these organizations are attempting to walk a line between being Arab and American, and, in the process, developing a new model of cultural practice and ethnic identity.

Being American vs. Becoming Americanized: Organizational Attempts at Cultural Hybridization

Virtually all immigrant and ethnic communities wish to preserve their cultural heritage. While they may welcome the chance to live in a new land rich with opportunities, they nonetheless still want to maintain what it is that makes them who they are. These groups fear a sort of cultural extinction, resulting in a loss of self through the loss of cultural traits and practices that define them as a distinct entity apart from others. At the same time, immigrant groups want their community, and especially their children, to benefit from the opportunities present in their new home. They do not want their children to be isolated members of society, alienated from others due to their conspicuous differences.[11]

Given the large number of organizations in the Arab community of greater Detroit and the breadth of services they offer, it might appear that the Arab American community is "institutionally complete,"[12] meaning that members of the community do not need to go outside of the community to receive any kind of services and are, thus, theoretically insulated from external influences that might dilute the Arab community's cultural character. On the contrary, the activities of these organizations reveal a complex picture of managed assimilation and acculturation, where organizations attempt to walk a line between being Arab and becoming American. In this way, rather than insulating the Arab community from mainstream society, the organizations serve as filters that attempt to monitor what gets through to the community in terms of cultural influences.

Today, in the Arab Muslim community of Dearborn, as well as throughout Metropolitan Detroit, attempts to reach a balance between being Arab and becoming American are particularly focussed on the youth. In general, community members are worried that their children will become "Americanized," referring to the internalization of what they see as the negative traits of American culture. Americanization means that the youth become culturally "lost" and eventually separated from the Arab community. Through a process called "mediated assimilation" the youth of the community are encouraged to be simultaneously Arab and American. The task for the community members and community organizations is to determine what is to be retained of Arab culture, what is to be accepted from American culture, and how the "cultural impurities" that they believe could cause ruinous results are to be filtered out. This is explained in the conversation below between one of the authors (A) and an organizational representative (B):

A: I hear the word "Americanized" a lot. People are worried about their children becoming "Americanized."

B: That's what they say when they feel like they lost them.

A: How do you lose them? What do the kids lose in their culture?

B: There are two important things I come up with. They feel that they lose them when they see their kids are not understanding their language. They lost their Arabic language. So they feel that they lost them because they lose their communication. And they feel that they lose them when their behavior also becomes different than their parents. That's how they start [to] worry about them.

In a sense, the children become unrecognizable to their parents because they speak a language the parents are not comfortable with (and do not speak the one they are at home in) and act in a way with which the parents are not familiar. Parents then become alarmed that the children they expected always to have are now gone forever.

This does not mean that parents want their children to be isolated. Organizational leaders and community members are concerned about American cultural activities outside of parental and organizational control that they fear will negatively impact their youth, such as dating, promiscuity, drinking, smoking, and violence. Yet they are also clear about the positive American traits that they want the youth to adopt. The following statement from an organizational leader illustrates what are considered to be positive and negative values in American society:

> We would like first of all for [the youth] to stay away from bad things. If you don't pro-
> vide good things, bad things will come. We want them to stay out of the streets. We want
> them to stay from around places where they speak bad language. We teach them the value
> of education. Talking about the importance of being able to read, and write and the excel-
> lent life. We want them to have good values and to learn good manners. To speak to each
> other with respect and to feel a sense of socialization. . . . *No question American culture has a lot
> of good things. You know the work ethic, the scientific management of things, the value of life. All these things
> are very important.* (emphasis added)

While the community's youth are learning the positive cultural traits from the United States, they are expected to simultaneously retain as much as possible of the positive traits from Arab culture. This is meant to result in the creation of a person who is uniquely adapted to exist and prosper in two cultures. One organizational respondent had the fol-lowing to say:

> Our youth are supposed to keep our traditions. Family traditions. And be proud of what we
> have given the world. Mathematics, algebra, geometry, chemistry, pharmacy. And in many
> fields of knowledge. If they are not proud of their heritage and what their heritage has given
> the rest of the world, they will stray away and hide away from being Arab American.

The issue of "keeping our traditions" is at the heart of concerns over assimilation. Com-munity members are concerned that the youth will not maintain what is positive in Arab culture, and, as a result, will be lost and misguided. This informant expresses the concern of the community that youth will "hide away from being Arab American." It is the belief of the community that being Arab and becoming American can be two sides of the same coin, and that they can in fact compliment each other. The following two statements il-lustrate this point clearly:

> I see no contradiction in identifying with Arab or Druze ancestry and with being in this coun-
> try and identifying with the values and traditions of this country. There isn't really a contra-
> diction. On the contrary there's enrichment. I'm somebody who if you say Arab American I'm

lucky and enriched by the fact that I can combine the two and take the better aspects of each and combine them in myself or in somebody that identified with the same culture.

We cannot deny the fact that they're American. They're born here. They were raised here. They're educated here. They live here. I cannot call them Arab Americans. They're American Arabs. Their heritage, their background. . . . When the kids go to school, associate with American kids, they are going to pick up the habits. What's home is home. You instill the values, you instill the system. But when the kids go to school, they really have to assimilate in the society and go on with their lives. They cannot stand out. This is a growing sentiment in the Arab Muslim community. Rather than preaching cultural exclusion and separation, community residents and organizational leaders are trying to find ways that cultures can be combined. What is occurring in Dearborn is the creation of a hybrid that is not fully "American" and not completely "Arab." Rather, it is a cross between the two that is unique to the situation in Dearborn, creating a unique ethnic group that fully belongs to itself and only partially belongs to the others.

"Arabics" and "Dearbornites": The Emergence of a Cultural Hybrid in Community Youth

Thus far, we have examined the impact of community organizations on the socialization and identity formation of the community's youth. Of course, the youth are not isolated from influences that are extraneous to the organizations. They receive messages from any number of sources, including peers, music, television, movies, books, and teachers. As a result, youth are also free to craft for themselves a sense of cultural identity and cultural pride that is out of the control of their parents and community organizations.

For instance, the youth of Arab ancestry in Dearborn refer to themselves as being "Arabics," reflecting the way the school system identifies the group in its census-taking procedures to ascertain languages spoken at home if other than English. This term, which began as a tool to identify educational needs of students, has evolved into an ethnic identity of children. When an Arab American student is asked "What are you?" he or she will probably respond "I am Arabic." While the designation "Arabic" may only appear to be a semantic juxtaposition to being "Arab," it underscores the separation between what it means to be Arab in the Arab World and what it means in Dearborn.

The majority of those who are "Arabic" in this context are of Lebanese background, since the Lebanese are the oldest immigrant group in Dearborn. However, the Arabic culture also extends to include other Arab youth in the city. Part of what makes the Arabic culture of Dearborn different from Arab culture in general is that Dearborn can be essentially likened to a village in southern Lebanon, in southern Iraq, or in Yemen. The majority of people in Dearborn come not from urban areas, but from small towns culturally far away from the cosmopolitan centers of the Arab world. This results in the youth getting a narrower version of Arab culture than is the case in the Middle East in general. The culture reproduced in Dearborn is essentially a variant of village life, not the multifaceted culture present in Arab countries. One manifestation of this is that Muslim youth born or raised in Dearborn are genuinely surprised to meet someone who is Arab and Christian. This is the case because the ethnic enclave in which they live does not expose them to Arab

Christians.[13] What is perhaps most remarkable about this is that most of the Dearborn youth hail from Lebanese ancestry, a country which is extremely diverse in religious terms. This legacy gets lost, and for the youth of Dearborn, the terms Arab and Muslim are interchangeable and synonymous.

Youth generally first receive their cultural and ethnic impressions from their parents. The parents have the dual aim of raising their children not only to be good Arabs and Muslims but also to be good Americans. Thus, it is important that the children be strong in their ethnic identity and at the same time, be able to adapt in their lives outside of the community. What parents emphasize in this process are readily observable cultural practices, such as those associated with religion, cuisine, and social mannerisms. As a result, for example, the issue of *halal* food becomes a major indicator of who is being culturally "faithful" and who is not. Dress is another indicator. The dress code revolves around the concept of modesty for both sexes, and especially for Muslim girls who wear the *hijab*, or "scarf" in the parlance of the youth. Language usage can also be a designation between who is "Arabic" and who has become "Americanized." The issue of cultural observance can be seen in interactions between the community's youth. This occurs to the extent that youth can be seen questioning each other's convictions if the "appropriate" behavior is not being exhibited. In one instance during a summer youth program, a group of boys challenged some girls for not wearing the *hijab*, thus questioning their legitimacy as members of the cultural group. Other instances include debates over whether a person's clothing choice was appropriate or if a person was indeed praying "the right way." So narrow is the interpretation of what is proper that anything can become questionable behavior.

A cultural distinction between Arab youth (recent immigrants) and "Arabic" youth (raised in Dearborn) can also be seen in the Dearborn Fordson High School cafeteria. Over 90 percent of the student population at Fordson (one of three public high schools in Dearborn) are of Arab ancestry. During their lunch period, students have the option of either eating on the campus or going off campus to any local restaurant or fast food establishment. The "Arabic" youth would never eat in the lunch hall, preferring to go out for burgers, pizzas, burritos, or even *shawarma* and *shish tawook* sandwiches at any of the numerous Middle Eastern restaurants in the area. The recent Arab immigrant youth, however, choose the bland fare of the cafeteria. As a result, the "boater" youth (those recently "off the boat") are viewed in condescending terms as unsophisticated and generally nerdy. Even though the recent immigrant youth are in many ways an authentic representation of Arab culture since they are recently from the Arab World, they are not of the "Arabic" culture and are therefore looked down upon as being strange and different.

The Arabic youth see themselves as being "100 percent" Arab, both genetically and culturally. In the minds of the Arabic youth, the cultural practices they manifest are true to what goes on "back home." In fact, many Arabic youth have a point of reference since family vacations are frequently taken to the "old country." Once the youth are "back home," away from the potentially harmful influences of American society, they frequently have greater freedoms than in Dearborn. Youth often recount how lenient their parents become during travels back to the Arab World, allowing them to stay out with friends and family members much later, travel without telling their parents exactly where they are going, and socialize in more liberated conditions. In many respects, the freedoms enjoyed by the youth when visiting "back home" are more than they would enjoy if they lived there. Thus, "back home" becomes a sort of cultural Disneyland. It is only in America, which can represent being torn from the group's culture, that children are carefully monitored by parents and each other.

The often carnival-like atmosphere of these family trips in some ways gets exported with the youth back to Dearborn. The high school prom is one example. The music and dancing of the night is a mixture of East and West—Arabic pop music, Western "house" music, American rap, European techno, and Latin songs that frequently can carry an Arab beat. These songs are matched with the appropriate steps, be they a *dabke*, salsa, or other dance steps that bear no name. The Arabic youth are completely at ease with all these styles and are able to flow seamlessly between them. In between songs, youth frequently steal away to the washrooms to take an illicit drink of something alcoholic. Even though Muslim youth know it is *haram* (forbidden) to drink, in the context of the prom, it is viewed as permissible. Likewise, while dating is not allowed by most community parents, students are able to circumvent this in a variety of ways. Some Arabic boys will take non-Arab girls. Arabic females will go with their Arabic cousins (or approved childhood friends). Some will go with friends of the same sex, only to meet up with their male and female counterparts at the prom. In the minds of the Arabic youth, none of this makes them "bad Muslims." Rather, they are simply carrying out their localized cultural variant of Islam.

Some aspects of the new Arabic culture, such as pagers and cellular phones, are shared by both boys and girls. Both are used to stay connected to one's friends, even though the community is so close-knit that staying out of touch is virtually impossible. Typically, it is parents who pay for these accessories that are claimed to be essential to living. Parents may get them for their children to keep better tabs on their activities. Youth, of course, have different ideas regarding how the technology should be applied, for example, for keeping in contact with secret boyfriends or girlfriends. It is easy to arrange dates without the knowledge of one's parents by using beepers and cell phones.

Other Arabic cultural traits apply more usually to boys. Recently, Arabic boys (age fourteen to twenty-five) have adopted the tattoo craze that has been sweeping American culture. While the form is American, the content is undeniably Arab and Muslim. One popular choice is the word "God" in Arabic calligraphy tattooed on one's upper left arm. Often Muslim boys wear a religious symbol such as Imam Ali's scimitar, *Dhul Fiqaar*. Some have sported the emblem of Hizbullah on their arms. To them, it is not so much a statement of political belief as one of solidarity with their overseas cousins in their resistance to Israeli occupation and hegemony. They know little about the political realities of Arab-Israeli relations. A Hizbullah tatoo is support for Arab culture (as envisioned by Arabic youth), not support for Hizbullah itself.

Given the strong presence of car culture in Detroit (the Motor City), it is not surprising to see the special meaning the car has for an Arabic male. His car is an emblem of his status and his future. Lebanese youth in the parlance of Dearborn are nicknamed "zoomers" because of the way they zoom around in fast cars like Mustangs and Z-28s. Cruising (driving up and down a main street repeatedly) has long been a pastime in the Detroit area. Arabic youth cruise Michigan Avenue, Ford Road, and Warren Avenue, meeting friends, flirting with the opposite sex, and generally being seen. On any given summer night, the streets are filled with these cars as they make the rounds. Here, the car is not a vehicle of physical as much as cultural transportation. It is also not uncommon to see flags of Arab nations and statements such a "Lebanon" or "Arab Pride," or even religious statements such as "The Qur'an is the Last Revelation." In the rearview mirror of many cars, one can see a Qur'an or some other religious talisman. For the Arabic youth, there is no inherent contradiction in expressing religious views in one's car, and using the same car for having physical encounters with members of the opposite sex, which, according to their parents, is against the religion. Again, the youth are able to flow between cultures, blending together a mixture that suits the pragmatics of being young in Dearborn.

The Arabic girl has different ways to express her Arabic culture. Instead of a tattoo, her emblem is likely to be the "cover," the local name for the *hijab*. It is as much a fashion statement as it is a religious one. Traditionally, the *hijab* is supposed to be a display of modesty in one's appearance. However, in the hands of the Arabic female, it becomes something else. It is common to see a young Arabic female wearing the *hijab* with full make-up, including bright red lipstick, pink blush, black eyeliner, and eye shadow. In terms of clothing, tight blue jeans and a tight top are also not uncommon at the same time one is wearing the head-cover. In fact, girls who do not wear the *hijab* are often dressed more modestly than those who are "covered." *Hijabs* are also worn that match one's outfit, in effect, becoming an accessory rather than a religious statement.

Dating is of interest to the Arabic girl, but must be carried out with care and away from the prying eyes of community adults. The best "hang-outs" are those places not frequented by adults, such as Starbucks Coffee Shop, where they will happen to meet their boy friends. Commonly, this can be a first stop in the evening and used to set up the rest of the evening's plans. Another place where parents are not likely to be is the local college library. Armed with their cell phone and beepers, even high school students will go there under the auspices of doing schoolwork. Once there, they will receive private calls and make plans to meet their current sweethearts. The library at the local university has served the romantic interests of many Arabics of the Dearborn community. It must be kept in mind that it is not the "bad girls" of the community who engage in this behavior. These girls believe that they are good Muslims and good Arabs. They respect their parents and do not want to disappoint them. They are merely trying to express their cultural variant of being Arabic. They do not want to be rebellious in the sense of forsaking all that they have learned of being Arab and Muslim. They are embracing both Arab and American cultures in the most creative ways they can.

It is important here to realize that the Arab culture and values being transmitted to the youth, shaped by the hopes and fears of parents and the collective community in Dearborn, form essentially a "new Arabic" culture that is only tangentially related to the ancestral culture of the homeland. The youth are therefore not Arab, or Lebanese, or Yemeni, but rather "Arabic" or "Dearbornites." However, even though this new culture is a hybrid, it is claimed by the parents to be not only authentic but a direct representation of the original ancestral culture. The belief or expectation of parents is that youth raised in this culture will grow up to be just the same as their cultural cousins overseas. Clearly, this is not the case. Despite the efforts of the parents, the Dearborn youth are different. Parents and the older members of the community tend to see these differences as meaning that the youth are culturally less authentic than themselves, which they attribute to the negative effects of American culture. The youth have noticed that they are different as well, and echo it in their public discourse about themselves. They cannot have the same experiences as their parents had back in the Arab World, and, therefore, cannot be culturally the same. While parents, to varying degrees, voice interest in some day "going back home," the youth do not share in any such illusions. Dearborn Arabics are fully at home in their environment, which makes them in another sense "Dearbornites," much in the same way that those who are from Lebanon are Lebanese, those from Yemen are Yemeni, and those who are from America are Americans. They see themselves not as immigrants, but as natives to their environment. While a cultural minority in the city of Dearborn, they are not alien to it and accept both their "American-ness" and their "Arabic-ness" as integral parts of their identity.

Conclusion

One vehicle of the process of cultural hybridization as illustrated in the Detroit/Dearborn area is the Arab community organization, which is uniquely situated as a mediating force between American society and the Arab community. This is most often seen in, but is not exclusive to, how the organizations orient to the community's youth. This finding goes against the traditional notion that ethnic organizations promote community cohesion and cultural maintenance by limiting the contact between community members and society at large. While the Arab and Muslim ethnic organizations in Metropolitan Detroit are trying to achieve both of those aims, they are likewise trying to create a new cultural property, a mixture of "Arab" and "American" that will result in a blended ethnicity. The organizations are taking it upon themselves to temper the mixture in such a way that it produces a positive result.

The movement toward mediated assimilation is a direct result of the acknowledgment on the part of the Arab community that it is no longer made up of immigrants who are in America only temporarily. Members of the Arab community in large part have dropped the belief that they will soon be returning to the Middle East and are ready to make the United States their new home. This does not mean, however, that they are, at the same time, forsaking the Arab World and their Arab and Muslim roots. On the contrary, they are, in essence, straddling two civilizations and trying to maintain a presence in both. This desire is becoming manifest in the work of the organizations as they try to walk a line between the two cultural forces. It remains to be seen if this will be successful.

In Dearborn one can see this cultural drama played out by the community and its youth, the "Dearbornites" and the "Arabics," who are not Arab in the way their parents would like and not American in the way that society may like. Their seeming lack of fit does not mean they are "lost" and do not belong anywhere. Rather, they constitute a new hybrid that is perfectly at home in the hybrid surroundings of Dearborn. For that matter, these hybrid surroundings are impacting the "Arab-ness" and "Muslim-ness" of their parents as well. They are taking pages and experiences from life in the United States, and this is creating the emergence of a new model of religious organization. The power within these religious institutions is being shifted to a more group-based approach where the community itself (through boards of directors) has a large say in the activities of the organizations. Also, the political and the religious are being separated to a greater extent, thus following the doctrine of "separation of church and state." In these ways, the experience of America is changing adults as well as youth.

It is, of course, premature to determine the lasting impact of these changes or where they will lead (or end). Community members who have immigrated in the recent past have resigned themselves to life in Metropolitan Detroit and America. At the same time, they wish to stay connected to the Arab world and their respective nations spiritually, ideologically, and physically. Given the advances in travel, telecommunications, and information technology, there is every reason to believe this can be done, at least to some extent. Even with these new tools and the firm resolve of community members and organizations, however, the Arabs of Metropolitan Detroit will continue to develop tangentially to their cultural cousins "back home." This is largely because "home" is, in reality, no longer there, but here.

Notes

1. S. Y. Abraham, "A Survey of the Arab-American Community in Metropolitan Detroit," in *Arab World and Arab-Americans*, ed. S. Y. Abraham and N. Abraham (Detroit, Mich.: Wayne State University Center for Urban Studies, 1981), 23–33; S. Y. Abraham, "Detroit's Arab-American Community: A Survey of Diversity and Commonality," in *Arabs in the New World: Studies on Arab-American Communities*, ed. S. Y. Abraham and N. Abraham (Detroit, Mich.: Wayne State University Center for Urban Studies, 1983), 85–108.

2. Philip M. Kayal, "Religion and Assimilation: Catholic 'Syrians' in America," *International Migration Review* 4 (1973): 409–425.

3. Alixa Naff, *The Arab Americans* (New York: Chelsea House, 1983).

4. For a description of the South End of Dearborn, see Barbara Aswad, ed., *Arabic Speaking Communities in American Cities* (Staten Island: Center for Migration Studies, 1974).

5. Gary David, *The Mosaic of Middle Eastern Communities in Metropolitan Detroit* (Detroit, Mich.: United Way Community Services, 1999); G. David, *Middle Eastern Community of Metropolitan Detroit Directory of Organizations* (Detroit, Mich.: United Way Community Services, 1998).

6. Raymond Breton, "Institutional Completeness of Ethnic Communities and Personal Relations of Immigrants," *American Journal of Sociology* 70 (1964): 193–205; Julia Kwong, "Ethnic Organizations and Community Transformation: The Chinese in Winnipeg," *Ethnic and Racial Studies* 7 (1984): 374–386.

7. David, 1998.

8. Gunder Baureiss, "Toward a Theory of Ethnic Organizations," *Canadian Ethnic Studies* 16 (1982): 22.

9. Breton, 1964; Lopata, 1964; Pyong Gap Min, *Caught in the Middle: Korean Communities in New York and Los Angeles* (Berkeley, Calif.: University of California Press, 1996); Kyeyong Park, *The Korean American Dream: Immigrants and Small Business in New York City* (Ithaca, N.Y.: Cornell University Press, 1997).

10. See Herbert J. Gans, "Symbolic Ethnicity: The Future of Ethnic Groups and Cultures in America," *Ethnic and Racial Studies* 2 (1979): 1–20.

11. Much of this section is from David's *The Mosaic of Middle Eastern Communities in Metropolitan Detroit*.

12. See Breton, 1964.

13. It is also interesting to note that many of the Christian groups in the region (e.g., Maronites, Chaldeans, and Copts) do not consider themselves to be ethnically Arab, which undoubtedly contributes to the present situation.

THE EUROPEAN EXPERIENCE II

Invisible Muslims: The Sahelians in France 8

SYLVIANE A. DIOUF

ALTHOUGH ISLAM IS THE SECOND RELIGION IN FRANCE, and Muslims are increasingly evident in the public square, one sector of the Muslim population has remained virtually invisible. Paradoxically, this community, which is made up mostly of Sahelians (Senegalese, Malians, and Mauritanians), enjoys a highly visible presence even though it is not recognized as a Muslim presence. It has been at the forefront of the *sans-papiers* (illegal immigrants) movement, its members squatting in a Catholic church for weeks to dramatize their plight. Sahelians have waged battles for decent housing, and when evicted from squalid buildings, have camped for months with hundreds of children on the Parisian sidewalks or in front of the Vincennes Castle.

This community is also often in the spotlight because some of its members practice polygamy and excision. Yet in spite of the fact that most of these men and women are Muslims, they are almost never mentioned when French authorities, media experts or academicians ponder about the "Islamic presence," "What Islam for France?" or the "Muslim community." One may argue that their numbers, when compared with the Maghrebis (North Africans), are low and that their relative invisibility can be explained by demography. The real reason, however, may rather be that in France, as is true more generally in Europe, Islam is viewed primarily as a (dangerous) problem. It is associated with the FIS (Islamic Salvation Front) of Algeria, with Iran and Afghanistan, and with fundamentalists who are accused of forcing young girls to wear headscarves in school and of putting bombs in the subway and in crowded stores.

Sub-Saharan Muslims, however, have never been identified with terrorism or fundamentalism at home or in Europe. Unlike other Muslims in France, they are not considered to be a violent threat to secularism, social peace, and French culture. Insofar as they are not seen as part of "the Islamic problem," they also tend not to be thought of as part of the "Islamic community" either. Sahelian Muslims are not perceived by French society as Muslims—except in two instances, discussed below, that have no repercussions on the larger society—but simply as Africans. Even within the Muslim community itself, they are often overlooked, due in part to their numbers, but also to the persistence of prejudice among North African, Middle Eastern, and Turkish immigrants against sub-Saharan Africans. Nevertheless, for most of the Sahelians, Islam is an essential component of their identity. In addition, Islamic schooling and the Muslim confraternities often play a significant role in the migration process. As a result of this "Islamic invisibility," research and studies on West African Muslims in France are very scarce; only a few articles have been published in the late 1980s and early 1990s. At the same time, books and articles dealing with African immigration refer to its social, economic, and cultural dimensions, but seldom to religion. Today, as Africans in France are increasingly from Central Africa, the Sahelians, once preponderant, receive less attention. Already invisible as Muslims, they are becoming less and less visible as Africans.

The Sahelian Community in France

The numerical force of the Sahelians, to start with, is unclear. The 1990 census (results of the 1999 census are not yet available) gives precise figures but does not take into account probably tens of thousands of illegal immigrants and people who are naturalized French. It is also likely that the largely illiterate population, unable to fill out census forms, has been undercounted. As Muslims, the Sahelians fare even worse. By law, French statistics cannot cover religion; therefore, various bodies—using diverse methodologies—arrive at different estimates. The *Haut Conseil à l'intégration* (High Council for Integration) estimates the number of Muslims at a maximum of three million.[1] But the *Secrétariat pour les relations avec l'islam* (Secretariat for the Relations with Islam) mentions a total of 4,140,000 Muslims, representing about 7 percent of the total population: 2.9 million Maghrebis; 300,000 non-Arab Middle Easterners; 250,000 sub-Saharan Africans; 100,000 Arabs from the Middle East; 100,000 Asians; 40,000 French converts; 350,000 illegal aliens; and 100,000 others.[2] Those numbers, however, do not coincide with the 1990 census, according to which there were about 210,000 Africans in France. Most of the 43,700 Senegalese, 37,700 Malians and 6,600 Mauritanians are surely Muslims, as are the Comorians, many Ivoirians and Guineans, some Burkinabe, and Cameroonians. Even if provision is made for the illegal immigrants, the Secretariat's figures (at least for 1990) seem high. Interestingly, number inflation is used by some to conjure up images of an Islamic threat and by the opposite camp to bolster their claims to representation and a significant share of the public space.

Because of differences in cultures, social traditions, history, and patterns of migration, a general study of the African Muslims in France has little relevance. The most homogeneous group is without a doubt the Comorians,[3] but the largest community with the longest history in France is that from the Sahel region. It is composed of different ethnic groups, which in some cases transcend geographic borders. For example, the Halpulaaren ("people who speak Pulaar," i.e., Fulani and Tukulor) can be found in Senegal, Mali, and Mauritania, as is true of the Soninke (also called Sarakole and Maraka). Mande people (Manding, Bambara, Malinke) are Senegalese, Malians, and Guineans. In France, African immigrants make the most of all their different layers of identity: they may be members of a village/town association, a national organization, and an ethnic association that groups people from the same ethnic group who are citizens of various countries. Thus, to speak of a Senegalese or a Malian community in France is to circumscribe it using a Western framework, whereas, for the people themselves, identity is multifaceted and has deeper roots than postcolonial realities. Therefore, the community described in this essay is by necessity transnational but also multiethnic. It is the community of Senegalese, Malian, and Mauritanian men and women who are Soninke, Tukulor, Fulani, Manding, and Wolof (the latter are found exclusively in Senegal) and who are linked by geography, history, traditions, cultures, brotherhoods, and languages. When referring to the transnational group, we will use the word "Sahelian" and ethnic or national designations when they are pertinent.

Sahelians have a long history of the practice of Sunni Islam of the Maliki rite. For the past one thousand years, native traders, rulers, clerics, and *jihadists* have spread the religion throughout West Africa. From the start, large numbers of West Africans espoused Sufism and many belong to brotherhoods. The oldest, the Qadiriyya of 'Abd al-Qadir al-Jilani (1077–1166), has lost significant ground in Mali and Senegal but is still dominant in Mauritania, especially among the Moors. However, most Mauritanian immigrants in France are Halpulaaren and Soninke who tend to belong to the Tijaniyya of Ahmad al-Tijani (1737–1815.) This *tariqa* is also widespread among Soninke, Halpulaaren, and Manding of Mali and Senegal. Nevertheless, some Senegalese, Soninke, Hapulaaren, and Manding, as well as large numbers of Wolof, belong to the *tariqa* that is the most dynamic in terms of associations, visibility, conversions, and wealth, namely the Muridiyya of Cheikh Amadou Bamba (Senegal, 1853–1927.) In Senegal, the Muridiyya and the Tijaniyya are about equally represented, while in Mali most people belong to the Tijaniyya and a minority to the Qadiriyya. In France, the Tijanis are predominant, followed by the Murids and the Qadiris.

French Demands and African Responses

The story of the Sahelian Muslims on French soil began more than eighty-five years ago. The first large group arrived in 1914. They were part of the "Black Force" of General Mangin: 170,000 young men sent to fight in the French army, many enrolled forcibly, with 134,000 battling in the trenches.[4] Some were "contributed" by the Muslim brotherhoods themselves. Cheikh Bamba, for example, sent young Murid men to France, as did other religious leaders.[5] Muslim soldiers were not the majority of the "Black Force," as the recruits came not only from Senegal, Mauritania, Sudan (Mali), Guinea, and Niger but also from Côte d'Ivoire, Upper Volta (Burkina Faso), and Dahomey (Benin) where Muslims were a minority. The soldiers from French West Africa were called, collectively and inaccurately, *Tirailleurs sénégalais* (Senegalese riflemen.)[6]

In an effort to please the religious leaders whose support was essential—the sultan of Turkey had asked the Muslims of West Africa to support Germany and engage in a holy war against France and its allies—accommodations were made for the Muslims' religious needs. "Mobile mosques" were sent from camp to camp, and imams were brought from Africa. In the military barracks of Fréjus, the Murids were given a space where they could meet and chant Cheikh Amadou Bamba's poems.[7] World War I marked the first time that large numbers of Muslims, including the Maghrebi soldiers, were present on French soil since Charles Martel had pushed back the Arabs at Poitiers in 732 C.E. After the war, during which

30,000 Africans were killed, several thousand former soldiers were living in France as sailors, domestics, factory workers, and students.[8] In 1926, Sahelian religious leaders were associated with the planning of the first mosque ever built in France since the eighth century.[9] Located in Paris and built in the Moroccan style, it was erected in honor of the Muslim soldiers of World War I.

When World War II erupted, once again, Muslim leaders came to the rescue. El Hadj Seydou Nourou Tall, a grandson of the *jihadist* El Hadj Omar, crisscrossed West Africa, exhorting the Muslims to join the army and help France's war effort. He was named *Grand Imam des troupes noires* (Great Imam of the black troops) in 1940.[10] Intellectuals and nationalists largely criticized his devotion to French interests. By June 1940, the date of the Armistice, 40,000 West Africans had been killed, wounded, or sent to prison camps. At war's end, 158,000 Africans had fought in France, and more than 5,000 had joined the Resistance.[11] In 1991, the city of Langeais resonated with the Muslim prayer to the dead when a street was renamed *Rue Addi Ba* in honor of the young Guinean Resister who co-founded the first *maquis* (guerilla base) in the Vosges, saved hundreds of lives, and served as a liaison between Resistance groups. Betting that the Gestapo would have difficulty deciphering his writings, Ba drew on his Quranic knowledge and jotted down the German positions in Arabic on his notepad as he biked his way between the free and the occupied zones to deliver news and plans to the *maquis.* When captured, twenty-nine-year-old Ba was horribly tortured, and when he refused to talk, was shot.[12]

As had been the case after World War I, the vast majority of the demobilized soldiers, Muslims and non-Muslims, went back home. Some, however, remained in France, working, like their predecessors, as stevedores, sailors, or laborers. Among the Muslims who chose to remain, some were educated in the French system and joined the ranks of professionals. There are no statistics on the subject, but it seems that most of these men married French women—there were no African women in France at the time—and did not pass on Islam to their children. The absence of mosques, of a structured community, of clerics and Quranic schools, added to the fact that their wives were Catholic or non-religious, are the reasons some give for the absence of an Islamic presence in the second generation. To the extent to which they practiced it at all, the Muslims lived their religion in private and did not form religious associations.

But the picture started to change in the 1960s. France was in the middle of an economic boom and needed more workers than were currently available. Recruiters were dispatched throughout Senegal, Mali, and Mauritania, and a 1960 multilateral agreement gave members of the Franco-African community full right to settle and work in France. For years, young men left their cities and villages and worked in France, usually for four or five years, before heading back home and sending a younger brother or nephew in their place. The strategy was for every man to have a chance to make money for himself and to help sustain the extended family. It was also part of a religious and historic pattern. For the Murids, emigrating emulates the exile or *hijra* of Cheikh Amadou Bamba who was deported to Gabon and Mauritania by the French colonial authorities. The *talibs* (disciples) must relive the pain of the *Shaykh* by going through their own exile.

Moreover, following the injunction of Serigne Bamba, they must learn what is useful in the ways of the Europeans. During their stay in the West, they must contribute financially to the development of the holy city of Touba and to the reinforcement of the brotherhood. Thus, while the French used the *Shaykh*'s exile as a tool to destroy the *muridiyya*, the self-imposed exile of the *murids* strengthens its power and influence. The Soninke, for their part, have been involved in trade for centuries, but the demise of the trans-Saharan and trans-Atlantic trades doomed their area, a commercial crossroads that was never agriculturally developed. Young men converted from traders to migrant laborers and went to the neighboring countries in search of work. The most adventurous left for Central Africa and Europe, to France in particular. With plenty of men eager to leave and with the rotation system, Sahelian families—who had been devastated by a persistent drought—thought they would be taken care of for a long time.

However, in 1974, a new policy brought an end to such hopes. France was no longer booming and did not need more laborers. No newcomers could enter legally, and the migrant workers who were already there had no choice, if they wanted to continue taking care of their families, but to stay.[13] The rotation strategy came to a halt. The government, however, authorized family reunification. Today, even though 70 percent of the men are bachelors or have not brought their families, the vast majority of the Sahelians live in familial units. The men who did marry have one or several wives, and the average woman has about six children. The community is now anchored and concentrated in one area: 70 percent of the Africans live in Ile-de-France (Paris, its suburbs, and satellite cities).

Besides a minority of students and professionals, many Sahelian immigrants are ex-farmers who come from the Senegal River Valley (an arid area that stretches between Senegal, Mali, and Mauritania) and from eastern Senegal; others are ex-farmers or petty traders from the "peanut belt" of Senegal, the *murid* stronghold. They share a traditional background that places a strong emphasis on religion and religious education and often regards the "French school" with suspicion. Many were enrolled in Quranic schools at home and can read and write in Arabic and in their language written with the Arabic alphabet, but are illiterate or barely literate in French.[14] This was already a serious handicap in their countries of origin where French is the official language, and in France it clearly impedes their chances of professional mobility. Following the laborers and traders, and to cater to their needs, some marabouts or clerics from well-known maraboutic families have also migrated to France. They serve as spiritual guides, moral authorities, advisors, and confidantes.

In the mid-1970s, another group of men, well versed in the language and religion of Islam, started to arrive. They were young Senegalese, fluent in Arabic, who had previously studied (mostly law, theology, and pedagogy) in the Universities of Tunisia, Morocco, Egypt, Syria, Libya, Saudi Arabia, Lebanon, and Kuwait, and wanted to perfect their French in Paris. They were a diverse lot. Some discarded religion and became involved in Marxist Leninist movements; others worked for a sort of "Islamic revival" in France, setting up religious classes for the Sahelian immigrants and their children and developing Islamic associations.

Organizations and Associations

The lives of the Sahelians revolve very much around associations, for three primary reasons: African societies are oriented toward the community; Islam in West Africa is predominantly based on brotherhoods; and a community structure was much needed by immigrants who came straight from villages and had no money, no urban skills, no (French) literacy and no knowledge of the host country. Sahelians have founded hundreds of associations; some are spiritual, others are secular and relate to development projects back home, and still others are sociocultural. The main Islamic associations were created in the early 1970s, and today number between fifty and seventy. The first to be formed, the *Association pour la Rénovation de l'Alliance Islamique* (ARAI- Association for the Revival of the Islamic Alliance) was begun by Senegalese students who came from the Arab world with the objective of "fighting against mutual ignorance by breaking boundaries," in particular those between Arabo-Berber and Sahelian immigrants.

The early 1970s were marked by numerous clashes, sometimes bloody, between Maghrebis and Sahelians living in workers' hostels. The Sahelians accused the Arabo-Berbers of racism and of treating them "like slaves." The students, who had an intimate knowledge of both worlds, tried to mend relations on the basis of Islamic confraternity. ARAI members, who are Senegalese, Malians, Moroccans, Algerians, Comorians, and Mauritanians, organize religious talks and prayers and give biweekly classes in Arabic, Qur'an, hadith, Islamic history and law to boys and girls from ages seven to sixteen, and to adults. The association has sent several dozen students to Syria and Pakistan to complete their studies.[15]

Another multiethnic, multinational, and transbrotherhood movement that has recruited in the Sahelian community is the Jamaat Tabligh, founded in India in the 1920s. In the late 1960s, the Jamaat, known in France under the name *Foi et Pratique* (Faith and Practice), started to tour the hostels, pushing the Muslims to demand prayer rooms in their residences and workplaces. Most of its Sahelian members are Soninke.[16] Some have established their own mosque in Paris, and they actively proselytize throughout the country, as well as in other European countries. Contrary to the Jamaat and to ARAI, many Sahelian Muslim associations are created around a particular ethnicity or a *tariqa*. In 1990, for example, former Quranic students of Soninke origin founded the *Association pour la coopération islamique de la communauté africaine* (ACICA-Association for the Islamic Cooperation of the African Community). For the most part, they are employed in menial jobs, but on weekends they turn into teachers and give classes to several hundred students in the eastern suburbs of Paris. They teach Arabic, Qur'an, and the foundations of Islam to children and teenagers and theology, grammar, and Islamic law to adults.[17] Another ethno/religious association is the *Kawral Juulbe*, recruiting specifically Fulani Muslims, whatever their country of origin.

Among the associations organized around a *tariqa*, the Muridiyya is probably the most vigorous, not only in Senegal, but also in France, Italy, Spain, and the United States, wherever its adepts have settled.[18] In 1977, they founded the *Association des étudiants et stagiaires mourides en Europe* (Association of Murid Students and Trainees in Europe) to propagate Cheikh Bamba's ideas and to bring together Murid students, laborers, and peddlers. It became the *Mouvement islamique des mourides en Europe* (MIME-Murid Islamic Movement in Europe) in 1983. Its members are Senegalese as well as converts from diverse nationalities, including many from the French Caribbean islands of Martinique and Guadeloupe. Murid men and women are also organized in a multitude of *dahira*, or circles of study and practice around a spiritual guide. They usually meet twice a week to exchange news, recite the Qur'an, pray, and chant Cheikh Bamba's poems. Serigne Mourtada Mbacké, the last surviving son of Cheikh Bamba—who spends most of his time visiting Murid communities throughout the world—has asked them to organize the *Fédération des mourides de France* (Federation of Murids in France) to coordinate the activities of the numerous Murid groups, to collect *zakat*, and to build a Murid community center.

In order to strengthen the African Islamic associations, the *Fédération des associations islamiques d'Afrique, des Comores et des Antilles* (FAIACA-Federation of the Islamic Associations of Africa, Comores and the Antilles) was founded in 1989. The common denominator of its members seems primarily to be their African origin. The predominance of Maghrebi Muslims, with their own Islamic cultures, politico-religious agenda, and, according to some, condescension for the sub-Saharans, led to the federation of Muslims of African descent.

Sahelians have numerous layers of identity, including ethnicity, caste, nationality, brotherhood, continent, and race, and their religious associations reflect all of them. This kind of layered identity is typical of the larger Muslim community in France. The ethnonational dimension of the more than two thousand officially registered Islamic associations is both their main characteristic and a primary source of weakness. These associations are structured along quite rigid national and ethnic lines, many also incorporating a political dimension that follows political divisions in the country of origin. In addition, they often reflect political and ethnic antagonisms between countries. This has resulted in an impasse in the dialogue with local and national French authorities. While the authorities want one interlocutor on religious matters (especially as they pertain to the public sphere: mosques,[19] Quranic schools, Muslim areas in the cemeteries, *halal* shops, public butchering of sheep, etc.), they are confronted with a multitude of ethno-politico-religious groups that are in fierce competition. It is significant that since 1993, because of those dissensions, no Muslim representatives have been invited to the annual presidential New Year's celebration. The Muslim "community" has not been able to find a minimum common denominator, but, on the contrary, continues to exacerbate the problem by emphasizing particularities over commonalities.[20] While the Sahelian associations do not fight one another, they nevertheless cultivate differences that prevent them from getting better representation.

Sahelian secular associations, it seems, have been more successful in uniting peoples and getting things done. They number several hundreds and serve as links to the regions or countries of origin. More than any other immigrant community in France, the Sahelians have very close ties to their home. Following African social traditions, they feel it is imperative to contribute to the well-being of their families and communities, and they send the equivalent of about two months' salary to their families every year.[21] In addition to these personal remittances, they give weekly or monthly dues to their religious, local, and national associations, leaving a significant mark on the development of their villages or cities (including holy cities).

When the village associations were born in the hostels in the 1960s, their first project was invariably the building of a mosque. It was a way of rallying everyone, of giving legitimacy to young men who, as such, had little weight in the village decision-making process, and of attracting divine blessings for the rest of the communal endeavors. Today, the immigrants are involved in their home countries in irrigation schemes, primary care centers, maternity wards, pharmacies, collective fields, solar energy projects, communication centers (phone, fax, rural radios, Internet), and food entrepôts. Given the multiplicity of projects, and the redundancy of some within a few square miles, the Sahelians have often federated their associations to cover a district or a region. The contributions of the immigrants and the work of the local populations have revitalized several areas, notably in the Senegal River Valley. As many men have left their spouse(s) and children home, these development projects are not only helping the community at large, but also their extended and nuclear families.

Sahelian Women, Family, and Cultural Practices

In the West, Sahelian women have been actively involved in associations of their own that reflect their particular type of socialization in the host country.[22] Men are primarily integrated through work; they are, above all, immigrant *workers*. The women's socialization, on the other hand, has wider ramifications within French society and the public sphere. Their coming to France means that their husband has moved from a self-contained, often geographically isolated, workers' hostel to an apartment. This entails an interaction with neighbors, neighborhood, stores, schools, and social and medical services that has significant repercussions, internally and externally. For the women, the basic unit is no longer the extended family, the village, or even the reconstructed village of the hostel, but the nuclear family. The freedom of movement they enjoyed in the village, where everyone is either related to or knows everyone else, is sometimes restricted by the husband; outside of the door lies an alien world he knows will not "keep an eye" on the women as relatives and neighbors would do back home.[23] His authority, which can no longer be questioned by neighbors, his own parents, the women's relatives, or elders, at times and in some families, becomes greater.

Outside the family, women enter into a variety of relations with French society, in areas that are the most susceptible to creating social friction, such as housing and children. Sahelian women are the most visible "alien presence" in the public space. Unlike the men and members of other immigrant groups, many wear their traditional clothes, which does not always sit well with the French, who generally do not like people to exhibit their cultural or religious differences.[24] In addition, they are often pregnant with two or three children in tow and one tied to their backs, presenting an image that speaks to the French of social and economic irresponsibility, and of "foreign invasion." It is their numerous children, their acceptance of polygamy, and their cuisine (one hopes), that President Chirac derided in his infamous 1991 lambaste of the Africans' noise, matrimonial arrangements, and odors.

Paradoxically, at the same time that the women are perceived by public opinion as the very symbol of why Sahelians cannot and do not want to be integrated in French society, they are the agents of change and acculturation within their families and communities. Through taking the children to school, shopping, and going to the health center, they socialize with other women, sometimes from the same ethnic group but not necessarily from the same area, region, or country. Many Sahelian women are involved in national female associations or village groups, but they are also engaged in associations of women from different African countries, varied social classes, and diverse religions, which work at the neighborhood and city levels. Indeed, African women are the only immigrants who have created multinational, multiethnic, and multireligious associations that, today, number in the hundreds.[25] Very savvy, they finance their activities with dues, sales of crafts and cultural artifacts, and funds from public, private, local, national, religious, and international donors.

As African women in general and Sahelian women in particular try to define a new place between modernity and tradition, ethnic and French cultures, Islam and secularism, they focus their initiatives on practical matters at the local level: housing, children's education, unemployment, health (including the fight against excision), adult literacy classes, professional training, citizenship, relations with the administration, family planning, family counseling, and improvement of the African woman's image in public opinion. Whereas men are involved in Islamic and ethno-cultural associations that maintain a *status quo*, which generally benefits them, and in economic development back home that brings them enhanced status, women try to improve their life in the host country through involvement in civic activities. In so doing, they introduce change within the household and the community. This sometimes creates tensions with husbands whose authority has been reinforced by the women's isolation from their families. But the women's support, solidarity, and mutual-aid networks and associations function also at that level: they mitigate the absence of the extended family—which in Africa is commonly an intermediary and a referee in case of conflict—by acting as advisors and mediators.

Despite their role in acculturation, the French public perceives Sahelian women as symbols of obscurantism and "unintegrability" mostly because of polygamy and excision, which public opinion links to Islam. They are seen not only as victims of a "retrograde and sexist religion" that is branded as a major obstacle to social integration or insertion, but as perpetrators of these two practices that are deemed particularly abhorrent. Senegal, Mali, and Mauritania, like most Muslim countries, authorize polygamy and their citizens have brought this tradition to France, where it is illegal.[26] As it is difficult to assess exact numbers of Muslims in the country, so estimates on polygamous families vary greatly. Some mention fewer than 10,000, while others assume up to 21, 000.[27] Charles Pasqua, the former anti-immigration Minister of the Interior, stated that in the mid-1990s, 200,000 African immigrants lived in polygamy, which means that almost all did.[28] But according to the 1990 census, there were only 33,000 African families in France, of which 4,500 were headed by one parent. Empirical observations and some research suggest that 25 percent of the Sahelian families involve more than one wife.[29]

What is certain, though, is that emigration to the West has exacerbated the problems that polygamy often generates. Because apartments in France generally are designed for two parents and a maximum of four children, polygamy has engendered extremely crowded situations with one man, two or three women, and up to eighteen children sharing, at the most, 800 square feet. In the worst cases, the husband and the wife whose "turn" it is sleep in one bed, while a screen is put in the same room to ensure privacy from the other wife and the younger children.[30] Lack of privacy—seldom an issue in Africa where women have separate lodgings—often provokes tensions, jealousy, or hate. Women may race to have more children than the other wives in order to remain in the husband's good graces and, ultimately, in France. These facts have been largely reported (and exaggerated) by the media and have fueled French anger at the men who impose what the public feels are degrading conditions on their families, at the women who accept and perpetuate them, and at the culture and the religion that permit them.[31]

The French official position on polygamy is ambiguous. It is forbidden to the French and punishable by a fine and a jail term of up to three years. However, a 1986 text stipulates that for foreigners whose national law authorizes multiple marriages, "the admission of a second wife is contingent upon adequate resources and housing conditions."[32] Such resources and conditions rarely pertain, and some men declare that their new wife is their daughter or a resident brother's wife so that she can immigrate; or the new wives come with a tourist visa and fall into illegality three months later. Notwithstanding the usually dire circumstances of co-wives in the West, there is no shortage of candidates. Emigrants are a good catch, and young women are generally eager to marry them, even if they come in third or fourth. For those who are already there, arrangements can be fairly easy: at least two consulates (Morocco and Mali) celebrate polygamous marriages, and French authorities have no choice but to accept these unions, which take place in France but technically on foreign soil. However, laws that pertain to social benefits do not recognize polygamy. A woman who has immigrated legally and holds a job automatically gets medical coverage, but generally only if she is the first wife. The husband covers a wife who is legally in France but does not work, but again coverage usually applies only to the first wife. Therefore, second, third, and fourth wives often use the identity of the first one to circumvent regulations—"one" woman may thus give birth twice a year, for free, in the same hospital—which only exacerbates the image of the freeloading immigrant.

Another highly charged issue is the *allocations familiales,* benefits given to every family, regardless of income, with at least two children. Men are supposed to give each wife a pro rata of the monies according to the number of her children. African women's groups have been asking, for years, that the benefits be given directly to the mothers to diffuse tensions about fair distribution and to prevent men from keeping the money, which some have been known to use as a dowry for another wife. Some associations go even further, urging the French authorities to forbid polygamy, send the co-wives back home, and strip the polygamists of their legal resident status and of French nationality when relevant.[33]

Excision is used as another symbol of the "otherness" of African Muslims, even though it is a cultural tradition not linked to Islam.[34] The Tukulor, the Fulani, the Soninke, and the Bambara/Manding/Malinke practice it, but it is unknown in Wolof culture, and Senegal has outlawed it. In France, the immigrants sometimes tout excision—as well as polygamy—as tangible proof of their respect for their own values in a society, which, they fear, wants them not only to integrate but to assimilate. Excision is illegal in France and is vigorously denounced by some African women's associations. Starting in 1984, several trials have resulted in probation for the *exciseuses.* However, in 1999, for the first time, a woman was condemned to eight years in prison for having excised at least forty-eight young girls—several hundreds according to the prosecution—and their twenty-six mothers received between two- and five-year probation sentences.[35] The *exciseuse* had already received probation in 1984 and the jury, by giving her more time than the prosecution had requested, wanted to send a firm message. The message was also for Mariatou, the young Malian law student who had sued the woman (who had excised her when she was eight) as well as her own mother when they were about to have one of her younger sisters undergo the operation. Mariatou came to represent the kind of African youth that France wants and for whom it can take credit: a girl from an illiterate, poor, traditional, Muslim family, elevating herself through "republican and secular" school, absorbing modern values, shaking off obscurantism, and having the courage to risk rejection by family and community. Mariatou became a symbol of successful integration, some have even called it "Frenchization." But for many African youngsters, the place of ethnoreligious values and the role of the family and school in the process of acculturation are more ambiguous.

Trajectories of Sahelian Youth

More than 30 percent of the Sahelians in France are under the age of fifteen, and the new census should find a significant increase in their numbers. Studies have shown that they often identify their main problem as a tug-of-war between family traditions and French values, the latter instilled primarily at school.[36] Parents customarily demand complete obedience and devotion to the family and community, while school develops individualism, autonomy, personal initiatives, and a critical sense. Torn between conflicting views of education, many children remain passive in school and take from one to three years longer than normal to graduate. Others (mostly boys) act out, because they see school as a space where they can exercise freedom. In the context of immigration, a father becomes the only authoritative figure, whereas in the African context, uncles share this responsibility. Unprepared to manage a nuclear family, men often demonstrate a tendency to rigidify the rules. Aware both of their low status in society and of their lack of prestige in the household, especially among the children due to such factors as poverty, unemployment, or menial jobs, and irresponsible polygamy, they tend to assert their power at home.

Boys who have difficulty accepting this type of authoritarianism leave school as soon as they can in order to earn money and be independent.[37] Parents know that school is necessary to get a good job, but their illiteracy in French and their ignorance of the educational system often prevent them from being actively supportive and from helping with homework. In addition, in polygamous families, lack of privacy and sometimes open conflicts between co-wives that extend to the children, are not conducive to good performances at school. On the whole, formal education has not yet been, for Sahelian children, the elevating factor it is for other groups. The youngsters from Central Africa, for example, have a much higher rate of success. Some observers attribute this difference to religion: Central Africans are Christians and would place a high value on a type of education that is not fundamentally different from theirs; Muslims used to Quranic schooling, where religious values are instilled and where students learn by rote and are expected to be docile, would see the French secular school as a place antagonistic to traditional values and religion. However, the main difference between Sahelians and Central Africans is that the latter's parents were mostly urban before they came to France, they have a much higher educational level, and often hold white-collar and professional jobs.

Sahelian girls' trajectories present some specific traits. Their first years of schooling are often as chaotic as the boys', but they tend to stay longer in school. Contrary to the boys, their emancipation from family can only be achieved through marriage, usually arranged, as is prevalent in the Islamic world. That perspective often leads them to remain in school as long as they can. For cultural and religious reasons, endogamy is strongly favored by Sahelian parents, and certain groups (French, Christians) are commonly regarded as unacceptable. Sahelian Islam is generally tolerant, practices are frequently adapted to local situations, women do not wear veils, and are free to go about, work in any capacity, and travel. But, especially among rural people, as far as girls' marriages are concerned, social customs, added to religious proscriptions, can be constraining. Young men are less restricted because Islam allows them to marry outside of their faith, for example, but girls may not. Religion is used by the parents as the ultimate weapon in favor of endogamy that they view as essential to the perpetuation of the family, the community, the culture, and the religion. The leaders of the women's associations commonly share these views and almost never intervene when girls come to them with problems relating to forced or arranged marriages.[38] A measure of change is nevertheless happening, one that takes into account the new reality of girls growing up seeing another matrimonial model. Forced marriages with men chosen by the parents, sometimes even before the girl was born, are decreasing and have given way to arranged marriages that take place at a later age, with someone selected by the parents but known to and accepted by the girl. With education and diplomas that offer better job opportunities, girls are sometimes in a position to negotiate some degree of autonomy and more say in their future marriage arrangements. According to one of the few in-depth studies of Sahelian girls, "School socialization and professional insertion free them from some constraints and give them, progressively, a position of power within the family. [Girls] appear to be the vectors of acculturation and they introduce innovations and adaptations that were not accessible to their parents."[39] In so doing, they clearly follow in their mothers' footsteps.

Generally, Sahelian youth, contrary to the Central Africans—who sometimes ignore their parents' ethnic background, often do not speak their language, and have seldom been "home"—are close to their roots. They usually have a good knowledge of their parents' ethnic culture, speak their language, participate in community events, and have gone to their country of origin. Showing the continued resonance of traditional models of identity, young Sahelians often define themselves as member of an ethnic group first, a national group second, and as Muslims third, rejecting constructions such as Afro-French or black French. Some belong to ethnic and Islamic associations and take classes in their native language and culture, as well as in Arabic and religion. Even for those who tend to rebel against parental authority, Islam is not an area of contention, and it represents a large part of the values that parents transmit to their children. However, for a growing number of youth, identification with Islam does not mean practice; and the emergence of a secularized Islam, one in which people have an individualized rapport with the religious tradition, is visible among the younger generations. In fact, according to researchers, within a few years, "the profile of the young Africans . . . is going to homogenize, at the level of identity and way of life, and come close to the profile of the young French of working class background."[40] Young Sahelians would thus increasingly affirm an identity based not on ethnicity, national origin, or religion—the latter present, but lived at the intimate level—but on youth culture and social class, and become a significant component of the mixed (French, Maghrebi, African, Caribbean, Asian) population and culture that are developing in the French working class.

Sahelian Muslims have been part of the French landscape for over forty years. Unlike the Maghrebis who, because of the Algerian independence war and the political turmoil of the 1990s, as well as the fear of Islamic fundamentalism and terrorism, have a rather negative image, Africans have enjoyed a positive—if quite paternalistic—image. However, as they invest the public space, they increasingly have to confront hostility, as immigrants, as Africans, and as Muslims. For the adults, participation in French social, economic, and civic life does not mean shedding ethnic, cultural, and religious specificity and group affiliation. But this is a concept to which the French are profoundly hostile, because France does not "integrate" groups, only individuals. There is no place for minorities in Republican, Jacobin France. Therefore, the challenge for the Sahelians, and the Muslims in general, is to transcend ethnonational affiliation to become "French Muslims," and no longer the representatives of (foreign) national interests, ethnic groups or races; to speak, as much as possible, in a single voice on religious matters, and develop an "Islam of France" as opposed to an "Islam in France"; and to reach out to the Christians and the nonreligious. Sahelians, perhaps more than other Muslims, are going in that direction. Their native countries do not intervene in the religious debate in France, directly or through the Ministry of Foreign Affairs, by appointing imams, financing mosques, and contesting who may do the ritual butchering. The fact that most Africans in France are not Muslims prevents any association of the religion with a particular race or ethnic group. In addition, West African Islam does not exhibit the "muezzin syndrome," as confrontational Islam is referred to in France; and the reality of migration will probably change its most problematic practices. Given the lack of appeal of polygamy *à la française*, for example, it is very doubtful that young people will keep up the tradition. Some groups, especially the Murids, are quite open to the larger society and invite non-Muslims to their celebrations and prayer meetings. The presence of mosques, Islamic associations, Quranic schools, and the development of religious classes, show that the community is strongly committed to seeing the new generations grow up as Muslims, contrary to the children of veterans who settled in the 1950s. But what kind of Muslims? There is no model, so far, and these generations will have to invent new identities as they negotiate between their ascendants' ethnicity, national origin, sense of hegemony of the community, and of all-encompassing religion on the one hand, and French rejection of the minority concept, insistence on individualism, and deep-seated secularism on the other. They will also have to become visible to, and make their voice better heard by, the rest of the Muslim community as it faces the challenge of creating a distinctive French Islamic culture.

Notes

1. Haut Conseil à l'intégration, *L'intégration à la française* (Paris: Robert Laffont, 1993), 99.
2. C. Barthélemy, et al. *Les dossiers du Secrétariat pour les relations avec l'islam* I (March 1996): 26–30.

3. See special issue *Hommes & Migrations* 1215, September–October 1998.

4. Myron Echenberg, *Colonial Conscripts: The Tirailleurs Sénégalais in French West Africa, 1857-1960* (Portsmouth: Heineman, 1991), 25.

5. Christian Coulon, *Le marabout et le prince: Islam et pouvoir au Sénégal* (Paris: Pedone, 1981), 177.

6. Philippe Dewitte, "Des tirailleurs aux sans-papiers: la République oublieuse," *Hommes & Migrations* 1221 (September–October 1999): 6–11.

7. Moustapha Diop, "Esquisse historique sur l'islam des Ouest-africains en Ile-de-France," *Sociétés africaines et diaspora* 4 (December 1996): 136.

8. Philippe Dewitte, *Les Mouvements nègres en France 1919-1939* (Paris: L'Harmattan, 1985), 26.

9. There were mosques in Narbonne in the South of France during the eighth century.

10. Maurice Rives, "L'apport de l'Afrique Noire et de Madagascar pendant la Seconde Guerre Mondiale," *Frères d'armes* 188 (1995): 18–39.

11. Maurice Rives and Robert Dietrich, *Héros méconnus 1914–1918 1939–1945* (Paris: Frères d'armes, 1993).

12. Ibid., 289–91. Philippe Sprang, "Addi Ba, résistant, noir et musulman," *L'Evènement du Jeudi* 12–18 (November 1992): 96–97.

13. They lost their status if they remained outside France for more than three months.

14. On the link between Quranic schools and migration, see Sylviane Diouf, "Islam, mendicité et migration au Sénégal," *Hommes & Migrations* 1186 (April 1995): 37–40; and "Senegal Upgrades its Koranic Schools," *UNICEF Features*, (April 1995).

15. Moustapha Diop, "Immigration et religion: les musulmans négro-africains en France," *Migrations Société* I (October–December 1989): 54–56.

16. Moustapha Diop, "Structuration d'un réseau: La Jamaat Tabligh," *Revue Européenne des Migrations Internationales* X, no. I (1994): 145–155.

17. Moustapha Diop, "Le Mouvement islamique africain en Ile-de-France," *Migrations Société*, 8, no. 4 (March–April 1996): 71.

18. For the Murids in the U.S. and Europe, see Sylviane Diouf, "Senegalese in New York: A Model Minority?" *Black Renaissance* I, no. 2 (1997): 92–115; Ottavia Schmidt di Friedberg and Reynald Blion, "Du Sénégal à New York, quel avenir pour la confrérie mouride?" *Hommes & Migrations* 1224 (March–April 2000): 36–45; Sophie Bava, "Reconversions et nouveaux mondes commerciaux des mourides à Marseille," *Hommes & Migrations* 1224 (March–April 2000): 46–55.

19. There are about a dozen large mosques in France that can accommodate a thousand people, thirty to forty can receive five hundred believers, and about a thousand "prayer rooms" are disseminated throughout the country.

20. Jocelyne Cesari "De l'islam en France à l'islam de France," *Immigration et Intégration: L'état des savoirs*, ed. Philippe Dewitte (Paris: La Découverte, 1999), 222–231. Moustapha Diop,"Negotiating Religious Differences: The Opinions and Attitudes of Islamic Associations in France," *The Politics of Multiculturalism in the New Europe: Racism, Identity and Community*, ed. Tariq Modood and Pnina Werbner, (London: Zed Books Ltd., 1999), 117–118.

21. See special issue, "Migrants acteurs du développement," *Hommes & Migrations* 1165 (May 1993). Reynald Blion and Véronique Verriere, "Epargne des migrants et outils financiers adaptés: Pratiques des immigrés maliens et sénégalais résidant en France," *Migrations Etudes* 82 (September–October 1998): I–16.

22. There were 73,000 sub-Saharan African women in France in 1990. According to the 1990 census, 52 per cent were under 25 and 33 per cent between 25 and 34.

23. Mahamet Timera, "Identité, langue et religion dans l'immigration soninké en France," *Journal des anthropologues* 59 (winter 1995): 73–76.

24. Maghrebi women's headscarves are often perceived as a refusal to respect France's secularism and as a provocation. The "Headscarves Affair" (girls who insist on wearing them in school and are expelled) is still creating widespread tensions.

25. Catherine Quiminal, Babacar Diouf, Babacar Fall, Mahamet Timera, "Mobilisation associative et dynamiques d'intégration des femmes d'Afrique subsaharienne en France," *Migrations Etudes,* 61 (October–December 1995): 1–12. See also Albert Nicollet, *Femmes d'Afrique noire en France* (Paris: L'Harmattan, 1992); Guy Boudimbou, *Habitat et mode de vie des Africains en France* (Paris: L'Harmattan, 1992).

26. There has been some discussion in Senegal about abolishing polygamy, but it has elicited a strong reaction from religious bodies.

27. Isabelle Gillette, *La polygamie en France et le rôle des femmes* (Paris: Edition G.A.M.S., 1993), 7.

28. Quoted by Christian Jelen, "Jeunes Africains: L'inquiétante dérive des enfants perdus," *Le Point* 1125 (April 9, 1994): 44–47.

29. Gillette, 114.

30. Philippe Dewitte, interview of Lydie Dooh-Bunya, "La condition des femmes noires en France," *Hommes & Migrations* 1131 (April 1990): 43–48.

31. Christian Jelen, "La polygamie en France," *Le Point* 1098, October 2, 1993, 42–51.

32. *Actualités Migrations* 343 (September 23, 1990): 16.

33. Edwige Rude-Antoine, "Trajectoires familiales, transformations des rôles et des statuts," in *Immigration et Intégration l'etat des saviours,* ed. Philippe Dewitte (Paris: Editions La Découverte, 1999), 200.

34. Isabelle Gillette, *L'excision et sa présence en France* (Paris: GAMS 1993.)

35. The verdict was widely denounced in Mali as too harsh. African women associations and the FAIACA (Federation of Islamic Associations of Comores, Africa, and the Antilles) ask for education programs as well as repression.

36. Rude-Antoine, *Trajectoires,* 201–203.

37. Jacques Barou, "Familles, enfants et scolarité chez les Africains immigrés en France," *Migrants-formation* 91 (December 1992): 12–23; Catherine Quiminal, "Qui sont ces 'jeunes Africains noirs?" *Migrants-formation* 91 (December 1992): 113–120.

38. *Migrations Etudes* 61, 1–12.

39. Catherine Quiminal, Mahamet Timera, Babacar Fall, Hamedy Diarra, "Les jeunes filles d'origine africaine en France: Parcours scolaires, accès au travail et destin social," *Migrations Etudes* 78 (December 1997): 1–10.

40. François Rigaldiès and Jacques Barou, "Modes de vie et intégration des enfants et adolescents issus de familles africaines sub-sahariennes," *Migrations Etudes* 88 (June 1999): 1–8. See also Michèle Tribalat, *Faire France: une enquête sur les immigrés et leurs enfants* (Paris: La Découverte, 1995); Christian Poiret, *Familles africaines en France* (Paris: CIEMI/L'Harmattan, 1996).

The Northern Way: Muslim Communities in Norway 9

SAPHINAZ-AMAL NAGUIB

> *Même si tu revenais, Ulysse . . . tu serais toujours l'histoire du départ. . . .*
> (Adonis, Terre sans retour)
> [Even if you were to come back, Ulysses . . . you would always have the history of leaving. . . .]

Introduction

THE KINGDOM OF NORWAY[1] has a total population of 4.4 million inhabitants, most of whom are members of the State Lutheran Church. Of the remaining 12 percent, around 60,000 are Muslims.[2] Except for an estimated four hundred "indigenous" Norwegians who have converted to Islam,[3] Muslims in Norway represent different nationalities and ethnic groups. They came to Norway understanding their identity to be as nationals of a given country rather than as Muslims. The reasons for immigration are many, the most common being labor migration and political and humanitarian asylum. The categories according to country of origin of persons who were registered as Muslims in 1998 is as follows (the numbers are approximate):[4] Pakistanis (21,000), mostly from the Punjab, form the predominant group, whose numbers increased as a result of chain migration, followed by Bosnians (12,000), Turks (9,000), and Iranians (9,000). In addition, there are Moroccans, who are mostly Berbers (4,800), Somalis (5,800), Iraqis (4,200), Lebanese (1,300), Palestinians, and other Asians (2,500), and Muslims from Algeria, Egypt and sub-Saharan African countries (2,500). No official figures for Albanians from Kosovo are available.

This chapter concentrates on Muslims of foreign origin who live in urban areas, in particular the capital, Oslo, and its surrounding districts, where the biggest agglomeration of Muslims is to be found. It focuses on Muslims from rural backgrounds in developing countries who came to Norway as a result of chain migration. In describing an expanding religious group and investigating the ways in which they have settled, adapted, integrated, and organized, I will provide some reflections on the flexible nature of roots and on processes leading to the formation of contemporary diasporas. My aim is not to give a detailed survey of this heterogeneous group. Rather, it is to contribute a few theoretical perspectives and some general considerations to the study of what could be described as the "ethnicization" of religion and to discuss its significance for the notion of citizenship among Norwegian Muslims. In order to allow for the multiplicity of Muslim voices and for their different articulations of the meaning of space and moments of being, I draw upon the concept of polyphony and address issues pertaining to the temporalities of cultural and religious memory, gender, and education.[5]

Spaces of Acculturation

Norway became an independent state in 1905. Until then, it had first been part of the kingdom of Denmark and Norway (1397–1814), then of the kingdom of Sweden and Norway (1814–1905). It has no colonial past. While Norway itself enjoys a long history as a seafaring country and was an important source of emigration to America at the turn of the nineteenth century and during the first decades of the twentieth, there has been little immigration into the country. Those who did come were generally from the neighboring countries of Scandinavia and northern Europe. The Same (Laps) in the north of the country constitute the autochthonous ethnic minority of Norway.

The more or less organized immigration of groups of Muslims from developing countries in Asia and Africa to Norway began at the end of the 1960s. The pattern is quite similar to that of other Scandinavian and European countries. Immigration was due primarily to the need for cheap industrial labor and was very much based on chain migration. In 1975 the Norwegian government decreed a stop to immigration, but did allow for family reunification. This entailed a shift of civil status among immigrants from single men to families. Labor migrants became resident immigrants and, after a period of seven years, many acquired Norwegian citizenship.

At present, it is possible to distinguish three generations of Muslims in Norway. The first generation consists of persons who came to the country as adults. They were born abroad of parents who were not Norwegian citizens. The second generation are those born in Norway of parents who were born abroad. The third generation is represented by individuals born in Norway who have at least one Norwegian parent. With the arrival of women, children, and sometimes parents, issues related to housing, education, and employment had to be faced. Finding work is a problem shared by many immigrants, not only Muslims. To treat such a complex question in detail would go beyond the limits of the present essay.

Immigration to Norway has entailed adaptation to a different way of life. The encounter with Scandinavian urban environments, a sophisticated social-democratic ideology and a welfare society of mainly secular character has compelled immigrants to reassess many of their own values and ideals in order to be able to accommodate them to their new situation. Choice of residence normally has been restricted by socioeconomic factors. Average Muslim immigrant families from rural backgrounds had to adjust to living in individual flats in apartment buildings. These are quite different in design from the living quarters they were used to. For example, flats do not adapt to gender segregation and offer no women's quarters. Kitchens are often situated beside the entrance door, while the living rooms are further inside. Bedrooms and bathrooms are not set according to a standardized order and might either be clustered at the entrance or at the back of the flat, or located in different parts of the apartment. In addition to the unfamiliar physical structures of the flats, immigrants have had to comply with "strange" sets of regulations about acceptable behavior for residents and how the apartments were to be maintained.

In the city of Oslo, immigrants from non-Western countries tend to cluster in and around an area where housing is relatively cheaper than in other parts of the city. This section of town is commonly known as *Oslo østkant*, that is, "east-end" Oslo. It is situated on the east bank of the river Aker where factories were built during the last century. Consequently, the area was mainly inhabited by factory workers and families with low incomes, many of whom were originally migrants who had left their provinces and come to the capital in search of employment. This pattern seems to have continued, and it is on the east side of Oslo that many first-generation foreign labor migrants have settled. The heart of *Oslo østkant* has often been considered a space of exclusion where the marginalized or "threshold people" live. In my opinion, the east side of Oslo should instead be viewed as a "space of adaptation," or more exactly of "transposition."

Transposition, meaning change while moving from one context to another, involves displacement in time and space. In the case of immigrants it is often tied to flexibility and to a sense of enterprise. Once families are better settled and their social and economic situation improves, they usually move to newer and more comfortable quarters in other districts of the city and its suburbs. The districts of east-end Oslo are neither ghettos nor genuine ethnic neighborhoods, but are quite mixed. As such, they allow for both formal and informal inter- and intra-cultural contacts that take place in living quarters, schools, clinics, shops, etc. The establishment of communities with a visible foreign background in east-end Oslo has resulted in noticeable cultural changes in the locality. East-end Oslo is now the "exotic" part of the city with most of the implications of the word. It is on the eastside of Oslo that a large number of Muslim communities live. It is also here that we find a concentration of mosques and Islamic centers.

Schooling is free in Norway. In addition to public schools, there are a few private educational institutions. These are either international schools that follow a foreign curriculum (French, German, American-British) and do not receive allocations from the state, or schools that are based on religious and philosophical principles. The latter follow the Norwegian curriculum and receive state grants, as for example the Kristelig Gymnas (Protestant), St. Sunniva (Catholic), or Montessori schools, and schools applying the anthroposophic system of Rudolph Steiner. The great majority of Muslim immigrants send their children to public schools in their district. Children who do not have Norwegian as their mother tongue are offered courses in their own home language (*morsmål*). The initial reason for such teaching was the belief that the knowledge of their mother tongue and original culture would help these children to learn Norwegian. In turn, it would lead to their smooth acculturation and integration into Norwegian society. Newer research, however, indicates that a significant number of young people of immigrant origin are proficient in neither language and are constantly "drawn between two cultures." This, according to recent studies, seems to be one of the main causes for poor achievement at school and for a relatively high percentage of unemployment among second-generation Norwegians. But these assertions are subject to dispute among specialists. The children of immigrants who do go on with higher education tend to choose studies that will lead to such professions as medicine, dentistry, biology, data technology, engineering, and nursing. Few choose the humanities or social sciences.

Among the controversies between school authorities and Muslim communities in Norway, those concerning mixed physical training and swimming (for girls), sex education lessons, participation in school trips, and the compulsory teaching of Christianity and life philosophy have been the subject of heated debates in the media.[6] Tensions over these issues, however, have never reached the dramatic dimensions of those related to the Islamic *foulard* (headscarf) in France. Generally speaking, contacts between homes and schools have been inadequate. Parents, especially mothers, remain cut off from their children's schooling. They show little interest in being involved and do not attend parent's meetings, explaining that they do not understand the language. Children, especially girls, are conspicuously absent from after-school activities, such as playing in the school band or participating on sports teams. However, Muslim girls seem to compensate for the restrictions imposed by their families by obtaining better school results than the boys of their communities. The request to establish a privately funded Islamic school in Oslo was rejected in 1995, primarily on the grounds that such a school would lead to the further isolation of Muslim children, especially girls, from the rest of society. Since then, no permission to start any other school based on religious denomination has been granted.[7] There are, however, a few Islamic pre-schools and youth clubs. These are often run by Norwegian converts who take it upon themselves to act as mediators between Muslim groups and the Norwegian authorities and society.

Carving an Islamic Space

The need to establish distinctive spaces where members of the various Muslim communities and their children can socialize, receive proper religious teaching, pray, and discuss current matters led to the formation of Muslim congregations and associations. To understand the complexities of this situation, it is important to know something about religious and philosophical societies in Norway.

Norway has an official Lutheran Church. It is worth noting that until 1851 Jews were forbidden to enter the kingdom and that, until 1957, Catholics and other Christian minorities (Baptists, Pentecostals, and members of various free churches) could not be appointed to higher positions in the state administration. While Catholics were, and still are, in the majority among Norwegian intellectuals, members of various minority Protestant sects generally have been found among the lower social classes.

The Norwegian state gives financial grants to the Lutheran church and also to other registered religious and philosophical societies. The subsidies are set in relation to the number of members. At the end of the year, in order to continue receiving the subsidies from the state, each group presents its updated lists of members, protocols of meetings, and books of accounts to the authorities. According to the statistics from January 1998, Muslims constituted the fourth largest religious/philosophical group in Norway, with 40,800 members spread among sixty different congregations.[8] They were preceded in number by the State Church, the Humanists (*Human-etisk forbund*) (with 69,900 members) and the Pentecostal churches (with 43,800 members). Catholics were the fifth largest group with 37,000 members. Although the number of Muslims seemed to have decreased compared to the figures of 1997, when 46,000 Muslims were registered, this is explained by the fact that many Muslim congregations did not apply for state grants in 1998.[9]

The majority of Muslims in Norway are Sunni. In addition, there are some Shiʻa groups and an Ahmadiyya group. The Barelwi movement is predominant among Pakistanis, but there are also a number of the Sufi brotherhoods such as the Christiyya, the Qadiriyya, and the Naqshbandiya. The biggest organization is the Jamaat Ahl-e-Sunnat which was founded in 1976; by 1998 it had 5,373 members. In 1995 the World Islamic Mission, founded in 1984, obtained the concession to build a mosque in Oslo.[10] Until then, this was the only mosque, uniting both the *masjid* and the *jamaʼ*, built in Norway. In addition, a plot of land in the suburbs of Oslo was reserved for the building of an Ahmadiyya mosque. All other mosques and Islamic centers are lodged either in converted flats or villas, or in the basements of apartment buildings.

These institutions serve as prayer halls (*musalla*), meeting places, and teaching centers. They are administered by an all-male board, headed by an imam. The latter is normally contracted for that purpose and is from the same region as the members of his congregation. These "foreign" imams, especially the Pakistanis and the Turks, have formal education and training in Islamic theology and law. The ban on immigration does not apply to specialists in religion, and imams are normally granted residency for a limited period, usually four years. As in other Western countries, imams in Norway are invested with greater authority and assume a much greater range of responsibilities than they do in Muslim countries.[11] In fact, they take on roles similar to those of ordained priests and rabbis and act as spokesmen for their congregations. The imams are expected to lead the prayers and to deliver the weekly *khutba* (sermon), which, in the Norwegian context, is often done on Sunday, since Friday is a working day. They give religious instruction, visit Muslim patients in hospitals and criminals in prisons, perform marriages and funeral services. Two imams told me that they also act as family counselors. The Islamic Council (*Islamsk Råd*) was created in 1992. It is a pan-Islamic body with offices in Oslo that seeks to become an umbrella organization and to represent the interests of all Muslim communities in Norway vis-à-vis the authorities. Its 20,000 members are spread all over the country.

In 1994, ninety-nine religious and philosophical societies were registered in the counties of Oslo and Akershus.[12] Of these, twenty-eight were Muslim. The ninety-nine societies comprised 216,923 members in all and received a financial support of 30.8 million NKr. from the Norwegian State.[13] The total number of members belonging to the twenty-eight Muslim mosques and Islamic centers amounted to 26,238 (12 percent of the total), and they received 3.7 million Nkr. (12 percent) in governmental grants. In 1996, one hundred religious and philosophical societies were registered in the counties of Oslo and Akershus. Of these, thirty-one were Muslim. The one hundred organizations comprised a total of 241,109 members, and received a state grant of 47,449,035 million Nkr. The total number of members belonging to the thirty-one Muslim mosques and Islamic centers amounted to 35,439 (14 percent of the total), and they received 7,321,545 million Nkr. (15 percent) in governmental grants. In 1998, there were 149 registered religious and philosophical societies in the counties of Oslo and Akershus. Of these, thirty-five were Muslim. The 149 societies comprised a total of 253,186 members, and received a state grant of 52,660,552 million Nkr. The total number of members belonging to the thirty-five Muslim mosques and Islamic centers amounted to 40,137 (16 percent of the total), and they received 8,448,544 million Nkr. (16 percent of the total) in governmental grants.

"Ethnicizing" Religion

It is commonplace in Norway to have negative coverage of Islam in the press and other media.[14] In the public debate about Muslims, there is a marked tendency to represent Islam as a threat to democracy and Muslims as a monolithic, undifferentiated group. By essentializing the religion in this way, the plurality of Islam is disregarded. Its many regional forms, the different ways it has been adapted to local conditions and traditions, are ignored. No religion, of course, is homogeneous, and ignoring its heterogeneity both contributes to its being stereotyped and "orientalized" and tends to transmute religion into ethnicity. In the most extreme cases, it appears to give way to fanaticism and to racist movements, many examples of which are appearing worldwide.

Ethnicity, that is, the sense of belonging and of being different, refers mainly to cultural patterns that characterize different communities. These patterns include language, common codes of behavior, value systems, social networks, group activities, and shared interests. Abner Cohen pointed out that ethnicity is a matter of degree and is influenced by power relationships and economic conditions. He made a distinction between ethnicity and ethnic identity, which he defined as the individual's sense of belonging to a group, of partaking in its past history as well as its present and future aspirations. As a result, ethnic positions and allegiances are never permanent.[15] In *Ethnic Groups and Boundaries*, Frederik Barth argued for the primacy of boundaries over cultural content in multicultural societies. He explained that ethnic distinctions involve mobility, by which processes of inclusion and exclusion are formed. Accordingly, ethnicity is mainly the product of interactions between different social groups.[16] Michael M. J. Fischer, on his part, noted that, far from being a depository of customs that either continue or disappear through assimilation, ethnicity denotes a fund of values and of inter-referential cultural knowledge that can and should concern the future more than the past.[17] These scholars, however, were more concerned with the cultural aspect of ethnicity as separate from religion. In a previous study I argued that ethnicity may be, and often is, correlated to religious identity. As a key to self-definition, ethnicity is expressed by systems of symbols that convey its religious dimension. These symbols are anchored in the history of a given group and are perpetuated by the community's religious memory. This memory, however, is not frozen in time. Rather, it is built on the deliberate and active search for and reevaluation of the past and its meanings. Hence, it is always in the process of being (re)interpreted and shaped in order to suit its contemporary context.[18]

If we accept Clifford Geertz's notion of religion as a dynamic cultural system[19] and Albert Bastenier's view of ethnoreligion as a form of social differentiation,[20] we may, on the theoretical level, understand the Norwegian Muslim identity, in particular that of the second generation, in terms of a symbolic ethnicity. Continuing in this line of thought, we may advance the idea that, while Muslims represent a great variety of national, ethnic, social, and cultural backgrounds, Islam as a symbolic ethnicity generates a sense of community, bonding, and cultural togetherness among its adherents. At the same time, religion—in this case, Islam—confers on them a certain measure of distinctiveness from the majority of the population. However, the empirical data of my research indicates that Muslims in Norway have yet to achieve this homogeneity.

In the process of settling down in the new country, Muslim immigrants in Norway have to reappraise their ties with their homelands, their kinship relations, and their cultural and religious traditions. In the diasporic context, Muslim immigrants to Norway must reflect upon their cultural and religious identities and question them. They have to make choices and decide which elements to keep and which to discard. As Eugen Roosen pointed out, "In order to see and use one's own culture as a right, one must first have gained distance from that culture. In other words, one must first have questioned it or must have been questioned by a process of forced acculturation."[21] By making these choices, Muslim immigrants gain greater mobility and freedom of action than if they had stayed "home," particularly in regard to private matters. This independence in making personal decisions also affects their religious attitudes. A wider spectrum of choices is offered to them. They may, if they want, leave one congregation and join another. They may even establish a new congregation.

Conflicts exist in the diaspora and reasons for discord inside and between Muslim congregations are many. They may be caused by the different ways Muslim immigrants from a similar background respond to their new environment, differences in religious interpretation, struggles for leadership, and shifts of allegiances and social status. Disputes between Muslims are also due to ethnicity. The question remains whether the plurality of mosques denotes a fragmentation of Islam that could lead to the possibility of sectarianism. In Oslo, as in most West-European capitals, mosques and Islamic centers are usually established on the basis of ethnicity, language and cultural background, nationality, and religious affiliation.[22] Mosques and Islamic centers organized on a pan-Islamic paradigm, as for example the Muslim Society in Trondheim, are the exception. According to its members, the latter model reflects the concepts of *tawhid* (unity) and *umma* (community) and expresses the diversity of Islam within its unity. Interestingly, it is this model of mosque-Islamic center that the younger generation of educated Norwegian Muslims aspires to institute.

The Predicaments of Youth

Until recently, discussions about Muslim immigration in Norway reflected little sense of change or development. Time seemed to stand still. Now after some twenty-five years, the voices of young Norwegian Muslims, the so-called second-generation immigrants, are beginning to be heard. Their message is an important one and may help us to see that, rather than a liability, multiple cultural identity could be turned into an asset. We need to ask how having a number of different roots, being familiar with more than one worldview, and knowing how to mix different lifestyles could, in fact, contribute positively to cultural synthesis, renewal, and innovation.[23] It is important to see, in this context, whether second-generation Norwegian Muslims are moving toward more self-conscious Islamic identity or are headed in the direction of increased secularization and religious indifference.

The narratives of first-generation immigrants constitute a crucial legacy in shaping the multivalent identities of their children. Second-generation Norwegian Muslims grow up absorbing different sets of collective memories and histories, worldviews, and codes of ethics. Their identities are imprinted with various interwoven systems of value and patterns of behavior. They have incorporated some of the identity and values of their parents and have been influenced by the historical and socioeconomic circumstances surrounding their expatriation from their country of origin. At the same time, they have assimilated the ways of being and thinking of the environment in which they live. To these multiple influences one should add global trends provided by current international events and developments and served up by all kinds of media. Understanding some of the dynamics of these often conflicting sets of influences, including the legacies of the parents and the realities and expectations of the present and future in which second-generation Norwegian Muslims are active agents, is a complex task. It involves the exploration of issues related to gender, to the implications of formal literacy, and to the waning of popular religion.

A great number of Muslim immigrants who came to Norway, came from rural backgrounds in developing countries and were semiliterate and, in the case of women, often illiterate. However, being unable to read and write is not synonymous with being ignorant. The most significant conceptual baggage Muslim immigrants brought with them was that embodied in the written word of the Qur'an and the teachings derived from it. The majority of Muslim immigrants, both men and women, knew before their emigration how to perform their prayers regularly, to observe Ramadan, and to conform to the principles of Islam. They had learned parts of the sacred text by heart. They were taught to internalize it and to recite the appropriate *sura* at the right time. Many stories belonging to the collections of hadiths and to the lives of prophets and saints, as well as various myths and folktales, had been memorized.

Nevertheless, in spite of their oral literacy, there were few among these first-generation immigrants who could, or would, actually read and question the text. Their religiosity was more in terms of popular Islam than of text-based religion. Most popular religion is deeply rooted in the lore and traditions of a given region and relies heavily on orality. Narratives, beliefs, and rituals are transmitted from one generation to the next through speech, corporal behavior, and symbolic gestures. These elements not only encompass the bulk of what Paul Connerton defines as a society's incorporated and inscribed practices,[24] they also constitute an essential part of its cultural, thus also its religious, memory. Inferentially, beliefs and rituals pertaining to popular religion tend to lose much of their significance when taken into a new context. To survive, they must be adjusted and translated to suit their new environment.[25] In the diasporic context, practices belonging to popular religion are often privatized and restricted to the intimacy of the home. This is particularly noticeable for rites of passage, such as birth rituals and marriages. Funerary rituals are among the last to adapt to change. Even after a lifetime as émigrés, many prefer to send their dead back home rather than bury them in the new country, even if the dead are children born in the diaspora. The symbolic bond that ties roots to soil, land, and geography is expressed clearly in times of death. Finding consecrated ground in which to bury one's dead is, in my opinion, one of the most eloquent signs of settlement and integration. Until it is able to do that, an immigrant community remains foreign. By modifying their rituals, first-generation Muslim immigrants have paved the way for second and future generations to pursue different options than those available in their original country. Consequently, second-generation Norwegian Muslims feel freer to decide which elements of religion to retain and how to transform them. The processes of reinterpretation and innovation result in the appearance of different forms of cultural syncretism.[26] Regional idiosyncrasies tend to melt into a pan-Islamic blend of Norwegian-Scandinavian character.

Young Norwegian Muslims who have completed the required minimum of nine years of schooling in Norway do not have the same frames of reference as their parents. Thus, although they have absorbed many of their parents' beliefs and practices, they have been shaped by a different educational system and have developed a different analytical approach to texts. In addition to attending public school, the majority of second-generation Norwegian Muslims have followed the religious instructions imparted through the Qur'an classes at the various mosques and Islamic centers. Not only do they learn to memorize the sacred text and to recite it accurately, they can actually read the Qur'an and collections of hadiths, if not in Arabic, at least in translation. In a non-Muslim environment where the symbols of their religion are not part of the landscape, young Norwegian Muslims have to rely primarily on the written texts to gain some knowledge of their religion. They reconcile different systems of education and learning while ascribing to the texts their own understandings that have been molded in a synthesis of a culturally embedded religion, a literate Islamic worldview, and a north-European, secular way of being. Their goal, especially in the case of girls, is to reinterpret and reevaluate the Qur'an and other fundamental religious and juridical texts in order to accommodate them to the Norwegian context. In fact, as in other west-European countries, second-generation Norwegian Muslims are asserting their right to individual interpretation or *ijtihad*.[27] During my fieldwork, I have found that the majority of second-generation Muslims who are pursuing higher studies, often members of associations of Muslim students, express their frustrations with "foreign" imams who are ignorant of local conditions and maintain "outdated" ideas and lifestyles.

One of the most visible consequences of this increased formal literacy among second-generation Norwegian Muslims is the gradual disappearance and abandonment of old practices of popular Islam. New forms of religious conventions are gradually replacing the culturally rooted religion of the parents.[28] These changes are not unique to Norway but comply with today's pan-Islamic, transnational movements. This does not happen without conflicts between parents and children, in particular, between parents and daughters.

The Metaphor of the Veil

Second-generation Muslim girls generally acknowledge their emotional tie to the culture of their parents as well as their allegiance to Islam. At the same time, they confess reacting negatively to the restrictions imposed on them by their families and their community. In trying to harmonize their loyalties to religion, family and community with their attempts to participate actively in Norwegian society, they resort to various strategies. The most common is to challenge parental authority through argument or open disobedience. Some decide to wear the veil over their parents' objections. Others find no solution other than moving out, or in the most dramatic cases, running away. Among second generation Muslim women, it is especially those pursuing higher studies that are involved in the process of renegotiating Islamic values and family relations and structures.

In the Norwegian context, the new Islamic veil, *hijab*, is the most conspicuous emblem of religious fellowship. It should be remembered that the modern Islamic dress is quite different from women's traditional costume in the various regions of the Islamic world. Actually, it is an excellent example of an invented tradition. During the last three decades, the *hijab* has assumed a central place in issues of gender and religious identity. As a consequence, it has also affected processes of integration of Muslim communities in the West. Today, in addition to dress, behavior, decorum, and appearance in public, the conscious decision to wear the *hijab* is charged with strong radical messages. The *hijab* is a gendered badge of religious and political allegiance and a way for Moslem women from various nation-states and social and cultural backgrounds to engage modernity in a new manner and within different parameters. Wearing the *hijab* today, in my view, is a political gesture as highly charged as was taking off the veil in the 1920s by Middle Eastern feminists such as Hoda Sha'rawi, Malak Hifni Nassef, Ceza al Nabarawi in Egypt, and Aswa Zahawi, Amina er Rahal, and "Red Rose" Kadduri in Iraq. The *hijab* is a form of protest that should be viewed according to the context and the time in which it appears. For women of my generation and cultural background, it is understood as an urban phenomenon, a reaction to the political systems in the Middle East that can be traced back to the aftermath of 1967, the time of postcolonialism, post-Nasserism, post-pan-Arabism, and post-Arab socialism. Further, it is also seen as a result of labor migration to oil-rich countries of the Arabian peninsula as well as a response to Western values and ideals. It is my contention that the new Islamic garb should also be interpreted within the framework of the renewed universalist tendencies of today's Islam. Far from implying seclusion, sheltering, concealment, and withdrawal as the Arabic root (*hjb*) of the term signifies, it provides now opportunities for public participation. Muslim women who have made the deliberate choice to wear the *hijab* do not see themselves as oppressed or marginalized. On the contrary, many become activists while keeping the outer signs of conformity to religious traditions and by following principles and methods that are widely accepted as Islamic. This is certainly true in the Norwegian context where the *hijab* confers upon those who wear it liberty of movement and a certain independence and authority in relation to families and communities. The strategies of second-generation Norwegian Muslim women are quite similar to those of their sisters in faith in other parts of the world. They include participation in women's groups, cluster-structured organizations, networking, and literacy classes. Women are also claiming their place in one of the most jealously guarded male bastions, the mosque.

The Nadia Case

The Nadia case, which took place in 1997–1998, exemplifies many of the issues related to immigration, religion, gender, generation clash, and citizenship. In the summer of 1997, Nadia, an eighteen-year-old, second-generation, young woman of Moroccan origin, phoned her Norwegian employer from Morocco and informed him that she had been drugged by her parents and brother and driven out of Norway while unconscious. The family traveled by car through Europe; during the whole trip Nadia was under constant watch. After their arrival in Morocco, she was locked up and kept under tight custody in the house her father had had built in his village of origin. Nadia claimed that she was being forced to marry someone of her parents' choice. The Norwegian embassy in Morocco was alerted, and, after much pressure from the Norwegian authorities, Nadia was released and allowed to return to Oslo. Since then, her whereabouts have been kept secret. The legal proceedings took place at the level of the Oslo city court. During the trial, Nadia's parents, who were themselves Norwegian citizens, living on social security, accused their daughter of "becoming Norwegian." She was, they said, losing touch with her own culture and religion, and they saw it as their duty to save her. According to Norwegian law, Nadia was an adult Norwegian citizen, while in Morocco, she was considered a minor and, as an unmarried girl, under the authority of her father. The verdict condemned the parents to a one-year suspended sentence. In addition, they had to pay an indemnity to their daughter for having abducted an adult Norwegian citizen against her will and for the distress they had caused her.

At the time of the trial, issues related to individual rights, personal choices, and the notion of (dual) citizenship were the subjects of heated debates in the media. Among the most thorny topics discussed was that of arranged/forced marriage among immigrants, especially in Muslim communities where the choice of the spouse seems to be a major source of conflict between generations. There are still very few intercommunity marriages among Muslims in Norway. As one Pakistani imam explained to me, "We have a caste system. That is why we have to marry persons who are of the same caste as us."

Nevertheless, it is worth noting that, although all the girls (between eighteen and twenty-five years of age) in our interviews declared that the worst possible choice of marriage partners would be boys from their own communities and congregations, they were positive about the idea of marrying a second-generation Muslim from another community. The great majority, however, said they did not want to upset their parents. They are convinced that, together, they will be able to find a compromise concerning the choice of the spouse. As one Muslim female student expressed it, "There are many things to take in to account like caste, education, country, work. The best would be an 'arranged love marriage' with a Muslim who grew up in Europe."[29]

New Dilemmas for Muslim Communities: The Elderly, Single Women, and Young Delinquents

Three issues and problems challenging Muslim communities in Norway need further inquiry.

The first concerns the situation of elderly Muslim immigrants, for whom much needs to be done in terms of care, accommodations, and activities.[30] Because the majority of Muslim communities are relatively young, these matters have not yet been put on the agenda of the various mosques and Islamic centers. Elderly care is still seen to be part of the individual family's responsibility. Generally, families of three generations try to live either in the vicinity of each other, or, if possible, in two-family houses. However, because of various contingencies such as employment, military service, studies, etc., second-generation Muslim immigrants are not always able to live with or near their parents and provide the necessary care. Further, if the elderly are disabled, they need the services of professionals and even of nursing homes. These homes are not yet ready to accommodate the specific requirements of Muslim patients. It appears from my own restricted studies among elderly first generation Pakistanis that the notion of "home" is gradually taking on new dimensions. It is more tied to the presence of children and grandchildren than to geography. Many grandparents stay on in Norway to help their children. It is not only kinship, of course, that keeps old immigrants in Norway but also their own individual developments and changes, habits that have become ingrained, friends, and connections they have made in the diaspora. Some return to their homeland, but, after some months, come back to Norway. They told me that they got sick in Pakistan and that there was too much pollution. When asked where they want to spend their holidays, they often say that they would like to visit the holy places of Islam, such as Mecca, Medina, or the grand mosque of Damascus, instead of going back home.

The second issue is that of single women. First-generation Muslim immigrants from rural backgrounds have normally kept strong ties with their original homelands. Women have tended to re-create their networks with other women of the same community. In this way, they have continued to live within a transplanted Pakistani or Turkish milieu, having very little contact with the Norwegian surroundings. During the first period of their stay, the support and care extended from members of the same community eased the different stages of settling down and finding their bearings in the new country. But in the long run, it has hindered the acculturation process for women and in many cases become quite oppressive. When the nuclear family disintegrates because of death, divorce, unemployment, or children who break out of the family and the community, women have to renegotiate both gender relations and family structures. An increasing number of Muslim women have to assume the role of breadwinner and/or single parent. Some decide to live on their own. Unfortunately, mosques and Islamic centers are not providing assistance to this group. For first-generation immigrants, not knowing the language makes their situation even more difficult. Special courses in Norwegian are offered to immigrant women, and the waiting list is quite long.

The third issue, which is also the one that has attracted the attention of politicians and the media, is the alleged high percentage of youth delinquency, gangs, and violence, particularly among boys, in the Muslim communities. Parents, mosques, and Islamic centers seem powerless to deal with this problem, for which they are unprepared. The imam of an Arabic speaking mosque told me, "They leave the mosque when they are thirteen, especially the boys. Instead, they hang around big shopping centers and get into trouble. We don't know what to do. We hope they'll come back before it's too late. "

"How Long Does It Take to Become 'Indigenous?'"

As noted earlier, religion may serve to confer an ethnicity in its adherents. Thus, being a Muslim immigrant in a non-Moslem environment might provide the grounds for a kind of "flexible citizenship."[31] As Clifford has noted, "Islam, like Judaism, in a predominantly Christian culture, can offer a sense of attachment, to a different temporality and vision, a discrepant modernity."[32]

However, so far, no common Muslim identity appears to have emerged among Muslim communities in Norway. In fact, the universalism of Islam, the concept of the Muslim *umma*, is not a determining factor for many communities that remain entrenched within the boundaries of their various national, political, linguistic, ethnic, and religious groupings. At the same time, second-generation Norwegian Muslims are striving to accommodate Islamic perspectives to the Norwegian context and to set up pan-Islamic networks and associations. Acquiring Norwegian citizenship involves both rights and duties that have to be assumed. In their attempt to participate actively in the construction of a multicultural and multireligious Norwegian society, Muslim communities are driven to reflect, ideally with honesty and self-criticism, on their own values and ideas. They have to examine in depth a number of important issues. Questions regarding the situation of the young and the elderly, problems of education, employment, violence, and youth delinquency, the subjugation of girls and women, the abuse of basic human rights, and, not least, the implications of citizenship for Norwegian Muslims need to be addressed. Integration is not an easy task and becoming a citizen is not the same as being an integral part of the nation. The latter might still take a few more generations.

Notes

1. Norway's name in Old Norse was *Nordvegr*, meaning the Northern way. This article is based on my research on mosques and Islamic centers in Norway and the iconography of Islamic spaces in a non-Muslim context. The research has been partly financed by The Research Council of Norway, Culture and Society Division, Culture Studies program. My approach is both qualitative and quantitative. It is based on field study and semi-structured interviews conducted by myself and by students at the Department of Culture Studies, section of History of Religions, University of Oslo. In addition, I make use of statistics and of the insights offered by the different immigration studies (*innvandrerstudier*) that have been carried out during the last two decades in Norway, as well as on current debates in the media. I am grateful to director of research, Lars Ostby, Statistics Norway, and special advisor, Vivien Wrede-Holm, Department of Primary Healthcare and Social Services, Municipality of Oslo, for reading and commenting on an earlier draft of this essay.

2. This is an approximate number. As mentioned below, not all Muslims are registered as such.

3. The majority of converts are women, cf. Lene Larsen, *Velkommen til en stor familie . . . Islam og konversjon i norsk kontekst*, unpublished M.A. thesis, University of Oslo.

4. The data is provided by Statistics Norway; the figures are from 1 January 98. In order to keep within the frame of a culture historical analysis, and since many immigrants have become Norwegian citizens, the figures used here include persons born abroad and persons whose parents were both born abroad.

5. Saphinaz-Amal Naguib, "The Era of Martyrs. Texts and Contexts of Religious Memory," in *Between Desert and City: The Coptic Orthodox Church Today*, eds. Nelly van Doorn-Harder and Kari Vogt, Institute for Comparative Research in Human Culture, Serie B: Skrifter XCVII (Oslo: Novus forlag, 1997), 121–141; *The Temporalities of Cultural Memory*, forthcoming in Proceedings of the Conference on Moving Matters, Cairo, December 1998.

6. Whereas, during the 1970s and 1980s, religion was not obligatory, the school reform of 1997 has introduced Christianity and life philosophy (*Kristendom og livssynsundervisning* or KRL-faget) as a compulsory subject at all levels. The curriculum is based on Christian values, in particular those of the Lutheran Church. There have been many protests, and various religious and philosophical groups have separately sued the state on the grounds of breech of human rights, with the intent of pursuing their cases as far as the Tribunal of Human Rights in Strasbourg. The lawsuit between the Humanists and the State began in January 1999 at the level of city court. The Humanists lost the case in April 1999 and it was subsequently submitted to the Court of Appeal.

7. A new and revised request has been presented in 1998. No decision about the founding of an Islamic school has been made yet.

8. In addition, there are 5,900 members of unregistered Muslim congregations.

9. The figures are provided by the web-site of Statistics Norway, <http://www.ssb.no>.

10. A land concession to build a pan-Islamic mosque and cultural center in Oslo was officially granted in 1979. However, due to internal strife among the different Muslim communities, it was never realized. Personal information provided by my father, the former ambassador of Egypt, Gamal Naguib, who was for a time involved with the project; see also Nora Ahlberg, *New Challenge*

—*Old Strategies. Themes of Variation and Conflict among Pakistani Muslims in Norway.* Transactions of the Finnish Anthropological Society No. 25, Helsinki: Gummerus-forlaget, 1990, 165f.

11. Compare with the roles of the imams in the United States, cf. Yvonne Haddad and Adair Lummis, *Islamic Values in the United States*, New York: Oxford University Press, 1987, 58f.

12. The Norwegian appellation *trosamfunn/livssynssamfunn* means "congregations/life-value oriented societies." I use, here, the translation provided by Statistics Norway. Information on the registered religious and philosophical societies in the counties of Oslo and Akershus during the period 1994–1998 was provided to me by the office of the Governor of Oslo and Akershus county which administers the "Law on religious congregations" ("Lov om trossamfunn"), from June 13, 1969, in these counties.

13. 1 US$ = ca. 8 Nkr.

14. However, there seems to be a change of opinion due to the recent events in Kosovo.

15. Abner Cohen, "Introduction: The Lesson of Ethnicity," in *Urban Ethnicity*, ed. Abner Cohen, A.S.A. monograph 12, 1974m, ix–xxiv.

16. Fredrik Barth, *Ethnic Groups and Boundaries. The Social Organization of Culture Difference* (Oslo: Universitetsforlaget, 1982), 9f.

17. Michael M. J. Fischer, "Ethnicity and the Post-Modern Art of Memory," in *Writing Culture: The Poetics of Ethnography*, ed. J. Clifford and G.E. Marcus (Berkeley: University of California Press, 1986), 197f.

18. Saphinaz-Amal Naguib, "The Era of Martyrs: Texts and Contexts of Religious Memory," in *Between Desert and City: The Coptic Orthodox Church Today*, ed. Nelly van Doorn-Harder and Kari Vogt, Institute for Comparative Research in Human Culture, Serie B: Skrifter XCVII (Oslo: Novus forlag, 1997), 121–141.

19. Clifford Geertz, *The Interpretation of Cultures* (New York: Basic Books, 1973), 90.

20. Albert Bastenier, "Migrations, choc de cultures et religion: à propos des communications de C. Lacoste-Dujardin et W. Clark Roof et C. Manning," in *Social Compass* 41, no. 1 (1994): 189.

21. Eugen E. Roosens, "Creating Ethnicity: The Process of Ethnogenesis," *Frontiers of Anthropology* 5 (London: Sage Publications, 1989), 150.

22. Jacques Waardenburg, "The Institutionalization of Islam in the Netherlands, 1961–86," in *The New Islamic Presence in Western Europe*, ed. T. Gerholm and Y. G. Lithman (London: Mansell, 1988), 13.

23. Saphinaz-Amal Naguib, "Kulturbrytning, tradisjonsendring og innovasjon," in *Kulturstudier: Kulturforståing, kulturbrytning, kulturpolitikk*, ed. Bjarne Hodne, Kulturstudier 1, Norges forskningsråd, 95–109.

24. Paul Connerton, "How Societies Remember," *Themes in the Social Sciences* (Cambridge: Cambridge University Press, 1989), 72f.

25. Saphinaz-Amal Naguib, "The Temporalities of Cultural Memory," forthcoming in Proceedings of the Conference on Moving Matters, Cairo, December 1998.

26. Ibid.

27. Chantal Saint-Blancat, "Hypothèses sur l'évolution de 'l'Islam transplanté' en Europe," in *Social Compass* 40, no. 2 (1993): 171f; Steven Vertovec and Alisdair Rogers, eds., *Muslim European Youth: Reproducing Ethnicity, Religion, Culture* (Aldershot, England: Ashgate, 1998), 11.

28. Saint-Blancat, 1993; Pnima Werbner, *The Migration Process: Capital, Gifts and Offerings among British Pakistanis* (New York: Berg, 1990).

29. Interview conducted by Inger-Anne Bergersen.

30. As for example the survey of Bjørg Moen, *Eldre innvandrere i Gamle Oslo*, Norsk gerontologisk institutt, rapport n. 4, 1993, on elderly immigrants in Oslo.

31. James Clifford, *Routes, Travel and Translation in the Late Twentieth Century* (Cambridge Mass.: Harvard University Press, 1997), 252.

32. Ibid., 257.

Turks in Germany: Muslim Identity "Between" States

10

JAMES HELICKE

Introduction

SAMUEL HUNTINGTON'S CONCEPT OF A "CLASH OF CIVILIZATIONS"[1] has had a profound influence on the thought of numerous policy makers, intellectuals, and members of the media, as well as private citizens. In the German context, Huntington's arguments have seemed to confirm what has been suspected: that conflict between Muslims and Christians is inevitable, as is evident in the difficult relations between German citizens and *Ausländer* (a word that often connotes Turkish workers) resident in Germany. For example, *Der Spiegel*, among the most widely read of German newsmagazines, featured a series of articles in its April 1997 issue that portrayed a growing sentiment of confrontation between Germans and *Ausländer*. One article, in citing Huntington's work, expressed the fear that Germany itself might become the venue for such a conflict in the presence of German social "disintegration" and the "ethnicization of social problems." This chapter attempts to explore the links between culture and politics, challenging the proposition that a cultural clash between "foreigners" and Germans is inevitable.

In recent scholarship about Turks in Germany, two primary approaches have prevailed. The first, a social-scientific approach, has generally attempted to understand the debate in terms of large-scale social, economic, and political forces, and has tended to reduce the impact of culture to rational human interaction. The second has utilized cultural methodology, which, as Yasemin Soysal points out, often obfuscates the more complex role of the host society in the process of integration by referring instead to contrasts based in a Turkish or Islamic model of organization.[2] I hope to avoid the pitfalls of both methods by stressing instead the interrelatedness of culture and politics, while not reducing the one to the other.[3] I will argue that political considerations, such as differing conceptualizations of citizenship of the Turkish and German states, have a profound effect on the culture of "Turks" within German society. Whereas the Turkish understanding of the nation is based on territoriality and the state, the German understanding of the nation has been defined in genealogical and exclusionary terms. Turks in Germany have been profoundly influenced by the cultural understandings of both states, but they have not been entirely connected to either.

The marginality of Turks living in Germany to both Turkish and German societies, as Ruth Mandel indicates, has provided the context for a newly defined Muslim identity.[4] I would extend her observation to include not only immediate social surroundings but also the connection of Turks in diaspora to the Turkish and German states. Turks in Germany have found themselves caught between the influence of these two differing political entities. Their concepts of national inclusion thus have provided for a space in which Turks living in Germany have been able to develop new understandings of what it means to be Turkish and Muslim in that context. Because neither the Turkish nor the German identity asserts absolute cultural hegemony over Turks in diaspora, they have developed a cultural identity that is rooted both within and apart from the two states.[5]

The Relation between State and National Identity in Turkey

The development of an independent Turkey necessitated the simultaneous development of a national culture to support the sovereign state. For Mustafa Kemal, the founder of the modern Turkish nation-state, the process of establishing a national consciousness involved nothing less than a cultural revolution. In essence, Kemal attempted to create a Turkish national identity, both as a vessel of his envisioned state and as the basis of state legitimacy. Ultimately, Turkish national identity can be understood as state-centered and territorial, with religion playing a significant (albeit extremely complex) role in the formation of national identity.

Mustafa Kemal's vision of a Turkish national consciousness was closely related to a strong, centralized state. His early Turkish republic imposed the notion of Turkishness on residents of Anatolia, rather than relying on existing civil-societal identities that were mainly rooted in religious communal and local affiliation. The Ottoman Empire had divided its population into distinct religious communities (*millets*) that functioned as the loci of identity until the Tanzimat reforms (1839–1856), which promoted modern notions of egalitarianism among citizens before the law.[6]

Nonetheless, religious identity continued to shape politics in Anatolia. During its final years, the Ottoman Empire became increasingly rooted in Anatolia with the loss of its European and Middle Eastern territories. In essence, Anatolian Muslims formed the final remnants of the Ottoman Muslim *millet*. In this context, it is unsurprising that Muslim identity played a prominent role in defining Turkish identity.[7] Anatolia, moreover, became increasingly Muslim in population as a result of the massive influx of Muslims from lands under former Ottoman domination and the disappearance of a significant Christian population.[8] Thus, in the absence of a single language and a popular national consciousness (the term "Turk" often implied "peasant"), Islam provided the most cohesive form of communal identity in Anatolia.

However, Mustafa Kemal did not regard Islam as the new state's ultimate source of legitimacy. Instead, he promoted a unitary state structure by turning to a territorially specific definition of the Turkish nation, rooted in Anatolia. Pan-Turkism, which sought to unite the Turkic speaking world, was also clearly refuted by Mustafa Kemal. Indeed, he rejected Pan-Turkism as an "ideological bind," instead turning to "natural" and "legitimate limitations" of a clearly defined Anatolian land mass.[9] In doing so, cultural understandings of the Turkish nation moved away from ethnic and religious identity to the political consolidation of an existing territorial entity.

The state began a series of reforms in order to create a Turkish society that would be separate from Islam and ultimately serve as a compliment to state ambitions.[10] This was accomplished by eliminating the caliphate, closing all *seriat* (Shari'a) courts, and eliminating *medreses* (Islamic schools). Sufi brotherhoods, which had served as the most important link between the ruling Islamic elite and the countryside, were banned.[11] The Kemalist state also implemented national forms of education to replace the educational hegemony of the Muslim clerics, changed the alphabet, and mandated a more "European" style of dress.

The significance of the state and the territorial features of Turkish national identity have continued throughout the life of the Turkish republic. The current constitution affirms that the Turkish nation is determined by the boundaries of the geographic nation-state, rather than by religious and other ethnic allegiances. Indeed, the constitution firmly rejects "the creation of minorities" in religious, cultural, or ethnic terms.[12]

However, Turkish political thought has been marked by a continuous tension with regard to religion. On the one hand, religiously oriented political movements (such as the Democratic Party of the 1950s, the National Salvation party of the 1970s, and the Welfare-Virtue party of the 1990s) and a variety of Turkish nationalist parties have attempted to establish a closer official connection between Turkish national identity and Islam. Popular support for these movements and the virtual absence of religious minorities in Turkey support the hypothesis that being Turkish inherently means being Muslim.[13] On the other hand, a secularist notion of Turkishness has generally prevailed at the level of the state and among military officers, who perceive themselves as guardians of the Kemalist state legacy. The latter have vehemently opposed the introduction of Islamic symbols in public life. Interestingly, however, even General Kenan Evren, who directed the 1980 military coup, used Quranic verses in order to support military intervention and the modern and secular Turkish state. Moreover, there is really no separation of state and religion in Turkey, as the state, in fact, has incorporated religious institutions into its Ministry of Religious Affairs.[14] Thus, while the Turkish state does not derive its legitimacy through Islamic reference, neither can it be characterized as strictly *laic*. Accordingly, Alevites, as well as more "fundamentalist" Sunni Muslims, have criticized the Turkish state for imposing a republican form of Sunni Islam on Muslim constituents that fundamentalists claim to be diluted, and Alevites claim is overtly Sunni in character.

The Relationship between State and National Identity in Germany

German conceptualizations of the relationship between state and national identity contrast starkly with the Turkish. Whereas the Turkish understanding of the nation is related to a particular territory and intimately connected to the Turkish state, the German is based on the nation as *volk*-centered and prepolitical. Rogers Brubaker, who explored the relationship between the notion of citizenship and state in the German context, argues that the German notion of citizenship extends beyond a particular geographic domain because of the political fragmentation of Germans. According to the German understanding, citizenry is a community of descent (*jus sanguinis*). Accordingly, *Deutschtum* (the abstract notion of all Germans) transcends the particular German state, insofar as some Germans live outside territorial Germany. In other words, the German notion of national identity is genealogically, not geographically, determined. By its nature, "German nationhood engendered an interest in civic exclusion"[15] by attempting to exclude Poles and other ethnic groups in the creation of a more ethnically defined "German" state (as is evident in the Kleindeutsch decision to exclude the Habsburg domain with its considerable Slavic presence). The Kleindeutsch decision, however, also implied that the Prussian-German state did not contain all ethnic Germans.

Religion has also played a complex role in the German notion of nation. Michael Minkenberg indicates that German nation building developed as religion and dynasty slowly lost authority in political communities. Nonetheless, the Prussian state, mainly Protestant in composition, still required religious support. The idea began to develop among Protestants that they had a special covenant with God following victory in the Franco-Prussian war in 1871.[16] Because Protestantism could not enjoy the status of state religion without alienating Catholics, the two religions were incorporated into the state's self-definition as a means of assuring religious legitimacy. Jews, many of whom perceived themselves as Germans, occupied a difficult position in this state structure. Although toleration sometimes prevailed, persecution was the general rule. It is clear, then, that the Third Reich marked a pivotal point in national consciousness by essentially removing any correlation of Germanness and Jewishness.

Despite the various attempts of the Federal Republic of Germany to distinguish itself from acute manifestations of German nationalism following the history of the Third Reich, an ethnically determined understanding of citizenship has continued to be strong throughout the history of the Federal Republic as well. The definition of citizenship given in the Basic Law indicates that "everyone is a German citizen in the eyes of the Constitution who holds German citizenship or who, as a refugee of German descent or spouse or children thereof, has fled to the Federal Republic of Germany from areas included in the Third Reich as existing on December 31, 1937."[17] Despite claims that Germany is not a land of migration, Brubaker indicates that the relationship between German identity and the German state provides for the immigration of "ethnic Germans" from Central and Eastern Europe at the same time that it promotes repatriation of Turks born in Germany. Moreover, the relation of religion to state has continued. The Federal Republic of Germany does not claim to be *laic* in nature, but rather is "*religionsneutral*," guaranteeing freedom of religion by acknowledging the status of Judaism, Catholicism, and Protestantism as "publicly recognized corporations (*Körperschaft öffentlichen Rechts*)."[18] Thus, church and state operate closely together, in that church schools and other agencies receive public funds, and the state even administers taxation on behalf of the church.

Motivations for Migration

In 1962 an agreement was reached between Germany and Turkey in which the latter would provide *gastarbeiter* (guestworkers) to Germany. This was the first step in the immigration of hundreds of thousands of Turks to Germany in response to German labor shortages and Turkish labor surpluses. The agreement is based on the understanding that the Turkish and German states should attempt to maintain their respective political tropes on national inclusion/exclusion. Foremost, both states appropriated the boundaries defined by German national identity, i.e., Turks would not become Germans. Permanent residence in Germany was never considered in the 1962 agreement, and the implicit understanding was that while Turks would "temporarily" reside in Germany, they would ultimately return to Turkey.

It is significant to recognize that the 1962 agreement was reached mainly through interstate relations. The German state established labor recruiting offices in order to get needed manpower. The Turkish state, moreover, posted available positions in Germany[19] and had final say in which of its citizens would be sent to fill them.[20] Germany required labor in order to promote a high level of growth. According to Nielsen, it is not coincidental that the bilateral agreement for recruitment was reached in 1962, shortly after the construction of the Berlin wall, ending the influx of East German labor.[21]

Turkey's interests were also fostered by its program of state-led development. In the words of an official report on a five-year plan issued during this period, Turkey aimed for "population planning" and "the export of surplus manpower" in order to pursue its economic improvement.[22] In the first place, the export of labor aimed to lower domestic unemployment. The Turkish state also saw an opportunity to improve the supply of foreign exchange reserves in the form of remittances paid by Turkish workers in Germany to their families in Turkey.[23] Finally, as Terry Monson indicates, Turkey saw a potential means of expediting the development of an industrial labor force from a dominantly rural and minimally educated population through training in Germany.[24]

The Status of *Gastarbeiter*

Germans understood that the Turks in the first generation of immigrant workers were only temporary laborers. Although they did receive social benefits and all of the employment rights of German workers (largely because of the fear of German unions that cheap Turkish labor might begin stripping Germans of jobs), the involvement of Turks in German society was not understood to go beyond the workplace. Workers were accommodated mainly in factory dormitories, and their lives were largely focused on their place of work. Most important, because these Turkish workers were almost all men, they lacked the social rootedness of family life.

Differences among "Turks" were apparent in the first generation of *gastarbeiter*. They represented the general demographic composition of Turkey. Accordingly, ethnic, linguistic, and religious distinctions between Turks and Kurds, Sunnis and Alevites revealed themselves most fully in their limited networks of acquaintances outside the workplace. Nonetheless, those in the first generation of *gastarbeiter* clearly also had a good deal in common. Their living arrangements, their lack of family life and institutional support, and their status as undifferentiated "Turks" among Germans initially created a more homogenous effect. They believed that they would soon be repatriated to their Anatolian homeland; thus, they lived on the fringes of the country where they temporarily found themselves working.

Nonetheless, change did occur in the German state conception of the foreigners within its boundaries that allowed for a change in the status of Turkish *gastarbeiter*. German companies began to prefer holding on to existing Turkish workers in order to avoid the inefficiencies and costs associated with retraining new workers. Meanwhile, the German state recognized that the presence of a large foreign minority could pose a challenge to German conceptions of exclusionary, genealogically based citizenship. In 1965 a new Foreigner Law was passed. Although not attempting to improve the rights of foreigners, but rather confirming existing notions of civic exclusion, the ambiguous wording of the law inadvertently created results that differed significantly from the intentions of its drafters. Section 2 indicated that a residency permit of a foreigner can be extended if this "does not injure the interests" of the Federal Republic of Germany. [25]Although the scope of the law applied to the whole Federal Republic, the actual enactment of the law was left to the discretion of local bureaucrats. Therefore, although the intention of the law was to confirm the Federal Republic's exclusionary understanding of society and its right to expel foreigners, the result was that it became necessary to prove that the presence of foreigners "injured" the German state. Moreover, the state's power vis-à-vis foreigners was relegated to local interpretation, thereby lessening to a certain extent the state's grip on the presence of a significant Turkish population in Germany.

Many Germans were becoming increasingly aware of a potential anomaly between the simultaneous profession of liberal notions of democracy and inclusion and German notions of citizenship as exclusionary. Willy Brandt's famous statement "to dare more democracy" with regard to the foreigners in Germany attempted to address this issue. Nonetheless, the year 1973 marked a dramatic change in policies regulating the presence of foreigners in Europe as a whole.

This was the year of the oil embargo, in which Europe suffered severe economic recession as its dependency on oil was revealed. As a result, unemployment grew and, with it, antagonism toward Turkish guestworkers increased. Accordingly, Brandt issued the *Bewerbestopp* to end the import of foreign labor. However, in contrast to other ethnic groups, such as Spaniards and Italians, who, as a result, left en masse, the number of Turks remained virtually unchanged.[26] The Turkish state suffered economically because of a reduction in foreign loans, thus reducing its ability to create jobs to meet the demand of a rapidly increasing population.[27] Fewer Turks in Germany were willing to return home, and even more families of Turkish workers wanted to migrate to Germany. Ironically, the oil embargo had a stabilizing effect on the Turkish presence in Germany by changing the composition of the resident Turkish population from primarily single men to a reconstituted family as the wives and children of the resident workers arrived.

Mitburger versus Living Here/Living There

Throughout the 1970s and 1980s, both the Turkish and German states held to the notion that the presence of Turks in Germany would remain temporary, despite demographic evidence to the contrary. This perception by the two states was to have a profound impact on the culture of the Turks in Germany.

The position of the German state has been expressed as follows: "The Federal Government is of the opinion that there is no necessity of providing special regulations for foreign workers with regard to naturalization. Naturalization presupposes a process of assimilation and therefore demands a time of residence which cannot be too short."[28] This statement is interesting for several reasons. First, the German state would not change its understanding of civic inclusion and citizenship to accommodate the large Turkish presence within its borders. Instead, they would remain "foreign workers." Second, citizenship would not be granted in the foreseeable future. Third, the definition of what it meant to be German was understood in static terms. Any possibility of acquiring German citizenship would entail "assimilation" into this given definition because the German state was not willing to accommodate.

These essential distinctions between "German-ness" and "Turkish-ness" are apparent in a 1977 statement by the Christian Democratic Union: "Integration does not mean an assimilation which works toward making foreign workers and their families into Germans." Instead, it means "the opportunity for foreign workers to live under the same conditions as German without having to abandon their national identity."[29] Despite support of the right of foreigners "to live under the same conditions," it was apparent that foreigners would remain excluded from German society because of an essentialized understanding of national identity. As Elcin Kursat-Ahlers points out, even though German integration rhetoric advocated preserving the homeland culture of a minority so as to assist in the process of reintegration, it was also expected that non-German minorities should adapt to German culture.[30] An essentialized and exclusive definition of German citizenship means that Turks living in Germany are prohibited from acquiring German citizenship unless they renounce Turkish citizenship— in effect, that they cease being Turkish.

It is interesting to recognize the ways in which the German state's trope of intrinsic difference between Turks and Germans manifests itself in the culture of the Turkish residents in Germany. Turks are excluded from German society in various ways. Only German citizens can participate fully in the German political process. Foreigners cannot vote, nor are they permitted to join German political parties. The most significant form of political participation for Turks in Germany occurs at a local level. Local advisory boards have acted, in a sense, as a foreign parliament in giving suggestions to local government agencies and institutions. However, these recommendations are in no way binding on governmental policy.

Economic as well as political marginalization has been the general rule for Turks in Germany. Unemployment has affected non-Germans much more starkly than Germans. Despite the fact that Germany has one of the highest per capita incomes in the world, Turks have generally been excluded from the affluence of German society as a whole. Indeed, there is hardly any Turkish middle class.[31]

In social terms, the rights of Turks to live within German society are also limited. Most have a Residency Permit rather than a Right of Residency. Whereas the former acknowledges one's right to reside in Germany, the latter can be revoked by the German state. Although such revocation has been rare in recent times, recanting permission remains at least a theoretical possibility. Furthermore, housing ordinances have functioned as a further means of excluding Turks from German society. According to a German law, any area with over 6 percent foreign population can be designated as an "overburdened settlement area"; with 12 percent a city can assert this designation without any need for higher authority.[32] This legal provision provides an attempt by the German state to disallow the development of Turkish "ghettos" and areas that might fall away from German cultural domination. In the words of Ray C. Rist, a large number of foreigners seems to "constitute an implicit assumption that the concentration of foreign workers is detrimental to German society." Rist, however, shows that Turkish space may assume a much smaller form, in that individual apartment buildings are generally distinguished between those in which Germans live and those inhabited by foreigners.[33]

However, Turks have been able to acquire "places of their own" within Germany as a whole. Berlin Kreuzberg, the most famous and largest Turkish neighborhood in Germany (now zoned as an overburdened settlement area), is commonly designated as "Small Istanbul." While the concentrated settlement of Turks in Berlin Kreuzberg has occurred partially because of German concepts of civic exclusion, it is also a result of Turkish interest in finding support and continuity with their homeland. Although Kreuzberg is located in the center of Berlin, it maintains a strong continuity of identity with Turkish society. Turkish-owned shops and coffee and tea houses provide ways to maintain ties with other Turks. Turks' residence in Kreuzberg is not accidental. Kreuzberg has been traditionally a peripheral area of Berlin. Formerly surrounded on three sides by the Berlin Wall, Kreuzberg is one of the most economically depressed areas in Germany.[34] In this sense, Kreuzberg represents one of the few areas that Turks are able to afford in Berlin.

Mandel provides an interesting cultural example of the attempt of Turks to "live" in Turkey, while residing in Germany, by making annual visits to Turkey. She writes that while migrants live and work in Europe for eleven months each year, they are waiting for the twelfth month in which they can "really live" by going home.[35] According to Mandel, "For many, if not most, migrants, Kleine Istanbul is not home. They dream of their final return to Turkey, plan for it, save for it, talk of it."[36] There is also a great deal of confusion when Turks living in Germany return to their homeland. Often they are no longer accepted as strictly "Turkish"—the identity that they have attempted to retain in Germany—and Turkish friends and family in Anatolia often refer to them as *Almancı* (someone from Germany). Many have indeed adopted aspects of German culture. This dynamic is particularly acute among later generations of Turks resident in Germany, who, similarly, are sometimes called *"deutsche Ausländer"* (German foreigners) or *"ausländische Einheimische"* (foreign natives) in German media.

Education and the State(s)

Education provides an important means of socialization for later generations of Turks who, unlike their parents, grow up in German society. To a significant extent, however, education reinforces the German notions of exclusion. At a national level, the widespread presence of Turkish students at the lowest streams of German education has pushed German students into higher streams of education.[37]

In accord with the notion of being *religionsneutral*, the German state requires schools to provide religious education for adherents of the officially sanctioned religions. However, the state leaves Islamic religious instruction to the discretion of the individual *Länder*. In so doing, the state confirms the idea that it is not its responsibility to attempt to assimilate and accommodate the particular needs of Turkish students. While religious education might serve as a means of socialization, developing a Muslim identity within German society and bringing ethnic Turks closer to the German state, according to prominent understandings of German identity, Turkish ethnic background and Muslim religious identity persist as signs of difference.[38] Moreover, very few states (notable exceptions include North Rhine-Westphalia and, recently, Berlin) have actually chosen to provide separate funding for Turkish language and Islamic religious education. Instead, most states have opted to provide educational programs provided by the Turkish state. Because this instruction is in Turkish, not German, Yasemin Karakasoglu points out that "Muslim children never acquire concepts enabling them to discuss religious concepts with Germans.[39]" Islamic religion, rather than becoming a means of integration into German society, becomes a means of separation by distancing Islam from German institutions and connecting it to Turkish ones.

Muslim Identity among Turks in Germany: Here and There

To some extent, Muslim identity is conditioned in response to the dominant and exclusive German, and Christian, culture. Turks understand themselves to be Muslim specifically as a way to locate themselves in relation and in contrast to Christian Germans. It is important to recognize that German society has contributed to this dynamic in several ways. Since the Second World War, West German society has attempted to pursue a close relationship between religion and state in an attempt to distance Germans from the atrocities of atheistic National Socialism (and perhaps equally important, from the "atheistic" East German state). Religion, therefore, has been understood by the West German state as a resource against totalitarianism.[40] However, the close partnership and legal recognition given to the Catholic and Protestant Churches has fostered the perception that being German is intimately connected to being Christian. Although Judaism is granted a similar status to the two Christian denominations, it is possible to argue that this status is closely related to West German attempts at reconciliation with Jews following the Second World War. Moreover, Judaism does not enjoy the numerical strength of Catholicism and Protestantism that allow for a parallel comparison.

As already indicated, the German state has been unwilling to grant Islam the same legal status as Protestantism, Catholicism, and Judaism in terms of state tax privileges, education, and cultural recognition.[41] It is possible to argue that purposeful exclusion of Islam from state cultural recognition is not surprising in a historical context. Numerous studies have attempted to relate German and Western perceptions of Islam (and Turks—oftentimes perceived as the same) as of the antagonistic "other."[42] Indeed, numerous German media suggest that Muslims and Turks should be understood as an undifferentiated civilizational whole that confirms Samuel Huntington's notion of a clash of civilizations. Turks, as Muslims, are often associated with fanaticism, backwardness, and terrorism. *Der Spiegel* in its series of articles in the April 1997 issue portrayed a growing sentiment of confrontation between Germans and *Ausländer*. The cover of the issue featured the juxtaposition of a Muslim girls' school, a girl protesting, and a series of apparently Turkish teenagers showing off their weapons, with the accompanying title, "Outsiders and Germans, DANGEROUSLY FOREIGN: The Failure

of the Multicultural Society."[43] The article, moreover, mentions sociologist Heitmeyer's finding that 57 percent of the Turkish youth polled responded affirmatively to the (both ambiguous and misleading) statement that "the Turkish nation is our body, our spirit is Islam.
A spiritless body is a corpse."—a statement which, according to the article, "sounds quite as-
tonishing to German ears." Jutta A. Helm points out that Turks have assumed the form of
"other" in another important means of social discourse: as the subject of jokes. For example,

> Question: What is the difference between Turks and Jews?
> Answer: The Jews already have it behind them.

Helm points out that this identification of Turks as the "new Jews" not only reveals
racist attitudes, but that the Turkish presence in Germany has become "an emotionally
perceived threat."[44]

Muslim identity, in this context of exclusion of the Turkish "other," serves as a means
of defining Turkish identity by contrasting Turks with those who they are not. Dursun Tan
and Hans-Peter Waldhoff describe this type of cultural and religious position as "culturally defensive," in which isolation from the decadence of German society acts as a means
of Muslim-Turkish group cohesion.[45] In this sense Germans appear as the "other" in the
consciousness of many Turks in Germany. Indeed, they often refer to Germany as "Gavuris-
tan" (the land of the infidel). External symbols worn by Turks, such as the headscarf, act
in this context as a means of resistance against the impiety (and perceived sexual promiscuity) of German society by isolating Turkish Muslim women from it. A recent Turkish
film juxtaposes promiscuity, crucifixes, and German society with the tragic lives of Turks
in Germany,[46] revealing the partially reactive significance of Muslim-Turkish identity in a
German context.

At the same time, increasingly intensified Muslim identity and Islamism provide a way
of connecting between here (Germany) and there (Turkey). Whereas the Turkish state has
linked Turkishness to territoriality and the Turkish state (with mythic historiography that
also serves to legitimize the state), a significant number of Turks in Germany have developed a new notion of Turkishness in terms of religious identity. For example, the organization Milli Görüs, which is outlawed in Turkey, is tied to movements within Turkey promoting the development of an intense Turko-Islamic identity. Somewhat ironically,
Turko-Islamist movements operating in Germany such as Milli Görüs can best be understood as intimately connected with Germany, both as a reaction to German state and society and as a dependence on space within Germany away from the hegemony of the Turkish state.

However, Muslim identity as a source of Turkishness contrasts with Turkish state definitions of identity. There are numerous explanations for this discrepancy. First, the Turkish state has never been able to assert absolute control over identity, even within the confines of its own territory. The 1970s in Turkey marked a time of severe social division with
the politicization of Islamist ambitions.[47] Necmettin Erbakan's National Salvation Party,
which favored an increased role of Islam in politics, enjoyed a large degree of support
throughout the 1970s, especially in the least developed parts of Turkey.[48] Many Turks in
Germany, mirroring this demographic composition, have also been attracted to this move-

ment. When the Turkish military engineered a coup in the early 1980s, the state was unable to extend its hegemony to the Turks living in Germany. Shortly after the coup, however, Turkey reached an agreement with Germany that increased the role of the Turkish Department of Religious Affairs (*Diyanet*) among mosques and in providing education for Turks in Germany.[49] This agreement has also provided a context for the Turkish community to perceive the close state cooperation as indicative of a "co-conspiracy" between Germany and secular Turkey. The diminishing capacity of the Turkish state to pursue etatist policies is growing increasingly apparent during a period of downsizing, liberalization, and privatization. These processes, in turn, allow for the development of a partially autonomous civil society within Turkey, a significant portion of which increasingly identifies itself in Islamic terms.[50] Ultimately, the inability of the Turkish state to monopolize the identity of Turkish workers and their families in Germany, and the German state's detachment from the affairs of the community, have provided a space for Turks in Germany to discover an identity "between" states, particularly in Islamic terms.

Alevite Muslims, the Anatolian adherents of a version of Shi'ite Islam, have attempted to develop an understanding of their identity not only as differing from German society, but also as distinct from Sunni Islam. Alevites in Turkey, fearing possible oppression from the Sunni majority, have remained the strongest supporters of a secular Turkey and are vehemently opposed to Sunni Islamist movements. In Germany, Alevites have often attempted to use integration in German society as a means of distinguishing themselves from Turkish Sunni Muslims. For example, Alevite women avoid the veil as a means of showing their willingness to integrate into German society. Alevites tend to see themselves as modern, progressive, secular and anti-fundamentalist, as a result of which they are viewed more positively by German society than Sunni Turks. Whereas both Sunnis and Alevites often hang Turkish flags as signs of their Turkishness, Alevites are more likely to put pictures of Mustafa Kemal Ataturk in Berlin shop windows as signs of their dedication to a secular Turkish republic. Exclusionary definitions of citizenship still apply to Alevites, however, especially because many Germans do not recognize the distinction between them and Sunni Muslims. Alevites themselves, less prone to center their activities in the mosque and often framing their identity in contrast to Sunni fundamentalism, seem to confirm the idea that the only possible means of integration occurs at an individual level by accepting German social institutions and ideas.

Islamic Institutions: Us or (Part of) Them?

Despite the fact that many Turks in Germany have used Islam as a means of framing identity in contrast to the German state, Turkish Islam in Germany has developed within a particularly German context. Because Turks have to survive within a German institutional framework, the institutional manifestations of Islam may actually provide a potential means of integration into German state and society.

From their earliest arrival in Germany, Turks have gathered together as Muslims. The German Basic Law (*Grundgesetz*) guarantees that "Every person [including foreigners] has the right to express his opinion in words, written material, and in pictures and also to publish and distribute these materials."[51] Nonetheless, the unwillingness of the German state to extend the formal religious recognition given to the Catholic and Protestant Churches to include Islamic institutions has provided a hindrance to the integration of Muslim Turks. Mosques, which have generally been local and low-scale in organizational terms, have not easily adapted to the hierarchical structure of German churches. Increasingly, however, many mosques have recognized the need to work together in larger organizational terms in order to achieve political recognition by German authorities. The Islamic Federation of Berlin, established in 1980, sought to bring together all Muslims, not just Turks, in the hopes of receiving recognition by German authorities. However, this organization was relatively short-lived.

Both Turkey and Germany have been interested in bringing Muslims under a greater degree of state control. The German state is interested in developing a single voice for Muslims for reason of more effective policy. Both states would like to bring the rather divided Turkish Muslim community under a greater degree of centralized control, as a way of moderating the contrasting, and occasionally radical, Muslim voices in Germany (which sound alarming to German ears and which rebuke the secular legitimacy of the Turkish state). The two states reached an agreement in 1981 that only imams and religious teachers approved by Turkey's Department of Religious Affairs (*Diyanet*) would be permitted to work with Turkish Muslims in Germany.[52] This has proved somewhat effective in moderating Islamic extremism among Turks.[53] Many Islamists, however, have instead gone through official channels, effectively "infiltrating" Turkish state control.[54] Although a large number of mosques (some 740) are under direct *Diyanet* control, other organizations also have significant membership. The Association for a New World View in Europe, which is Islamist in orientation, has 262 member mosques. The Grey Wolves, regarded by both Germany and Turkey as the most extremist in orientation, have 180 member mosques.[55] Although German acceptance of *Diyanet* serves to reinforce the ties of domestic Turks with the Turkish state, the connection also provides a greater means of consolidation for Turkish Muslims, with the potentially greater opportunity for integration into the German system.

Muslims in Germany belonging to different organizations, Turks and non-Turks alike, have sought to achieve legal recognition, similar to the Christian churches, by forming a central authority. In 1994, the Islamic Council for the Federal Republic of Germany was formed on the model of the Central Council of Jews in Germany. This organization aspires to represent the needs of the Muslim community as a whole by operating within a German legalistic framework, while attempting to avoid competition with any Islamic organization. The Council has adopted German religious, social, and political discourse. Discussions are framed in terms of human rights, modern individual needs, religious freedom, and human dignity, concepts which the German state and court system can understand.[56]

Mosques in Germany respond to the needs of Turks in German society. Unlike in Turkey, where mosques function primarily as places of prayer, German mosques assume functions more like those of German churches, providing welfare services and serving as the locus of funerals, weddings, and social gatherings. In addition, mosques take on roles not generally associated with either mosque or church in providing needed services for a community between states. *Halal* (Islamically acceptable) meat is often provided by butchers at a local mosque. Mosques offer courses responding to the needs of the local community, such as German language and computer courses and translation services. As a community center, the mosque responds not only to the spiritual concerns of Turks in Germany but acts as a gathering place for maintaining connections to Turkish culture as well as responding to more "secular" needs.

Although the German state at a national level has generally attempted to maintain the links of Turkish Islamic institutions to the Turkish state, some local communities have recognized the integrative potential of Islam. For example, the city of Mannheim, home of Germany's largest mosque, has co-financed integration programs for Turks in the mosque.[57] However, Mannheim's mosque has recently become the center of local controversy because of the decision to replace the mosque's liberal, pro-integration leader with a member of the ultranationalist Grey Wolves organization, who opposes the integration of Turks into German society. Interestingly, this move was supported by the Turkish state "as pressure against Germans critical of Turkey and as a bulwark against Islamists."[58]

Reunification and Contemporary Issues

Following German reunification in 1989, several new issues have emerged that affect the status of the Turkish minority in Germany. Politically, reunification has meant less the establishment of a new German state than the integration of the former East German republics into West German institutions. Whereas most Turks who have lived in Germany for decades still do not have German citizenship, former East Germans have acquired citizenship instantly. Unlike Germany's treatment of its Turkish population, unified Germany has made considerable efforts at integrating the new citizens and their institutions. "On the one hand the Turks are more 'foreign' than the Germans of the eastern 'new states,' yet in many cases the Turks are much better integrated into the western German social and economic structures."[59] More important, the collapse of the Soviet bloc has led to thousands of "ethnic Germans" seeking refuge in the German state. Although the latter have come only very recently to Germany and occasionally lack complete competence in the German language, they, too, have automatically qualified for citizenship. The rapid attempt at East German integration, and the willingness both to accept and accommodate ethnic "Germans" from the former Soviet bloc, has led to a more profound sense of being foreign in contrast to being German among Turks in Germany. The increase in xenophobic attacks against Turks following the reunification, particularly among former East Germans, has further added to the sense of isolation among Turks in German society.

Currently, more than two million Turks live in Germany, the majority of whom continue to be without German citizenship.[60] Moreover, only one-fourth of Turks actually have the right of residency; the rest still possess a permit that can at least theoretically be removed upon expiration. Nonetheless, some progress has been made toward the fuller incorporation of Turks into the German state apparatus. For example, the 1990 Foreigner Law recognized the right (not privilege) of many Turks who have grown up in German society to German citizenship at the age of eighteen. However, many have not taken advantage of this because it would require renouncing Turkish citizenship, and with it a sense of cultural and familial connection. An important citizenship law passed in 1999 further expanded foreigners' citizenship rights by reducing the required time of residence in Germany from fifteen to eight years, granting automatic citizenship to children born in Germany of foreign parents (who have resided in Germany for more than eight years), and even permitting dual citizenship until the age of eighteen. Although this law has significantly amended existing citizenship legislation by introducing citizenship rights based on residence in Germany, genealogically defined understandings of citizenship have also been maintained and will continue to affect popular notions of who is and who is not a "German." Moreover, Turkish youth are confronted with the difficult choice between German and Turkish citizenship at the age of eighteen. Although a growing minority of Turks has chosen to become German citizens,[61] an overwhelming majority (1.6 million of 2.1 million Turks) prefers dual citizenship and would apply for it if the possibility existed.[62] Regardless of citizenship, there is little evidence to suggest that large numbers of Turks living in Germany will return to Turkey. This is especially true of second- and third-generation Turks who have grown up in Germany and lack a formal memory of the "home" country.

Although services and businesses that orient themselves to the needs of Turks living in Germany have slowly developed, most Turks have remained employed by German businesses (especially industry). Despite a relatively constant level of Turks in the country, the number of Turkish-owned businesses has increased from 33,000 in 1990 to some 47,000, employing over 200,000 workers (a large portion of whom are Turks). According to a study conducted by the Center for Turkish Studies at the University of Essen, job security and independence are the most frequently mentioned reasons for the trend toward self-employment among Turks in Germany. It is possible to argue that this trend seems to indicate that Turks, in "setting up shop," are confirming the permanent nature of their lives in Germany.

Turkish-owned businesses generally try to remain independent from German state control as a way of affirming their sense of separation from German society. However, business also represents a possible means of integration. As Turks become more economically rooted in German society, their need to operate according to rules more clearly defined by the German state increase as well. A recent survey indicates that 81.2 percent of the Turkish-owned businesses in Germany fulfill the formal requirements dictated by the German state for the training of apprentices.[63] It is also becoming more difficult to discern Turkish from German consumption. Many German consumers find Turkish produce of much higher quality than that offered by German grocers, and therefore patronize "Turkish" markets.[64]

Conclusion

I have illustrated the complex relation between culture and politics in the lives of Turks residing in Germany. The understanding of German nationality in static and essential terms has entailed an understanding of the presence of Turks as external to the German nation. Germany has, instead, largely turned over Turkish religious institutions, education, and other means of transmitting identity to Turkey in an attempt both to distance Turks from the German state and to maintain cultural and political allegiance with Turkey. However, this attempt has not proven entirely successful. The presence of Turks in Germany appears to have become permanent, calling into question the German understanding of the nation that has excluded them. Moreover, Turkish understandings of nation, intimately connected to the territorial Turkish state, have not been able fully to survive "extraterritorially." Instead, Turks living in Germany have attempted to discover identities of their own, that, while influenced by both states, are not entirely connected to either. Many Turks in Germany have redefined the notion of "Turk" in religious terms, which runs counter to the secular understanding of the Turkish state. In this sense, Turks in Germany have discovered identity "between" states.

Notes

1. Samuel Huntington, "Clash of Civilizations," *Foreign Affairs* 72, no. 3 (Summer 1993): 22–49.

2. Yasemin Soysal, "Workers in Europe: Interactions with the Host Society," in *Turkey and the West: Changing Political and Cultural Identities*, ed. Metin Heper et al. (London: Tauris, 1993), 236.

3. As Rogers Brubaker points out, particular "cultural idioms" manifest themselves in political conceptualizations of citizenship. *Citizenship and Nationhood in France and Germany* (Cambridge: Harvard University Press, 1992), 16.

4. Ruth Mandel, "Shifting Centres and Emergent Identities: Turkey and Germany in the Lives of Turkish Gastarbeiter," in *Muslim Travellers: Pilgrimage, Migration, and the Religious Imagination*, ed. Dale F. Eickelman and James Piscatori (London: Routledge, 1990), 153–71.

5. I am not suggesting that Muslim identity has been the Turks' only response, but wish to illustrate the ways in which Islam has served as a form of "Turkish" identity in German society. Ethnic Kurds, who comprise approximately one-fourth of Turkish workers, have also been influenced by a similar space "between" states encouraging "Kurdishness" (as well as Muslim identity).

6. Albert Hourani, "Ottoman Reform and the Politics of Notables" in *Civil Society in the Middle East*, ed. Augustus Richard Norton (Berkeley: University of California Press, 1995), 103–4.

7. Consider the fact that the Turkish National Pact, which stated the goals for the Turkish Nationalists during the Turkish War of Independence, never made reference to "Turks" or a "Turkish Nation," but rather to the "Ottoman Muslim majority." See also Erik Zuercher, *Turkey: A Modern History* (London: I. B. Tauris & Co., 1993), 154, 158–9.

8. According to Erik Zuercher, the population of Anatolia climbed from being approximately 80 percent Muslim in 1918 to more than 98 percent after the Turkish War of Independence. Ibid., 171–73; It is also worth noting that this trend would continue in the following years as a result of property taxes that were disproportionately applied to non-Muslims. According to official statistics, Turkey is currently 99.8 percent Muslim.

9. Patricia M. Carley, "Turkey and Central Asia: Reality Comes Calling," in *Regional Power Rivalries in the New Eurasia: Russia, Turkey, and Iran*, ed. Alvin Z. Rubinstein and M. Smolansky (Armonk, N.Y.: M. E. Sharpe, 1995), 177–79.

10. Serif Mardin, "Religion and Secularism in Turkey," in *The Modern Middle East*, ed. Albert Hourani et al. (Berkeley: University of California Press, 1993), 369.

11. Roderic H. Davison, "Turkish Attitudes Concerning Christian-Muslim Equality in the Nineteenth Century," in *The Modern Middle East: A Reader*, ed. Albert Hourani et al., (Berkeley: University of California Press, 1993), 75.

12. Turkish Industrialists' and Businessmen's Association, *Perspectives on Democratisation in Turkey* (Istanbul: Tüsiad, 1997), 45.

13. Bernard Lewis, *The Emergence of Modern Turkey* (London: Oxford University Press, 1961), 15.

14. Binnaz Toprak, "Civil Society in Turkey" in *Civil Society in the Middle East*, ed. Augustus Richard Norton (Leiden: E. J. Brill, 1995), 627.

15. Brubaker, *Citizenship*, 15.

16. Michael Minkenberg, "Civil Religion and German Unification," *German Studies Review* (February, 1997): 66.

17. Ray C. Rist, *Guestworkers in Germany* (New York: Praeger Publishers, 1978), 136.

18. Jorgen S. Nielsen, *Muslims in Western Europe* (Edinburgh: Edinburgh University Press, 1995), 26.

19. Rist, *Guestworkers*, 61.

20. Ibid., 91.

21. Peter O'Brien expands on this notion, noting that "the strong emphasis on rapidly developing the West German economy became inextricably linked to the yearning for the unification of all Germans. With familiar irony, though, the maturing German economy soon fell dependent on foreign labor." "Continuity and Change in Germany's Treatment of Non-Germans," *International Migration Review* (Fall 1988): 115.

22. Rist, *Guestworkers*, 90.

23. Tufan Kolan, "International Labor Migration and Turkish Economic Development" in *Manpower Mobility Across Cultural Boundaries: Social, Economic, and Legal Aspects, The Case of Turkey and West Germany*, ed. R. E. Krane (Leiden: E. J. Brill, 1975), 138–60.

24. Terry D. Monson, "Differences in Industrial Learning Behavior of Turkish Workers at Home and Abroad: Causes and Consequences" in *Manpower Mobility Across Cultural Boundaries: Social, Economic, and Legal Aspects, The Case of Turkey and West Germany*, ed. R. E. Krane, (Leiden: E. J. Brill, 1975), 95–123.

25. O'Brien, "Continuity and Change," 116.

26. Rist, *Guestworkers*, 65.

27. Alan Richards and John Waterbury, *A Political Economy of the Middle East: State Class, and Economic Development* (Boulder: Westview, 1990), 247–48.

28. In Rist, *Guestworkers*, 76.

29. In O'Brien, "Continuity and Change," 123.

30. Elcin Kursat-Ahlers, "The Turkish Minority in German Society" in *Turkish Culture in German Society Today*, ed. David Horrocks and Eva Kolinsky. (Providence, R.I.: Berghahn, 1996), 113–14.

31. Eva Kolinsky, "Non-German Minorities in Contemporary German Society" in *Turkish Culture in German Society Today*, ed. David Horrocks and Eva Kolinsky (Providence, R.I.: Berghahn, 1996), 98–99.

32. Rist, *Guestworkers*, 81.

33. Ibid, 80.

34. Ruth Mandel, "A Place of Their Own: Contesting Spaces and Defining Places in Berlin's Migrant Community" in *Making Muslim Space in North America and Europe*, ed. Barbara Daly Metcalf (Berkeley: University of California Press, 1996), 147–66.

35. Mandel, "Shifting Centres," 156.

36. Mandel, "Place of Their Own," 163.

37. David P. Baker, et al., "Effects of Immigrant Workers on Educational Stratification in Germany," *Sociology of Education* 58 (October 1985), 213–27.

38. Eva Kolinsky, "Conclusion" in *Turkish Culture in German Society Today*, ed. David Horrocks and Eva Kolinsky (Providence, R.I.: Berghahn, 1996), 183.

39. Yasemin Karakasoglu, "Turkish Cultural Orientations in Germany and the Role of Islam" in *Turkish Culture in German Society Today*, ed. David Horrocks and Eva Kolinsky (Providence, R.I.: Berghahn), 1996, 164–5.

40. Minkenberg, "Civil Religion," 67.

41. A variety of other religious groups have also been denied such recognition. On the one hand, Germany's treatment of Islam is much better than that of some other religious groups, such as Scientologists and Jehovah's Witnesses, whose status as religions have been challenged. On the other hand, no other religion of comparable numerical strength has been denied public recognition.

42. See M. E. Yapp, "Europe in the Turkish Mirror," *Past and Present* (November 1992): 134–55.

43. *Der Spiegel* (April 14, 1997).

44. Jutta A. Helm, "No Laughing Matter: Joking about Turks," *German Politics and Society* (Spring 1994): 51.

45. Dursun Tan and Hans-Peter Waldhoff, "Turkish Everyday Culture in Germany and its Prospects" in *Turkish Culture in German Society Today*, ed. David Horrocks and Eva Kolinsky. (Providence, R.I.: Berghahn, 1996), 141.

46. Mandel, "Place of Their Own," 154.

47. Nilufer Gole, "Authoritarian Secularism and Islamist Politics: The Case of Turkey " in *Civil Society in the Middle East*, ed. Augustus Richard Norton. (Leiden: E. J. Brill), 36–37.

48. Toprak, "Civil Society," 637.

49. Jorgen S. Nielsen, "Muslims in Europe in the Late Twentieth Century" in *Christian Muslim Encounters*, ed. Yvonne Yazbeck Haddad and Wadi Zaidan Haddad (Gainesville: University Press of Florida, 1995), 319.

50. Binnaz Toprak, "Civil Society," 101, 106–12.

51. Rist, *Guestworkers*, 145.

52. Nielsen, *Muslims in Western Europe*, 30.

53. Karakasoglu, "Turkish Cultural Orientations," 169.

54. Nielsen, *Muslims in Western Europe*, 31.

55. Karakasoglu, "Turkish Cultural Orientations," 169.

56. Soysal, "Workers in Europe," 236.

57. "Mit den Wolfen heulen" *Der Spiegel* (April 27, 1998), 58.

58. Ibid., 61.

59. Mandel, "Fortress Within," 115.

60. For recent employment and residence statistics, see Institute for Turkish Studies, University of Essen <http:\\www.uni-essen.de\zft>.

61. In 1997, approximately 220,000 out of 2,049,000 opted for German citizenship. These figures do not indicate if the latter are Sunni , Alevite, or even possibly Kurdish in background. The Turkish state has accommodated those who have chosen to become German by issuing them so-called Pink Cards, allowing former Turkish citizens to keep many of their former citizenship privileges (including inheritance privileges, but excluding voting rights).

62. Faruk Sen, "Turkish Communities in Western Europe" in *Turkey Between East and West: New Challenges for a Rising Regional Power*, ed. Vojtech Mastny and R. Craig Nation (Boulder: Westview, 1996), 252.

63. Institute for Turkish Studies, University of Essen <http:\\www.uni-essen.de\zft>.

64. Mandel, "Place of Their Own," 152.

THE EXPERIENCE IN AREAS OF EUROPEAN SETTLEMENT

Muslims in Australia: The Building of a Community

I I

ANTHONY H. JOHNS AND ABDULLAH SAEED

Introduction

> Never had I participated in an Eid gathering as big as the Lakemba celebration. I was stunned
> by the size of the crowd, the sounds, the buzz in the air. The scene tapped many buried mem-
> ories. I had an awkward rush of nostalgia as thoughts of my youth rose up. I savoured the rit-
> ual of prayer and the emotional charge that always lingered from its strange blend of vulner-
> ability, submission and solidarity. People had been gathering since dawn. . . . By 7 a.m. Wangee
> Road was jammed with an excited, happy throng. People spilled into front gardens and on to
> balconies or perched on walls. All wanted to be together for Eid ul-Adha. The next day, news-
> papers reported that more than 7,000 people had attended the Lakemba mosque. . . . I was
> spellbound. From my vantage point opposite the mosque, I could see over people's heads. The
> scene was far different from anything I had imagined. Inside the mosque, the religious and
> political aspects of Lakemba life were unfolding. Dignitaries, community leaders and politi-
> cians were paying their respects (and being seen paying them), and there were dignified prayers
> and speeches. But outside it was a festival—an unofficial youth festival with wave after wave
> of laughing, chattering young people. The allure and sheer magnetism of the occasion were
> irresistible.[1]

THIS VIVID DESCRIPTION OF THE 'ID AL-ADHA CELEBRATION in Lakemba in 1994
gives an idea of the vitality of the Muslim community in Australia and the role
of one of its best known Australian mosques. The community, however, is not
large, nor has its establishment as one of the viable religions of the continent been easy.
Like that of coreligionists who have immigrated to many other parts of the non-Muslim
world, the transition has often been fraught with difficulties, not the least being the suspicion and lack of welcome with which they have been greeted by native citizens.

Muslims in Australia in the year 2000 were a network of cohesive groups forming a
distinctive community in a diverse population. In 1996 over 200,000 Muslims were resident in Australia, comprising 1.1 percent of the population.[2] The accuracy of the figure is
uncertain, in part due to the reluctance of immigrants from particular parts of the world
to provide more personal information about themselves than is required by law. Figures on

mosque attendance and membership in Islamic organizations suggest that 400,000 may be a more realistic figure. But even 200,000 would make Islam the largest religion in Australia after Christianity, though fewer in number than the nearly three million persons who claim no religious allegiance, over 16 percent of the population. Numbers alone, however, give little information about or insight into the human dimension of Muslim communities in Australia, the challenges they face, the pains and joys they experience. This needs to be seen in the context of the background and history of Muslim migration, the structure of Australia as a nation-state, and the distribution of Muslims within it.

Australia comprises six vast states and two territories. The population is largely urban, and loyalties are expressed in the rivalries between the capital cities of these states and territories: Adelaide, Brisbane, Canberra (the Federal Capital), Darwin, Hobart, Perth, Melbourne, and Sydney. Each state has a large number of smaller towns, villages, and settlements in country areas. Sydney and Melbourne account for almost a third of the Australian population and are on the verge of becoming megacities with their own corporate pride and character. They are also composite entities consisting of subsets of identification and loyalty, often distinguished by the ethnicity, social class, professions, employment patterns, and social status of their inhabitants. It is within the interstices of this structure that the Muslim 1.1 percent has its place.

Although not large, the figure is significant when compared with census figures for 1947,[3] for which no Muslims were indicated, and only 0.5 percent of the population was listed as not belonging to a Christian denomination. (At that time, Aboriginals were not included in the census). It is not until 1971 that Muslim residents were recorded, when they constituted 0.2 percent of the population. The 1996 figure of 1.1 percent reflects a steady and continuing growth curve. Equally important, the individuals the statistic represents are not evenly distributed, and it is in this respect that the breakdown of Australia into states and cities is significant. Half of Australia's Muslims are in Sydney, 32 percent in Melbourne, and only 4.3 percent live outside the major cities.

Compared with the rest of the population, Muslims comprise 2.1 percent of the population of Sydney and 1.6 percent of that of Melbourne. Yet in some Sydney suburbs, Muslims are 5 percent of the population, and, in a few, up to 10 percent,[4] sufficient in number for a Muslim community to be visible and identifiable as such. In fact they have established a critical mass, a visibility, a demographic, social and industrial importance, and the capacity to make an individual and distinctive contribution to the shaping of Australia. This, however, does not take into account the number of Muslims in Australia holding strategic positions as professionals. For many of these Muslims, primary contacts are with their professional peers, their relationships with other Muslims perhaps marginal or even incidental to their ethnicity or religious commitment.

According to the 1996 census, 72,161 or 35.9 percent of the Australian Muslim community was born in the country, the largest single group. Of those born abroad, the biggest group is those born in Lebanon, 27,125 (13.5 percent) followed by Turks at 22,270 (11.1 percent). In descending order of size are 6,939 from Indonesia, 6,651 from Bosnia-Herzegovina, and 5,221 from Iran, followed by Muslims born in Fiji, Cyprus, Malaysia, Egypt, Macedonia, India, and Singapore, down to the United States, represented by 242! Those born in Australia largely remain in the ethnic communities of their parents.

Not all are children of first generation migrants: there are a few old established Muslim families, as well as a number of Australian converts. But the characteristics of Australian-born Muslims—relative youthfulness, stability of family life, number of children, and the lowest rate of religious out-marriage in Australia—are indicators of a strong and continuing growth of the Muslim community in Australia, and of the indigenization of Islam as a religion in Australia.[5] At the same time, it must be stressed that the Australian Muslim community is very diverse. Media headlines, stereotypes, and popular cliches about Islam suggest that there is a single Muslim entity, when in fact there are many communities of Muslims making up the fabric of Australian Islam.

Migration and Muslim Settlement

There are indications that Macassar fishermen from the southern Celebes sailed on a regular basis to Northern Australia in search of *trepang* (*beche de mer*) from as early as the sixteenth century. Some may have settled in parts of Northern Australia, intermarrying with local Aboriginal communities and possibly introducing Islam to them. Muslim graveyards from an early period can be found even today in Arnhem Land.[6]

It was, however, the Afghan camel drivers brought to Australia between 1860 and 1910 who were the earliest of the many ethnic groups that have come to constitute a Muslim presence in today's Australia; they have become part of Australian history and folklore. The story began when Thomas Elder and Samuel Stuckey became aware of the feasibility of using camels for transport across and exploration of the interior of Australia, and in 1866 imported 124 camels and thirty-four Afghan attendants. Commenting on the importance of these Afghan camel drivers, Christine Stevens writes:

> For nearly fifty years these Muslim men and their animals crisscrossed three-quarters of the Australian continent to service and sustain life and industry in the harsh interior. Without the exceptional skills and perseverance of these hardy Muslims—among the first Muslims to become part of the cultural mix of contemporary Australian society—much of Australia's traditional wealth would have remained undeveloped for many decades.[7]

The first teams were settled at Beltana sheep station in the Flinders Ranges.[8] Reports indicate that, during this period (1860–1910), between 2,000 and 4,000 men were brought to Australia to work in this camel-based transportation industry. These Afghans worked in the desert inland sections of the then separate colonies of South Australia (including Northern Territory), Western Australia, Queensland New South Wales, and Victoria, providing a vital lifeline between the developing settlements scattered across the continent and the major settlements of the south and east coastal regions.

The Afghans formed tight but isolated communities on the edges of outback towns. They were viewed as temporary sojourners only (and indeed most of them planned to stay only a few years before taking their earnings back home) and so were not accompanied by their families. At first, due to prejudice against outsiders, they were denied access to either Aboriginal or European women. Later, however, some of them were to find wives among marginalised groups of women: deserted wives or Aboriginal women who had been disowned by their cultural groups or were landless.[9]

Hanifa Deen, a descendant of one of these original Afghan Muslims, tells of what she heard from her father about the fortunes of these Afghans in her book *Caravanserai—Journey Among Australian Muslims*. When they returned home after a few years in Australia, some to the northern Punjab, where they had been recruited, they told stories of life in the great South-land. They were a source of inspiration for others who were suffering economic hardship to go to seek their fortunes there. New workers made their way to Australia via Singapore and Hong Kong. Eventually, in the 1880s, they began to settle in Perth, Sydney, and Melbourne, congregating in particular suburbs, including Redfern in Sydney. Many of them worked as hawkers. As they traveled, supplying goods needed outside the main centers of population, they established a mutual credit system among farmers in the outback. While, in Stevens' account, they were despised in some areas, Hanifa Deen relates that they were regarded with affection and respect for their honesty as well as the role they played. Having arrived before the introduction of the White Australia policy, they were also able to establish themselves in rural areas, such as the La Trobe valley, as farm laborers; some of them tended banana plantations in Queensland.[10] On a small scale, this interaction was an early instance of mu-tually beneficial interaction between Muslim immigrants and the Christian settlers in Aus-tralia who had preceded them.

The introduction of mechanized transport in the late nineteenth century led to the collapse of the camel trains. When, in 1901, a Federation was created out of the former colonies into which the Australian continent had been partitioned, its early commitment to the White Australia Policy excluded most non-Europeans from the right to apply for naturalization and further marginalized the Afghans. Denied citizenship, and with em-ployment opportunities becoming fewer, many of those still remaining chose to return to their homelands.[11] Some, however, lived out their lives in places such as Wyndham, on Aus-tralia's northwestern coast. This reduction in numbers made it all the more difficult for those who remained to retain their Islamic identity. By 1921 there were fewer than three thousand Muslims resident in Australia. Alienated both religiously and racially from the dominant white Anglo-Celtic society, many of this generation of Muslims lost their Is-lamic faith.[12]

They did not, however, vanish without a trace. The camels they left behind in the Aus-tralian outback flourished and have regularly been exported to Saudi Arabia and the Gulf States for racing. More importantly, some of the mosques they built have survived. One of the oldest, built in 1889 and still in use, is in Adelaide; another, built in 1891 at Bro-ken Hill in New South Wales, is now a museum maintained by the Broken Hill Histori-cal Society.[13] The remains of a number of the mosques can be seen on the old route to the northwest between Adelaide and Brisbane. The camel traders left their mark on the Australian landscape in other ways: today, in Alice Springs, there are still Mahomet and Khalick Streets, as well as the Charlie Sadadeen School. The popular name for the Trans-Australian Railway is the Ghan, so named after the Afghan cameleers who helped estab-lish the first transport system across arid central Australia in 1879.[14] Indeed, one original Afghan, who came in 1885, lived on until his death in 1962 at the age of 106.[15]

Nevertheless, a minor tributary of Muslims from the Indian subcontinent continued even during the years of the White Australia policy. In 1920 there was a slight relaxation in the application of the Immigration Act, allowing a number of limited family reunions.

With the independence of the Indian subcontinent and the creation of Pakistan, a number of these Muslims or their descendants returned to their former or ancestral homelands, while others remained in Australia.[16]

Generally speaking, federation in 1901 marked an end to Muslim entry to Australia. Most immigrants were from Britain and Europe; religiously, they represented the Judeo-Christian tradition and thus contributed to the development of a homogenous Australia. One exception was the small number of Albanians, former citizens of the Ottoman Empire, who made their way to Australia throughout the 1920s and 1930s. As Europeans, they were not subjected to the restrictions imposed on earlier Muslims by the White Australia policy.[17] They were a trickle rather than a stream. Between 1930 and 1939 only some four hundred of them arrived in Australia, predominantly single and male, some as young as fifteen. They worked as casual laborers in Western Australia, and Queensland as well as Victoria. A small number settled in Melbourne. The best known Albanian mosque is on Drummond Street in the Melbourne suburb of Carlton.[18] A new and larger stream began to flow in the 1940s, namely the immigration on a small scale of Turkish-Cypriot Muslims, facilitated by the fact that they had British passports.

There was, however, no significant increase in the immigration of Muslims until the late 1960s, although the ground was prepared for it soon after the end of World War II. A need to rebuild the Australian economy led to the development of a vigorous new immigration policy, with the slogan "populate or perish." Immigration Minister Arthur Calwell, overcoming the suspicions of the trade unions, pioneered a policy that brought thousands of immigrants to Australia. They came first from Britain, which was economically prostrate after the war. A British immigrant could travel by ship to Australia for £10. Immigrants were actively recruited from Italy and other areas of Europe. The launching of the "Snowy Mountains" scheme brought thousands of immigrants to the country, including displaced persons from Yugoslavia, Bulgaria, Cyprus, Poland, Hungary, and Russia.[19] These may well have included European Muslims, who would not have been excluded by the White Australia Policy, but the range of ethnic backgrounds went far beyond the traditional Anglo-Celtic mix that was the backbone of the Australian population.

At the same time, there were various factors at work leading to a modification in practical terms of the White Australia Policy. Foremost among them was the emergence of the new Asian nations of Indonesia, India, and Pakistan to Australia's north and northwest, the move towards self-government and independence of Malaya and Singapore, the Communist Revolution in China, and the economic emergence of Japan as a major trading partner. Australia's geographical position on the rim of Southeast Asia was crucial, as was a positive engagement with its Asian neighbors. At a political level, this engagement began in response to the struggle for Indonesian Independence from 1945 on, continued through the Indonesian campaign for West New Guinea, and, then, Indonesian confrontation of Malaysia. Finally, there was participation in the Vietnam war.

This engagement with Asia, however, was to be much more than political. It soon became clear that educational needs in Australia could not adequately be served by the tradition of the humanities derived from Europe and that it was educationally, politically, and, in the longer term, even economically prudent to include the study of the languages and cultures of Asia in the curricula of the various levels of the Australian educational system. This provided an opportunity for reciprocal human relationships between Australia and its neighbors and served to prepare the ground for the social acceptance and welcome of individuals from different backgrounds.

The Colombo Plan brought significant numbers of Asian students to study in Australia and, in some cases, facilitated Asian scholars teaching in Australian institutions. Closer contacts of this kind at a personal and official level, and the increasing number of Asian nations with diplomatic representation in Canberra, gradually made clear that the White Australia Policy was incompatible with positive relations between Australia and its neighbors. Thus, even before it was formally abandoned, there were transient Muslims in the diplomatic corps in Canberra and at consulates in the state capitals as newly recognized nations established missions in Australia, and as Australia founded its own Department of Foreign Affairs, independent of Britain. Significant numbers of students who came to Australia for technical training and university study from 1951 under the Colombo Plan acquired skills that could later be practiced in Australia, and, alongside them, numbers of professional people were granted "Certificates of Exemption."

Scholars appointed to Australian universities to teach the languages and cultures of Asian nations found a place in the Australian educational system. Some became members of the academic elite, with the capacity to introduce Australians to higher levels of Islamic culture.[20] There was considerable diversity of social class, level of education, skills, and training in the various Muslim groups that were being established in Australia. Thus, by the early 1960s, although the White Australia Policy was officially still in place, selection criteria had been relaxed to enable the entry of refugees, professional and skilled workers, and family members into the country, irrespective of race.[21]

Another factor contributed to the demise of the White Australia Policy. The Australian economy in the 1960s was booming and needed workers. But with the recovery of the European economies, the supply of European immigrants began to dry up. New sources of immigrant labor were essential. One response to this need was the signing of an immigration agreement between Australia and Turkey in 1968. Turkish Muslims represented the first wave of large-scale Muslim immigration to Australia and laid the foundations for the growth of significant Muslim communities in both Melbourne and Sydney. The first planeload of 186 Turks arrived at Sydney airport in November that year and were dispersed to automotive assembly lines and clothing and textile factories, in Victoria. Between 1967 and 1971, over ten thousand Turks were to emigrate from Turkey.[22] Older Muslim settlers in Australia recognized a historical significance in their arrival, seeing in it continuity with the immigration of Muslims over a hundred years before. A number gave them a ceremonial welcome at Sydney airport, including Shaikh Fahmi el-Imam, who had arrived in the 1950s, a pioneer of interfaith dialogue, who is still imam at the Preston mosque in Melbourne.[23] Others were reminded of the Anzacs at Gallipoli in 1915, when an expeditionary force composed largely of Australian and New Zealand military attempted to invade Turkey, and was defeated. No grudges followed that defeat, and the welcome of Turks as new Australians had an almost poetic irony. There is an additional irony in that it was an Australian need that brought an earlier generation of Muslims to Australia, the Afghans, as it opened the door to the Turks in 1968. With their arrival, the door was also opened for the entry of non-European and non-Christian immigrants into Australian economic, political, and social life; the official abolition of the White Australia Policy in 1972 was an inevitable consequence.

In the early 1970s, a large number of Muslims began to arrive from the Middle East, some as a result of war and civil unrest. In the wake of the Arab-Israeli war in 1967 and the continuing Palestinian tragedy, the war in Cyprus in 1974, the outbreak of civil strife in Lebanon in 1975, and the breakup of Pakistan, leading to the establishment of Bangladesh, Muslim immigration to Australia increased dramatically. By 1981 Australia had received about 16,500 Lebanese-born Muslims, who today form the largest group within the Australian Muslim community.[24] More recent immigrants include refugees from Somalia, Afghanistan, and Bosnia; between 1991 and 1995 Australia accepted 14,000 Bosnian refugees.[25] Since 1998, significant numbers of Muslim boat people from the Middle East have been reaching Australia. Many of them are currently detained, waiting for a decision on their refugee status. Some are highly qualified professionals. Of course, not all Muslims came as a result of war. Immigration programs were structured according to an annual quota, and filled according to a mix of criteria which might vary from year to year but generally included professional skills, knowledge of English, sponsorship, family reunions, refugee status, and age.

As a corollary to the new immigration policy, there was a change in the concepts of "social engineering" that governed the acceptance of new immigrants. The assimilationist model was replaced by a policy of multiculturalism, in large part due to the representations of an emerging vocal immigrant community. It recognized the value of diverse cultural traditions living in harmony, and so provided opportunities for giving a voice to various ethnic, linguistic, cultural, and religious minorities within an Australian context. In the 1970s, new publicly funded institutions arose that were designed to support the multicultural idea: a government Department of Multicultural Affairs, government-funded research projects on settlement in Australia, the Special Broadcasting Service (the SBS) with radio and television programs in the languages of all the major ethnic communities, and the Adult Migrant Education Program. Translation services and classes in English were established.

Thanks to this policy of multiculturalism, Muslim Australians have gained a voice and an identity. It is natural to speak of the Muslim "community," but it does not mean that Islam should be understood in a unitary sense. There are a number of Muslim communities, and to appreciate the potential and reality of their contribution to Australia, it is necessary to stress their richness and diversity. Muslims are distributed across the whole range of professions and fields of employment, with varying levels of education, opportunities, and drive for upward mobility. Ethnic loyalties are still preserved, as is characteristic of the Islamic tradition. Thus, there is always a fusion of the universal forms and doctrines of Islam with local beliefs and lifestyles, with ethnicity remaining an important element in the composition of the Muslim *umma* in Australia.

Australian Muslims brought with them a range of cultural richness and diversity of background, and this diversity was also expressed in their different responses to the new environment. Many felt uprooted and traumatized at finding themselves in the unfamiliar situation of being a religious minority and were forced to adopt different kinds of strategies for survival. Initially, neither state nor local community could give them any support, let alone offer recognition of their faith or of the rituals that identified them as a community.

They brought a faith expressed through cultures with deep historical roots, a variety of kin and associated supportive networks, and a consciousness, however vaguely formulated, of being bearers of a great tradition of learning, art and culture. Yet, as newcomers, they found themselves counting for little, and facing disregard, if not hostility. Culture shock, bewilderment, and disorientation were the common response at arriving in a land where the local way of life seemed sterile, boring, and empty, and family relationships attenuated and underdeveloped. Over and against such personal concerns, of course, loomed broader issues: the challenge of survival and the establishment of institutions that would give a corporate presence to Muslim life in the new country.

Muslim Community Building, Post-1970

Until the end of the 1960s, there were not enough Muslims in Australia to establish the kinds of institutions that serve as the cornerstone of Islamic life. Nevertheless, the potential was always there. Muslim communities in Australia had little to start with other than these inner resources and needed to establish a place for themselves among other communities with differing ways of life and spiritual priorities. The effort to establish themselves, and define their own identity, often had to be carried out in the face of open hostility on the part of other Australians.

There were two sources of support in facing this challenge. One was the aforementioned shift from "assimilationism" to "multiculturalism." The second was the support made available to Muslim communities from overseas for building mosques and prayer facilities, providing imams, and establishing educational facilities for Muslim children. Fortuitously, this coincided with the time when there was an explosion of oil prices, and so-called petro-dollars for charitable projects were plentiful; the various Muslim communities took full advantage of these opportunities.

The mosque has a central role in the life of a Muslim community in both its social and its prayer life. It serves as a center for worship and for the expression, interpretation, inculcation, and celebration of Muslim belief and practice. Thus it is a community reference point and provides the means for self-identification in the new homeland.

Gary Bouma gives a lucid and sympathetic account of mosques in Australia, although, since his book was published in 1994, much of his information is now somewhat outdated.[26] He notes that at the time of writing, there were fifty-seven mosques in the country. The first was probably that built outside Adelaide in 1889 by the Afghans; another came to New South Wales about 1891 in Broken Hill. A number of Australian mosques are over a hundred years old. One was constructed in the national capital of Canberra during the 1950s to serve the diplomatic staff of the embassies of Muslim countries and Muslim students from overseas. The first mosque in Sydney was built in the late 1960s; in Sydney and New South Wales there are more than twenty mosques, the majority of them built since 1968. Of these, the largest, and for some the most beautiful, is the Imam Ali Mosque at Lakemba. Another is the King Faisal Mosque, built by the Islamic Society of New South Wales.

The city of Melbourne has more than twenty-five mosques. The largest, in Preston, Victoria, was opened in 1976 by the Assistant Secretary General of the World Muslim League in the presence of a personal representative of the Prime Minister Malcolm Fraser, the then Leader of the Opposition Gough Whitlam, and religious leaders, including the Roman Catholic Archbishop of Melbourne. Thus, the event was regarded as significant in the development of Australia as a nation and was welcomed by the government and community, as well as by the older established religions in Australia.[27] There are now mosques in all the other capital cities, each with its story to tell, and others being built.[28] These mosques are largely the result of support by local communities, although, in some cases, assistance comes from the governments of Muslim states. (See table 11.1 for mosque distribution in Australia.)

Approval for the building of mosques has not always been easy to obtain. Some people have complained to local authorities about the traffic jams during worship times or the disturbance of the early morning tranquillity by the dawn call to prayer. In 1995 an abandoned Presbyterian church in the Sydney suburb of Bankstown was bought by the Bangladesh Islamic Centre. The Bankstown Council, which had given permission for the church to be built in 1954, opposed its use as a mosque. In 1998 the matter went to the Land and Environment Court, which supported that opposition, ruling that a mosque, while a place of worship, is not a church, which it defined as a place of worship in the Christian tradition. This ruling was successfully challenged on the grounds that the judge failed to consider broader dictionary definitions, some of which include a mosque or a temple in their meanings of the word "church, and, therefore, insofar as "church" refers to a place of worship rather than a physical structure, a mosque would fit this description. The announcement that the original decision was overturned coincided with 'Id al-Adha, a timing particularly pleasing to the Australian Federation of Islamic Councils.[29]

During the 1970s and 1980s, the new immigrants, divided both by residence and by state (Australia being a federation), set to work to consolidate their position. Islamic societies mushroomed, each located at a mosque or prayer facility and structured to meet the needs and concerns of communities. Such societies by definition were pioneering in nature and uncertain in their organization. But by the 1980s they became well-established and effective. In each state, the various societies established state Islamic councils to work on such concerns as welfare, educational and religious facilities, and coordination of statewide community-related functions. The Islamic Council of Victoria, for example, has a board of imams, mechanisms for representing Muslims at the level of state government, and a range of activities including interfaith dialogue.

The Islamic councils of all the states have been represented at the federal level since the 1970s by the Australian Federation of Islamic Councils (AFIC), an umbrella organization

Table 11.1   An estimate of the current distribution of mosques in Australia.[30]

Australian Capital Territory	1
New South Wales	28
Queensland	10
South Australia	4
Tasmania	1
Victoria	29
Western Australia	7
TOTAL (2000)	80

for all Australian Muslims. It has been funded by support from the local communities, from oil-rich Muslim countries, from revenue generated by the issuing of *halal* certificates, and, as its capital resources increased, from its own investments. Utilizing these funds, AFIC was able to provide sufficient monies to support the varied activities of the Muslim community, both at local and national levels, and to make contributions toward the further building of mosques and prayer facilities, the provision of imams, and the establishment of educational facilities for Muslim children. The organization survived the decline in world oil prices of the late 1980s and the subsequent reduction in petrol dollars available for the "propagation of Islam" worldwide thanks to the generous support provided in the previous decade. In maintaining all the organization's activities, the Saudi Kingdom played a special role.

Religious Leadership

The effectiveness of the mosque as an institution depends on the qualifications and quality of leadership that the imam serving it can provide. The 1980s saw, among those entering Australia, a significant number of graduates in Islamic disciplines, mainly from Islamic universities in the Middle East and the Indian subcontinent. Formally, they were qualified to serve as religious professionals, although often they were not familiar with Australian conditions. A number of them were sponsored in their move to Australia by the governments of countries such as Turkey and Saudi Arabia. Indeed, from the beginning of large-scale Turkish migration in the late 1960s, there was official Turkish interest in the religious life of the expatriate community in Australia. The Turkish government expressed this interest by sending imams to a number of Turkish mosques and by providing funding for mosque building. Saudi Arabia has also been extremely active in funding similar projects. Even with the decline in world oil prices, significant funds were provided to the community in the late 1980s and 1990s to establish this infrastructure.

The relatively large-scale immigration of Muslims in the 1980s, and well into the 1990s, meant that religious leaders were arriving from a variety of communities and cultures. The policy of multiculturalism made it relatively easy for religious leaders who had the support of their respective communities to gain visas, and the governments of countries such as Egypt and Turkey supported Imams serving societies comprised of their nationals.[31]

Effective religious leadership is essential for a sense of religious identity. If it cannot be homegrown, it must be imported. Although these "imported" leaders have generally provided excellent leadership,[32] others who are unfamiliar with conditions in Australia, including local culture and the demands placed on the local community within a secular environment, have been controversial.[33] Such unfamiliarity at times has led to difficulties with the religious community as well as with some segments of the wider society.

In fact, a continuing problem for the Muslim communities in Australia is that of the evolution of a professional religious leadership that is knowledgeable about both Islamic and Australian culture. Some well-established imams have spent a considerable amount of time in Australia and understand the tension between preservation of identity and adaptation to the wider culture. These established religious leaders use their local knowledge and their fluency in English to be active at local, state, and federal levels in promoting the needs of Muslims and in playing a significant mediating and facilitating role between the wider society, the government, and the Muslim communities. Imams more recently arrived and not yet familiar with the local culture are somewhat handicapped in this regard. Though there are signs of the emergence of a small number of younger religious leaders born and educated in Australia, it may take some time before a homegrown professional religious leadership emerges.

Educational Facilities

As early as the 1950s, there were moves among the older generation of Muslims, few as they were, towards establishing an organizational framework for the maintenance of Islam in Australia. The setting up of "Sunday Schools" signified the recognition by parents of the need to provide for their children's Islamic education. One of the earliest schools opened in Melbourne in 1957 with fifteen children.[34] It was, however, in the early 1980s that the first regular Islamic schools were established. Australian government (commonwealth and state) support for community-based schooling provided a strong incentive for Muslims to establish their own Islamic schools. Unlike other Western countries such as the United States, where there is no taxpayer-funded Islamic school system, and Britain, where there had been none until recently, Australia gives substantial support to private schools, provided that they meet certain conditions. As a result of this support, which was first won for the Catholic school system in the 1960s, private schools of various kinds have multiplied. They include elite secular schools, schools with an ethnic base, and a number of fundamentalist Christian schools. The number of children in such schools grew by more than 50 percent between 1986 and 1994. This level of enrollment can be expected to grow even more since the federal government ended the minimum and maximum enrollment limits on private schools, adjusting the education funding formula in their favor.[35]

It was in this context that, from the early 1980s, Muslims were able to begin the establishment of primary and secondary schools to teach the core curriculum areas of the state in which they were located, along with Arabic and Islamic religious instruction. In other words, they were providing a secular education within an Islamic environment. With the initial infrastructure for the schools coming largely from outside sources, the subsequent funding from the commonwealth and state governments was used to expand the Islamic education system considerably.

A number of these schools serve as the final two years of secondary education, and some of them are able to include languages such as Turkish in their curriculum. Despite initial difficulties, standards have gradually improved, and the well-established ones, such as the King Khalid Islamic College in Melbourne, the Malik Fahd Islamic School in Sydney, and the Islamic College of Perth, compete with other established prestige schools to provide a high quality education. At the King Khalid Islamic College of Victoria, for instance, all students who graduated in 1998 obtained university places, a success rate far above the average for Victoria and a striking example of upward social mobility in the new generation of Muslim immigrants. Today there are twenty-three Islamic schools, with a student population of around 10,000 (See table 11.2). In addition, many weekend Islamic schools and Qur'an classes are held at most mosques and Islamic schools.

One would expect Sufi orders to play a role in Islamic education in Australia, but it is difficult to find detailed information about them. An Australian Centre for Sufism was established in Sydney in 1999, with the mission "to promote the message and the beauty of Sufism and Islam in Australia through raising the awareness of God in day to day life using the teachings of Sufism to define the journey of life."

Many other organizations, some of them ad hoc, meet various needs in the community and are an expression of its vitality. There are committees to discuss and formulate policy on issues of importance, such as announcing the beginning and ending of Ramadan[36] or ensuring that *halal* food is available. Brunswick, for example, an inner-city, working-class suburb of Melbourne, features *halal* Turkish clubs, restaurants, coffee houses, and bakeries.[37] There are also committees formed to discuss issues of dress and whether it is obligatory for women to wear a headscarf. There are friendship organizations, such as the El Sadeaq Society, based in Melbourne. It has a community center and small mosque for its mainly Egyptian members, and functions as a surrogate family, embracing Egyptians of all ages, dedicated to serving their religious, educational, recreational, and social needs that neither state nor society provide. Other groups, such as the Arabic Speaking Welfare Workers Association and the Arab Women's Solidarity Foundation, are dedicated to social welfare, community support, and matters of community concern.

Of particular significance, because it is based in the national capital, is the Canberra Islamic Centre. It was incorporated in December 1993 to epitomize Islamic culture and lifestyle, provide social and cultural facilities, and be a liaison with the Australian government and countries of Muslim embassies in Canberra on behalf of Muslims. Because the Islamic Centre does not depend on any of the Muslim embassies for financial support but aims to be self-funding, it is registered as a charity to which donations are tax deductible. It is not a member of AFIC, although it has contacts with it. Its constitution ensures that no particular ethnic group can dominate it. It has been granted a prime site by the ACT (Australian Capital Territory) government, plans are approved, and building construction has begun. It will house an Australian National Islamic Library, for which a thousand books have already been collected, as well as recreational facilities such as a swimming pool

Table 11.2   Islamic Schools[38]

	1982– 1989	1990– 1995	1996– 2000		% primary
Australian Capital Territory	0	0	0		
New South Wales	3	1	6	4,000	65%
Queensland	0	1	0	250	100%
South Australia	0	0	1	100	100%
Tasmania	0	0	0		0
Victoria	2	2	3	3,000	65%
Western Australia	1	2	1	1,900	65%
TOTAL (2000)	6	6	11	9,250	

for women. Launched with an inaugural address by the Governor General in 1997, the Centre holds monthly meetings, and has some two thousand members.

Muslim organizations of one kind or another are active in the all states and territories of Australia, including convert support groups and educational institutions. Many social and educational Muslim institutions take the initiative to work with travel agents in organizing group tours for those wishing to make the Hajj or 'Umra at reasonable prices.[39] Various communities have also established Islamic banking on a small scale,[40] although there is only one local Islamic financier, The Moslem (sic) [Muslim] Community Co-operative of Australia, which is in the process of upgrading its status by becoming a credit union.[41] Many women's organizations have been formed for devotional or educational purposes, as support groups, and to help women deal with life in Australia. A Muslim Women's National Network of Australia publishes a regular newsletter.

As well as participating in the mainstream media, Muslims run small-scale radio stations in the major metropolitan areas of Melbourne and Sydney. Local Muslim newspapers and magazines are also gaining a following. *Australian Muslim News* is a long-running publication under the banner of AFIC. Other publications include the magazine *Salam*, *Nida al-Islam*, and a series of student newsletters. Most of these are based in Sydney or Melbourne.

Muslims Living in Australia

Despite the fact that Australia is ostensibly a Christian nation, it shares the social permissiveness associated with "post-Christian" Europe. It is secularized to a far greater degree than statistics of religious affiliation would suggest, with widespread evidence of family breakdown, sexual license, violence, and a general lack of interest in the practice of religion. It is not often, except on special occasions, that Anglo-Celtic or Euro-Australians meet Muslims as Muslims. They meet individuals whom they may identify as "Asian," meaning Indonesian, Pakistani, Philippine, or Chinese. Religious denomination at such a level of acquaintance is not often relevant. The public ethos is overwhelmingly secular. To refer to God in public is seen as embarrassing. Religious allegiance is excluded from all application forms for jobs and need not be indicated on national census forms. (Religious affiliation may be indicated for admission to a hospital so that religiously acceptable services may be provided or appropriate funeral rites performed.) In Australia the practice of religion is a private matter, apart from occasional rituals such as the recitation of the Lord's prayer at the opening of Parliament, and may even be regarded as evidence of a certain social and intellectual backwardness.

Some Muslims are totally at home within the mainstream secular Australian community, relating to their fellow religionists through their ethnic communities at Friday prayers or during the religious observations during Ramadan or Hajj. Active participation may vary from simply personal identification as a Muslim to full participation in the social and religious activities of the community. Some simply drop out, while others, in the face of these challenges, rediscover a Muslim identity that had lain dormant. For many Muslims, the experience of living and working in what is publicly a secular society presents real problems. Islam is a religion with a ritual law that requires visible, outward signs of commitment. Thus, issues of religious observance inevitably arise, including prayer, fasting, dress, and regulations relating to food and drink. Islam has its own twelve-month lunar calendar marked by its own sacral points and celebrations, all of which identify Muslims as "a people set apart." To the secular world, or even to religious traditions that do not have such a ritual law, this may command respect or it may arouse resentment.

The five daily ritual prayers, fasting, and the role of festivals in Muslim community life have implications for the workplace. Through interviews with Muslim respondents, Bouma reports that often employers and coworkers respond to these religious concerns with increased respect for the Muslim workers and for Islam, though it is difficult to be sure how representative these are.[42] Without a proper recognition in the work place of the Muslim way of life, Muslims are likely to feel members of a fringe group in Australia. The traditional Christian festivals of Christmas and Easter marked by public holidays are so familiar to traditional Australians as to be religiously neutral. But this does not help Muslims who have their own religious celebrations. Interrupting the working day for prayer times is a new problem for employers. It is not only a question of time, but also of the need to provide a private space in which to pray, as well as facilities to perform the required ablutions for males and females, which may require special plumbing.

The fast presents greater difficulties. It imposes a heavy burden, especially during the summer months when the long days mean up to seventeen hours of fasting, made more difficult by high temperatures. This requires some concessions or at least recognition on the part of management. Although the rules of *fiqh* (jurisprudence) in regard to the fast have a realistic flexibility, for most Muslims, the fast is to be accepted, no matter how severe the difficulties. The ending of the fast is one of the great festivals of the Muslim year. It and the festival marking the climax of the pilgrimage ceremonies in Mecca are part of the lifeblood of the Muslim community, and inability to take part in the celebrations, whatever the reason, is disruptive of family life and causes a loss of psychological well-being. Muslim workers need to be able to participate in these rituals and festivals without experiencing financial loss.

Food requirements are likewise a problem. Not every work canteen can provide *halal* meat, and although fish, egg, and vegetarian dishes may be available, for some, even the proximity of pork dishes to those lawful for them to eat is a problem. Alcohol plays a major role in social life for many Australians during recreation and relaxation after work. Taking a turn to shout a round of drinks is an important part of social bonding. While non-alcoholic drinks are available, the general atmosphere of a hotel, the air heavy with the smell of beer, and the heightened gregariousness due to the effects of alcohol, are difficult for Muslims to cope with.

Then, there is the matter of dress. In general, this affects women more than men. For some women, a total covering of the body apart from the face or hands is regarded as a sign of commitment to Islam and is a matter of conscience. This style of dress may appear intolerably ostentatious, potentially alienating prospective employers either out of prejudice or through concern that members of the public may find it disconcerting.

The situation is duplicated when children go to school. Parents are concerned that their children have the opportunity to pray with facilities for ablutions, and that *halal* food be available. Some of the most popular sandwich fillers for Australian children include pork products. Problems may arise with participation in social activities such as visits to McDonald's, excursions, or barbecues, or sleeping over with friends. For girls who have reached the age of adolescence, problems may become acute: whether they should "cover" or be in mixed classes, what clothing they should wear for physical education, or if they should swim in mixed company. Members of the Muslim community are more concerned about such matters for their children than for themselves, since children need support and protection in their faith and are vulnerable in ways that adults are not. A number of schools do provide the necessary facilities. Some teachers ask for guidance as to how Muslim children may be integrated in schools and help students know where prayers can be performed.

There are no instant solutions to such issues, particularly since Muslims as a minority are finding their way and there are differences in Muslim communities themselves as to how they should be accommodated. Some prefer to be closely associated with the wider Australian community and have an open, confident attitude to the outside world. Others feel the need for an Islamic space in a community of their own, where they can be themselves. Some prefer to interpret broadly, some more conservatively, the norms of conduct set out in particular traditions of Islam. All, in one way or another, have to find ways to respond to new situations, and yet maintain what is of the essence of the transcendent values of Islam. Particularly painful are issues of interfaith marriage, especially the marriage of a Muslim girl to a non-Muslim, when there is the risk of an irretrievable family breakdown.[43]

This engagement of Muslims with non-Muslim Australia is a continuing process. Much of what passes as documentation of its progress or lack of progress is either based on interviews, which may or may not be representative, or is anecdotal. Yet, in some cases, there is a legal base for the protection of religious minorities. The New South Wales Public Service, for example, has issued a circular to heads of departments to make sure no one is denied time for religious obligations. Many private employers take the same view.[44]

Australian Attitudes to Islam

There is a pecking order in the popular assessment of religions in Australia. Buddhism is intellectually chic, and there is a broad appreciation in educated circles of the sacred sites and spirits and reverence for land and nature of Aboriginal spirituality. Islam, on the other hand, is widely viewed through stereotypical lenses, and conversion to Islam (as opposed to Buddhism, for example) is regarded as an aberration. There is a degree of sympathy for certain aspects of Sufism. But the Sufism that is admired is often not that of the spiritual giants of Islam growing out of the Qur'an and the Islamic tradition, with its spiritual discipline of prayer, meditation, and ascetic practice, but out of an aesthetic appreciation of the poetry and theosophy of the Ibn 'Arabi tradition, productive of a warm inner glow. Islam, in such circles, is regarded as a kind of optional extra to Sufism.

There are other reasons for this attitude to Islam. Islam as a politically loaded stereotype based on media images dominates the public consciousness. It is not widely realized that Islam means submission to the will of God in all things, a Muslim being one who makes this act of submission, and who works to realize the moral values and social virtues epitomized in the Qur'an. This is not to suggest that there is necessarily any widespread personal animosity to individual Muslims in Australia, but there is enough latent resentment for concern. There have been objections voiced to the growth of Islamic education in Australia, partly, of course, on the grounds that increased funding of private schools would inevitably be at the expense of the public school system. Those with misgivings about multiculturalism in general are also unhappy with state-supported religious schools being established. Some feel that criticism of Muslims and Islamic schools could be part of a latent racist discourse, creating a less tolerant society by accusing those who are culturally different.[45]

Hanifa Deen gives a number of instances of such resentment at a personal level. She tells of a couple she met at a cafe in Sydney who, learning that she was writing about Muslims in Australia, began to denounce the arrogance of Muslim women wearing the veil. "Just who do they think they are? Where do they think they are living?"[46] She tells of the experience of a Lebanese woman, who regularly wore the veil, enrolling in a community development course at her local college. She had expected to be able to meet and talk with non-Muslim women. But each time she attended classes, she was asked such questions as, "What's it like wearing that bag?" "Won't your husband take a second wife, then a third as you get older?" or "Do you wear it in bed?" In a discussion class on gay relationships and adoption, she said that she could envisage a lesbian couple adopting children, but had difficulties with a male couple doing the same thing. A lesbian classmate walked out, reported the view she had expressed to the college administration, and the lecturer instructed her to read the rules concerning respect for the beliefs of others.[47]

On the one hand, Muslims are often dismissed as a minority fringe sect, with all the connotations that such an association implies, without a history, culture, or civilization; on the other, they may be seen as potential members of a menacing international conspiracy. The values that Muslim living exemplifies pass unnoticed. Muslims also suffer from quite widespread, subconscious, atavistic Australian distrust of things not Anglo/Celtic/North European, which, in times of tension, may unexpectedly erupt. The Gulf War was one such occasion. It was a special case, but it provoked irrational behavior in odd pockets of Australian society, including some Sydney suburbs, when individuals of possibly Arab appearance were harassed in the streets.

No account of such difficulties would be complete without reference to sections of the Australian media, whether print or electronic, and their tendency to reduce complex issues to stereotypes and to delight in presenting images people love to hate. Among these images is Islam as an abstract noun, used as a portmanteau term to elicit reactions of distrust and fear, with no reference to Islam as signifying a commitment and dedication to divine and human values. This is not to deny that there are a number of exclusivist Muslim groups with an ideological hostility to Australian (and Christian) society who, on various occasions, express their views. But that is no more than to say that there are Muslim counterparts to Australian rednecks. Appeals to ethnicity and religion unfortunately are a ready standby for the power-hungry no matter what their affiliation.

Positive Attitudes to Islam and Muslims

As far as the mainstream churches in Australia are concerned, the sectarianism of the first half of the twentieth century has largely been replaced by an awareness of each other as communities on complementary, rather than competing, journeys of faith. Warmth and friendship has largely replaced old rivalries and resentments. This change in attitude has extended to religious traditions outside the Christian fold. For many, it encompasses Judaism, and equally, with important and growing communities of immigrants from outside Europe, religions such as Islam, Hinduism, Buddhism, Sikhism, and the like—faiths new to what used to be mainstream Australia. This is a counterpart to developments in Europe, where, on church doors in Luxembourg and Belgium, one may see posters announcing lectures on Islam: "Get to know your new neighbours." In many cases this goes beyond tolerance and takes the form of an outstretched hand of welcome and support to these communities of faith in a new environment. It is then no accident that Gary D. Bouma, the author of *Mosques and Muslim Settlement in Australia*, is an Anglican priest. His book, which has been a valuable source for the preparation of this chapter, presents Muslim settlement as an enrichment of Australian life and society.[48]

Many Christian communities, in fact, make it a matter of concern to understand and appreciate the theology, moral values, and social discipline of Islamic teaching. They refer to Muslims as members of the broader monotheistic community, recognizing Muslims as among the people of God in the so-called bidding prayers of a Sunday liturgy as communities on whom God's blessing is invoked. And where there have been Muslim guests at functions attended by mixed faith communities such as weddings, baptisms, and funerals, passages from the Qur'an are now sometimes read.

A variety of organizations are dedicated to the goal of mutual religious understanding, giving Muslims a sense of belonging in Australia. Among them is the World Conference on Religion and Peace (WCRP), which has a pioneering role in stimulating support groups for new immigrants. It has arranged a number of conferences and issued various booklets laying the groundwork for interreligious understanding and mutual respect in practical matters, for example, assisting the settlement of people, and examining the adequacy of government provision for newcomers. The titles of their publications are an indication of their goals: *With Other Faiths—A Guide to Living with Other Religions*; *Religious Pluralism in a Liberal Society*; *Faith to Faith—Belief in a Pluralist Society* and *Guidelines on Dialogue with People of Living Faiths*.[49] The first booklet gives an account of two local initiatives, one of them having to do with community relations in the city of Springvale, near Melbourne. A gathering of faith leaders organized a number of meetings, one for a day of prayer, and another to coincide with the annual mayoral induction. These initiatives led to regular monthly meetings. The other was a series of discussion programs hosted at the Preston mosque in Melbourne. One, led by a Muslim and a Christian, was on the theme "Religious Understandings of Human Dignity." The mosque leadership and local clergy and members of their congregations together made a commitment to support these meetings.[50]

In New South Wales and Victoria, the heads of faith communities hold biennial meetings to discuss local issues such as racism and racial vilification, and in Victoria, a group works on a common approach to euthanasia. Interfaith units, on behalf of UNICEF, are addressing issues relating to children in the Pacific and Southeast Asia. About three years ago, the WCRP invited Malaysian Professor Chandra Muzaffar to Australia to address a meeting on "Religious and Human Dignity: Rights and Responsibilities." Up to the present, however, there have been few meetings dedicated to theological dialogue, due in part to the fact that Muslim communities in Australia at this stage are concerned principally with issues of survival, and also because they do not have the same proportion of middle-class intelligentsia as Muslim communities in Europe.[51]

Although the numbers are still small, there is a growing awareness in Australia of the values and religious insights in the theology of minority religious traditions, and of the human and social values expressed in their cultural traditions. One indication of this is the way in which some of the themes and motifs of Islamic literary culture are finding their way into Australian literature in English. Such an understanding of common elements in diverse traditions has to be inculcated through the education system, and teachers of religious studies have a special responsibility, along with the authors of textbooks, for such courses at various levels.[52] It is necessary to go beyond tolerance of areas of diversity to a sense of realization that there are elements that can be shared.

Conclusion

The general picture of Muslims in Australia is of a predominantly urban, intricate mosaic of communities and relationships at various stages of development. Islam is represented in all its principal traditions, Sunni as well as Shi'a, and smaller communities such as the Ismaelis and the Ahmadis, both Lahore and Qadiani. They vary in the style and intensity of their religious observance, and in their social interaction with non-Muslim communities. All these communities are proceeding in various ways and different speeds in a process of indigenization and vernacularization. Overall, it is a success story, a remarkable achievement. In less than forty years, Muslim communities have established themselves and created social and community structures to support an Islamic way of life. Mosques, many of them of real architectural beauty, are no longer an exotic feature of the Australian landscape, and behind one or two of them, there is a century or more of history. They are genuinely places of prayer and the celebration of a Muslim identity.

Islamic Schools have had significant successes measured against the standards of the wider community, despite problems in the development of an appropriate Arabic language curriculum and teaching materials, and recruitment of competent teachers familiar with modern methods of instruction. They have provided for many Muslims a way of retaining and strengthening their religious and cultural traditions within an Australian context, seeing it as part of their mission to nurture the generation of Muslims who are at home with Australian society as well as with Islamic tradition.

While Islam may not be well understood, or its relationship as a monotheistic faith to Judaism and Christianity appreciated, Muslims are recognized as part of the religious landscape, a far cry from the Afghan pioneers who, despite the services they gave, were often considered aliens.[53] Even though pockets of intolerance still exist, the wider Australian community is not simply tolerant, but fully accepting of Muslims as persons, as it largely is now of individuals of any ethnic background or skin color. This acceptance is backed by a number of laws and institutions that protect ethnic minorities. Among the Commonwealth Acts in this regard are the Equal Employment Opportunity (Commonwealth Authorities) Act 1987, the Human Rights and Equal Opportunity Commission Act 1986, the Racial Discrimination Act 1975, the Racial Hatred Act 1995.

A significant proportion of Muslims is middle class, and well represented in the professions. According to the 1996 census, 27 percent of families fully owned their homes, and 20 percent were purchasing their homes, a significant index of commitment to Australia. The statistics do not indicate how many of them have taken out Australian citizenship; whether to do so or not appears more a matter of ethnicity than religious commitment. It is also a matter of generation, the second generation taking advantage of a simple and straightforward ceremony of naturalization. It is not possible to estimate accurately the number of Muslim immigrants and their families who are naturalized or to determine whether one ethnicity is more likely to accept Australian citizenship than another.

There are a number of advantages to holding an Australian passport, although citizenship also carries responsibilities. Voting in national and state elections is compulsory, and failure to vote is punished by a fine. The major Australian political parties take into account the so-called ethnic vote—which, by definition, includes Muslims—in their campaigning, particularly in fringe electorates. Among Muslims, there seems no discernible movement to support one political party rather than another. Social class, need, and the relevance of electoral policies to their circumstances are the crucial factors. Even an issue such as that of Palestine does not have a defining role, since the position of the two major parties, Liberal and Labor, on this issue is so close. Certainly, AFIC does not sponsor any party political agenda. There is currently no study of the role of individual Muslims in particular parties or of Muslims in prominent positions in the bureaucracy or public life. But the communities are still young.

The numerous Islamic organizations show a variety of interests and concerns, all directed in different ways to establishing a network of valid Islamic responses to life in a new world without the weight of tradition that plays such a role in British and European life. One aspect of this is a gradual opening out of ethnic communities, most directly through marriage. If an Australian male converts to Islam and marries a woman of a particular ethnic group, he may well be accepted as a member of that ethnicity. At the same time, to some degree, he may carry his wife and in-laws into his own family circle and widen the horizons of all concerned. There is increasing intermarriage between Muslim ethnic groups, partly attributable to the spontaneous encounters between these subcommunities that occur at the mosque on the great festivals. It should not be overlooked that there are conversions to Islam in the wider community among those searching for, or reassessing, a previously held religious faith. Among such converts, women significantly outnumber men. Converts will make a notable contribution to the indigenization of Islam in the country.

Ideological orientation in some groups is taking the place of ethnic alignment, as individuals devise various approaches to living in the new country. There are lively debates in the various communities, and these have been carried onto the university. This has been particularly noticeable since the late 1980s and early 1990s, most major Australian universities having their own Muslim students' associations. Generalization in this area is difficult. A distinction has been drawn between so-called *salafi* and non-*salafi* Muslims, between imams reflecting a Saudi stance, and those sent out by the *diyanet* bureaucracy in Turkey. That there is a *salafi* movement is true, and it is propagated through organizations such as the Islamic Information and Services Network of Australasia. It is, however, not limited to Saudi Muslims. There are *salafis* among Jordanian, Indian, and Lebanese Muslims, as well as among Australian-born Muslims, and locally trained imams. But they represent one trend among many, and it is probably misleading to single out particular groupings and tendencies in a pluralistic situation that ranges from the radical and conservative to the highly eirenic and adaptive. Despite these differences, however, across the entire spectrum there is a sense of belonging to the Islamic *umma*.

The life and activities of these Muslim communities shows how Australia has changed since the end of World War II. In 1945 it was a monochromatic, monolingual country with a population of less than nine million. Politically, it had hardly escaped from the tutelage of Britain; racially, it was largely Anglo-Celtic, its skin pigmentation protected by the White Australia Policy (the Aboriginal population had been pushed to the fringes, and was not even counted in national censuses); religiously, it was dominated by three largely competing traditions of Christianity: Roman Catholic, Anglican, and the Free Churches; educationally, the fields of study that could be pursued were limited, and students with their eyes set on higher degrees had to go overseas. In the year 2000 Australia had more than doubled in population to more than eighteen million. The White Australia Policy has been abolished, and the country is home to a remarkable range of ethnicities, languages, and religious traditions whose rights and traditions are recognized under an umbrella policy with the admittedly ungainly title of multiculturalism. It has a sophisticated immigration policy—the 2000 target was 80,000 new immigrants per year. In addition, it has its own role in the community of nations, as well as its own pattern of engagement with Europe. The mother country, Britain, is now only a part of Australian identity, along with the Americas and the diverse nation states of postcolonial Africa, Asia, and Oceania, especially those that are its near neighbors. This is the Australia to which Muslims contribute as equal partners and in which they find a stimulus to develop and extend their ethnic traditions in their own way.

All in all, the picture is one of great vitality on the part of Muslims, who, from many quarters, are welcomed by an older established citizenry. There are grounds for hope that the multiple convergences among peoples of different backgrounds who now share a common homeland will continue to lead to a clearer perception of common core values behind variegated cultural forms. People need to make the effort to reach out and across traditional cultural divisions and recognize the values and ideals they share. Then, it will become possible to see how diverse religious traditions provide an ultimate, transcendent authority for such values and provide the means by which they can offer principles of order in social life.

Notes

1. Hanifa Deen, *Caravanserai: Journey among Australian Muslims*, (St. Leonards, New South Wales, Australia: Allen & Unwin, 1995), 121.

2. *Census of Population and Housing* conducted by the Australian Bureau of Statistics.

3. Gary D. Bouma, *Mosques and Muslim Settlement in Australia* (BIPR: Commonwealth of Australia, 1995), 27.

4. Ibid.

5. Bouma, *Mosques*, 37.

6. Fousiya Bismi, *Arab News* (Melbourne issue), Wednesday, 27 April 1994.

7. Christine Stevens, "Afghan Camel Drivers: Founders of Islam in Australia," in *An Australian Pilgrimage: Muslims in Australia from the Seventeenth Century to the Present*, ed. Mary Lucille Jones (Melbourne: Victoria Press, 1993), 62.

8. Stevens, "Afghan Camel Drivers," 52.

9. Stevens, "Afghan Camel Drivers," 53.

10. Deen,*Caravanserai*, 3–14.

11. Mary Lucille Jones, "The Years of Decline, Australian Muslims 1900–40," in *An Australian Pilgrimage: Muslims in Australia from the Seventeenth Century to the Present*, ed. Mary Lucille Jones (Melbourne:Victoria Press, 1993), 63.

12. Jones, "Australian Muslims," 68.

13. Bismi Fousiya, *Arab News*, 27 April 1994.

14. Ibid.

15. Laurence P. Fitzgerald, "Christians and Muslims in Australia," in *Islamochristiana* 10 (Rome, 1984), 163.

16. Deen, *Caravanserai*, 8–10.

17. Jones, "Australian Muslims," 78–79.

18. Deen, *Caravanserai*, 36.

19. Jones, "Australian Muslims," 87.

20. Among them was Dr. Abdul Khaliq Kazi who came from Pakistan in 1961 to teach Arabic and Islamic Studies at Melbourne University. In 1961 Dr. S. Soebardi (an Indonesian), the first tenured Muslim academic in Australia, was appointed to the Australian National University in Canberra to teach the Indonesian language and Islamic culture in Indonesia. In 1968 the first Muslim academic was appointed in Perth.

21. Jones, "Australian Muslims," 88.

22. Jones, "Australian Muslims," 94.

23. Deen,*Caravanserai*, 15.

24. Jones, "Australian Muslims," 94.

25. *The Age*, 3 July 1995, 3.

26. Bouma, *Mosques*, 56. See also Fitzgerald, "Christians and Muslims," 167–69.

27. The current imam is Shaykh Fahmi. Mosque facilities include an administrative section, classrooms, library, and catering area.

28. Bouma tells of a new mosque currently being built at Auburn to accommodate 5,000 worshippers, designed along classical lines with pillars, domes, and two 39-metre minarets. Bouma, *Mosques*, 56–57.

29. *Sydney Morning Herald*, 17 March 2000, 5.

30. This table is based on personal communications of Abdullah Saeed with imams of the various states.

31. Deen, *Caravanserai*, 73.

32. Sheikh Fahmi, for example, is highly respected among religious leaders of all faiths.

33. One such example is Taj al-Din al-Hilaly.

34. Jones, "Australian Muslims," 98.

35. Pamela Bone, "A New School of Social Division," *The Age*, 13 December 1996, 15.

36. Deen, *Caravanserai*, 63.

37. Deen, *Caravanserai*, 15.

38. Based on Dr. Saeed's communications with imams of the various states.

39. An inclusive price for the Hajj with three weeks in the Holy Land is under Aus$4,000.

40. Abdullah Saeed, "Islamic Banking Moving Towards a Pragmatic Approach," ISIM Newsletter, vol. 3 (1999), 7.

41. *The Australian*, 7 April 2000, 34.

42. Bouma, *Mosques*, 46–49. The author also documents a number of negative experiences.

43. Deen, *Caravansarai*, 160.

44. Bouma, *Mosques*, 49.

45. Irene Donohue Clyne, "Those Preaching Tolerance Failed to Extend it Religious Schools," *The Age*, August 1, 1997, 11.

46. Deen, *Caravanserai*, 125.

47. Deen, *Caravanserai*, 165–66.

48. Bouma, *Mosques*, 88. He notes that the opposite is the case: "The more religious people were, the less likely they were to object to foreigners, immigrants, or members of minority religious groups as neighbours."

49. See John Baldock, *With Other Faiths: A Guide to Living with Other Religions*. World Conference on Religion and Peace (WCRP), Religion in Australia Series, no. 4 (Melbourne, 1995).

50. Baldock, *With Other Faiths*, 25–25, 34–35.

51. Hanifa Deen, personal communication to Anthony H. Johns.

52. A recent contribution to religious studies in senior high schools in Australia is Beck et al., (Eds.), *Exploring Religion* (OUPANZ: Melbourne, 1997). A pioneering new tertiary-level work published in the United States is J. Renard, ed., *Windows on the House of Islam: A Source Book of Muslim Spirituality and Religious Life* (Berkley: University of California Press, 1997).

53. Christine Stevens, *Tin Mosques and Ghantowns: A History of Afghan Camel drivers in Australia* (Melbourne: Oxford University Press, 1989), 150.

Muslim Women as Citizens in Australia: Perth as a Case Study

12

SAMINA YASMEEN

I SLAM HAS BEEN A FEATURE OF THE AUSTRALIAN LANDSCAPE for a number of centuries. Formal contacts between Muslims and Australia began in the 1860s with the arrival of camel drivers from the Northwestern Frontier Province of British India.[1] Commonly referred to as Afghans, or Ghans, their number increased to about two thousand by the early twentieth century. They established the most reliable and efficient system of transportation between different colonies on the continent, and, in the process, built a number of mosques around the country. According to the prevailing laws, Asians were not permitted to bring their wives into Australia. Thus, they either remained bachelors or married Aboriginal or Anglo-Saxon women at the periphery of society. Their offspring were the first known Australian-born Muslims. Their number remained limited until the early 1920s, when Australia began to allow Muslim migration.

Initially, these immigrants came in small numbers as refugees of the two world wars from Albania, Yugoslavia, Poland, Hungary, and Russia. Liberalization of Australia's immigration policy and the political upheaval in Lebanon in the 1970s increased the numbers of Muslims immigrants. Today, Australia hosts 200,885 Muslims of diverse origin who have come from the Middle East, Africa, Southeast Asia, South Asia, and former Yugoslavia. Muslims account for 1.09 percent of the total Australian population, of whom 47.5 percent are women. With nearly half of its population now female, the Australian Muslim community looks very different from the early days of Muslim settlement when the emigration of women was banned. Not only has the total number of Muslim women migrating into Australia increased by nearly elevenfold during the period from 1971 to 1996, but the proportion of Australian-born Muslim females has also risen to 37 percent.[2] Of these women, four out of five are under forty years of age.[3]

Despite their obvious presence, little or no literature exists on the role of Muslim women as citizens in Australia. To some extent, this lacuna stems from the tendency among those engaged in the citizenship debates in Australia to define multiculturalism in terms of ethnic rather than religious diversity. Even when the role of religion is acknowledged, the dominant trend remains one of treating religious communities as single entities with little or no reference to the gender dimension. Muslim women, therefore, are often viewed as part of the Muslim community rather than as both Muslim and women. This chapter is an attempt to depart from this dominant trend and to assess the manner in which Muslim women participate and operate as citizens in the multicultural liberal democracy that is Australia. To this end, it focuses on Muslim women in the Perth metropolitan area and their experiences as citizens. It draws upon the findings of a large-scale research project on gender-based assessment of settlement needs of Muslims living in Perth in 1994–1995 and the research currently being conducted as part of the Women and Citizenship project at the University of Western Australia.

Islam in Western Australia

Islam was brought to Western Australia by people of Malay origin and by Afghan camel merchants during the second half of the nineteenth century. In the early 1870s the discovery of pearls and pearl shells in Nickol Bay prompted a number of Australian pearl dealers to recruit Asian divers, especially Muslims of Malay origin. Their total number in West Australian waters was estimated to be 1,800 by 1875. During the next few decades, the northern pearling town of Broome emerged as a major center of Malay Muslim population. Although brought in as contract labor under agreements concluded with Dutch authorities, these divers left a mark on West Australia's northern shores. Not only did they introduce Malay culture and cuisine but they also built a mosque in the 1930s in Broome.[4]

Meanwhile, Afghan cameleers arrived in western Australia from the eastern states. Most of these Afghans had already been employed in South Australia where they had established "Ghan towns" in Port Augusta, Maree, Beltana, Farina, and Oodnadatta.[5] The 1890s gold mining boom in western Australia attracted some of them. More arrived from Broken Hill and Bourke in New South Wales, crossing by land into Kalgoorlie, western Australia.[6] The port of Fremantle provided a second point of entry. Once in the state, they either traveled north along the coastline to reach the remote northwest areas or moved into the more arid interior. As in other states, they also began to establish their Ghan towns in the eastern and northern gold fields, with more than five hundred arriving by 1897.[7] By 1897, the total number of Afghans on these western Australia gold fields had exceeded five hundred. Within the next eight years, they were able to raise enough funds to build a mosque in the center of Perth City on William Street.

As their numbers grew, some of the new arrivals distinguished themselves as leaders of the Muslim community. The two best known Afghans of the early twentieth century were Faiz Mahomet and Musa Khan.[8] Outside the community itself, however, Muslims were disliked by the majority of the Anglo-Saxon settlers, who viewed them as barbarians who followed different customs. The criticism was partly due to the relationship between Afghans and European women. Since they were not permitted to bring their wives to Australia, and West Australian law prohibited marriage between Asians and Aborigines, they normally cohabited with or married "marginal" European women.[9] The children born into these relationships raised the issue of how part-European children (especially girls) and their mothers were to be treated. Often, Afghans were accused of the barbaric treatment of the females in their families.[10] The situation persisted until the Afghans were gradually allowed to bring women from their country of origin.

In the 1920s, Albanian Muslims began to immigrate to Australia for economic reasons. They entered western Australia through the Fremantle port. While their European origin secured them better treatment than their Afghan counterparts, they also experienced hardships. Finding jobs was not easy, and some were compelled to return home. Others stayed and were employed in, for example, timber plantations.[11] After the end of World War II, more Muslim immigrants arrived from Europe, especially from the former Yugoslavia and Turkey, parts of the Middle East, and Southeast Asia.[12] Until 1971, however, there were only 535 Muslims in western Australia, and only 3 percent of them had been born in Australia.[13]

The number of Muslims living in the western region began to increase after 1971. Muslims from Southeast Asian states, the Middle East, and, especially, Lebanon and South Africa arrived. By 1985, their total number had increased fivefold to 2,724.[14] Since then, against the background of political upheavals in a number of Indian Ocean region states, more than five thousand more Muslims have arrived from areas such as Palestine, Somalia, Ethiopia, and Iraq. According to the 1996 Census, the total number of Muslims living in the state has increased to 12,583 from 8,225 in 1991. Although the increase has followed a wider Australian trend, the ethnic origins of Muslims in western Australia differ from those of the rest of the country. Instead of Lebanese and Turkish Muslims dominating the scene, nearly 20 percent of those living in western Australia come from Malaysia, Indonesia, and Singapore. Immigrants from Turkey, Lebanon, and Bosnia-Herzegovina account for 12 percent of this population, with those from South Africa, Iran, Egypt, Pakistan, and Iraq constituting other major ethnic communities. In line with the national trend, however, nearly 40 percent of these Muslims are under twenty years of age, with those between twenty-one and forty comprising the second largest group (38 percent). Approximately 33 percent of this population are Australian born.[15]

The Muslim population of western Australia is concentrated in a number of cities and towns, including Port Hedland and Goldsworthy in the north, Geraldton on the west coast, Kalgoorlie-Boulder in the east, Katanning, Busselton and Harvey in the south. Over 87 percent of Muslims live in the capital of Perth, however. Constituting less than 1 percent of the city's population, they are by no means the largest religious community.[16] In the past they were spread widely across the northern and southern suburbs of the Perth metropolitan area, but recently they have begun to congregate in particular suburbs. The southern suburb of Thornlie has the largest concentration of Muslims (578), while other suburbs in the area such as Gosnells, Rivervale, Victoria Park, and Bentley are fast becoming the main settlement areas for Muslims. Suburbs north of the River Swan, such as Ballajura, Mirrabooka, Dianella, Girrawheen, and Mount Lawley, are home to more than one hundred Muslims.

The growth of the community in Perth recently has become evident with the development of Muslim institutions. Until the 1960s, the mosque on William Street, established by Afghan cameleers, provided the venue for Muslims to congregate for social and religious activities, as well as offering religious education to children on Sundays. The new immigrants from the former Yugoslavia, Turkey, and the Christmas and Cocos Islands have been engaged in erecting ethnic mosques to serve their various communities. By 1997 the number of mosques had increased to seven. With the exception of one mosque for which Saudi Arabia provided funding, the rest have been built through the efforts of the local ethnic communities who often identify closely with one specific mosque. Hence, while one mosque in Welshpool is referred to as the Turkish mosque, another one south of the river in Rivervale is patronized primarily by those from Southeast Asia. Similarly, immigrants from South Africa support the Mirrabook, a mosque north of the River Swan. The most interesting case has been the conversion of a church into a mosque in a northern suburb. The church was purchased by a local Iranian immigrant and is now mostly used by Shi'ite Muslims from Afghanistan, Iran, Iraq, Burma, and Lebanon.[17]

A noticeable change has also occurred with respect to the availability of *halal* food. Until the 1950s, the small Muslim community had difficulty obtaining *halal* meat. Initially, they solved the problem by obtaining meat from a slaughterhouse in Midland, half an hour's drive from the Perth City center. Later, these Muslims found a creative solution: some of them secured a *fatwa* from Pakistan that decreed that Jewish kosher meat was also permissible. Thereafter, Muslims began to rely on a Jewish butcher close to the mosque for the supply of *halal* meat. Since then, Muslim dietary needs have been catered to through outlets for obtaining *halal* meat, found in at least thirty shops spread across the Perth metropolitan area. Some main chain stores as well as small retailers have begun to stock and provide *halal* meat to a number of restaurants run by Muslims. Muslim student organizations at various universities and educational institutions have also made arrangements for being supplied with such meat.

Muslims have also gradually established Islamic schools in Perth. The first of these was established in the 1980s. Later, an Islamic College was opened and another Islamic School, al-Hidaya, caters to Muslims in the southern suburbs. At the same time, a number of local associations have emerged, such as the Australian Muslim Information and Education Service (AMIES), which are affiliated with mosques and provide information to Muslim immigrants about Islamic educational institutions, libraries, practicing doctors, and *halal* food outlets.[18] The WA Islamic Council (WAIC), which was established in 1976 as part of the Australian Federation of Islamic Council (AFIC), plays a role in this process.[19] In addition to issuing a newsletter and compiling a list of Muslims living in Perth, it has been active in inviting speakers from around the world to discuss issues affecting Muslims living in non-Muslim societies. Muslim men, however, have dominated the Council, with women playing only an indirect role in council activities.

Muslim Women and Citizenship

Muslim women are an important part of the West Australian Islamic picture. In marked contrast to the early decades of the twentieth century, when they were denied entry into the country, the total number of Muslim women has steadily increased. While there were only 174 Muslim women in the state before 1971, their number rose to 5,989 in 1996; they now account for 47.5 percent of the total Muslim population.[20] In line with the general settlement pattern in western Australia, 87 percent of these women are based in Perth, where their total number was estimated in 1996 to be

5,258.[21] Of these, 40 percent are under twenty years of age, with those between twenty-one and forty forming the second largest group (39 percent).[22] While about a quarter of them were born in Australia, the rest have migrated from overseas and belong to more than thirty-eight different ethnic communities. Approximately 62 percent (or 3,284) of all Muslim women living in the metropolitan area were born as Australian citizens or have acquired Australian citizenship.[23]

Primacy of the Private Sphere

Two studies conducted between 1994 and 1998 on Muslim women from Afghanistan, Pakistan, Egypt, Iran, Palestine, Indonesia, Malaysia, India, Singapore, and Cocos Islands[24] demonstrated that Muslim women viewed their relationship to Australian society differently than their male counterparts.[25] The findings of the two research projects and the available statistical data reveal that a large majority of Muslim women living in the Perth metropolitan area operate primarily in the private sphere. Their main focus remains on the family unit, with networks of friends and acquaintances occupying a secondary place. Muslim men, on the other hand, are assigned the role of operating in the public sphere and of being the breadwinners.

Female emphasis on the family unit is partly a function of immigration patterns: an overwhelming majority of all women immigrants enter Australia as part of a family.[26] The decision to immigrate is normally taken by husbands and fathers seeking a better economic life or better opportunities for their children. Wives, and other female members of the family, accede to the decision even if it proves difficult during the initial stages of immigration. Once settled into Australia, the family remains the first reference point for these women. Interestingly, culture takes precedence over religion in perpetuating this close identification with the family. This is not to suggest that Islam becomes irrelevant to their sense of identity. But it is culturally based notions of the rights and responsibilities of individuals that mainly define the spaces that male and female family members occupy. Different interpretations of Islamic injunctions are used to reinforce the validity of these role definitions. While most Australians define family in terms of a nuclear unit, for Muslim women, it includes members of an extended family as well as friends living in the house for some period of time.[27]

Given this close identification with the family unit, the gender-based definition of roles within that unit, and the large proportion of Muslim women who get married at an early age, bringing up children becomes the major priority. Those with younger children prefer to stay at home and bring up their children "properly." Generally they feel that participating in the work force would deny children much-needed attention during their early childhood. This focus on woman's role as mother makes the issue of childcare facilities largely irrelevant for Muslim women. Even when employed mothers need access to childcare, they tend to rely on extended families or networks of friends to provide it. The same applies to care for the elderly. Muslim women perceive their role as including care for their elders and tend not to explore alternative arrangements.[28]

The emphasis on the family also defines other major concerns of Muslim women. They generally focus more than their male counterparts on ensuring that the everyday needs of the family are met satisfactorily. Decisions about the location and design of the house, availability of *halal* food, access to health facilities, education, and safety engage their attention more than they do Muslim men. These concerns are explained in both cultural and religious terms. For example, nearly all the Muslim women interviewed during 1994–1995 explained their need for *halal* food in religious terms. For them, *halal* means not only properly slaughtered meat but also the availability of processed *halal* foods and of restaurants where *halal* food is served.[29] Similarly, women who expressed a preference for going to female health practitioners (approximately 70 percent) referred to the religious injunctions which prohibit Muslim women from disrobing in front of non-Mahram men.[30] A classic case is of a young woman who refused to consult a doctor for abdominal pain until she was assured access to a female physician.[31] In contrast, their views on house design are mainly determined by cultural backgrounds. While most Muslim women are satisfied with Australian architectural styles, some Kurdish and Afghan women insist that they prefer houses where spaces for preparation of meals and entertainment are clearly demarcated and separate from each other.

Gender-based definition of roles in the family unit, however, does not totally determine the behavior of Muslim women in the private sphere. While acting as nurturers, these women retain a sense of identity distinct from the family unit. When asked, they are willing to discuss their personal needs candidly and with a clarity that is often absent among their male counterparts. Muslim women tend to place relatively less emphasis on relationships in the larger Islamic community than Muslim men who place the family unit within the larger context of the Muslim community and focus on the need to perpetuate its Islamic identity within a predominantly non-Islamic society.[32] These differences are perhaps most apparent in discussions of educational needs. Nearly 83 percent of the women in the study focused on their personal educational needs rather than those of their children. Specifically, they referred to their desire to become proficient in English, which they felt was necessary to operate both as effective parents and as "good members of the society." When they did discuss the educational needs of their children, the emphasis was on the quality of education and the availability of appropriate transport facilities and *halal* food in educational institutions. Some women expressed concern at the inclusion of sex education in the school curricula at a very early age which, in their view, might serve to make premarital relations seem more acceptable. This, they argued, ran counter to their Islamic values. The great majority of Muslim men, on the other hand, discussed education exclusively in terms of the quality of instruction available to their children. Many were concerned that the state and private schools do not provide Islamic education to their children. They suggested appointing Muslim teachers who could rotate between different schools and impart Islamic knowledge to Muslim children.

A strong emphasis on the family unit is not specific to Muslim women. Some analysts argue that multiculturalism in general promotes the perpetuation of cultural traditions different from those prevalent in the larger society and that this process indirectly contributes to the relegation of women to the private sphere.[33] Hence, irrespective of their religious background, women from Iran and Egypt accord equal importance to their role as nurturers within the family environment. Similar views can be found among non-Muslim women from Southeast Asia.[34] These similarities notwithstanding, Muslim women do operate in a slightly different family environment than women from other ethnic and reli-gious backgrounds. These differences stem from the economic situation in which most Muslim men find themselves after immigrating to Australia.

Australia's stringent immigration laws mean that only individuals with high profes-sional and or educational qualifications normally gain entry into the country. Most of these men, however, find it difficult to find appropriate jobs in the new country. Statistics reveal that Muslim men encounter this difficulty more than other immigrants. While 8.8 percent of all Australian men are unemployed, the figure is as high as 25.3 percent for Muslim men in the labor force.[35] The labor force participation rate for all Australian men is 73 percent, but for Muslim men it is 62.4 percent.[36] The national trend is evidenced in Perth, where 22 percent of the Muslim men in the labor force are unemployed.

The human picture behind the statistics is even more sombre. Muslim men with good professional experience, who have sometimes occupied senior managerial positions in their countries of origin, often find it difficult to secure appropriate jobs. Often, men either re-sign themselves to living on the stipend provided by the social security system or opt for jobs that are unrelated to their professional qualifications. The ensuing frustration affects the quality of life within their respective family units. For Muslim women, it creates two sets of difficulties. On the one hand, the inability of the traditional breadwinner to per-form his role obviously creates economic problems for the family. Equally significant, but not so obvious, is the impact upon the space available to women within their family units. Unlike the conditions in their home countries, where they, at least, have predominant ac-cess to and control over the family space, Muslim women in Australia find this space be-ing taken over by the male members who are dissatisfied with their status in the larger so-ciety. Such a situation results in a high incidence of depression and a sense of helplessness among Muslim women, especially if they do not have members of the extended family around.

To overcome these difficulties and their effect on everyday life, Muslim women tend to establish close networks of friends and companions. Chosen primarily from their re-spective ethnic communities, these friends do not necessarily live in the same suburbs. The choice is guided by a sense that a common culture makes it easier for these women to be understood without detailed explanations about the assumptions and motives of their norms and behavior. A shared language, however, remains the major reason for this choice. In some cases, the circle of friends extends to include "other" Australians as well. The manner in which these friendships are discussed, however, reveals an inherent categoriza-tion of Australian citizens by Muslim women. If the friends are Muslims, their identifi-cation is normally preceded by a reference to their ethnic origin, such as Turkish or Bos-nian Muslim. An ethnic-based differentiation is also made for non-Muslim Australians. The term "Australian" is used to refer only to white Anglo-Celtic Australians, whereas all other non-Muslims are identified on the basis of their ethnicity. For example, a number of women interviewed for both projects would say, "I have friends from my community. I have some other Muslim friends as well. I also know some Australians." Such categoriza-tion is indicative of a sense of strong cultural identity as well as a feeling of alienation from the larger society in which most of these women operate as citizens.[37] It can be ar-gued, of course, that women from other ethnic backgrounds make similar distinctions and that in a multicultural society like Australia the tendency is unavoidable. Nonetheless, a majority of Muslim women living in Perth operate primarily in culturally bound private spheres, in which they do not always perceive themselves as citizens.

Muslim Women and the State

The participation of Muslim women in the state sphere has been limited. Their strong identification with the private sphere generally determines the extent and nature of this participation. It also determines their notions and understanding of their rights and duties as Australian citizens. At one level, their notion of citizenship means compulsory voting in elections.[38] While they regularly perform this duty, they generally do so informed by males as to which political party or candidates to support. The underlying assumption remains that men operate in the public sphere and are, therefore, more capable of making such decisions. Very few Muslim women go beyond this minimal engagement. They seldom join political parties or pressure groups formed to influence state or federal governments or legislatures and often remain silent observers of the political system. Such attitudes were obvious during the 1998 debate in western Australia on women's right to abortion. While the issue attracted heated debate from within and outside the state legislature, Muslim women did not voice their opinion on the issue. The task was left predominantly to a few Muslim men who presented their views on the admissibility or inadmissibility of abortion.

At another level, Muslims generally take citizenship with great seriousness. Linked to their focus on the family unit, they view citizenship in terms of their obligation to bring up their children to be good citizens who can contribute to the Australian society. The distinction between "good" and "bad" citizens is based on cultural and religious values, including inculcating in children habits of respect for elders, obedience and loyalty to the family unit, and respect for the laws of the state. It also includes ensuring that children do not learn about or engage in premarital sex and that they stay with parents until they are married and set up their own family units.

The notion of rights as citizens, on the other hand, is generally absent among a majority of Muslim women. To some extent, this absence can be explained by the experiences of these women in their respective countries of origin. Often coming from states with varying degrees of political unrest, authoritarianism, or dictatorships, these women have little or no conception of their rights in a liberal democratic state like Australia. The problem is compounded by their limited proficiency in English, which makes accessing appropriate information difficult. This absence is even apparent among a number of second-generation women who have grown up in the country.

Limited knowledge of rights and Australian laws sometimes has implications for the family unit. Inadvertently, it draws women into interaction with state structures, sometimes resulting in sad consequences. This overlapping of state and private spheres is apparent in the laws about child-rearing practices. Some mothers subscribe to the notion that their culture permits them to discipline their children by using physical punishment. This has sometimes resulted in them being accused of child abuse. Some mothers have even lost their children to foster care against their will. That the foster parents in some cases are not

Muslims further adds to the trauma of these women. One woman narrated a story of her encounter with the legal system:

> One day, we went to Scarborough Beach. I smacked my kid, didn't know Australian law. Po-
> lice visited next night and said wants to visit me and my husband. Police said you hit your
> child. Husband replied we hit our children to teach them. Me and husband went to police
> station, till early hours of the morning. We were shown a video, and asked if we were guilty
> or not. I said not. We were warned that if we hit our children again they would take our
> children away. I asked for an interpreter to understand better, but Police didn't get one. I
> said I want to go home for the breast-feeding time of child. We went to Margaret Hospi-
> tal, husband said wife will go to baby. We were at the Police station from 9.30 p.m. till 3.30
> a.m. Police said we'll bring you a letter, for another appointment with the police in March
> 1995. I'm afraid of losing my children—if they take them what will I do? If I'd known
> Australian law, I would never have touched my children."[39]

The impact of the state on the family unit has led some Muslim women to increase their level of engagement with state institutions. Generally, this activism has been lim-
ited to individuals approaching the relevant state bureaucracy or political representatives. Afghan women dominate in this category. Despite the fact that they are relatively new immigrants, their higher educational level, coupled with the need to "make it work in Australia," has prompted them to be more vocal in communicating their needs to governmental institutions.[40] At the same time, a few leading women have taken it upon themselves to represent other coreligionists. They have contacted various governmental agencies and institutions to educate them about the Muslim faith and the needs of Muslim women, with specific reference to the family unit. While, in the northern suburbs, women of Lebanese, Bosnian, and South African origin have been active in this sphere, moves in the southern suburbs have primarily been made by women of Afghan, South-
east Asian, and Iranian origin. This limited activism, however, has not as yet translated into an attempt to influence the views of political representatives by presenting Muslim women as a single united entity. Essentially, therefore, the picture is different not only from that existing in other western liberal democracies, but also from that in eastern states of Australia where Muslim women have been more proactive in presenting themselves as a united group.

Muslim Women in the Market and Public Spheres

The limited participation of women beyond the family unit is also apparent in the mar-
ket and public arenas. Of a total of 3,649 Muslim women above the age of fifteen living in Perth, only one-third is in the labor force. Of these, nearly two-thirds are employed, with 34 percent and 36 percent of the total working in full-time and part-time jobs respectively. Nearly half of those in the labor force are employed as intermediate clerical, sales, and service workers and laborers. Only 140 (or 15 percent) are working as profes-
sionals. Most of these women are employed in the health and community services sectors or in the hospitality industry. A small proportion of Muslim women (8 percent) is employed in educational institutions.

Health and community services and the hospitality industry are the two main sectors employing women in Australia. Some Muslim women are also employed in these sectors, but beyond that, they tend to be underrepresented in the market sphere. While the percentage of Australian females over the age of fifteen who are not in the labor force is 53.8 percent, the figure is as high as 64 percent for Muslims. Similarly, the unemployment rate for Australian women is 8 percent while that for Muslim women living in Perth and Australia in general is 26 percent.[41] Part of the explanation can be found in the structural barriers that limit Muslim women's participation in and engagement with the labor market. Only 31 percent of Muslim women over fifteen have educational qualifications equivalent to or above bachelor degrees. Another 16 percent have undergraduate or associate diplomas, and only 15 percent possess skilled or basic vocational qualifications. With their lack of knowledge about the job market, and growing unemployment in the country, these women find it difficult to get appropriate jobs. However, the fact that even women with bachelor degrees or higher educational qualifications do not participate fully in the labor market indicates that the barriers are more than structural in nature.

Non-structural barriers to Muslim women's participation in the labor market can be identified in two areas, the first being the emphasis on the family unit and the gendered role definitions. Most of these women accept and perpetuate the notion that they need to care for the family instead of looking for jobs. This attitude is not just restricted to first-generation or older women. Younger and second-generation women also tend to define their roles in cultural terms and opt out of the labor market as soon as they get married. Those who do not subscribe to gender-based role differentiation often face pressure from their family members. They are reminded of their duty to act as nurturers and not to entertain notions of operating in the labor market.

The biggest obstacle to increased participation by women in the labor market, however, comes in the stereotypical images of Islam common among Australians. Despite the long history of association between Muslims and Australia, Islam remains a misunderstood religion. Muslims are often viewed as fanatics and fundamentalists who are determined to undermine the West. Biased reporting in the media reinforces such negative images. Muslim women are viewed more negatively than their male counterparts. Convinced that Islam discriminates against women, Australians see Muslim females as weak, oppressed, subjugated, and incapable of making independent decisions. Such negative imagery is even more pronounced in the case of women subscribing to traditional dress standards, and especially those who wear the *hijab* (head cover).[42] Despite the fact that wearing the headscarf may be a conscious choice by some Muslim women, it is frequently associated with subjugation and absence of independence.[43] It is also equated, quite unrealistically, with the inability of these women to operate effectively in the job market. Understandably this affects Muslim women's access to jobs. For instance, an Australian-born woman in her early twenties said,

> I find a barrier in finding a job myself because I do not have degrees, and I wear a scarf. I can only work as a secretary or a salesperson. [But] in these jobs *hijab* is not acceptable for fear of customers. They think that the customer may not take it too well. I had applied for secretarial position. . . . They asked me, "Will you be wearing your scarf all the time?" I said, "Yes, I would not change that to suit other people." Then I was not employed.[44]

The prevailing anti-Muslim prejudice has prompted some women to become more active in the public sphere. They are beginning to form formal or informal associations to support and represent Muslim women. Compared to eastern states, this phenomenon of forming organizations is relatively new in western Australia. While Muslim women in Sydney had formed a "Mu'minah" (Muslim women) association as early as 1981, the same process started relatively late in Perth. Initially, it involved informal gatherings of females to discuss their problems or socialize with other Muslim women.[45] Since the Gulf War, when the stereotypical images of Muslims gained currency, the process has gained momentum. To some extent, the impetus has been provided by the decision to establish the countrywide Muslim Women's Association (MWA), which held its first national conference in October 1992. The process, however, has also been aided by the influx of refugees from Iraq, Jordan, and Bosnia in the 1990s. Their greater numbers allow potential for the growth of Muslim women's organizations.

On one end of the spectrum, such movement has resulted in the formation of organizations that situate Islam at the center of their conception of citizenship. The Muslim Women's Support Group, established in 1987 and incorporated in 1992, is an example. Run by an elected body, the group aims to bring Muslim women and those sympathetic to Islam together in a supportive environment. It has succeeded in securing a $26,000 grant from the West Australian government for employing a social worker to assist Muslim refugee women living in the northern suburbs. The group organizes regular activities for its members, as well as for their children during school holidays. It has also been raising funds to acquire land and build a Muslim Family Centre in Perth. The Sisters in Islam Multiethnic Association (SIMA) has undertaken similar activities in southern suburbs. Established in 1992, the group draws its membership primarily from women of Southeast Asian background. While it has not been registered as an incorporated body, the members of the group have engaged in extensive networking and have held talks and lectures on issues facing Muslim women.

Apart from the organized groups, a few Muslim women have also individually organized activities for and made representations on behalf of Muslim women. In the northern suburbs of Beechboro and Lockeridge, for instance, Lebanese and Bosnian women have established close links with state government institutions and assisted them on issues involving Muslims. More recently, these women have initiated moves to contact local parliamentary members or approach members of the state cabinet.[46] At the same time, with a view to enabling other Muslim women to engage in recreational activities, they have arranged swimming lessons specifically for Muslim females. Another relatively new but significant development has been the holding of *dars* (religious study groups) by a number of Muslim families. Muslim women participate in these lessons, which are organized informally among friends. The sessions are devoted to discussing Islamic teachings and the issues faced by the Muslim community. Men and women are segregated, and men give the lessons.[47]

On the other end of the spectrum, some Muslim women have organized activities that emphasize the liberal-democratic notion of being a citizen in Australia. While acknowledging their identity as Muslims, they focus on the need to access knowledge about their rights and duties in a multicultural society so that they can operate as effective citizens.

Funded by a state government grant, they hold regular meetings that enable other Muslim women to come in contact with state and federal representatives and officials. These contacts serve as a channel for learning about services for immigrant women as well as for articulating their concerns to government authorities.[48] Others have used the media, such as community radio, to talk to other Muslim women about rights and duties in their respective ethnic languages.

Although established with the view of representing Muslim women as a united group, some of these activities are actually promoting division. This is largely due to the different interpretations of Islam, Islamic identity, and the links between Muslims and the larger civil society supported and promoted by different groups. The Muslim Women's Support Group, for instance, publishes a regular newsletter that propagates an orthodox interpretation of Islam. Encouraging the restricting of woman's role primarily to the family sphere, it sometimes includes advertisements from Muslim men looking for Muslim wives. Articles are often published that warn members against, for instance, watching television, filing teeth, or living their lives in a manner that would make it difficult for them (in a hypothetical sense) to welcome the Prophet Mohammed in their homes. These notions of the relationship between Muslims in Perth and the larger society are questioned by some who place Islam in the center of their discussion of citizenship but refuse to subscribe to orthodox interpretations. Those emphasizing the liberal-democratic notion of citizenship also question these interpretations on the grounds that they could turn Muslims away from the religion without making their assimilation into the society easier. Although these differences are in their infancy, and seemingly at odds, they have the potential to develop into better-defined interpretations of what it means to be a Muslim, a woman, and a citizen in Australia.

Conclusion

With the approaching centennial of the Australian Federation, the discussion of citizenship and related issues has gained prominence. However, the emphasis on the Republic debate has inhibited any discussion beyond links between immigration and ethnicity. Gender issues are raised, but they are normally couched in terms of the western feminist agenda. The interplay of religion, culture, gender, and ethnicity is seldom explored. Nonetheless, it remains significant for understanding the manner in which different citizens conceive of and define their notions of citizenship. It also has implications for the way that these conceptions are practically and operationally manifested in the civil society. The research on Muslim women living in the Perth metropolitan area supports this view.

Coming from diverse cultural backgrounds but united by their adherence to the religion of Islam, most of the Muslim women exhibit what could be identified as contradictory notions of citizenship. At one level, they view themselves as Australians who have entered into a legalistic relationship with their adopted state. The relationship enables them to live in Australia but also imposes the obligation of acting as "good citizens." For a large majority of Muslim women, this value-laden notion is translated to mean the duty to bring up children who will be good citizens and still conform to the religious and cultural norms. The focus on the family unit, therefore, remains the main area of operation for most Muslim women. It also circumscribes the extent of their participation in the state, market and public spheres. At another level, these women see themselves as outsiders who are not Australians. Widespread prejudice in Australian society about Muslims, and particularly about Muslim women, also plays a significant role in this self-image. The dominant cultural norms in society, and the inability of their male counterparts to participate fully in the labor force, also reinforce this sense of alienation.

The negative images of Islam and Muslims, however, have prompted a change: gradually, some activism by Muslim women in the public sphere is becoming apparent. The need to articulate their needs and views has resulted in the emergence of formal and informal associations and organizations among Muslim women. Their diverse notions of the place accorded to Islam in their conception of citizenship, however, carry the seeds of future division among the very group they intend to represent. The prevalent notions of what constitutes a Muslim woman (often defined as one committed to orthodox interpretation of the religion and wearing the *hijab*) are likely to empower those who do not necessarily represent the majority of Muslim women in the city. The *hijab* may be accepted and portrayed as representing the "real Muslim woman," attenuating the identity of other Muslim women who chose not to follow orthodox interpretations of appropriate dress code. In the long term, therefore, even if second- and third-generation Muslim women increase their participation in the market and state spheres, greater legitimacy may still be accorded in the public sphere to those women who dress "Muslim." This, in turn, may perpetuate nascent differences and undermine the ability of Muslim women to operate as a unified group in the public sphere of Australia's civil society.

Notes

1. Mary Lucille Jones, "Muslim Impact on Early Australian Life," in *An Australian Pilgrimage: Muslims in Australia from the Seventeenth Century to the Present*, ed. Mary Lucille Jones (Melbourne: Victoria Press, 1993), 31–37.

2. Australian Bureau of Statistics, 1991 Census of Population and Housing, Ethnic Communities Package-Religion Profile (Islam in State WA) [Hereafter cited as 1991 Census-Islam in WA], Catalogue No. 2803.5, Table No. 5; and Australian Bureau of Statistics, 1996 Census of Population and Housing-Ethnicity, Thematic Profile Service for Islam in Australia, [Hereafter cited as 1996 Census-Islam in Australia, Table No. E03].

3. Nearly 43 percent of these women are less than twenty years of age; those between twenty and forty constitute the second largest group (37.5 percent).

4. Jones, "Muslim Impact," 31–37.

5. The following discussion relies heavily on the information provided in Pamela Rajkowski, *Linden Girl: A Story of Outlawed Lives* (Perth: University of Western Australia Press, 1995), 43–45. For more details, see, Pamela Rajkowski, *In the Tracks of the Camelmen* (Sydney: Angus and Robertson, 1986), 15–18.

6. According to Rajkowski, "They crossed into Western Australia either through the far north of South Australia from Marree via Oodnadatta, or from Port Augusta across the Nullabor Plain via Eucla and Ooldea." *Linden Girl*, 43–45.

7. The list includes, among others, the Ghan town at Fly's Flat near Coolgardie, and those "adjacent to Laverton, Leonora, Mount Morgans and Bummer Creek in the eastern goldfields

and in the northern goldfields adjacent to Port Hedland, Marble Bar, and Cue." Rajkowski, *Linden Girl*, 43–45.

8. Jones, "Muslim Impact," 60.

9. Rajkowski, *Linden Girl*, 47.

10. Rajkowski, 47–50.

11. Jones, "Muslim Impact," 78–79.

12. Other immigrants included those from Austria, Bulgaria, Russian Federation, Netherlands, and Britain. 1991 Census of Population and Ethnic Communities Package, Product 4, Islam-WA, Table No. 14.

13. Information derived from , Islam-WA, Table 14.

14. 1991 Census-Islam in WA, Table No. 5.

15. Australian Bureau of Statistics, 1996 Census of Population and Housing-Ethnicity Thematic Profile Service for Islam in Western Australia, [Hereafter cited as 1996 Census-Islam in Western Australia], Table No. E01.

16. There are, for instance, more Buddhists than Muslims in western Australia and, by implication, in Perth.

17. The mosque is known as Isa Ibn Maryam Mosque, or St. Mary's Mosque, to indicate that the church was originally known as St. Mary's Church.

18. *Muslims Western Australia*. A pamphlet distributed by the Australian Muslim Information and Education Service, Cloverdale, 1997.

19. For details, see, Qazi Ashfaq Ahmad, "Islam and Muslims in Australia," in *Islam, Muslims and the Modern State: Case Studies of Muslims in Thirteen Countries*, ed. Hussin Mutalib and Taj ul-Islam Hashmi (London: Macmillan Press, 1996), 317–38.

20. By 1985 there were 1,497 women living in the state, which increased to 3,891 in 1991. 1996 Census-Islam in Western Australia, Table No. E01.

21. For demographic details of Muslims living in Perth Metropolitan Area, see Australian Bureau of Statistics, 1996 Census of Population and Housing-Ethnicity Thematic Profile-Islam in Perth [Hereafter cited as 1996 Census-Islam in Perth], Catalogue No. 2020.0, Table No. E01.

22. Only a very small proportion of these women (1.8 percent) is over sixty-five years of age.

23. 1996 Census-Islam in Perth, Table No. E07.

24. A gender-based assessment of settlement needs of Muslims living in Perth Metropolitan Area was undertaken in 1994–95. It investigated the extent to which needs of Muslim women differed from those of Muslim men. To this end, detailed qualitative interviews were conducted with 114 women and 92 men over 16 years of age. They were asked to rank, in order of significance, a number of settlement needs. These initial findings guided the research methodology for a larger research project on Women and Citizenship in Australia undertaken from 1995 to 1998. In-depth qualitative interviews were conducted with a number of ethnically diverse women over eighteen years of age to assess their views on being an Australian citizen. See Samina Yasmeen, "Women as Citizens in Australia," *ISIM Newsletter*, published by the International Institute for the Study of Islam in the Modern World, Leiden, Netherlands, no. 2, 1999, <http://isim.leidenuniv.nl/newsletter/2/index.html>.

25. For details, see Samina Yasmeen and Salma Al-Khudairi, *A Gender Based Need Assessment Study of Muslims Living in Perth Metropolitan Area*, a report prepared for the Australian Department of Immigration (Perth: University of Western Australia, 1998).

26. See, for example, Ruth Fincher, Lois Foster, and Rosemary Wilmot, *Gender Equity and Australian Immigration Policy* (Canberra: Australian Government Publishing Service, for Bureau of Immigration and Population Research, 1994).

27. See, for example, Qazi Ashfaq Ahmad, *Islam and Muslims in Australia*, 333.

28. Yasmeen and Al-Khudairi, *A Gender Based Need Assessment Study*, 32–35.

29. For instance, one Australian-born woman in her early twenties stated, "I have lots of problems. We cannot eat certain foods. The numbers and ingredients used in products are difficult to understand. For example No.471 means fatty acid and we cannot have it. . . . We go to *halal* or vegetarian restaurants. In fish and chips shops one has to ask, 'What kind of oil do you use?' Some people do not tell you what kind of oil is used just to sell their food. In supermarkets, you have to read ingredients. Then you get used to brand names and stick to them." Yasmeen and Al-Khudairi, *A Gender Based Need Assessment Study*, 21.

30. "Mahram" refers to a male chaperone who is legally proscribed from marriage to the woman.

31. Interview with an immigrant woman in her mid-thirties. Yasmeen and Al-Khudairi, *A Gender Based Need Assessment Study*, 16.

32. For instance, one Muslim man who migrated to Australia in 1991 said, "For the Muslim community, education is the most important issue because at stake is the future of the Muslim Community. [We] need to reduce the Western cultural influence on our kids. The Australian kids take drugs, drink alcohol, and have unlawful sex relationship. We would not like our Muslim kids to be influenced by this corrupt society." Yasmeen and Al-Khudairi, *A Gender Based Need Assessment Study*, 12.

33. See, for example, Mary Kalantzis, "Ethnicity Meets Gender Meets Class in Australia," in *Playing the State: Australian Feminist Interventions*, ed. S. Watson (Sydney: Allen and Unwin, 1990), 39–59.

34. A sample survey of women from Southeast Asia, for instance, revealed that they did not identify with the dominant feminist discourse in Australia that focuses on equal employment opportunities for men and women. Instead, they preferred to stay at home and take care of their children. Angelina Tang, *Citizenship, Gender and Ethnicity in Australia: Perspectives from Southeast Asian Women in Western Australia*, Honors dissertation, 1996.

35. *Australia Now—A Statistical Profile Labor Characteristics of the Labor Force*, Australian Bureau of Statistics, Table No. 6.4 & 6.5; and Australian Bureau of Statistics, 1996 Census of Population and Housing-Islam in Australia, Table E17.

36. It represents the proportion of the population aged fifteen and over who are in the labor force.

37. It may also reflect the views held by male members of the Muslim community who often make similar distinctions between "the Australians" and themselves.

38. These views were apparent in the qualitative data collected from 1994 to 1998.

39. Interview with a woman who immigrated in 1991, interviewed in 1994.

40. For instance, one Afghan woman who migrated to Australia in April 1993 stated, "I went actually once to our Parliament members. Me and my husband went to complain because he had been applying for eight years for Homes West Accommodation. When we did get it was not fit accommodation, it was more like a rubbish bin, it needed rebuilding. They did listen, they offered us this house, which was much better than the ones they offered before and we moved in. It is still small, but they say our boys should share a room. Still, I feel I have this right to go to them and complain."

41. Data from Labor Employment, *Australia Now-A Statistical Profile*, Table No. 6.7, Information based on the 1996 Census, <http://www.abs.gov.au>.

42. For instance, one woman in her early fifties who had lived in Australia since 1981 stated that she felt very discriminated against especially because she covered her hair. "I was harassed in Karratha, the kids used to put broken eggs in the front of the door or flour and rocks were thrown on our windows. I went to the Police but after that it became worse." (Interviewed in 1993).

43. See, for example, Angela Wellington, "Life behind the Muslim Veil," *The West Australian*, 19 April 1999: 9.

44. Interview, July 1994.

45. A "new" Muslim woman, Zaleena Kennedy, who initially offered her home as the meeting place, aided this process. Later, the meetings were shifted to a school south of the River Swan.

46. Information supplied by a Lebanese woman who is leading these moves. April 1999.

47. Information provided by a South Asian Muslim woman. May 1999.

· 48. Occasionally, some non-Muslim immigrant women have also attended these meetings.

Muslims in New Zealand

13

WILLIAM SHEPARD

T HE MUSLIM COMMUNITY IN NEW ZEALAND is small, remote, and relatively new,
but in the last quarter century it has become effectively organized and has grown
vigorously.[1] New Zealand, a member of the British Commonwealth, is located in
the South Pacific and consists of two main islands, the North Island and the South Island. Its current population is about 3.8 million, the majority of which live in the North
Island and about a million live in Auckland, its largest city and commercial capital.[2]

All New Zealanders, or Kiwis, as they commonly call themselves, are in a significant
sense, immigrants. Even the indigenous inhabitants, the Maori, now about 15 percent of
the population, recount the stories of how their ancestors came from elsewhere during the
last millennium. British (including Irish) settlement began in the 1820s and 1830s, and
immigration from Britain has continued to the present. Thus the majority of the current
population is of British background and may still mean Britain when they say "home."
These New Zealanders, along with much smaller numbers from other (predominantly
Northern) European countries, are commonly called "Pakehas." There is also a significant
number of Pacific Islanders (Samoans, Fijians, etc.), accounting for about 5 percent of the
population. While dozens of other ethnic groups live in New Zealand, they are present in
very small numbers. The largest Asian groups are the Chinese, with 2.3 percent of the
population, and the Indians, with 1.2 percent.[3] In recent years there has been some discussion of multiculturalism, but the dominant commitment is to biculturalism (relations
between Maori and Pakeha) which should not, but sometimes does detract from multiculturalism.[4]

The Muslim community in New Zealand is rooted in South Asian (Indian, Pakistani,
Bangladeshi, and Fijian Indian) immigration, with Fijian Indians particularly prominent.
It now includes, however, some thirty-five nationalities, among which are Arabs,
Malaysians, Indonesians, Iranians, Somalis, people from the Balkans, and some Pakehas.[5]
The community has increased numerically almost ten-fold in the last twenty years and
more than doubled in the last five. According to the latest census, that of 1996, there were
13,545 Muslims in New Zealand, representing 0.37 percent of the population.[6] Muslim

leaders today estimate a figure of over 20,000, which is not unlikely in view of the most recent growth. The majority of Muslims are in the Auckland area, while most of the rest live in the nation's capital of Wellington or four other major cities.[7] Of these, up to a thousand are overseas students, most of whom will leave after completing their studies. Many of these students contribute significantly to the community while they are in New Zealand.

History of the Community

The census records report small numbers of Muslims from 1874 on, but those that came before the early twentieth century have left no further record. Some may have been Chinese, working in gold fields in the south of the country.[8] The continuous and remembered history of the present community goes back to a handful of Gujarati Indian men who arrived in the early decades of the twentieth century. They opened small shops, mainly in towns south of Auckland. In time, they brought their sons to New Zealand to help in the shops, while their wives, daughters, and younger sons, for the most part, remained in India, where they were frequently visited by the men who had emigrated.[9] At that stage, they do not appear to have viewed their stay in New Zealand as permanent. In 1920 the government adopted what amounted to a "White New Zealand" immigration policy, though it was not called that, which precluded further significant Asian immigration. The Muslim population of New Zealand remained at less than a hundred until after the Second World War. In the early 1950s, however, the children of the first arrivals did bring their wives and children and settled on a more permanent basis. The third and later generations of these families have been raised in New Zealand, although they appear to keep in close contact with members of their extended families elsewhere in the world. After the Second World War the government accepted a limited number of war refugees coming to the country for purposes of immigration. Among these were some Muslims from Turkey and the Balkans, including perhaps twenty or thirty who came to the Auckland area, where the resident Indian Muslims helped them to settle in. This group appears to have been more inclined to assimilate into Pakeha society and attenuate their Muslim identity. Some, however, have remained actively and ethnically identified with Islam and have publicly expressed their concern over such international events as the recent crises in Bosnia and Kosova. The censuses of the 1950s reported about two hundred Muslims in the country.

Further limited but significant Muslim growth began in the mid-1960s, when a period of liberalized immigration policy opened the way for a small number of mainly South Asians and Fijian Indians, including some professional and white collar workers. A few overseas Muslim students also came to the universities.[10] The number of Muslims reported in the census between 1961 and 1971 trebled, from 260 to 779. Relatively rapid growth continued in the 1970s and 1980s with Muslim numbers, as recorded in the census figures, reaching 2,500 by 1986; the actual number may have been higher than what the census indicated.[11] The years from 1977 to 1980 saw major Muslim organizational developments at both local and national levels, which will be described below.

Since the late 1980s, numbers have risen dramatically, partly as a result of political events elsewhere and partly due to changes in the government's immigration policy. The

1987 coup d'etat in Fiji caused a considerable influx of Fijian Indians, many of them Muslims, particularly to the Auckland area. Since 1993, at least two thousand refugees have come from Somalia, and Somalis currently form the single largest Muslim ethnic group in at least two centers, Christchurch and Hamilton.[12] Smaller numbers of Bosnians, Kosovars, Kurds, and Afghans have also come as refugees. The uncertain situation in Fiji (as of October 2000) will probably bring more Fijian Muslims to New Zealand. Apart from refugees, new immigration regulations put in place by the government in November 1991 established a "point" system that favors immigration by wealthy or well-educated people from any ethnic background. A number of Muslim professional people have entered under this system, especially from the Middle East. Unfortunately, many of these have found that their qualifications are not recognized in New Zealand, with the result that some are moving on to places such as Australia where opportunities are better. According to the census figures, the number of resident Muslims had increased to 5,772 in 1991 and to 13,545 in 1996; today there may now be as many as 20,000, as indicated above.

A few Kiwis have also become Muslims, often in the context of marriage to a Muslim, although in some cases their interest in Islam had begun before meeting their future spouse. They are probably less than 5 percent of the community, but some have made significant contributions to it, including at the leadership level.[13]

The Community Today

The recent immigrant character of most of the community is reflected in the fact that only about 20 percent of Muslims have been born in New Zealand (as compared to over 80 percent for the general population).[14] There is a preponderance of males over females, but much less than was once the case. According to the 1996 census, 55 percent of Muslims were male, as compared with 49 percent for the New Zealand population as a whole. The Muslim population is also younger than the population as a whole. Almost 60 percent of the Muslims are under thirty years of age while in the general population the percentage is about forty-five. The numbers over sixty-five years old are particularly low, 1.5 percent compared to 11.7 percent.[15]

The Gujeratis who came early in the twentieth century were almost all small shopkeepers. Many Muslims are still owners of small businesses, some of which are doing quite well. More fall into the category of unskilled or semi-skilled laborers, particularly in Auckland, but there are also a fair number of professionals, as already indicated. Those raised in New Zealand often have acquired tertiary qualifications that have allowed them to get good jobs. The 1986 and 1991 censuses reported a median income for New Zealand Muslims only slightly below the average for the country as a whole and the unemployment rate among men who had settled in also did not seem much different.[16]

For those who have come in the last decade or so, however, the situation is generally more difficult, but this varies from one ethnic group to another. Fijian Indians on the whole have probably had the least difficulty, since there was already a strong community established. At the opposite extreme are the Somalis, who have suffered particularly severe trauma prior to arrival and have a high incidence of health problems and gaps in the education of their young people. Moreover, the gulf between their culture and the Pakeha culture is greater than it is for most other Muslim immigrants.[17] Very few Somalis have been able to gain employment, even though they generally come from well-educated middle or upper-class backgrounds.[18] Added to this is the high cost of bringing in relatives who are not technically in the category of refugees according to the government.[19] In between are groups such as the Bosnians and the Kosovars, who have some countrymen in New Zealand and whose culture is European. Those professionals who have come in under the "point system," but whose qualifications are not recognized, have had to earn their living in some other way, such as working in ethnic restaurants. Some rely on unemployment benefits while they seek to pass the necessary professional exams (which often require levels of English they have not reached or local knowledge not relevant to their skills as such) or train for some other occupation.[20] For them, as well as for the Somalis, the loss of status has been hard to bear. One Somali has commented, "Somehow, you can turn from a hero at home to a fool here. I mean I was a very important man in my village at home, and here I cannot get a job."[21] It is thus not surprising that the relative median income for Muslims in the 1996 census is considerably lower than in the previous two.[22]

Muslim women who are not recent arrivals appear to be employed in the labor force in fairly large numbers, though at a rate somewhat less than that of the general population.[23] Allowing for family responsibilities and cultural traditions, women among the newer arrivals may not be too much worse off than the men, but Somali women are generally less willing or able to work than those from other groups. Due to the circumstances that brought them to New Zealand, they have a high proportion of families headed by women.

In moral and cultural terms, Muslims have some problems adjusting to a society that has traditionally prided itself on "rugby, beer, and racing." Beer and the betting involved in racing clearly run counter to Muslim moral values. Few Muslims relate to rugby, but other sports such as cricket and soccer are popular in the countries from which they come. As is true elsewhere, clothing and particularly women's clothing has been an issue. Many, but not all, Muslim women wear distinctively Islamic garb, or at least a headscarf in public, and this makes them quite noticeable. Somalis appear to be particularly insistent on this. Informants differ on the degree to which this makes it harder for them to get jobs, but it surely does to some extent. School uniforms for girls are skimpy by Muslim standards, but, for the most part, state schools seem to have been reasonably accommodating at this point, allowing headscarves and some variants to the uniforms and even to bathing suits. The issue of long trousers, rather than regulation shorts, for boys also has been raised and successfully addressed in some schools. Schools also appear to be accommodating on matters of diet and allowing time for *salat* (daily ritual prayer) and time off for the boys to go to *jum'a* (Friday congregational prayer). At least a few schools set aside space for *salat*. The situation varies from school to school, however, often depending on the attitudes of the headmaster, as well as on the degree to which the students or their parents insist. In some cases the presence of a Muslim on the teaching staff has made a significant difference. Schools do not, however, provide any specifically Islamic education and they perforce reflect the general community mores.

The ways in which children and young people respond to the conflicting pressures for conformity to Kiwi norms, to Islamic norms, and to family expectations, indeed the degree to which these conflict in practice, vary so much from group to group and from individual to individual that generalization is impossible. I have been told that the problem of getting Muslim girls to wear headscarves is greater than the problem of getting schools to allow it and that some girls, even among the Somalis, remove their scarves once they get to school, i.e. without their parents' knowledge. On the other hand, I have also been told that some second-generation Muslim girls have insisted on their rights concerning dress in school and on other matters, reflecting in this a certain self-confidence vis-à-vis Kiwi culture. I am aware of one young woman who, upon getting married, put on heavy Islamic garb much to the disapproval of her parents. At the opposite extreme, a Fijian-Indian Muslim woman won the title of "Miss India-New Zealand" in May of 2000, a development described as "shocking" by at least one prominent Muslim man. A similar diversity exists in other areas.

There have been some problems for Muslim workers getting time to perform *salat*, or attend *salat al-jum'a*, but mainly in assembly-line conditions where the temporary absence of even one person stops the whole line. I am told that office workers rarely have problems today.[24] Matters of this sort are usually handled in an informal and low-key manner. Such an approach, for example, was used in relation to the issue of female genital mutilation. With the arrival of the Somalis, many of whom do practice female circumcision, New Zealand Health authorities became concerned. Such practice was actually made a criminal offence at the beginning of 1996, but it was done with virtually no publicity or media discussion. The emphasis is on education more than prohibition.[25]

Racial and religious discrimination is illegal in New Zealand, and Kiwis on the whole are tolerant. But they are not well-informed about Islam, and therefore prejudice and negative stereotypes do exist in the minds of many people. This is partly because the media, drawing heavily on overseas sources, tend to stress the violence and extremism that does exist in certain parts of the Muslim world. Still, local Muslims get some positive attention from the local media, especially the press and radio, and efforts to counter negative reporting are sometimes successful. In some cases, Muslims are on quite good terms with the local press. Some efforts by the national federation along this line will be discussed below.

There have been scattered cases of discrimination, harassment, and violence directed at Muslims. For example, Somalis have suffered personal assaults in several cities; in Christchurch, a group of Egyptian Muslims was harassed while picnicking and in Auckland, a Fijian was badly bashed.[26] Incidents of this sort, however, are isolated and result more from racial than religious motives. They, too, are handled in a very low-key manner, both by the Muslims and by the local authorities, and their importance is generally downplayed by Muslim spokespeople.

There has sometimes been local resistance to granting building permits for building mosques. In 1990, during the Gulf War, graffiti was sprayed on the Islamic center in Wellington, but the Muslims received considerable support and sympathy from the local churches, a Jewish congregation, and other agencies. The most serious incident of this sort took place in Hamilton in 1998 and shows New Zealand at both its worst and its best in this respect. There had been considerable resistance to the building of a mosque in 1997, and about six months after it was opened, it was burned and gutted in an arson attack. The city was deeply shocked by this event and people rallied to assist the Muslims. The City Council provided space for prayers while they were rebuilding, and donations from the community, spearheaded by some church groups and the local Jewish community, assisted them in building a protective fence and installing a security system. One Muslim leader has commented that the whole event showed them how many friends they have.

Some Muslims have attained high positions in their professions, such as medicine and scientific research, but few so far have participated prominently in politics. In fact, even the largest Asian ethnic group, the Chinese, got its first Member of Parliament only in the 1996 election when what is called Mixed Member Proportional Representation was introduced. Under this system half the members of Parliament are elected from single member districts and half from national party lists. The party list gives ethnics a greater chance, and the Chinese representative is from a list. In 1999 a Muslim of Pakistani origin was on the Labour Party list and came close to winning a seat. This same man has been active in ethnic affairs and has been national president of the New Zealand Federation of Ethnic Councils for two years. While he is a Muslim and has been active in one of the associations, he sees his political involvement as separate from his religious concerns and describes his choice of the Labour Party as motivated by a concern for the underdog. He believes that being a Muslim and an Asian may have both hurt him and helped him in politics, but, in the long run, that it has probably helped because he gained votes for the party. Two other Muslims stood for one of the smaller parties, the United Party, but with no real chance of winning.[27]

Local Islamic Organizations

The local or regional Islamic institutions in New Zealand consist of seven associations affiliated to the national organization, The Federation of Islamic Associations of New Zealand (FIANZ), along with several unaffiliated associations, student groups, trusts, and a school. The oldest local association is the New Zealand Muslim Association (NZMA), which was established in 1950 in Auckland. Initially, its membership consisted of the few Gujerati families present at the time, joined shortly by a few families coming from Turkey and the Balkans. Fijian Indians and others were added from the1960s on. In the early years, its meetings were held in homes or shop premises; then, from 1963, in houses owned by the association. For larger celebrations, such as Eids, a hall would be rented.

By the mid-1970s, three other Muslim groups had also been formed in Auckland. The Anjuman Himayat al-Islam was a mainly Fijian-Indian group. The New Zealand Council of the World Muslim Congress was led by a businessman of Albanian background and seems to have focussed mainly on publicizing Muslim social and international political concerns. There was also a "Sufi" group led by a Kiwi convert who was much influenced by Gurdjieff and whose following was mainly Pakeha. The existence of these several groups in a small community posed problems, and a visiting delegation from Saudi Arabia in 1976 advised them to unite. As a result, the Anjuman and the NZMA did unite that year to form a new New Zealand Muslim Association. The other two groups went their separate ways and, to my knowledge, are no longer active.[28] The new association promptly began to plan and raise funds to build a mosque. The foundation was laid on

March 30, 1979, and, by 1983, the main prayer hall, with a capacity of four hundred worshippers, and the ablution block had been completed and furnished. A meeting hall and flat for the imam were completed by 1990.

The NZMA has grown in recent years and, at the turn of the twenty-first century, had an average five hundred worshippers at *salat al-jum'a*. Other associations and groups have come into being in the Auckland area, as Muslims have grown in numbers and spread to various areas of the city. Beginning as an offshoot of the NZMA in the early 1980s, the South Auckland Muslim Association became a separate association in 1989 and, when it had some four hundred registered members, began to build a mosque. Several other centers were established after the late 1980s. A mosque was built in West Auckland under the aegis of the NZMA. The Mount Roskill Center (Masjid-e-Umar), run by an Islamic trust, formed in 1989 independent of the other associations and of the national federation. After meeting in a purchased house for several years, they acquired a church building where they have the largest attendance at *salat al-jum'a* of all Auckland groups, about eight hundred on average. There are as many as six or seven other places where *salat* is performed in the Auckland area, at least one of which is under the aegis of the NZMA.[29] In 1999 and 2000, *salat* for Eid al-Fitr was held in a park; in 1999 about four thousand attended and the following year there were nearly eight thousand.[30] For Eid al-Adha in 1999, some three thousand persons attended a similar outdoor *salat*.

Several other Muslim communities are active in the North Island. The Muslim community of Hamilton dates more or less from the 1970s and for a time was associated with the NZMA in Auckland. They founded the Waikato-Bay of Plenty Muslim Association in 1980, which developed into a very active association and in 1997 constructed a mosque. The Muslim community of Palmerston North also dates from the 1970s and was, for a time, affiliated with the association in Wellington. Its Manawatu Muslim Association was incorporated also in 1980. Many of their activities are held in a mosque recently built on the campus of Massey University, which is located in Palmerston North.[31] Beginning as outreach efforts from the associations based in Hamilton and Palmerston North respectively, groups have been formed very recently in the cities of Tauranga and Wanganui. Efforts have also been made to form associations in Hastings and Rotorua.[32]

The International Muslim Association of New Zealand (IMAN) was established in Wellington in 1966.[33] Initially it was made up mostly of university students, but this is no longer the case. It has an Islamic center and has been planning to build a mosque for some years, but has had difficulty working out its plans. The growth and spread of the community has led to the opening of two or three new facilities in the greater Wellington area, one under the aegis of IMAN and at least one independent. *Salat al-jum'a* is also held at the headquarters of the national federation in Wellington. The average attendance at *salat al-jum'a* for all of these centers combined was about five hundred to six hundred in 2000. IMAN seems somewhat more committed than other associations to emphasizing the international dimension of Islam, as opposed to particular ethnicities, and to making English the language of its activities.

In the South Island, Muslim communities are found in Christchurch and Dunedin. The Canterbury Muslim Association was established in Christchurch in 1977 and, though a small group, was able to build a mosque in 1985. This association suffered seriously from internal division, although it has grown in numbers. Its average attendance for *salat al-jum'a* is 300 to 400. It has drawn some leadership over the years from graduate students at the two universities in its area, Canterbury and Lincoln, although the universities are not always heavily represented. Since the late 1970s, there has been a students' association at the University of Otago in Dunedin, composed mainly of Malaysians, but the present Otago Muslim Association was incorporated only in 1995.[34] It works very closely with the student association and people connected with the university form a large proportion of its constituency. In 2000 it comprised twenty different nationalities and was planning to build a mosque or purchase a building for a mosque, although funding presented a problem.

Depending on numbers and resources, these associations provide for the main religious services, including regular *salat*, *salat al-jum'ah*, and prayers and activities for Ramadan, and the main festivals, and various social activities. Especially in the earlier days, the concern to pass on the faith to the next generation that was growing up in a non-Muslim environment appears to have been one of the major motives for the founding of the associations.[35] They all provide basic religious teaching and Arabic instruction for children and adults as circumstances and resources permit. The Mt. Roskill Centre in Auckland has a children's *madrasah* (school) in the evenings with as many as two hundred children learning the Qur'an. Such instruction appears most often to be given in English, certainly where there is a mixture of ethnic groups. In some cases, most notably among the Somalis, an ethnic group will have separate classes in its own language. Some associations have organized the provision of *halal* food, although this is also often obtainable from some shops in the larger cities or informally by other means. Most have marriage celebrants and burial space in a local cemetery. Many, but not all, of the centers in Auckland have full time imams, among them, NZMA, the South Auckland Muslim Association, the Mt. Roskill Centre, and Al-Madinah School (see below) in Auckland. Mt. Roskill has a second trained imam running its children's Madrasah. The long-serving and highly respected imam of IMAN in Wellington died in 1999. The Canterbury Muslim Association has had a full-time imam off and on over the years.

In recent years many of the associations, as well as the national federation, have adopted *shura* (consultation) as the way of conducting their business, rather than the Western-style majority rule and balloting. In part, this is an effort to be more Islamic and, in part, it reflects a feeling that the Western way encourages disruption and disunity. What it means in practice evidently varies, but it commonly seems to involve something like consensus decision making along with a strong role for the leader.

Women are active in the local associations, and some of these have women's groups, more or less formally organized. In some of the centers outside Auckland during the 1980s women would perform *salat* in the back of the same room as the men, but now they use a separate room or perform the prayer at home. This is partly because growing numbers have put pressure on facilities. Most of the communities have programs for youth, especially sports activities, which may or may not be organized by the associations. Youth camps and family camps are also held with some frequency.

Since the state-run schools provide neither Islamic education nor an Islamic atmosphere, some Muslims want a Muslim day school to provide these things. At least three significant efforts have been made, all in Auckland, to meet this need. The most successful is Al-Madinah School, backed by the Islamic Education and Da'wa Trust, which began on a "home schooling" basis in 1989 and became a government-supported "integrated" school in 1996. In 2000 it had about three hundred students at the primary and secondary levels. Government funding brings a measure of government control, and the Education Review Office has raised questions about the quality of its administration and teaching, which the school is working to address.[36] Auckland Muslim School for younger students ran for a few years but was discontinued due to financial problems. Zayed College for Girls was expected to open in 2001.[37]

Islamic Organizations at the National Level

The Federation of Islamic Associations of New Zealand (FIANZ) was formed in 1979 to coordinate the activities of the individual associations and to regulate contacts between New Zealand Muslims and Muslims abroad, especially in such matters as the solicitation of donations and representation at international gatherings. Its offices are in Wellington, and its membership consists of seven local associations: NZMA, South Auckland Muslim Association, IMAN, and the associations in Hamilton, Palmerston North, Christchurch, and Dunedin. The other newer groups in Auckland and Wellington, as well as those in Tauranga and Wanganui, do not, or do not yet, belong. The local associations select representatives to its Council, which in turn chooses the officers and Executive committee.

The objectives of FIANZ are described in the following terms:
- To establish and maintain the highest standard of Islamic practice in accordance with the teaching of the Holy Qur'an and *Sunnah*;
- To undertake *da'wa*, education, welfare, and other Islamic activities;
- To strengthen Islamic unity and assist in the development of the Muslim community of New Zealand;
- To establish and foster good relationships with Muslim countries and international Muslim organizations and institutions.[38]

Among other things, the organization assists local associations in fund raising and undertakes some troubleshooting. It holds annual Qur'an recitation competitions for children. It has a committee to determine the dates of Eids, a matter on which there has been some controversy in the past. It arranges visits by overseas speakers, distributes books, videos, and other literature both to Muslims and to non-Muslims, issues press releases and otherwise seeks to make Muslim concerns and positions public where appropriate, both on its own and in support of efforts by local associations. This includes publicizing Muslim viewpoints on overseas issues specifically concerning Muslims, such as the situations in Kosova and Chechnya. The association avoids comment on other political issues, however, as do the local associations. In 1990, AMANA Corporation was established as the wholly owned business arm of FIANZ, with the goal of generating revenue for the Muslim community and making FIANZ financially self-sufficient. So far as I am aware, however, it had only limited success in its first decade.[39] There has been some talk of establishing Islamic banking.[40]

Both FIANZ and the local associations publish newsletters with varying degrees of regularity, which present religious teachings, news of the associations, and other news of interest to Muslims. In the 1980s FIANZ produced a fairly long newsletter called *The Muslim*, which emphasized articles on religious, cultural, and historical topics. In the 1990s it produced a shorter newsletter, in a glossy and more professional format, that emphasized news items and community activities.[41] FIANZ and two university associations have web sites on the Internet.[42]

On several occasions FIANZ has taken vigorous and sometimes high-profile action vis-à-vis the media for its treatment of Islam. FIANZ lobbied vigorously, though largely behind the scenes, against the airing of the television docu-drama "Death of a Princess" in 1980. This probably had some effect on the decision not to air the program, although concern for Saudi trade was undoubtedly the major factor.[43] FIANZ also had some involvement in protests against the film "The Last Temptation of Christ." In March 1987 a particularly outrageous article, entitled "The Sword of Islam," was published in the *NZ Listener*, a widely circulated media-related magazine. As a result, FIANZ initiated a $7 million defamation suit, which was settled out of court. Among other things, the settlement gave FIANZ the right to a lengthy reply in the *Listener*, although this opportunity was not taken up.[44] In September of the same year, the two-part documentary, also entitled "The Sword of Islam," was aired on New Zealand television after FIANZ narrowly failed to get an injunction stopping it. Later, a Muslim response to this documentary was published in the *Listener*.[45]

FIANZ also took considerable interest in the controversy over Salman Rushdie's *Satanic Verses*. The approach was relatively low-key and focussed largely on making both Muslims and the general public aware of Muslim concerns about the book. This included organizing a letter-writing campaign, a variety of statements, articles, and interviews in the media, including at least one television interview, and helping to organize a series of public debates at the universities.[46]

FIANZ has not mounted comparable actions in the last ten years. Part of the reason may be the considerable cost of such efforts along with some doubt that such activity is really of value. Another part may be that the media have "gotten the message" at least to some degree and have not screened new "Swords of Islam."[47] Still another may be a change of priorities in the face of the influx of refugees and immigrants during this period. Finally, one of the key individuals leading these efforts no longer lives in New Zealand although he still has connections with the country. Muslims have, however, been involved in actions on an interfaith basis, and the Muslims in Dunedin were successful in getting a speedy apology from the Otago University Students Association for scurrilous material about Islam in one of their publications in early 2000.[48]

Both FIANZ and other organizations among the Muslims have undertaken to publicize international Muslim concerns, such as those relating to Palestine, Iraq, Bosnia, Kosova, and Chechnya. This has included press releases, articles in newsletters and *al-Mujaddid* and on Web sites. During the Kosova crisis, a long time member of NZMA, speaking for the Albanian Civic League of New Zealand, got prominent coverage on national television. The League also set up a charitable fund for refugees. In March 2000 a group of FIANZ leaders met with the Russian ambassador to express their views on Chechyna. More than one hundred Muslims in Christchurch marched after *salat al-jum'ah* on October 6, 2000, to protest the violence occurring at that time between Palestinians and Israelis.[49] Other efforts have included organizing collections for Muslim victims of the earthquake in Columbia in January 1999 and of goods and money for Kosova. *Al-Mujaddid* has published advice on how to send parcels to Iraq.[50]

Since 1990, there has been an active national women's organization, The Islamic Women's Council, affiliated with FIANZ, which holds one or more conferences and camps a year. In April 1999, the national conference was held in Hamilton on the theme "Education in Islam," with about 120 in attendance.[51] Two seats out of nineteen on the FIANZ governing council are reserved for women.

While Muslim university students have contributed to these associations, there have also been Muslim student associations at the universities, varying in size, activity, and continuity, over the years. In the year 2000 there were as many as two thousand Muslim students in universities and about the same number in polytechnics, and all of the New Zealand universities and a number of the polytechnics have Muslim student associations. In 1997 a nationwide university students' organization was formed, and at the end of 1999, it took the name, Muslim Students and Youth Organization of New Zealand.[52] While focussing on university students, it also seeks to encourage activities among polytechnic and high school students. Some involved have studied in the United States, and the organization draws considerable inspiration for its programming from Muslim student activities there. In February of 2000 they held a camp with forty-two participants aged fifteen to twenty-five with a program structured on the concept of "greater Jihad."[53] A New Zealand Muslim Sports Association, affiliated with FIANZ, has organized major tournaments around Easter and raised money to send a soccer team to Fiji in 1999 for a five-nation, Muslim tournament. In addition to soccer, the tournaments include golf, volleyball, and squash. The Women's Council has organized netball for girls.[54]

The associations, both local and national, have received significant financial assistance from sources in Muslim majority countries for their major building projects such as mosques and Al-Madinah School, and for salaries for some of the imams. This has come especially but not exclusively from Saudi Arabia and the United Arab Emirates. The associations are active in transnational organizations, such as Muslim World League, the World Assembly of Muslim Youth, and the Regional Islamic Da'wah Council of South East Asia and the Pacific (RISEAP). A South West Pacific Islamic organization is being formed to further cooperation with Muslims in Australia and Fiji.[55]

An important economic development for New Zealand in the last quarter of the twentieth century was the introduction of *halal* meat slaughter. Sheep meat has been one of the main New Zealand exports for more than a century, and, until the 1970s, most of this went to the United Kingdom. Excess production and the growth of the European Economic Community required it to seek other markets and, following the lead of Australia, it began to look to Middle Eastern and other Muslim countries. Exports to the Middle East began in 1976. When, in 1979, the revolutionary government in Iran signaled a willingness to purchase large quantities of New Zealand lamb on the condition that it be *halal*, the New Zealand meat industry moved promptly, and with relatively little opposition, to comply. A small group of farmers objected that this was anti-Christian and got brief media attention but had little effect. In the process, a considerable number of New

Zealand export processing plants shifted to *halal* slaughter, and New Zealand is now the world's largest exporter of *halal* lamb. At present there are forty-one meat processing plants throughout New Zealand approved for *halal* slaughter, representing 76 percent of the plants in the country and employing about 170 slaughterers. Sales to Iran have decreased in recent years but have been replaced by sales to other Muslim countries, with Saudi Arabia the largest market. At the beginning, most slaughterers were brought on a temporary basis from overseas, but now, most are local Muslims. There are two certifying agencies. One is FIANZ, which has offered this service as its main economic activity since 1984. It is qualified to certify for the whole Muslim world and is the sole certifier for the United Arab Emirates, Saudi Arabia, and Kuwait. The other certifying agency, New Zealand Islamic Meat Management, is an independent Wellington-based company run by a Muslim of Egyptian origin. It has been certifying since the late 1970s and has done most of the certification for countries other than the United Arab Emirates, Saudi Arabia, and Kuwait. Iran has made its own separate arrangements with the meat processors. The meat industry authorities believe that having more than one certifier increases the credibility of the certifying process, as well as controlling costs.[56]

Da'wa and Community Relations

Da'wa refers both to efforts to reach non-Muslims and to efforts to strengthen the commitment and activity of those who already are Muslims. In the latter category we may put the Tabligh movement, which began with the work of Maulana Ilyas in India in the 1920s and has since spread throughout the world. Its major concern in New Zealand and elsewhere is to recall Muslims to regular practice of the major obligations of Islam, such as *salat*, and it has tended to avoid involvement in political issues. In addition to regular local meetings, groups of volunteers travel about within a country and internationally to spread their message and stimulate existing activity. This movement is quite strong among New Zealand Muslims. There is Tabligh activity in most local areas and an informal national network. Such activity is distinct from the local associations and FIANZ, although there is cooperation and many of the same people are involved. Since 1979, there has been an annual national gathering (*ijtema*) and there is also an effort to hold other meetings on a national or regional basis.[57] A number of Tabligh groups have visited New Zealand from overseas over the years, and Muslims from New Zealand have travelled overseas for Tabligh work. The movement appears strongest in Auckland and Hamilton, and some associations and groups emphasize it more than others, but Tabligh activity is found in all or most centers. Tabligh meetings are mostly held in English, but other languages such as Gujerati and Urdu are also used.

Some criticize Tabligh as being a conservative force and too associated with Indian ethnicity, but it may be well suited to many people in the New Zealand situation. The meetings reaffirm and strengthen the Islamic identity and commitment of those involved. The level of teaching and discussion is very basic so that it can both be understood and carried out by relatively untrained laymen. One participant remarked to me that the purpose of the groups is not so much to learn something new as to provide a means of doing something for Islam and to keep participants from being carried away by the "world."

The "lay" character of the activity means that the financial costs to the community are not great since the work is done on a volunteer basis, with much of the expense sustained by the volunteers themselves. The apolitical character of the activities fits the desire of most Muslims in New Zealand to keep a low profile politically. It does seem to be a very "Indian" phenomenon in cultural form, appealing particularly to ethnic Indian Muslims in New Zealand, but, in fact, the Tabligh movement is found throughout the Muslim world, and there is some evidence that it can appeal to Pakehas.[58] In the longer term, these strengths may also be weaknesses. Its appeal to the more educated seems limited,[59] and it can make more demand on participants' time than many will be willing or able to give. To the extent that the community becomes more educated and more characterized by a Kiwi lifestyle, its value may decrease, but it appears to play a positive role in maintaining the community.[60]

A movement called Milaad has come to New Zealand quite recently. It appears to combine elements of popular Sufism and Fijian Indian folk practice, as well as to take a strong position favoring the celebration of the Prophet's birthday. Although it is critical of the Tablighis and they of it, and some centers in Auckland are identified with one or the other, members of both groups cooperate within the associations.

All of the communities are engaged to a greater or lesser degree in da'wa activities directed toward non-Muslims. This takes various forms, such as advertisements and announcements in the local press, receiving visitors to the centers and providing them with literature, and inviting speakers from outside. The Dunedin community held an "Islam Awareness Week" in 1999 which included a radio program, films, an exhibition of Islamic artifacts, a public forum, and an invitation to the general public to witness salat al-jum'a.[61] There is an Islamic Da'wah and Converts Association of New Zealand, which is concerned to invite non-Muslims to Islam and to support them afterward. It claims up to a hundred members, mostly in Auckland. One Muslim leader estimates that there were 150 converts to Islam from 1998 to 2000.

Prominent figures from overseas are brought from time to time by FIANZ and the associations to speak in one or more places. These have included Muzammil Siddiqi, Jamal Badawi, and Merryl Wyn Davies. Ahmad Deedat, from South Africa, came at the beginning of 2000 for the fiftieth anniversary of NZMA but also toured the other centers.[62] These visits can be considered a form of da'wa directed both to Muslims and to non-Muslims, though primarily the former. In some cases some non-Muslims have attended, but most of the audience have been Muslims.[63]

Significant interfaith dialogue activities take place, at least in Auckland, Wellington, and Hamilton. In Auckland the Council of Christians and Muslims was formed in 1998 and meets four times a year, including one meeting held jointly with the Council of Christians and Jews. In Wellington, there are at least two interfaith groups in which Muslims participate and discuss theological and other topics, one involving the Iranian Embassy and the Council of Churches and another sponsored by Anglicans. Interfaith activities also take the form of cooperation in matters of mutual concern. When the Department of Religious Studies at Victoria University in Wellington was under review, Muslims cooperated with others to support it, with favorable results. The Auckland Council of Christians and Muslims recently discussed three television programs that were considered to denigrate

Islam, and the Christian members lodged a complaint. Early in 1998 both Christians and Muslims demonstrated against an offensive display in the National Museum in Wellington, and a Muslim spokeswoman participated in a televised debate on this. Beyond the formal events, the personal contacts and acquaintances developed are invaluable.

Ethnicity and Sectarianism

Unlike the situation in many countries, the New Zealand associations are not divided along ethnic lines. This is primarily because of the small size of the Muslim community, but it also reflects the policy and efforts of the leadership. Ethnic feelings are certainly not absent, and along with personality factors, they contribute to some intracommunity disputes and tensions.[64] There is some resentment at the perceived predominance of South Asians, although this is far from universal, and the leadership does make efforts to be ethnically inclusive. Leaders recognize the possibility that ethnic mosques may appear some day, but not in the immediate future, and they appear committed to trying to avoid this development.

As to whether individuals have a greater sense of ethnic or of Islamic identity, in the 1980s several leaders told me that Islamic identity was more central at that time than had been the case earlier. The worldwide "resurgence" of Islam undoubtedly contributed to this, as did the community's need for outside support for many of its projects. The founding and growth of FIANZ and several of the associations both reflected and stimulated this tendency. Developments in the 1990s stimulated both ethnic and Islamic awareness, in most cases mutually reinforcing. Certainly concerns for such matters as Islamic dress in schools appear to be greater now. The Somalis present an interesting and probably extreme case. Their ethnic identity is extremely strong so that they form quite a distinct group within the Muslim communities where they are numerous. At the same time, to be Somali is to be Muslim, and, in New Zealand, the mosques form the main focus of their communal activity. Somalis appear to be more insistent than others on such matters as Islamic dress. There is reason to believe that Somalis in New Zealand (and probably elsewhere in diaspora) are more consciously Islamic than they were in Somalia. In part, this is probably a continuation of an Islamic revival that began before they left Somalia, which had had a secularist regime for many years under Siad Barre, in part it may reflect a quest for spiritual support in the face of their experiences as refugees, and in part it may reflect an accentuation of an aspect of their ethnic identity that is more "usable" in New Zealand. At the other extreme would be many Eastern Europeans who, as noted earlier, tend to assimilate more quickly and for whom religion may never have been very important. Also at this extreme, though different, would be those Iranians who dislike the present regime in Iran but have a strong sense of their Iranian identity.

There are a number of ethnic associations that involve Muslims. These include the Albanian Civic League mentioned earlier, longstanding Indian associations and associations of Somalis and Ethiopians. There are also associations of Bangladeshis, Pakistanis, Iraqis, Egyptians, and Iranians. In sectarian identity, New Zealand Muslims are overwhelming Sunni although some Shi'is are present. The associations appear to be strongly, but not officially, Sunni in ethos, and Shi'is are not very much involved in them. The NZMA limited its membership to Sunnis until 1980. An Iranian mullah, who had been sent to oversee the *halal* slaughterers and was assisting in the teaching activities of the association at the time, appears to have played a role in changing this. A group called Ahl al-Bayt Foundation was founded in 1993, but little information is available about them. In the mid-1990s there were a number of Iranian Shi'i students in Dunedin who participated in the associations to some extent, although accounts of the situation differ.[65] There has been an Iranian embassy in Wellington since the 1980s that sometimes conducts events with IMAN, as well as the interfaith involvement mentioned above. The ambassador once gave an *iftar* in Dunedin. Presumably, these are better described as "ecumenical" than Shi'i efforts. Other Shi'i groups include a few Ismailis who came to New Zealand from Uganda after they were expelled in 1972. In at least two cases, they sought to bury their dead in the Muslim section of cemeteries and, after some investigation, permission was granted by the associations. It also appears that Ahmadis, strong in Fiji, have appeared in Auckland in the last few years.

At another level, there have been debates within the community over the propriety of celebrating the Prophet's birthday and the permissibility of drinking Kava, a Fijian drink said to be alcoholic. Sermons by the late imam of IMAN have been circulated opposing both of these.

This chapter has, of necessity, focussed on the organized Islamic associations and those involved with them. There are, however, many Muslims who are not connected with the associations, and a few words are in order about their perspective. The variations among them are undoubtedly enormous, but there must be many who would fit the following profile, which is based on general impression and a couple of detailed conversations. They would have a fairly Westernized background in their country of origin but be comfortable identifying themselves as Muslim, taking pride in Muslim history and culture and recognizing it as their heritage. They would probably have family connections with people more practicing than they, and this would strengthen their Muslim identity. In many countries this would be further reinforced by outsiders' perception of them as Muslims, but such would be less likely to be the case in New Zealand. They would believe in One God and the finality of Muhammad's prophetic mission but would de-emphasize the superiority of Muhammad to other prophets or the superiority of Islam to other religions. Islam would primarily mean for them those universal ethical obligations that Muslims share with others, along with a stance on sexual and family issues that is "conservative" by current Kiwi standards. They would rarely or never perform such Islamic obligations as *salat* and the Fast of Ramadan, though they might appreciate the symbolic values enshrined in these acts, and they might even practice their own personal variations of them. They would be likely to view the associations as too inclined to emphasize the externals of Islamic practice and perhaps as too given to petty quarrels. They might, however, give financial support to some of the projects of the associations, such as mosques or donations to help refugees. While not active in the associations, such people form a part of the environment of the associations and may be potential members under the right circumstances.

Whither the New Zealand Muslims?

In the early 1980s, I was told that the main purpose of the recently formed associations for their members was "to keep them Muslims." That goal continues to be relevant but is somewhat easier now given the increased numbers. But how firmly rooted is this larger community? At the collective level it has reached a size and a degree of activity such that its continued and reasonably flourishing existence seems assured. At the individual level, however, I would judge that the majority of the Muslims are not firmly rooted in New Zealand. Even many of the South Asians who are of the second or third generation have family connections and overseas interests that could draw them away. Some of the more recently arrived would return to their homelands if and when things settle down or would move elsewhere if they cannot find suitable employment in New Zealand. The country, however, has limited economic opportunities for immigrants. In fact, many Kiwis also emigrate for economic and professional reasons.[66] For some Muslims the main advantage gained from their stay in New Zealand may be acquisition of a New Zealand passport that can open doors elsewhere in the world. This has serious implications for the character of the community and, in particular, for the continuity of its leadership. Especially in the smaller centers, the loss of a single individual or family can cause considerable setback. All of this inhibits the process of taking root.

Some time ago, some community leaders drew a distinction between being Muslims in New Zealand, that is, an immigrant community surviving in an alien environment, and being Muslims of New Zealand, or a community developing forms of Islamic expression appropriate to the local society and interacting significantly with that society. This represents the hopes of some within the leadership. Such a hope looks for a community of Muslims all the more committed to their faith by virtue of having chosen to become or remain Muslim in an environment where Islam is not "in the air" as it is in the home countries. In this community people would relate to each other primarily on the basis of their Islam rather than their ethnicity, and their interpretation of Islam would slough off or modify the distinctly ethnic interpretations and build on the common core of belief and practice shared by all Muslims.[67] Such a goal, however, was distant in the 1980s and even more distant in the 1990s, given the influx of immigrants and refugees and the immediate needs and problems they brought. Though distant, such an ideal could still guide the way in which the community and its leaders deal with today's needs and problems. Some time in the future it might become achievable if the development of ethnic mosques is avoided, if the rate of immigration in relation to the size of the resident community levels off, and if a sufficiently large core of longtime and reasonably stable residents builds up.

An alternative scenario would see a predominantly shifting Muslim population, as immigrants move in and out, in which the community would constantly have to "reinvent the wheel" for new groups coping with the initial problems of adjustment.

Let me close with an agricultural analogy. The Islamic seed has been well sown in New Zealand and is growing vigorously, but it is still in the process of striking its roots and adapting to its environment. How firmly circumstances will allow it to strike roots remains to be seen.

Appendix: Muslim Population of New Zealand 1874-1996 Based on Census Reports

Year	Muslim Population (% Males in parentheses)	
1874	17	(100%)
1878	39	(100%)
1881	07	(100%)
1891		(Not available)
1896	43	(100%)
1901	41	(100%)
1906	17	(94%)
1911	12	(100%)
1916	47	(87.2%)
1921	65	(100%)
1926	76	(98.7%)
1936	51	(98%)
1945	67	(88.1%)
1951	205	(89.3%)
1956	200	(75.5%)
1961	260	(n/a)
1966	551	(78.5%)
1971	779	(71.5%)
1976	1415	(60.2%) [1341]
1981	2004	(63.2%) [1701]
1986	2544	(58.2%)
1991	5772	(56.4%)
1996	13545	(54.7%)

Based on official census figures. The percentage of males is given in parentheses. Through 1971 the figures are for "total population." For 1976 and 1981, the "total population" figures are given in the main column and "usually resident population" figures are given in brackets. From 1986 on, the figures are for the "usually resident population."

Notes

1. This chapter was completed in June 2000, with a few updates in October 2000. Much of the information for this chapter was obtained through personal interviews with members of the Muslim community and others, over a period of about twenty years. This material is usually not footnoted. I wish to express my appreciation to those who have kindly taken the time to answer my questions and share their knowledge with me. I have also included or summarized material from my earlier articles on this topic, especially "Muslims in New Zealand," *The Journal of the Institute of Muslim Minority Affairs* 16, no. 2 (1996): 211–232; and "Australia and New Zealand," with Michael Humphrey, in *Islam Outside the Arab World*, ed. David Westerlund

and Ingvar Svanberg (Surrey: Curzon Press, 1999), 278–94. Two helpful recent articles by members of the New Zealand Muslim community are: Qamer Rahman, "Muslim Women in New Zealand: Problems and Prospects," *Al-Nahdah* 16, no. 1–2 (Jan.–June 1996): 34–35; and Leila Adam, "Muslim Community in New Zealand" *Al-Nahdah* 19, 1 (1999): 38–41. Useful information is also available on the Web site of the Federation of Islamic Associations of New Zealand, <http://www.angelfire.com/biz2/FIANZWEB1/>.

2. The 1996 census reported a total population of about 3.6 million, about 2.7 million in the North Island. The figure of 3.8 million comes from a report from the Statistics New Zealand on television, April 29, 2000. Census figures come from *Census 96, 1996 New Zealand Census of Population and Dwellings, National Summary* and *Regional Summary* (Wellington: Statistics New Zealand)

3. For ethnic figures, see *Census 96, Ethnic Groups*, 108, 111, 114, 117, etc. The census lists fifty ethnic groups on the basis of self-identification, with more than a thousand representatives; of these seventeen could be considered Northwest European.

4. The New Zealand government has a Human Rights Commission, which deals with individual complaints of discrimination in areas of religion, race, and ethnicity, and a Race Relations Office, which deals with issues between groups but does not include religion in its brief.

5. The figure of thirty-five nationalities appears in the recently published (October 2000) booklet, *New Zealand Muslims Endeavour to Success*, and also on the FIANZ Web site. The Auckland Muslim newssheet, *Al-Mujaddid*, however, claims forty nationalities (March 2000: 11) The following breakdown is derived from the table on "Ethnicity and Sex by Religious Affiliation" in the 1996 census figures: Indian: 4,110, 30.3 percent; Other Asian: 1,758, 13 percent; Middle Eastern: 2,982, 22 percent; European: 1,176, 8.7 percent; Other Southeast Asian: 1,125, 8.3 percent; African: 1,017, 7.5 percent. Pakistanis and Bangladeshis here are included under "Other Asian" rather than "Indian." A source from the FIANZ office estimates the following: Indian, 50–60 percent; Arab, 10 percent; S.E. European and Turkish, 5 percent; Southeast Asian, 10–15 percent; African/Somali, 20–25 percent; Pakeha, 5 percent. "Indian" includes Indian, Pakistani, Bangladeshi, and Fijian Indian.

6. See *Census 96, Ethnic Groups*, Ethnicity and Sex by Religious Affiliation, 108, 111, 114; cf. *Census 96, 1996, National Summary*, 37 and elsewhere. The New Zealand figure may be compared to 0.83 percent for Australian Muslims (Humphrey and Shepard, "Australia and New Zealand" in *Islam Outside the Arab World*, 278).

7. The Muslim population of main urban areas according to the 1996 census along with the percent of the total: Auckland: 7,454, 55 percent; Hamilton: 579, 5.4 percent; Napier-Hastings: 267, 2 percent; Palmerston N: 408, 3 percent; Wellington: 1,539, 11.4 percent; Christchurch: 831, 6.1 percent; Otago, 405, 3 percent; other urban areas: 1,795, 13 percent; rural areas: 267, 2 percent. Based on *Census 96, 1996 New Zealand Census of Population and Dwellings, Information Summary* (Wellington: Statistics New Zealand), 82–102.

8. Information in the 1874 census reports suggests that fourteen of the seventeen Muslims reported were in this category.

9. Part of this information is based on my interviews with the descendants of the earliest arrivals, along with J. V. Leckie, *They Sleep Standing Up: Gujaratis in New Zealand to 1945*, Ph.D. thesis, University of Otago, Dunedin, 1981. The three early arrivals most often mentioned are Ismail Bhikhoo and Joseph Moses (Isap Musa), who settled in the North Island, and Muhammad Suleiman Kara, who settled in Christchurch. Kara may have come as early as 1907. Bhikhoo probably arrived between 1909 and 1914.

10. Under the Colombo plan, according to "Muslim Community in New Zealand," but I have not been able to get further information on this. One of my sources suggests that there

was a relatively liberal period between 1960 and 1975, but another limits this to the period of the third Labor government, 1973–75.

11. This was commonly claimed by Muslim leaders in the 1980s. See Shepard, "Muslims in New Zealand," 1996, n. 3.

12. Technically most of these are not refugees, since those who have come as refugees have brought members of their families under "family reunion" provisions of the law, but in reality they are all refugees. The 1996 census recorded only 348 Somalis, but this figure is certainly out of date. My figures are based on Community Service as well as Muslim sources and estimate 600 for Christchurch, 600 for Hamilton, and 800 for Auckland, with smaller numbers elsewhere.

13. The estimate is that of one of the current leaders. I have received varying estimates over the years of numbers of recent converts.

14. *Census 96, People Born Overseas*, 65. In 1986 26 percent of Muslims were born in New Zealand.

15. The following are based on prepublication figures from the 1996 census but are not significantly different from the published figures: age 0–14, 29.7 percent, 23 percent general population; 15–29, 29.4 percent and 22.3 percent; 30–64, 39.4 percent and 43 percent; 65+, 1.5 percent and 11.7 percent.

16. Extrapolating from the census figures that I have, 1986 income figures appear to put Muslim median income at $10,000–$12,500 and that of the general population at $12,500–$15,000. I calculate that in 1991 the Muslim and general medians were both in the $10,000–$15,000 bracket, but the Muslim median was nearer the bottom.

17. In the case of women, most informants say simply that most Somali women do not go out to work, but a community worker in Christchurch tells me that Somali women could work in nursing homes if they were willing to wash male patients.

18. This is the view of most of my sources, although others tell me that a fair proportion come from the countryside and do not have such a high level of education. Some complain that slaughterers are often brought in from Malaysia and Fiji in preference to them. Louise Humpage cites a figure of 95 percent unemployment for Somalis, *Refuge and Turmoil, Somali Refugee Adolescents in Christchurch Schools*, M.A. thesis, University of Canterbury, 1998, 65.

19. Those who come in under the "family reunion" (see n. 12) category must pay the cost of transportation and a deposit to the government.

20. From November of 1991 to October of 1995, the point system considered general level of education but took almost no cognizance of the degree to which particular skills were needed. There is also a separate category for immigrants with entrepreneurial skills and considerable capital, but I have no information on how many Muslims have come in this way. The general impression is that people from such places as Taiwan and Hong Kong have arrived via this means.

21. Katherine Hoby, "More to Multiculturalism Than Just Eating Chinese Food," Christchurch *Press*, March 21, 2000.

22. The 1996 figures put the Muslim median in the $5,000–10,000 bracket and the general population in the $15,000–20,000 bracket. 1996 statistics for Asians over fifteen years indicate that 47.7 percent are employed full or part time, 7.8 percent are unemployed, and 44.5 percent are not in the labor force, as compared with 60 percent, 5 percent and 35 percent for the general population.

23. According to the 1986 census, 44 percent of Muslim women were in full or part-time employment, as compared with 53 percent of women in the general population (*1986 New Zealand Census of Population and Dwellings*, Series C, Report 14, 44–45). One current estimate for the community as a whole is 30 percent.

24. I understand that in the past, one or two cases have gone to the Human Rights Commission (see note 4).

25. Education not only of Somalis, but also of New Zealand health professionals, according to the article "Long, Delicate Process" in the *Christchurch Press*, 3 October 2000, which also states, "there is no evidence of the procedure being performed here."

26. The case of the Egyptians is from the minutes of the Christchurch Refugee and New Migrant Forum for April 17, 1998; the others are personal reports.

27. One stood for a district and one on the party list. The two major parties are National and Labour. Under MMP they will usually have to govern in coalition with one or more smaller parties. National and Labor are generally labelled "center right" and "center left" respectively. There are 120 members of parliament.

28. There are several Sufi groups and/or teachers who follow the teachings of Inayat Khan, but they appear to consider Sufism as a form of universalism rather than specifically Islamic. To my knowledge, they have no connection with any of the Islamic associations.

29. "New Zealand Muslims Endeavour to Success" lists eight mosques or Islamic centers in the Auckland area; one or two others have been mentioned to me by individuals.

30. According to *al-Mujaddid* (December 1999, 11; March 2000, 12) and personal communications. *Al-Mujaddid* is a recently founded Muslim newspaper issued quarterly in Auckland but not officially connected with any association, though it contains news of their activities.

31. The mosque was built in 1998 on land leased from the university. The funds were raised by Muslim staff and students at the university and it is run by a management committee which, as I understand, owns the mosque.

32. There is also, evidently, an association in New Plymouth, in the North Island, according to a report in the *Daily News* (further detail not given) on July 24, 2000 and passed on via the Internet by a FIANZ staff person.

33. "New Zealand Muslims Endeavour to Success" gives dates of 1962 for Wellington, 1981 for Hamilton, and 1982 for Palmerston North. The dates I give come from earlier sources.

34. "New Zealand Muslims Endeavour to Success" gives dates of 1980 for Christchurch and 1994 for Palmerston North.

35. I have been told this in the case of Canterbury, and the circumstances of the founding of the NZMA suggest this. IMAN, on the other hand, originated from the needs of the university students, as did the Otago Association.

36. See *al-Mujaddid*, October 1999 and October 2000, and the November 1999 and August 2000 reports of the Education Review Office (Internet: <www.ero.govt.nz>). In New Zealand parents are allowed to instruct their children at home under certain conditions rather than sending them to school. An "integrated school" is one with a special character that receives state funding and must meet certain requirements while retaining its special character; most of these are Roman Catholic.

37 See *al-Mujaddid*, October 1999.

38. "New Zealand Muslims Endeavour to Success," 3. See also the Profile on the FIANZ Web site.

39. According to "New Zealand Muslims Endeavour to Success," 12, and the FIANZ Web site, the AMANA Corporation was created in 1990. Its limited success is suggested by articles in the FIANZ newsletters for January 1999 and March 2000.

40. There is a notice of an effort in this direction, claiming FIANZ support, in *al-Mujaddid*, March 2000, 10. A group called the Islamic Information Service, formed about 1998 and independent of FIANZ, has been conducting discussions of Islamic wills. One in Auckland is reported in *al-Mujaddid*, October 2000, 4, and I was present at one in Christchurch in the same month.

41. My information is based on incomplete reports and on newsletters from NZMA, IMAN and the Canterbury Association.

42. FIANZ is <http://www.anglefire.com/biz2/FIANZWEBI/> and the Ackland University group is <http://members.muslimsites.com/auckland-I/>.

43. See, for example, "Caucus Strongly against Movie," *The Evening Post* (Wellington), May 29, 1980 and "'Stupid' to show film," *The Press* (Christchurch) 31, May 5, 1980. FIANZ presumably used this argument in its own lobbying. See also D. Willie, "Muslims Down Under" (1989), 14–15.

44. The article, published on March 7, 1987, reported the views of John Laffin in a totally uncritical manner. I do not believe that this could happen today. So far as I have been able to determine, FIANZ did not finally take up the right of reply, considering that it would not be productive.

45. Abdur Rahman Khan, "The Shield of Islam," *NZ Listener*, October 1987. See "Bid fails to stop 'Sword of Islam,'" *The Press* (Christchurch), September 8, 1987 and other articles at about the same time.

46. Much of this is summarized in an internal report to FIANZ, "Status Report on the Response by the Muslims," by G. I. A. R. Khan. According to Khan some effort was in process to get the book "scheduled" under the Race Relations Act, but so far as I know, nothing came of it.

47. Wille says that FIANZ spent NZ $100,000 in legal fees on the injunction against the TV documentary "The Sword of Islam" and at least $16,000 on its campaign against the *Satanic Verses*, with several Muslims mortgaging their homes to finance the first effort. Although the legal effort failed, they felt that "FIANZ did signal to the media its willingness to use the courts in the pursuit of its interests." ("Muslims Down Under," 16 and *passim.*)

48. The e-mail messages, which are the source of this information, state that similar things have happened at the Universities of Auckland and Waikato, but I have no further information about these.

49. Christchurch *Press*, October 7, 2000, 2.

50. For the meeting with the ambassador see *al-Mujaddid*, March 2000; for the collections for Columbia see *al-Mujaddid*, March and July 1999. For the Albanian Civic League see, *inter alia*, the 1999 FIANZ Annual Report on its Web site.

51. *Al-Mujaddid*, July 1999. I have seen slightly varying forms of the official name of this group. The national conference for 2000 was planned for Palmerston North at the end of September.

52. This organization plans to be associated with FIANZ in the same manner as the women's association, but I do not know if this arrangement has been completed.

53. Described in *al-Mujaddid*, March 2000, 4.

54. *Al-Mujaddid*, July 1999. The five nations are Australia, New Zealand, Fiji, Canada, and the United States. I am informed that there are plans to link the Sports Assocation to the Muslim Students and Youth Organization.

55. I have seen this referred to as South West Pacific Islamic Regional Conference (SWPIRC) and as the South West Pacific Islamic Forum. Its second gathering was hosted by the NZMA in October 1999, according to the 1999 FIANZ Annual Report.

56. On *halal* slaughter in New Zealand, see, inter alia, "Halal, lawful and safe," in *The New Zealand Meat Producer*, Last Quarter, 1996. In 1999 NZIMM certified about twice as much meat tonnage as FIANZ. FIANZ dealt with 26 meat plants employing about 130 *halal* slaughterers and NZIMM dealt with 24 plants employing over 100 slaughterers. There is overlap in these figures since a number of plants are certified by both FIANZ and NZIMM. Under tender arrangements that begin this year these proportions could change and, in the longer term, new agencies might come into the picture.

57. According to one informant, the *ijtema* is held around Christmas time and two *jor* around Eastertime and Labor day (October 23).

58. I have personally encountered the movement in Egypt and it is also strong in Malaysia, from which a number of New Zealand Muslims come.

59. A member of the Auckland community said to me that it is only the "humbler" people who come to the Tablighi meetings, but I do, in fact, know of some educated people of Indian and other backgrounds who are involved.

60. For more detail on the Tablighi movement in New Zealand, including descriptions of some meetings I attended in the early 1980s, see Shepard, "Muslim in New Zealand," (1982), 70; "Muslims in New Zealand," (1996), 220–21.

61. *Al-Mujaddid*, October 1999. An independent witness from Dunedin reports that it was quite well received but did not attract as many non-Muslims as had been hoped.

62. *Al-Mujaddid*, March 2000, gives a glowing account of his visit. According to the October 2000 issue, six Saudi scholars came in July and August for a well attended eleven-day seminar in Auckland.

63. In Christchurch, Siddiqi's 1985 visit in connection with the opening of the mosque was well attended by non-Muslims as was Badawi's first visit the following year. Badawi's second visit, in 1998, attracted few non-Muslims and Deedat's, in 2000, virtually none.

64. I have been told more than once by someone from one ethnic group that another group confuses its customs with Islam.

65. I have been told that at one point they were meeting separately because the Otago Muslim Association had taken an aggressive Sunni position and that the Iranian ambassador sought to intervene in some manner, but the current leaders of the Association are unaware of this and say that the relations have always been good.

66. There is currently (October 2000) a lively public discussion about the "brain drain" of talented young New Zealanders. For at least a generation, many young Kiwis have gone overseas for what is called an "O.E." (overseas experience), but most, though not all, eventually return. Whether fewer are not returning is one of the issues of the current debate.

67. These hopes are suggested by Leila Adam, a member of the Wellington community, in her article "Muslim Community in New Zealand," (see note 1). The phrase "Islam is not 'in the air'" is found on p. 40.

Muslims in South Africa: A Very Visible Minority

14

TAMARA SONN

Introduction

WHAT MAKES MUSLIM COMMUNITIES in the industrialized West an important topic to study is that they act as pioneers in the struggle to reconcile Islamic principles with life in technologically developed and pluralistic societies. They face challenges that will inevitably be faced by Muslims in all developing countries.

Industrialization and technological development bring socioeconomic changes that impact the individual, the family, and society at large. Industrialization is a feature of urbanized society, and urbanization brings with it a transition from reliance on the extended family to reliance primarily on the nuclear family. That transition, in turn, results in shifts in the roles of males and females in families, with women often taking a greater share of responsibility for the family overall than in more traditional settings. These shifts are augmented by increased literacy and the greater participation of women in the work force, also associated with industrialization and generally resulting in increased autonomy for the individual. Concomitantly, as individuals and nuclear families gain autonomy in industrialized society, social and political associations change. The rural pattern of primary socialization within the extended family gives way to the urban pattern of association based on shared interests and values. The crucial shift here is that associations no longer primarily reflect a particular religious affiliation, as is the case in rural societies. Urbanization brings far greater interaction with people of different faiths—interaction that often proves essential for the common good.

Such issues as the changing roles of individuals, especially those of women, and the nature of relations with people of other faiths are matters of significant concern to Islamic law. Therefore, life in industrialized society inevitably raises religious questions. Since the majority of the Muslim world is working toward industrial and technological development, eventually it will have to face those challenges head on. Muslim thinkers over the past century have acknowledged as much, predicting scenarios and solutions. Muslims actually living and participating in the economies of the industrialized world are confronting those challenges on a daily basis. It is in that sense that they are pioneers, a vanguard of sorts.

Muslim communities in South Africa fall into this category. South African society is dominated by an urban elite. While the country's Muslims unquestionably suffered under apartheid, they nonetheless lived primarily urban lives as members of South Africa's modernized society. However, unlike Muslim communities in most other industrialized countries, they were not singled out as immigrants. The oldest Muslim community in South Africa was established by slaves brought by Dutch colonialists from their domains in South Asia, including East India and what is now Malaysia, and other parts of Africa in the mid-seventeenth century. The Dutch are the oldest European ethnic stock in Southern Africa. They and their former Muslim slaves, many of whom intermarried with the indigenous African population, exhibit a strong sense of belonging to the area. Some two centuries later, British colonialists brought Indian laborers and traders into the region, many of whom were Muslim, thus establishing the second oldest European and Muslim ethnic communities, respectively. A small group of Muslim former slaves, commonly known as "Zanzibaris," arrived in Natal in the last quarter of the nineteenth century, and many Africans and some Europeans in South Africa have become Muslim as well. But the predominant ethnic groups among South African Muslims are the so-called "Malays" and Indians. Despite the questionable nomenclature, both are distinctly South African.[1]

Thus, South African Muslims do not see themselves as temporary inhabitants of their society, as do many Muslims in Europe and America. Although they recognize, and in some cases, valorize their religious and cultural distinctiveness, they tend not to harbor collective dreams of returning to some more Islamic abode.[2] In 1961, for example, Cape Muslims rejected an invitation from the Malaysian government to move there in the face of forced relocation to designated "group areas."[3] It is not so much the minority status of South African Muslims that is relevant, therefore, as the fact that they are Muslims forging lives in a pluralistic, industrialized society. As such, their example may be instructive, not only to the ever increasing number of Muslims living in industrialized countries, but even to Muslim majority communities still in the process of industrial and technological development.

The fact that until recently, at least, South Africa's government was one of the most blatantly unjust in the industrialized world makes its Muslim community even more interesting for students of contemporary Islam. This is not to say that South Africa was the only or the most unjust state in the industrialized world, but that its official apartheid system, institutionalizing in 1949 what had been a de facto separation of the population into a minority of European rulers and a majority of non-European marginalized groups, made it the most obvious.

In the discourse of twentieth-century activists and reformers, Islam has at its core the value of social justice. The challenge of human life, in this view, is to demonstrate one's submission to the divine will through contributing to the creation of a just society, one that reflects the equality of all human beings in the eyes of their creator. What could be a greater challenge to Islamic values, thus conceived, than South Africa's apartheid system? The response of South Africa's Muslims to that system, which epitomizes the evils attributed to "the West" in contemporary Islamic popular discourse, is therefore doubly instructive. Not only are they grappling with issues of individual autonomy—especially women's—and pluralism, but they are citizens of a polity based on distinctly un-Islamic principles.

Not all South African Muslims became engaged in this set of issues. For many South Africans overall, meeting daily responsibilities was sufficiently challenging to preclude social and political activism. For some South African Muslims, the ideological challenge required to make common cause with non-Muslims, especially with women who did not fit the traditional stereotype, was too great to overcome. This essay describes efforts of representative South African Muslim activists who were able to meet that challenge; many of them, as a result, continue to play leading roles in post-apartheid South Africa.

The Development of Islamic Resistance

Some Muslims were active in secular movements opposed to the de facto apartheid system, including the African National Congress (ANC, founded in 1912 as the South African Native National Congress),[4] from the early years of the twentieth century, but they were not considered Islamic activists as such. It was not until the 1950s and 1960s that many in the younger generation of Muslims began to look to their religion for the organizational and ideological bases of resistance. Several organizations were founded expressing this generation's discontent with the complacency and defeatism of the many Muslims who did not join in the resistance. The first such organizations were the Cape Muslim Youth Movement and the Claremont Muslim Youth Association, both arising in the Muslim community around Cape Town. In 1961 a general "Call of Islam" movement was launched in the Cape, setting the tone for Islamic activism against injustice with the publication of its principles:

> For too long a time now have we been, together with our fellow-sufferers, subjugated, suffered humiliation of being regarded as inferior beings, deprived of our basic rights to Earn, to Learn and to Worship. We therefore call upon our Muslim Brethren and all brothers in our sufferings to unite under the banner of Truth, Justice and Equality to rid our beloved land of the forces of evil and tyranny.[5]

While Muslims had protested interference with their religious practice in earlier years, this call for Islamic resistance was unique in a number of ways. First, unlike earlier protests, the new resistance was not against specific rulings, but was aimed against an entire system deemed essentially unjust. Second, and more significantly, the injustices being protested were not those suffered by Muslims alone, but by all victims of oppression, regardless of religious affiliation. The traditional focus on religious exclusivity was giving way to the overarching value of social justice for all human beings. Islamic resistance organizations from this time on focused on explicating this core value, seeking the roots of injustice wherever they lie, articulating the methods for extricating those roots, and defining the entire process as essentially religious activity.

Imam Abdullah Haron was a leading figure in this movement. Active in several Islamic resistance organizations, he also edited the Cape's *Muslim News*. An outspoken critic of apartheid, Haron was taken into police custody in 1969 and held for four months. There he died, undoubtedly due to torture. The security forces predictably attributed the death to accidental causes. Imam Haron's funeral was a public event, with thousands of people marching in the procession. Thus, one of the earliest leaders of this new Islamic resistance became a hero not just of Islamic activists, but of the anti-apartheid movement overall, and the Islamic resistance movement became a feature on the national landscape.

Farid Esack relates the story of a hunger strike undertaken by a Christian, Bernard Wrankmore, demanding an inquiry into the death. After sixty-seven days, the government showed no signs of relenting and Wrankmore ceased his strike. But the solidarity of all those motivated by social justice—regardless of communal affiliation—had been demonstrated.

In the 1970s, more Muslims were attracted to the liberation agenda. New organizations appeared, including the Muslim Youth Movement and the Muslim Students Association. The Muslim Youth Movement spun off a number of other organizations, including the Women's Islamic Movement. The 1980s saw the establishment of two more important organizations: Qibla and the Call of Islam (originally called Muslims Against Oppression, this group later adopted the name Call of Islam; the identity in name with the 1961 declaration of principles was a coincidence).[6] Although there are important ideological differences among these groups, they are alike in motivating Muslims to join the struggle against social injustice and articulating principles whereby that struggle is seen as religious.

Articulating Key Issues

People in these movements found inspiration in their renewed understandings of Islamic teachings. Islamic "study circles" (*halaqat*) proliferated as did university programs in Arabic and Islamic studies.[7] As in the rest of the Muslim world, encouraging believers to demonstrate their commitment to egalitarian values through social action was a central theme. The writings of Egyptian activist Sayyid Qutb, for example, Iranian ideologue 'Ali Shari'ati, and Pakistani Abu'l A'la Mawdudi were studied with enthusiasm.

But South Africa produced some unique challenges, ones for which Islamist activists from the likes of Egypt, Iran, and Pakistan provided no solutions. As noted above, Muslims in South Africa are a very small minority. Of a population of around 40 million people, Muslims make up less than 1.5 percent. Natural communal exclusivity had been intensified by forced segregation, and many Muslims had come to accept this segregation as compatible with their belief in the prohibition of associating with "non-believers" (*kuffar*). By contrast, for Muslim activists, as noted, social justice came to replace communal cohesion and exclusivity as the central religious value. Their cause was the same as that of the significant numbers of the rest of South Africa's population—especially its three-quarters "African" community, but also the roughly 17 percent ethnically European population—who were deeply involved in the struggle against apartheid. Yet, because of traditionalist opposition to making common cause with non-Muslims, articulation of the centrality of the struggle for social justice, even if it meant working with non-Muslims, became a dominant feature of South African Islamic liberation discourse.

A major figure in this discourse is Mawlana Farid Esack, a cofounder of the Call of Islam.[8] A scholar and activist of exceeding courage, Esack and the Call of Islam worked closely with other activists, particularly the United Democratic Front (UDF). The UDF was established in 1983 and devoted itself to developing broad, grassroots organizations to fight the unjust sociopolitical order. Articulating not simply a justification for working with non-Muslims but the religious imperative of doing so became a central theme in Esack's work. As he put it:

> The formidable presence of religious figures and organizations and, especially, the unprecedented Muslim-Christian religious solidarity that now formed an integral part of this struggle, ensured that questions of identity, affiliation and community assumed a stark new dimension.
>
> The formation of the UDF in 1983 and the subsequent visible participation of Muslims side by side with the religious Other, led to considerable debate and acrimony amongst some of the organized and activist Muslims who opposed this affinity with the religious Other. Fundamental theological issues, such as the nature of faith and the meaning of fellowship of the *ummah* (community), arose and were regularly alluded to but were seldom examined in a systematic manner.[9]

Following an incident when nineteen leaders of various religious faiths were arrested in a show of solidarity with people in the black township of Gugulethu, cooperation among liberation-minded religious leaders increased. Interfaith services proliferated and the line between religious and political movements was all but erased. Muslims could be seen addressing Christian congregations, and anti-apartheid activist Alan Boesak, for example, addressed Call of Islam meetings.

In 1984, the South African chapter of the World Conference on Religion and Peace (WCRP) was formed under the aegis of Bishop Desmond Tutu and convened by Archbishop Trevor Huddlestone, with active participation by Muslim leaders, including Esack. In 1992, as the apartheid system was reaching its end and South Africans were attempting to forge a new basis for their future, WCRP members drew up a "Declaration on Religious Rights and Responsibilities." The Declaration was to serve as a guide for the new South African constitution, then under negotiation. As such, it reflected the shared values of its diverse religious signatories. It affirmed "the rightful and lawful existence of diverse religious communities" and called upon the state to "recognize them and guarantee their autonomy."[10] At the same time it called upon religious communities "to promote spiritual and moral values, reconciliation and reconstruction, in accordance with their own teachings." Similarly, it affirmed that "people shall enjoy freedom of conscience;" "religious communities shall be equal before the law;" "religious communities have moral responsibilities to society" and that "people have the right to religious education." Further, "people in state institutions shall enjoy religious rights;" "religions have the right to propagate their teachings;" "religious communities shall have access to the public media;" "the state shall recognize systems of family and customary law;" "the holy days of religious communities shall be respected;" and "religious institutions may own property and be exempt from taxes." These ten principles formed the basis for the WCRP's proposed clause for the new South African constitution's bill of rights:

I. All persons are entitled:

    1.1 to freedom of conscience;

    1.2 to profess, practice, and propagate any religion or no religion;

    1.3 to change their religious allegiance;

2. Every religious community and/or member thereof shall enjoy the right:
   2.1 to establish, maintain and manage religious institutions;
   2.2 to have their particular system of family law recognized by the state;
   2.3 to criticize and challenge all social and political structures and policies in terms of the teachings of their religion.

The declaration played a major role in negotiations for South Africa's new constitution. It does not appear as such in the final draft of the constitution that was adopted in 1996, but its ideas were incorporated into several of its sections.[11]

The inclusion not only of religious rights but also of religious responsibilities in what is generally supposed to be a strictly political document illustrates the impact of another major position held by Islamic activists in South Africa. As expressed by Farid Esack at a 1994 conference on Islam and civil society in South Africa, "There is no such thing as anything being purely political or purely theological."[12] In other words, while some may consider working with non-Muslims for the betterment of society to be activity marginal to Islam at best, for activists like Esack, this activity is quintessentially Islamic, following directly from the Qur'an's teaching on justice.

This position is in direct conflict with the view of many of the traditionalists with whom Esack grew up. In the 1994 conference, he related the story of being taught as a child in South Africa to greet non-Muslims with *"samm alaykum"* (poison be on you), instead of the traditional Muslim greeting *"as-salamu alaykum"* (peace be upon you). According to this view, supported by some religious sources, working with non-Muslims may be necessary at times, but these are exceptions. Under ideal circumstances, Muslims should only associate with Muslims. Esack therefore recognizes the necessity of reinterpreting the traditionalist view. Rather than allowing the traditionalists' interpretation of religious sources and the terms used to identify Muslims and "others" to go unchallenged, Esack advocates "the rediscovery and re-appropriation of the meaning of these terms" as "the prerequisite to liv[ing] the Qur'an with integrity and also liv[ing] with [non-Muslims] with integrity."

> It is possible to re-deploy these terms in a way which enables one to live alongside others with integrity. Because ultimately the Qur'an is concerned and presents Allah as a being that is concerned with something that people do and with the people who do it, rather than with an abstract entity called faith. . . . Thus, *muslim* and all its positive connotations (including eschatological) cannot refer to the biological accident of being born in a Muslim family. Similarly, *kafir* cannot refer to the accident of being born outside of such a family.[13]

The overall spirit of Qur'anic teaching is personal accountability, Esack asserts, not group identity—personal accountability for actions, their motivations and consequences. But actions are by nature dynamic: "[E]very deed that we do or refuse to do is a step in our personal transformation." There is no single action or set of actions that encompasses an entire life; moral behavior is an ongoing enterprise, evident in every interaction and choice. It is ongoing effort, not a *fait accompli*. It is continuous responsiveness to injustice in all its forms. Thus, "[t]o affirm the dynamic nature of theological categories (*islam* [submission], *iman* [faith], and *kufr* [unbelief]), and their nuances, is to affirm the basic elan of justice in the Qur'an."[14]

This "re-appropriation" of Islamic terms in the service of the overall teaching of justice in the Qur'an is central to Esack's "project," as he calls it, the "search for the etiology of religious pluralism and for liberation." But it is integrally related to yet another aspect of liberation in industrialized, urban society, namely women. As noted above, the changing nature of the family, increased literacy, and increased economic independence result in increased autonomy, for women as much as for anyone else. Like other religious communities, Muslims are faced with the challenge of integrating religious teaching with social reality. Undeniably, traditional religious interpretations have reflected a social context in which women were economically dependent, generally less educated than men, and therefore less active in the public arena. In the face of changes in these circumstances, there is significant discourse among Muslims about the rights, responsibilities, and roles of women.[15]

But for South Africans, the challenge is somewhat more immediate since the demise of the apartheid government. In accordance with the WCRP's declaration on Religious Rights and Responsibilities, recognition of Muslim family law by the state has been under discussion. In its current form, however, Muslim law allows polygamous marriage, greater rights to divorce for men than for women, paternal custody for children in case of divorce, a greater share in inheritance for men than for women, the right of men to discipline their wives and, in general, men being "in charge" of women. Yet like other aspects of traditional Islamic law, these rulings dealing with women are contested by many Muslim activists. Although these activists struggled for the inclusion of religious rights within the "new South Africa," they did not necessarily accept the wholesale inclusion of traditional Islamic family law into South African law. Because of the contested nature of that traditional law, therefore, a committee was established to discuss "Muslim Personal Law" (MPL).

Little progress has been achieved in reaching an agreement on the form of MPL that should be recognized by the South African state; the committee disbanded in disagreement. Recent efforts to revive the issue of recognizing religious marriages by the South Africa Law Commission have likewise foundered over concerns such as reciprocal duties of support, divorce rights, and the status of offspring. But issues relating to women's roles in society continue to emerge. For example, in 1997, an uproar was raised concerning Muslim women in broadcasting. The controversy surrounded Shamima Shaikh, chairperson of the Muslim Community Broadcasting Trust. The Muslim Community Broadcasting Trust runs "The Voice," a Johannesburg-area Muslim radio station. When Shamima Shaikh's voice was heard over the airwaves, some Muslims protested vehemently, arguing from the traditional position that women's voices are not to be heard in public. In response, a petition was drawn up, signed by Muslim community activists, and submitted to the Independent Broadcasting Authority of South Africa, the country's broadcasting regulator:

1. We, the undersigned South African Muslims, are deeply concerned about the message of discrimination against women being conveyed by the current controversy around the issue of women on radio.

2. Islam is a religion of justice and promotes the equality of men and women. We, therefore, believe that discrimination on the basis of gender goes against the very spirit of Islam.

3. We are also concerned about the implications of a discredited minority religious opinion that purports that women may not be heard in public. This position implies that women are perpetual social minors and goes against the spirit of Islamic teachings. Perpetuating such a view not only lacks religious credibility, but militates against the hikmah (wisdom) the Qur'an exhorts all Muslims to employ in public life.

4. As citizens, Muslims have made significant contributions to South Africa's liberation struggle and its general socioeconomic development and are an inseparable part of this country. The current controversy not only reinforces negative stereotypes that portray Islam as an anti-women religion and all Muslim men being women-hating fundamentalists. It also has the potential to erode the positive gains Muslims have made in this country for centuries. This is not the best way of exposing others to the beauty of Islam.

5. We urge all Muslims who have just rejuvenated themselves in the holy month of Ramadan to continue with the process of social transformation aimed at upholding the dignity and equality of all of humankind. This is the vision of the Qur'an and was actively promoted by the Prophet Muhammad (peace be upon him).

6. We call upon all our Muslim fellow citizens to commit themselves to a democratic South Africa with the entrenched ideals of non-racialism and non-sexism and to deal with their differences with dignity and integrity.

The petition points out the interrelated nature of concerns for social justice and gender equality in industrialized society. Shamima Shaikh was a tireless worker in the anti-apartheid struggle. An active member of the Muslim Youth Movement, she met her husband while in police detention for handing out pamphlets. She became a member of the National Executive of the Muslim Youth Movement and later editor of the progressive Muslim monthly, *Al-Qalam*. Like many other Muslim women, Shamima Shaikh struggled valiantly along with others committed to social justice. The idea that, once the apartheid government was replaced, these women should retreat into silence seemed preposterous. Indeed, opposition to women playing public roles emerged even in the thick of the struggle, prompting the creation of the Gender Desk of the Muslim Youth Movement, spearheaded by Shamima Shaikh with widespread support. As was brought out repeatedly at the 1994 conference on Islam and civil society in South Africa, there is little difference between discrimination on the basis of skin color and discrimination on the basis of gender. Arguments supporting both positions turn on the superior humanity of those "in charge." Therefore, concern for progress in one area of discrimination almost inevitably results in concern for progress in the other.

As head of the gender desk of the Muslim Youth Movement, Shamima Shaikh consistently brought concerns for gender equality to the attention of the now defunct Muslim Personal Law Board. Putting her concerns into practice, she protested the eviction of

MUSLIMS IN SOUTH AFRICA   263

women from their standard mezzanine position in the mosque during crowded gatherings. As often happens during Ramadan, when more space was needed for men, they occupied the women's quarters upstairs and set up tents for women outside. During Ramadan in 1994, Shamima Shaikh led the women from their tents back into the mosque. Ultimately, she joined with a growing number of South African Muslims to establish a congregation where gender equality was an integral part of Islamic teaching on social justice.

In South Africa, as elsewhere, greater headway has been made in the struggle against racism than against sexism. Yet with the efforts of people like Shamima Shaikh, some progress is evident. When Shamima Shaikh died of cancer in January 1998 at the age of thirty-seven, funeral prayers were led by a female friend, an unprecedented act, at least in modern Islam. Even more shocking to traditional ways, women not only attended funeral prayers at the mosque, but they prayed on the main floor with the men, not sequestered upstairs. Despite traditional practice, women also attended the burial service, praying with the men.

Conclusion

Activists such as Farid Esack and Shamima Shaikh have clarified two points. First, the topics of social justice, pluralism, and gender equity are integrally related. Active commitment to the value of social justice, which dominates contemporary Islamic discourse, entails not only accepting the rights of multiple religious communities and at least two genders, but also working with those who share that value, regardless of communal or gender identity. Secondly, these issues, which inevitably arise in industrialized society, can be addressed in the context of Islamic principles.

This does not mean that the path followed by the South African Muslims discussed above is the only path available to Muslims in industrialized societies. In fact, as circumstances change, so will people's ways of understanding and implementing religious ideals. As Esack put it, "We know that our theology, wherever else it may also be located, is very much rooted in the basic experiences of people."[16] It is to be expected that other communities will draw their own inspiration from revelation and determine the best ways of implementing its teachings.

Still, the example set by the South African Muslims is inspiring. Once scorned minorities, Muslims have now achieved significant visibility in the new South Africa. Following the first all-race elections in 1994, when Nelson Mandela was elected president, a number of key posts went to Muslims. Not only were they elected to provincial posts, Muslims were also appointed to federal positions. Dalla Omar was appointed minister of justice, the first Muslim to hold such a position in a non-Muslim majority country, and Ahmad Kathrada was appointed minister of housing. Both Omar and Kathrada struggled alongside Mandela, enduring decades in jail as well. Farid Esack has completed his tenure as chair of the Commission on Gender Equity. This representation by Muslims in South Africa's government, disproportionate to the community's 1.5 percentage of the overall population, indicates that the challenges of "Western" life can be met within the context of Islamic values, and that doing so earns the respect of the population at large.

Notes

This chapter is dedicated to Shamima Shaikh, devoted wife, mother, friend, and Muslim activist. Shamima was a member of the National Executive of the Muslim Youth Movement, founder and former head of the gender desk of the Muslim Youth Movement, former editor of the progressive Muslim monthly, *Al-Qalam*, and chair of the Muslim Community Broadcasting Trust, which runs "The Voice," a Johannesburg-area radio station. Shamima died in January 1998, leaving the world a better place than she found it and countless people grateful for having known her.

1. For a history of Muslim populations in Southern Africa, see Y. DaCosta, "The Spatial Origins of the Early Cape Muslims, and the Diffusion of Islam to the Cape Colony," *Journal for Islamic Studies* 10 (1990): 45–67; Achmat Davids, *The Mosques of the Bo-Kaap* (Athlone: South African Institute of Arabic and Islamic Research, 1980) and *The History of the Tana Baru* (Cape Town: Committee for the Preservation of the Tana Baru, 1985); Fatima Meer, *Portrait of Indian South Africans* (Durban: Avon House, 1969).

2. This is not to deny a sense of affinity with India on the part of South African Indians, or a strong Indian cultural identity, as Fatima Meer demonstrates in her *Portrait*. A growing concern with Malaysian identity has also been observed among the Cape Muslims, e.g., by Shamil Jeppie in "Commemorations and Identities: The 1994 Tercentenary of Islam in South Africa," *Islam and the Question of Minorities*, ed. Tamara Sonn (Atlanta: Scholars Press, 1996): 73–92.

3. See Farid Esack, *Qur'an, Liberation, and Pluralism* (Oxford: Oneworld, 1997), 30.

4. For a survey of such organizations, see Esack, *Qur'an, Liberation, and Pluralism*, 20–30.

5. Published in Cape Town's *Muslim News* (31 March 1961): 4.

6. See Farid Esack, *Qur'an, Liberation, and Pluralism*, 47 n. 24.

7. See Tamara Sonn, "Islamic Studies in South Africa," *American Journal of Islamic Social Sciences*. 11, no. 2 (Summer 1994): 273–81.

8. Dr. Esack's views on religious pluralism in the cause of social justice are eloquently articulated in his *Qur'an, Liberation, and Pluralism*.

9. Ibid., 37.

10. See manuscript "Declaration on Religious Rights and Responsibilities."

11. According to Constitutional Assembly negotiators, as reported in personal communication from Farid Esack,

12. Farid Esack, "Between Mandela and Man Dalla: Rethinking Kaffirs and Kafirs," unpublished proceedings of Islam and Civil Society in South Africa: Prospects for Tolerance and Conflict Resolution, University of South Africa, 5–7 August 1994.

13. Ibid.

14. Ibid.

15. Reflecting the current tenor of this discourse, it may be noted that among the more popular formulations of what is considered a progressive approach to the topic is Amina Wadud-Muhsin's *Qur'an and Woman* (Kuala Lumpur: Penerbit Fajar Bakti Sdn., Bhd., 1992). The use of the essentialist term "woman" in this title is problematic. In his recent presentation at a conference in South Africa on "Violence Against Women," Farid Esack noted that such usage presents "a clear possibility of perpetuating that very stereotyping at the heart of gender injustice. As Spelman has cogently argued, failing to address the heterogeneity of women results in underwriting cultural and racial hierarchies (1990: 135–59)." (Unpublished proceedings.)

16. Farid Esack, "Between Mandela and Man Dalla: Rethinking Kaffirs and Kafirs."

Muslims in the Caribbean: Ethnic Sojourners and Citizens   15

JOHN O. VOLL

MUSLIMS IN THE CARIBBEAN region represent distinctive styles of minority and diaspora experiences. While they have a clear identity in terms of faith, their actual communal identity is frequently not based primarily on their religious identity. In this way, while Muslims in South Africa have been called "a most visible minority,"[1] Muslims in the Caribbean might be described as "a most invisible minority." The case of Muslims in the Caribbean region is a strong reminder that minority and diasporic identities may have many different dimensions and are not simply monolithic. The Caribbean experiences of Muslims might even suggest that, at least in this region, immigrant and diasporic identities are based more on language and culture than they are on religion. Stated more explicitly, although there *are* Muslims in the Caribbean region, in the most commonly understood usage of the terms, there may *not* be "Muslim minorities" or "Muslim diasporas" there.

In the Caribbean, immigrants play important historic roles, but the understanding of those roles and the definition of the identity of the peoples involved are topics of considerable debate. The immigrants represent a wide spectrum of experiences ranging from the voluntary movements of colonial elites to the forced migration of slaves, especially from Africa, and the rigidly controlled movements of indentured labor, especially from South Asia. In general terms, there is a growing body of scholarship that examines diasporas and migrations into the Caribbean region. Most of this literature concentrates on particular groups of people as they exist in specific countries. Recently some scholars, especially those studying the African diaspora, have conceptualized a broader regional network of diasporic interaction. On a grand scale, this is reflected in the work of Paul Gilroy and his concept of the 'Black Atlantic."[2] However, this concept has also been criticized by scholars like Colin Palmer, who argues, "There is no one Black Atlantic. . . . The term runs the risk of defining a people by an ocean."[3]

While it is important to avoid creating an overgeneralizing grand conceptualization, it is also useful, especially when dealing with diasporas and migrations of smaller magnitude than the African, to keep broader regional and global networks in mind. An approach that takes into consideration both these regional contexts and the particulars of local conditions is especially important when examining the Muslims in the Caribbean. Muslim immigrants came to countries in the Caribbean from a number of different areas, most notably South Asia and the Syrian-Lebanese Levant. Under very specific local circumstances, there are also Muslims of African origin in the region, but they represent a very small proportion of Caribbean Muslims. In general terms, those Muslims identified themselves with other immigrants from their place of origin rather than with other Muslims. As a result, historically, there has been virtually no "pan-Muslim" identification or activity in the region as a whole. While some scholars might speak of a "Black Atlantic" or more narrowly of an African-based "transnational Caribbean identity,"[4] it is not possible to identify anything that might be called a "Caribbean Muslim" identity. Similarly, while some scholars might speak of "African Islam" or "Malaysian Islam" as religiocultural traditions,[5] it is not possible to speak of "Caribbean Islam."

The Muslims and Their Communities

Muslims in the Caribbean live in the island societies and the countries on the northern coast of South America. They are not a very visible element in those societies. The *Britannica Book of the Year* for 1998, for example, provides statistical summaries of religious affiliations for the countries of the world; it explicitly notes Muslims in only three countries in the Caribbean region —Guyana, Suriname, and Trinidad, and Tobago—all of which are on the north coast of South America.[6] Although almost three-quarters of the Muslims in the region live in these three countries, over a decade ago it was reported the more than one hundred thousand Muslims live "on at least a dozen Caribbean islands, including Barbados, Grenada, Dominica, Puerto Rico, the U.S. Virgin Islands, and Jamaica."[7] In most of these areas there are sufficient numbers of Muslims to support mosques and effective communities, even though the numbers in proportion to the populations as a whole may be small. The majority of the estimated 2,500 Muslims in Puerto Rico, for example, live in Rio Piedras, a suburb of San Juan, where there is a mosque and an active Muslim community life.[8]

Most Muslims in the Caribbean are part of one of three different groups in the region. The majority are of South Asian origin. Their ancestors came in the nineteenth century after the abolition of the slave trade made it necessary to secure indentured labor for workers in the major plantations of the region.[9] The British Parliament had passed the Act of Abolition in 1833 and provided for a period of "apprenticeship" until 1840 for the newly freed slaves working in the plantations. It became clear that the former slaves were unwilling to continue to work under plantation conditions, and owners began to look elsewhere for cheap labor. In 1836, John Gladstone, a merchant involved in the plantation economy and the father of William Ewert Gladstone, the prime minister of Great Britain later in the century, arranged with a British firm in Calcutta to provide contract labor for plantations in the British Caribbean.[10] Although the initial arrangements made by Gladstone were so exploitative that the operation was suspended, by 1843–45, the indentured labor system was resumed. Between 1845 and 1917, more than four hundred thousand indentured laborers were brought from India to Trinidad and British Guiana,[11] and Indian laborers arrived in significant but smaller numbers in Jamaica and at least five other smaller island colonies between 1840 and 1861.[12] The Dutch and French also brought such workers from South and Southeast Asia to their colonies in the Caribbean.

The majority of these indentured workers were Hindu, resulting in Hindus being possibly the largest religious community in Surinam and almost the largest in both Guyana and Trinidad and Tobago. However, in all of these places, Muslims represented a significant proportion of the imported workers. One British colonial official, for example, estimated in 1884 that about one-fifth of the Indians in Trinidad were Muslim.[13] Although specific proportions would vary, Muslims were, and are, a significant minority in any Indian community in the Caribbean.

The second major identification of Muslims is "Syrian," or, more generally, Arabic-speaking peoples from the Eastern Mediterranean/Levant region. Most of these people came to the region beginning in the late nineteenth century "as part of a much larger migration from the Levant."[14] Again, the majority of the immigrants from this region to the Caribbean were not Muslim. Most were Christian, coming primarily from Lebanon or Greater Syria. However, in virtually every "Syrian" or Lebanese community in the Caribbean there are at least some Muslims. The "Arabs" did not come in large groups like the South Asians, but usually arrived individually. They became important as peddlers, local store owners, and merchants rather than as a significant part of the agricultural labor force. In Trinidad, for example, by around 1930, the Syrian-Lebanese immigrant community had "carved out a secure niche as a closed ethnic group involved exclusively in retailing cloth, clothes, and household goods. Some families prospered, laying the foundations for their post-World War II emergence as an important element in Trinidad's economic elite."[15] Even though the numbers of "Arabs" in the Caribbean are small, their influence has traditionally been quite large.

Muslims of African origin comprise the third and smallest group of Muslims in the Caribbean. While many of the Africans who had been forcibly brought to the area had come from Muslim communities in Africa, the trauma and oppression of the slave trade and slave labor made it extremely difficult for them to maintain an Islamic identity. In Brazil, there was a Muslim communal identity that was short-lived but sufficient to foster a series of slave revolts in the form of Islamic jihads in the first half of the nineteenth century.[16] However, in the Caribbean, the critical mass for movements of slave revolt to take Muslim form did not exist at that time. Most Afro-Caribbean Muslims represent relatively recent conversions, although this may have been accomplished in the context of a broader "quest for an identity . . . [among people who] have realized that their forefathers were Muslims."[17] Some of the most concerted efforts to affirm a separate Muslim identity have been made by Afro-Caribbeans, especially in Trinidad.

In general terms, the Muslims of the Caribbean have been primarily identified in communal terms by the larger immigrant communities of which they are a part. As a result, an analysis of Muslims in the Caribbean must primarily be an examination of the place of their larger communities in Caribbean societies and what special role, if any, Muslims play within those communities and societies. In the Caribbean societies in which Muslims lived in significant numbers, there were many ethnic tensions and divisions. Remarkably, in most of these conflict situations, while Muslims participated, they did so as part of their larger community of identity. At times, Muslims achieved positions of political importance or social prominence, but in such situations it was their communal rather than their religious identity which was the important factor. When a Muslim became the Speaker of the House of Parliament in Trinidad, for example, it was as a part of the assertion of "Indian," not Muslim, political influence. The Muslim experience in the Caribbean is a reminder of the many different dimensions in building communal diaspora and immigrant identities and also an indication that religion is not always a primary factor in intergroup ethnic tensions in pluralist societies.

The distinctive character of the experience of Muslims within a variety of diasporas provides informative insights into both the nature of those diasporas and the nature of Muslim experiences in the Caribbean. The path from "sojourner to citizen" for Muslims in the Caribbean was not a path defined primarily by the Muslims' religion. Instead, it was their communal ethnic identity that defined the nature of their path from immigrant to participant in the societies to which they came. Four specific cases can provide an introduction to the great diversity of experiences reflecting the complex nature of the life of Muslims in the Caribbean: the transformation of an explicitly Shi'ite festival into a Trinidadian holiday, the common experience of "Syrians" regardless of religious affiliation, the divisions among Muslim minorities based on ethnic origins (as seen in Surinam) rather than unity through shared religion, and the distinctive situation of a "Muslim" coup attempt to control the government of Trinidad.

Trinidad's Hosay

The experiences of Muslims in Trinidad provide many important examples of how Muslims live as both sojourners and citizens in Caribbean societies. One element of the Caribbean Muslim experience is the integration of distinctively Islamic activities into the broader framework of social life. "Caribbean" life styles are remarkable syntheses of elements brought to the region by a variety of immigrant communities. The majority of the South Asians who came to Trinidad were Hindu; among the Muslims the Shi'ites were a minority within a minority. However, the Indian Shi'ites in Trinidad brought with them the celebration of a religious holiday that in most of the world is distinctively Shi'ite. This is the commemoration of the killing of Husayn, the grandson of the Prophet Muhammad, in a battle at Karbala in 680 C.E. Ritual reenactments of the battle and parades in memory of Husayn's martyrdom are carried out annually in many parts of the world.

In Trinidad during the late nineteenth century the Shi'ite Muslims maintained a very low visibility, but they did organize ceremonial processions on the occasion of the memorial of Husayn's death. Relatively rapidly, these parades became public festivals in which a significant number of Trinidadians, both Muslim and non-Muslim, participated. Already by 1884, the celebration of Muharram, or "Hosay," as it was called locally, was of sufficient magnitude that there was a major incident when police fired upon a Hosay procession that was apparently in violation of an ordinance prohibiting certain types of public demonstrations.

The official investigation of the "Hosein riots of 1884" was undertaken by Sir H. W. Norman, a former officer in the Indian (British) Army who was then serving as the Governor of Jamaica. Based on his experience in India with Muharram celebrations, Norman emphasized the non-Islamic nature of the Trinidadian festival in his report. He noted that "the ceremony, although it is purely appertaining to the Mahomedans, is one in which most of the persons engaged are Hindoos," and he added, "the whole celebration has in Trinidad long been regarded as a sort of national Indian demonstration of a rather turbulent character."[18]

This situation in the late nineteenth century reflects the processes of what one scholar has called "Creolization of an Indo-Trinidadian performance."[19] The practice of celebrating the commemoration of the death of Husayn was brought by Indian Shiʻi Muslims to Trinidad in the middle of the nineteenth century. Shiʻi Trinidadians affirm that the observance of the celebration has continued from the arrival of the very first Indians on the island and "assert that no performative change has occurred in the observance."[20] However, over the years, a wide variety of activities has come to be associated with the celebration as more local people participated. Increasingly, as indicated already in the report on the disturbances in 1884, many non-Shiʻites took part. The other participants came to include Sunni Muslims, Hindus, and Christians of South Asian origin. This transformed the basic nature of the celebration in the Trinidadian context. The "religious aspect was downplayed in favor of the event's Indianness. For many, it is simply a way of identifying with the homeland in a purely secular fashion. . . . Whether Indo-Trinidadians performed Hosay out of a firm religious commitment or out of nostalgia for the homeland in the past, they all identified one way or another with being 'Indian.'"[21]

One remarkable aspect of the Hosay celebrations is that, by the late twentieth century, they had "become nationalized, a regular feature of Trinidad's cultural landscape," a tourist attraction of some significance, and "a multicultural phenomenon, lending itself to many different interpretations."[22] Muslims in Trinidad have provided a distinctive part of the developing Trinidadian identity in which it has been possible to maintain a complex set of identities. Muslims continue to be Muslim but within a framework in which identity is "multivalent."[23] The containment of the Muslim dimension of personal identity within a different cultural or ethnic identity is common among Muslims in the Caribbean.

The "Syrian" Experience

Throughout the Caribbean basin, there are immigrant communities who have come from Arabic-speaking areas of the eastern Mediterranean. Although they are relatively small in number, they are a significant part of the economic elite in virtually every country where they have settled. The most common identification of these immigrants is "Syrian," although this refers to the geographic Syria rather than to the more limited territory of the contemporary Syrian republic. Many were from what is now Lebanon and others from Palestine. Most of these "Syrians" were Christian, but in descriptions of virtually every "Syrian" or "Lebanese" community in the Caribbean there is the note, as in one observation of Lebanese in Trinidad, that "most were Christians . . . although a few of them were Muslims."[24] One analysis of Syrian migration to the Western Hemisphere estimates that among the people who emigrated from the Ottoman Empire to the Americas between 1860 and 1914, Muslims comprised about 15 percent to 20 percent of the total.[25] This proportion is similar to the situation in Syrian migrant communities in other parts of the world at that time. In the early twentieth century, for example, French officials estimated that some 20 percent of the Lebanese-Syrians were Muslim, as were about 30 percent of the Lebanese and Syrians living in Cote d'Ivoire in 1931.[26]

The Muslim Syrians did not make a special effort to identify themselves as Muslims and at times appear to have "preferred to pass as Christians" as a way of avoiding Ottoman restrictions on Muslim emigration and also in the Americas as a way of "gaining easier acceptance" in society.[27] In places where there were non-Syrian Muslims, as was the case in Trinidad, no major pan-Muslim associations or affiliations were created. Instead, South Asian Muslims worked with other South Asians and Arab Muslims were part of the Syrian community.

One example of the firmness of this identification with ethnic rather than religious community is the experience of Syrians in Haiti. Syrians had come to Haiti in the late nineteenth century and, as was often the case, became first peddlers and then merchants and shopkeepers. As the Syrian community became established, the few Muslims were "accepted by the Christian Arabs."[28] The local mercantile elite, which had its own ties to outside powers, viewed the arrival of the Syrians as a threat. There were efforts to restrict their entry, limit their ability to operate commercially in Haiti, and, ultimately, expel them. This anti-Syrian mood was very important at the beginning of the twentieth century when "Levantine businesses were attacked by mobs and their owners were physically assaulted."[29] Syrians faced similar opposition in many areas because their success as traders and merchants sometimes challenged local economic elites. At the same time that Syrians were being attacked in Haiti, "the Chambre de Commerce de la Cote d'Ivoire had issued warnings [in 1912] concerning 'le peril syrien.'"[30]

Many of the so-called Syrians in Haiti were naturalized citizens of the United States and a number of other countries. Great pressure was placed on the Haitian government to repeal a 1903 law that prohibited entry into Haiti of "any person styled a Syrian, or so called in popular language," or to ensure that other anti-Syrian measures like the proclamation in March 1905 that "all Syrians must close their stores and leave the Republic April 1" would not apply to naturalized citizens of the United States and other major European powers.[31] Such disputes and anti-Syrian measures continued with varying degrees of enforcement until the United States occupied Haiti militarily in 1915. During this period, the Ottoman Empire also became involved in the diplomatic exchanges since some of the Syrians were still Ottoman citizens. In 1912 the Ottoman Ministry for Foreign Affairs attempted to coordinate its efforts with those of the United States. When the United States declined, the Ottomans were able to work out an arrangement with the French, who were reported by the American ambassador to be "protecting Turkish interests."[32]

In all of this correspondence, even that from the Ottoman Ministry for Foreign Affairs, there does not appear to be any direct identification of the Syrians in terms of their religion. The Ottomans do not seem to have expressed special concern for the Muslims, even though in terms of emigration laws, the Ottomans did distinguish between Muslim and Christian emigrants.[33] This gives further support to the conclusion that Muslim immigrants from Syria in the Caribbean region identified themselves and were identified by others as Syrians rather than as members of a Muslim community.

Indians and Indonesians: Muslims in Suriname

The distinctive case of Muslims in Suriname provides an important confirmation of the tendency of Muslims to identify with their ethnic immigrant group rather than to create Muslim organizations and identities that go beyond those ethnic groups. As was the case in Trinidad, most Muslims came to Suriname in the late nineteenth century as a part of the importation of indentured workers to European colonies. Most of this labor came from British India; the Dutch were allowed to open an agency in India in 1873 to recruit labor for their Latin American colonies.[34] As a result of this migration, "East Indians" became one of the two largest elements in the population, along with Suriname Creole, with each comprising about 35 percent of the population, according to a 1964 census.[35] However, because the colonial power in Suriname was the Netherlands, there was an additional major source for indentured labor in Dutch areas: the Dutch-ruled islands of Southeast Asia. A significant number of indentured workers were brought from Java into what was then Dutch Guiana, and they became a distinct element in the population. In the 1964 census, Indonesians were about 15 percent of the population.

The Indonesians were virtually all Muslims, but Muslims were a minority among the Indians. Indian Muslims are about 5 percent of the total population, so Muslims represent about 20 percent of the population of Suriname, with about three-quarters of the Muslims being of Javanese origin. Although all Muslims identified themselves as Muslims, they tended to maintain community institutions identified with their region of origin. Distinctive Javanese customs were maintained in Suriname. The Javanese, for example, requested their own mosque in Marienburg in 1927 since "the existing one was British Indian," and the first "Javanese mosque" was opened in 1932, with several more to be opened in the following years.[36]

When political parties began to be established at the end of World War II as a prelude to the politics of gaining independence, there was a brief attempt to establish a Muslim political party, the Moeslim Partij, "formed in 1946 . . . to unite East Indian and Indonesian Moslems."[37] However, the political scene rapidly came to be defined by parties based on more ethnic constituencies. In preparation for the first major elections in 1949, various Creole groups came together in the largest single party in the country, the Nationale Partij Suriname (NPS), and predominantly Indian groups merged to form the Verenigde Hindostaanse Partij (United East Indian Party—VHP). While the NPS supported the formation of an Indonesian party, an independent Indonesian party was organized as the Kaum Tani Persuatan Indonesia (Indonesian Peasant Party—KTPI). The first elections to the twenty-one-seat assembly resulted in an NPS majority of thirteen seats, with the Indian VHP winning six seats, and the Indonesian KTPI winning two.[38]

The election of 1949 showed the basic pattern for Suriname politics:

> Although the smaller ethnic parties played important roles in some governments, the dominant parties are still [1994], as they were in the late 1940s, the NPS, VHP, and KTPI. These three, together with the smaller parties, have generally directed their election appeals and clientage services exclusively to members of their ethnic constituencies. In return, as far as can be inferred from the correlation of voting and census figures . . . political support for these parties followed the country's ethnic proportions.[39]

These ethnic parties interacted in coalitions that significantly reduced the possibility of open conflict among the ethnic groups. A major aspect of this was a "Creole-Hindustani coalition," created by a longstanding political alliance between the NPS and the VHP operating under the theme of *verbroedering* (brotherhood).[40] The consociational system of *verbroedering* politics "can be seen as an ideological means of keeping Surinam's ethnic groups separate"[41] while creating structures for intergroup coalitions and cooperation.

Party politics in Suriname were, and are, highly competitive, and building coalitions and alliances is a key to political success. In this context, one remarkable feature is the almost total absence of attempts by the Indonesian parties to expand their political base by appealing to "fellow Muslims" among the Indians. This appears to have been true even in a time like the period before and following the 1977 elections, when the Indonesian party, KTPI, was becoming divided by factions that sought support from a variety of different groups.

Muslims from both the Indian and Indonesian communities clearly identified themselves as Muslims. However, this Islamic identification did not provide the basis for communal organization or political action. Muslims in Suriname were not a distinguishable minority as a group. They were, instead, part of other major societal groups, defined more by the culture and traditions of the lands from which they originally emigrated than by the religious faith that they professed.

A Muslim Coup in the Caribbean

One of the rare times when a group of Caribbean Muslims engaged in a highly visible political action explicitly as Muslims was a failed coup attempt to take control of the government of Trinidad during the summer of 1990. At that time, an organization called the Jamaat al Muslimeen took control of the Parliament building and the state television station. For five days they held members of parliament, including the prime minister, A. N. R. Robinson, and most of the cabinet, hostage. The announced goals of the movement were to bring an end to the "atrocities" of the government, which included "frittering away" hard-earned taxes at a time when people were "hungry and destitute on a daily basis."[42] The coup was perceived by the Muslimeen "as a response to a 'divine calling' aimed to eliminate social ills and religious inequalities."[43] The coup failed, and the Jamaat evacuated the buildings after five days. The leaders were soon put on trial, convicted, and sentenced to prison terms.

The Jamaat experience in Trinidad reflects the importance of the ethnic realities of Muslim community life in the Caribbean and the disinclination for Muslims in the region to identify themselves with other Muslims outside of their own ethnic communities. The Jamaat did not develop within the established Muslim groups of East Indians or Syrians. Instead, it was basically a movement of Afro-Trinidadians from urban areas, especially the capital, Port of Spain, many of whom were unemployed or economically disadvantaged. The group was established by a charismatic former member of the police force, Yasin Abu Bakr, in the early 1970s.

It was Abu Bakr who defined the teachings and set the tone for the movement. He was described as "a comsummate [sic] believer in the fundamentalist interpretation of the Koran" and he believed that Trinidadian society "guarantees the oppression of the weak by the strong."[44] Abu Bakr believed that "his mission was to chart a new national direction inspired by the will of Allah. Guided by such strongly held religious convictions, and believing that the recession-devastated and deprived masses would put him 'at the helm of a new popular movement,' [Abu] Bakr decided to 'confront the state authorities, violently and frontally.'"[45]

In many ways, Abu Bakr and the Jamaat sound similar to many movements in other parts of the Muslim world in the 1970s and 1980s. At the time of the coup in 1990, some news reports alleged that the Jamaat was funded by Muammar Qaddafi and Libya.[46] However, Abu Bakr "described as 'malicious propaganda' statements that the Muslimeen were financed by Libya's Muammar Qaddafi. 'We have been to Libya. Colonel Qaddafi is our friend but we have also been to other Arab countries. We've also been to other countries. I myself have been to America, to England, to France, to Germany, to Rome, I've been all over the world; I am a missionary.'"[47] In the course of the negotiations to free the parliamentary hostages, there were reports that the Muslimeen were asking to be flown to Libya, but Abu Bakr said, "I am a Trinidadian and I want to stay here."[48] This, in fact, emphasized that the success or failure of the movement depended upon developments in Trinidad, not the broader Muslim world.

As a Trinidadian movement, the Jamaat was distinctively Afro-Trinidadian. There is no indication that at any time during the development of the movement, or during the coup, any of the East Indian or Syrian Muslims made any expression of support. The Jamaat had occupied some land in Port of Spain that had been vacated by the Islamic Missionaries Guild of the Caribbean and South America in the 1970s. There was a long series of legal battles, and the buildings belonging to the group were raided by police in 1988. In 1990 the Trinidad government decided to have the army occupy the compound of the Jamaat. It appears to have been a court dismissal of the appeal of the decision made by the Jamaat that precipitated the coup.[49] However, even in the context where it appeared that the government was prepared to demolish an operating mosque, there was no protest from Muslims outside of the Jamaat.

The Jamaat accused East Indian and "Syrian" Muslims of wanting to destroy the Muslimeen organization, saying that their program was one of isolation from the other Muslims rather than of trying to recruit them.[50] This reflected a long-standing tension between activist and possibly revolutionary groups among the Afro-Trinidadians and East Indians in general. In the partisan politics leading up to independence in the late 1950s, there were tensions between the emerging People's National Movement (PNM; the nationalist Afro-Creole party led by Eric Williams) and the party presenting the views of the East Indians, the Democratic Labour Party (DLP). The East Indians resisted moving toward political independence because of the "fear that once the British withdrew from Trinidad's internal politics nothing could prevent the PNM from establishing a racial dictatorship. Williams did not assuage these fears."[51]

A more dramatic expression of the tensions between the communities came with the development of a "black power" movement in Trinidad in 1970. The black power movement in the United States at that time owed much to the writings and activities of Caribbean-born radicals like Frantz Fanon. Stokeley Carmichael, himself born in

Trinidad, and others in the United States worked to build ties with radicals in the Caribbean. High unemployment among young people and an articulate group of radical intellectuals among the faculty and students in the university provided the foundations for the emergence of the black power movement in Trinidad in 1970. Although the origins of the movement came from blacks, "almost all the leaders of the movement were . . . committed to the idea of Afro-Indian unity, and to an interpretation of black power which could include the Indian masses."[52] However, the "black power leaders underestimated the importance of . . . [the historic tensions between Africans and East Indians], and failed to do the necessary groundwork among the Indian community."[53]

In this context, an event that was meant to be a symbol of solidarity came to be a sign of the communal divisions. In March 1970 the black power leaders organized a march to the great sugar fields where labor was largely East Indian. This was to be "a demonstration of solidarity, by the largely urban-dwelling African youth of the movement, with the 'suffering and exploited' Indian sugar workers."[54] However, Indian labor union leaders saw this as a direct threat to their organizations and as an attempt by the African labor unions to expand at their expense. Although the march took place with limited opposition, demonstrations in the following weeks did involve some violence. The government felt threatened by the developing situation and the possibility of growing support for the black power movement; in April 1970, it declared a state of emergency. Leaders of the black power movement were arrested. Soldiers from the defense force joined with the opposition in a quasi-coup attempt that appeared to pose a major threat, but it was quickly suppressed.

The Jamaat coup fits into this tradition of black power in Trinidad. It was smaller and less visible internationally, but the source of its support was similar. It was also similar in terms of the way in which it fit into the historic patterns of relations between blacks and East Indians in Trinidad. Like the events in 1970, the Jamaat coup was "an event that exposed, among other things, the ethnic and class cleavages of the society."[55] It also showed explicitly that there was no sense of Muslim unity that crossed communal boundaries in that time of crisis.

The ethnic communities in Trinidad are both inclusive and exclusive in the identities that they affirm. In these identities, religion may help to support a mode of expression of identity within a community, but it does not appear to provide a means for creating a group identity that crosses those communal frontiers. In this way, the Jamaat al-Muslimeen was explicitly Muslim, but in terms of power relationships in Trinidadian society, it remained a movement within the Afro-Trinidadian community and gained no significant response among East Indian and "Syrian" Muslims. By 1996, after a court-approved amnesty, the Jamaat had become a distinctive grouping in the society with some significance. When Baseo Panday became the first East Indian to hold the position of Prime Minister, he is reported to have met with Jamaat leaders as part of his efforts to create a sense of "national unity." The Jamaat, however, was viewed as having no connection with the East Indian political community. Instead, it was reported that "the group remains active, operating security and other companies, and is widely feared by both Indians and blacks."[56]

A reflection of the religiously inclusive nature of the communal identities may be seen in the politics of group pride following the coming to power of the first East Indian Prime

Minister. By that time, a Hindu "fundamentalist" group, the Sunatan Dharmanan Maha Sabah, had become highly visible. The leader of this group, Sat Maharaj, had gained notoriety by opposing a number of official Christian symbols, an apparent example of Hindu exclusivism. Maharaj annoyed people by boasting about the Indians who held high posts following the coming to power of Panday. However, the inclusiveness of ethnic identity is shown by the fact that this Hindu "fundamentalist" included in his boasting the fact that an Indian who was a Christian, Winston Dookeran, became the Governor of the Central Bank and another Indian with the clearly Muslim name of Noor K. Mohammed was Commissioner of Police.[57] In this situation, the Muslims of Trinidad are practicing Muslims, but that does not mean that they are a part of a "Muslim minority" or a "Muslim diaspora." Their diasporic identity is based on their geographic region of origin, not their religious faith.

Conclusion

Muslims live in many different countries in the Caribbean region. There are active communities and mosques, and in a few countries, such as Trinidad and Suriname, Muslims represent a significant proportion of the total population. However, for most of these Muslims, their place in society and sociopolitical identities are not determined primarily by their religious commitment. Instead, it is their ethnic identity that defines how they make the transition from sojourner to citizen. Most Caribbean Muslims are part of diasporas, but these diasporas are identified by the country of origin rather than religion. The majority of Muslims in the region are of East Indian origin, and that fact, rather than their Islamic faith, shapes which political parties they support and what their place in society is. In this way, it is possible to say that while there are Muslims in the Caribbean, there are no "Muslim minorities" or "Muslim diasporas."

Notes

1. See the presentation by Tamara Sonn in the conference on "Muslim Diasporas in the West" sponsored by Center for Muslim-Christian Understanding of Georgetown University, 17 April 1998.

2. See Paul Gilroy, *The Black Atlantic, Modernity and Double Consciousness* (Cambridge: Harvard University Press, 1993).

3. As quoted in Karen J. Winkler, "Historians Explore Questions of How People and Cultures Disperse Across the Globe," *The Chronicle of Higher Education* (22 January 1999): A12.

4. See, for example, the discussion on "Cultural Diasporas: the Caribbean case," chapter 6 in Robin Cohen, *Global Diasporas: An Introduction* (Seattle: University of Washington Press, 1997), 150.

5. See, for example, David Westerlund and Eva Evers Rosander, eds. *African Islam and Islam in Malaysian Islam* (Vancouver: University of British Columbia Press, 1984); David Westerlund and Eva Evers Rosander, eds. *African Islam and Islam in Africa: Encounters Between Sufis and Islamists* (Athens, Ohio: Ohio University Press, 1997); and Judith Nagata, *The Reflowering of Malaysian Islam* (Vancouver: University of British Columbia Press, 1984).

6. The percentages are 20 percent of the population in Suriname, 9 percent in Guyana, and 6 percent in Trinidad and Tobago. *1998 Book of the Year* (Chicago: Encyclopedia Britannica, 1998), 615, 714, 725.

7. Larry Luxner, "Muslims in the Caribbean," *Aramco World* 38, no. 6 (November–December 1987): 3.

8. Luxner, "Muslims in the Caribbean," 11.

9. For the broader global historical dynamics of indentured labor in the nineteenth century see David Northrup, *Indentured Labor in the Age of Imperialism, 1834–1922* (Cambridge: Cambridge University Press, 1995).

10. A discussion of the early Gladstone experiment can be found in Madhavi Kale, "Projecting Identities: Empire and Indentured Labor Migration from India to Trinidad and British Guiana," in *Nation and Migration, The Politics of Space in the South Asian Diaspora*, ed. Peter van der Veer (Philadelphia: University of Pennsylvania Press, 1995), 74–80.

11. Kale, "Projecting Identities," 73.

12. See, for example, the discussion and maps in Gerard Chaliand and Jean Pierre Rageau, *The Penguin Atlas of Diasporas* (New York: Penguin Books, 1995), 152.

13. Kale, "Projecting Identities," 84.

14. David Nicholls, "Lebanese of the Antilles: Haiti, Dominican Republic, Jamaica, and Trinidad," in *The Lebanese in the World: A Century of Emigration*, ed. Albert Hourani and Nadim Shehadi (London: I. B.Tauris, 1992), 340.

15. Bridget Brereton, "Social Organisation and Class, Racial and Cultural Conflict in 19th Century Trinidad," in *Trinidad Ethnicity*, ed. Kevin Yelvington (Nashville: University of Tennessee Press, 1993), 39.

16. Joao Jose Reis, "Brazil," *The Oxford Encyclopedia of the Modern Islamic World*, ed. John L. Esposito (New York: Oxford University Press, 1995), I: 231–32.

17. Luxner, "Muslims in the Caribbean," 6.

18. Quoted in Kale, "Projecting Identities," 85.

19. Frank J. Korom, "Memory, Innovation, and Emergent Ethnicity: The Creolization of an Indo-Trinidadian Performance," *Diaspora* 3, no. 2 (Fall 1994): 135–155.

20. Korom, "Memory," 141.

21. Korom, "Memory," 141–42.

22. Korom, "Memory," 142–43.

23. Korom (in "Memory," 149) says that "ethnicity must be multivalent," but the necessity of multivalence in not confined to ethnic identities. In the case of Muslims in Trinidad, both religious and ethnic identity is multivalent.

24. Michael Anthony, *Historical Dictionary of Trinidad and Tobago* (Lanham, Md.: Scarecrow Press, 1997), 344.

25. Kemal H. Karpat, "The Ottoman Emigration to America, 1860-1914," *International Journal of Middle East Studies* 17, no. 2 (May 1985): 183.

26. Henry Christian Bierwirth, "The Initial Establishment of the Lebanese Community in Cote d'Ivoire, ca. 1925–45," *International Journal of African Historical Studies* 30, no. 2 (1997): 330.

27. Karpat, "Ottoman Emigration," 182.

28. Nicholls, "Lebanese of the Antilles," 351.

29. Nicholls, "Lebanese of the Antilles," 349.

30. Bierwirth, "Initial Establishment," 340.

31. Correspondence relating to these discussions in 1905 can be found in United States Department of State, *Papers relating to the Foreign Relations of the United States [1905]* (Washington: Government Printing Office, 1906). This source, for different years, will be cited as FRUS with the appropriate year noted. The law was quoted in J. N. Leger [Haiti Minister of Foreign Affairs] to F. B. Loomis, Acting Secretary of State [U.S.], 9 June 1905, 539; The Proclamation was described in W. F. Powell, American Legation, Port au Prince, to Secretary of State, 21 March 1905, 534.

32. For correspondence on this, see FRUS 1912, 53538.

33. See, for example, the discussion in Karpat, "Ottoman Emigration," 182–83.

34. K. O. Laurence, *A Question of Labour: Indentured Immigration into Trinidad and British Guiana 1875–1917* (New York: St. Martin's Press, 1994), 43.

35. Edward M. Dew, *The Trouble in Suriname, 1975–1993* (Westport, Conn.: Praeger, 1994), 4.

36. Rosemarijn Hoefte, *In Place of Slavery: A Social History of British Indian and Javanese Laborers in Suriname* (Gainesville: University Press of Florida, 1998), 169.

37. F. S. J. Ledgister, *Class Alliances and the Liberal Authoritarian State: The Roots of Post-colonial Democracy in Jamaica, Trinidad and Tobago, and Surinam* (Trenton: Africa World Press, 1998), 142.

38. Ledgister, *Class Alliances*, 142–44 provides a clear description of the emergence of these parties and the political system based on their interactions.

39. Dew, *The Trouble*, 2.

40. Dew, *The Trouble*, 2–3.

41. Ledgister, *Class Alliances*, 147.

42. Caribbean News Agency (CANA) broadcast, 28 July 1990. Foreign Broadcast Information Service, *Daily Report, Latin America*, FBIS-LAT-90-146 (30 July 1990): 7. In subsequent citations, the Daily Reports will be cited as FBIS-LAT with appropriate dates and issue numbers.

43. Kathleen M. Collihan and Constantine P. Danopoulos, "Coup d'Etat Attempt in Trinidad: Its Causes and Failure," *Armed Forces and Society* 19, no. 3 (Spring 1993): 442.

44. Herb Addo, "The Crisis of Shock: the 1990 Muslimeen Insurrection in Trinidad and Tobago," *The Caribbean Quarterly* 37, nos. 2 & 3 (June–September 1991): 5 and 8, as cited in Collihan and Danopoulos, 441.

45. Collihan and Danopoulos, 441–42, also citing Abbo, 8–11.

46. See, for example, CANA reporter Debra Ransome's noting these allegations in CANA broadcast, 28 July 1990. FBIS-LAT-90-146 (30 July 1990), 6, and the assertions in the CANA report on Deputy Prime Minister Winston Dookeran's response to the coup in another CANA broadcast on 28 July 1990. FBIS-LAT-90-146 (30 July 1990), 8.

47. CANA broadcast, 29 July 1990. FBIS-LAT-90-146 (30 July 1990), 15.

48. CANA report by Reudon Eversley, 29 July 1990. FBIS-LAT-90-146 (30 July 1990), 13.

49. Collihan and Danopoulos, 442–43.

50. Collihan and Danopoulis, 441.

51. Ledgister, *Class Alliances*, 111.

52. David G. Nicholls, "East Indians and Black Power in Trinidad," *Race* 12, no. 4 (1971): 453.

53. Nicholls, "East Indians," 446.

54. Nicholls, "East Indians," 449.

55. Kevin A. Yelvington, "Introduction: Trinidad Ethnicity," in *Trinidad Ethnicity*, ed. Kevin A. Yelvington (Knoxville: University of Tennessee Press, 1993), 14.

56. Larry Rohter, "For New Trinidad Chief, Race Question Looms Big," *New York Times*, 1 January 1996, 7.

57. Larry Rohter, "High-level Name-Calling Across the Racial Fence," *New York Times*, 20 August 1997, 4.

Bibliography

Abraham, Sameer Y. "A Survey of the Arab-American Community in Metropolitan Detroit." In *Arab World and Arab-Americans*, edited by Sameer Y. Abraham and Nabeel Abraham, 23–30. Detroit, Mich.: Wayne State University Center for Urban Studies, 1981.

———. "Detroit's Arab-American Community: A Survey of Diversity and Commonality. " In *Arabs in the New World: Studies on Arab-American Communities*, edited by Sameer Y. Abraham and Nabeel Abraham, 85–108. Detroit, Mich.: Wayne State University Center for Urban Studies, 1983.

Adam, Leila. "Muslim Community in New Zealand." *al-Nahda* 19, no. 1 (1999): 38–41.

Addo, Herb. "The Crisis of Shock: The 1990 Muslimeen Insurrection in Trinidad and Tobago." *The Caribbean Quarterly* 37, nos. 2 & 3 (June–September 1991): 1–12.

Ahlberg, Nora. *New Challenges—Old Strategies. Themes of Variation and Conflict among Pakistani Muslims in Norway*. Transactions of the Finnish Anthropological Society, no. 25, Helsinki: Gummerus-forlaget, 1990.

Ahmad, Mumtaz. "Islamic Fundamentalism in South Asia: The Jamaat-i-Islami and the Tablighi Jamaat." In *Fundamentalism Observed*, edited by Martin E. Marty and R. Scott Appleb, 457–530. Chicago: University of Chicago Press, 1991.

Aijan, M. M. "The Mohammedans in the United States." *Muslim World* 10, no. 1 (1920): 35.

Ajami, Joseph. *The Arabic Press in the United States Since 1892: A Socio-Historical Study*. Ph. D. dissertation. Athens: University of Ohio, 1987.

Altareb, Belkeis. "Development of a Scale to Measure Attitudes Toward Muslims." In *Islam in American: Images and Challenges*, edited by Phylis Lan Lin, 51–61. Indianapolis: University of Indianapolis Press, 1998.

Anthony, Michael. *Historical Dictionary of Trinidad and Tobago*. Lanham, Md.: Scarecrow Press, 1997.

Aswad, Barbara, ed. *Arabic Speaking Communities in American Cities*. Staten Island: Center for Migration Studies, 1974.

Austin, Allan. *African Muslims in Antebellum America: A Sourcebook*. New York: Garland Publishers, 1984.

———. *African Muslims in Antebellum America: Transatlantic Stories and Spiritual Struggles*. New York: Routledge, 1997.

Baer, Hans A. and Merrill Singer. *African-American Religion in the Twentieth Century*. Knoxville, Tenn.: University of Tennessee Press, 1992.

Baldock, John. *With Other Faiths: A Guide to Living with Other Religions*. World Conference on Religion and Peace (WCRP), Religion in Australia Series, no. 4. Melbourne, 1995.

Barou, Jacques. "Familles, enfants et scolarité chez les Africains immigrés en France." *Migrants-formation* 91 (December 1992): 12–23.

Barth, Fredrik. *Ethnic Groups and Boundaries. The Social Organization of Culture Difference.* Oslo: Universitetsforlaget, 1982.

Barthélemy, C. et al. *Les dossiers du Secrétariat pour les relations avec l'islam* I (March 1996): 26–30.

Bastinier, Albert. "Migrations, choc de cultures et religion: à propos des communications de C. Lacoste-Dujardin et W. Clark Roof et C. Manning." *Social Compass* 41, no. 1 (1994): 185–92.

Baureiss, Gunder. "Toward a Theory of Ethnic Organizations." *Canadian Ethnic Studies* 16 (1982): 21–42.

Bava, Sophie. "Reconversions et nouveaux mondes commerciaux des mourides à Marseille." *Hommes & Migrations* 1224 (March–April 2000): 46–55.

Benhabib, Sayla. *Critique, Norm and Utopia.* New York: Columbia University Press, 1987.

Beyer, Peter. *Religion and Globalization.* London: Sage Publications, 1994.

Bierwirth, Henry Christian. "The Initial Establishment of the Lebanese Community in Cote d'Ivoire, ca. 1925–45. "*International Journal of African Historical Studies* 30, no. 2 (1997): 330.

Bitzer, Lloyd. "The Rhetorical Situation." In *Readings in Rhetorical Criticism,* edited by Carl R. Burghardt, 51–61. State College, Pennsylvania: Strata Publishing, Inc, 1995.

Blion, Reynald and Véronique Verriere. "Epargne des migrants et outils financiers adaptés: Pratiques des immigrés maliens et sénégalais résidant en France." *Migrations Etudes* 82 (September–October 1998): 1–16.

Bone, Pamela. "A New School of Social Division." *The Age* (13 December 1996): 15.

Bontemps, Arna and Jack Conroy. *They Seek A City.* Garden City, N.Y.: Doubleday, Doran and Company, Inc., 1945.

Books on Islam and the Muslim World: Catalog 1998-B. Falls Church: Halalco Books, August 1998.

Boudimbou, Guy. *Habitat et mode de vie des Africains en France.* Paris: L'Harmattan, 1992.

Bouma, Gary D. *Mosques and Muslim Settlement in Australia.* BIPR: Commonwealth of Australia, 1995.

Braibanti, Ralph. "Islam and the West: Common Cause or Clash?" *Occasional Paper Series,* The Center for Muslim-Christian Understanding: History and International Affairs, Edmund J. Walsh School of Foreign Service, Georgetown University, 1999.

Brereton, Bridget. "Social Organisation and Class, Racial and Cultural Conflict in 19th Century Trinidad." In *Trinidad Ethnicity,* edited by Kevin Yelvington, 33–55. Nashville: University of Tennessee Press, 1993.

Breton, Raymond. "Institutional Completeness of Ethnic Communities and Personal Relations of Immigrants." *American Journal of Sociology* 70 (1964): 193–205.

Bringham, John. *The Constitution of Interests: Beyond the Politics of Rights.* New York: New York University Press, 1996.

Brown, Wendy. *States of Injury: Power and Freedom in Late Modernity.* Princeton: Princeton University Press, 1995.

Brubaker, Rogers. *Citizenship and Nationhood in France and Germany.* Cambridge: Harvard University Press, 1992.

Butler, Keith. "The Muslims are no Longer an Unknown Quantity." *Corrections Magazine* (June 1978): 55–63.

Cainkar, Louise. "Immigrant Palestinian Women Evaluate Their Lives." In *Family and Gender Among American Muslims: Issues Facing Middle Eastern Immigrants and Their Descendants,* edited by Barbara C. Aswad and Barbara Bilgé, 41–58. Philadelphia: Temple University Press, 1996.

Carley, Patricia M. "Turkey and Central Asia: Reality Comes Calling." In *Regional Power Rivalries in the New Eurasia: Russia, Turkey, and Iran,* edited by Alvin Z. Rubinstein and M. Smolansky, 177–79. Armonk, N.Y.: M.E. Sharpe, 1995.

Census 96, 1996 New Zealand Census of Population and Dwellings, National Summary and Regional Summary. Wellington: Statistics New Zealand, 1996.

Cesari, Jocelyne. "De l'islam en France à l'islam de France." In *Immigration et Intégration: L'état des savoirs*, edited by Philippe Dewitte, 222–31. Paris: Editions La Découverte, 1999.

Chaliand, Gerard and Jean Pierre Rageau. *The Penguin Atlas of Diasporas*. New York: Penguin Books, 1995.

Clifford, James. *Routes, Travel, and Translation in the Late Twentieth Century*. Cambridge: Harvard University Press, 1997.

Cohen, Abner. "Introduction: The Lesson of Ethnicity." In *Urban Ethnicity*, edited by Abner Cohen, ix–xxiv. A.S.A. monograph 12 (1974).

Cohen, Robin. *Global Diasporas: An Introduction*. Seattle: University of Washington Press, 1997.

Collihan, Kathleen M. and Constantine P. Danopoulos, "Coup d'Etat Attempt in Trinidad: Its Causes and Failure. "*Armed Forces and Society* 19, no. 3 (1993): 442.

Connerton, Paul. *How Societies Remember.* Themes in the Social Sciences. Cambridge: Cambridge University Press, 1989.

Coulon, Christian. *Le marabout et le prince: Islam et pouvoir au Sénégal.* Paris: Pedone, 1981.

Cover, Robert. "The Supreme Court 1982 Term, Forward: Nomos and Narrative." *Harvard Law Review* 97 (November 1983–October 1984): 4–68.

DaCosta, Y. "The Spatial Origins of the Early Cape Muslims, and the Diffusion of Islam to the Cape Colony." *Journal for Islamic Studies* 10 (1990): 45–67.

Dannin, Robert. "The 'Holy War' on Crack." *The City Sun*, 23 August 1988.

———. "Island in a Sea of Ignorance: Dimensions of the Prison Mosque." In *Making Muslim Space in North America and Europe*, edited by Barbara Metcalf, 131–46. Berkeley: University of California Press, 1996.

David, Gary. *Middle Eastern Community of Metropolitan Detroit Directory of Organizations*. Detroit, Mich.: United Way Community Services, 1998.

———. *The Mosaic of Middle Eastern Communities in Metropolitan Detroit*. Detroit, Mich.: United Way Community Services, 1999.

Davids, Achmat. *The History of the Tana Baru*. Cape Town: Committee for the Preservation of the Tana Baru, 1985.

———. *The Mosques of the Bo-Kaap*. Athlone: South African Institute of Arabic and Islamic Research, 1980.

Davison, Roderic H. "Turkish Attitudes Concerning Christian-Muslim Equality in the Nineteenth Century." In *The Modern Middle East: A Reader*, edited by Albert Hourani, 61–82. Berkeley: University of California Berkeley and Los Angeles, 1993.

Deen, Hanifa, *Caravanserai—Journey Among Australian Muslims*. St. Leonards. New South Wales, Australia: Allen & Unwin, 1995.

Devine, John. *Maximum Security.* Chicago: University of Chicago Press, 1996.

Dew, Edward M. *The Trouble in Suriname, 1975–1993.* Westport, Conn.: Praeger, 1994.

Dewitte, Philippe. *Les Mouvements nègres en France 1919–1939.* Paris: L'Harmattan, 1985.

———. Interview of Lydie Dooh-Bunya, "La condition des femmes noires en France." *Hommes & Migrations* 1131 (1990): 43–48.

———. "Des tirailleurs aux sans-papiers: la République oublieuse. " *Hommes & Migrations* 1221 (1999): 6–11.

Diop, Moustapha. "Esquisse historique sur l'islam des Ouest-Africains en Ile-de-France." *Sociétés africaines et diaspora* 4 (1996): 135–42.

———. "Immigration et religion: les musulmans négro-africains en France." *Migrations Société* 1 (1989): 45–57.

———. "Le Mouvement islamique africain en Ile-de-France."*Migrations Société* 8, no. 44 (March–April 1996): 67–76.

———. "Negotiating Religious Difference: The Opinions and Attitudes of Islamic Associations in France." In *The Politics of Multiculturalism in the New Europe: Racism, Identity and*

Community, edited by Modood, Tariq, and Pnina Werbner, 111–125. London: Zed Books Ltd., 1999.

———. "Structuration d'un réseau: la Jamaat Tabligh (Société pour la Propagation de la Foi.)." *Revue européenne des Migrations Internationales* 10, no.1 (1994): 145–55.

Diouf, Sylviane. "Africans in France: What Future?" *West Africa* (4–10 March 1991): 295–96.

———. "Islam, mendicité et migration au Sénégal." *Hommes & Migrations* 1186 (April 1995): 37–40.

———. "Senegal Upgrades Its Koranic Schools." *UNICEF Features*, April 1995.

———. "Senegalese in New York: A Model Minority?" *Black Renaissance* 1, no. 2 (1997): 92–115.

———. *Servants of Allah: African Muslims Enslaved in the Americas*. New York: New York University Press, 1998.

Duval, Soraya. "New Veils and New Voices: Islamist Women's Groups in Egypt." In *Women and Islamization. Contemporary Dimensions of Discourse on Gender Relations*, edited by Karin Ask and Marit Tjomsland, 45–72. Oxford: Berg, 1998.

Echenberg, Myron. *Colonial Conscripts: The Tirailleurs Sénégalais in French West Africa, 1857–1960.* Portsmouth, UK: Heineman, 1991.

Eickelman, Dale E. and James Piscatori. *Muslim Politics.* Princeton: Princeton University Press, 1996.

Esack, Farid. "Between Mandela and Man Dalla: Rethinking Kaffirs and Kafirs," unpublished proceedings of Islam and Civil Society in South Africa: Prospects for Tolerance and Conflict Resolution, University of South Africa, 5–7 August 1994.

———. *Qur'an, Liberation, and Pluralism*. Oxford: Oneworld, 1997.

Findley, Paul. "The Muslim Bloc Vote." *Washington Report on Middle East Affairs* 20, no.1 (January–February 2001): 25.

Fischer, Michael M.J. "Ethnicity and the Post-Modern Art of Memory." In *Writing Culture: The Poetics of Ethnography*, edited by J. Clifford and G.E. Marcus, 194–233. Berkeley: University of California Press, 1986.

Fitzgerald, Laurence P. "Christians and Muslims in Australia." *Islamochristiana* 10 (Rome, 1984): 159–176.

Fukuyama, Francis. "The End of History?" *The National Interest* 16 (Summer 1989): 3–19.

Gans, Herbert J. "Symbolic Ethnicity: The Future of Ethnic Groups and Cultures in America." *Ethnic and Racial Studies* 2 (1979): 1–20.

Gates, Henry Louis, Jr. and Cornel West. *The Future of the Race*. New York: Vintage Books, 1996.

Geertz, Clifford. *The Interpretation of Cultures*. New York: Basic, 1973.

Gerholm, Thomas and Yngve Georg Lithman. *The New Islamic Presence in Western Europe*. London: Mansell Publishing Ltd., 1988.

Gillespie, Dizzie and Al Fraser. *To BE, or not...to BOP.* New York: DaCapa Press, Inc., 1979.

Gillette, Isabelle. *L'excision et sa présence en France*. Paris: GAMS 1992.

———. *La polygamie en France et le rôle des femmes.* Paris: GAMS, 1993.

Gilroy, Paul. *The Black Atlantic, Modernity and Double Consciousness*. Cambridge: Harvard University Press, 1993.

———. *Small Acts: Thoughts on the Politics of Black Cultures.* London: Serpent's Tail, 1993.

Glazer, Nathan. "Emergence of an American Ethnic Pattern." In *From Different Shores: Perspectives on Race and Ethnicity in America*, edited by Ronald Takaki, 13–25. New York: Oxford University Press.

Göle, Nilüfer. "Authoritarian Secularism and Islamist Politics: The Case of Turkey." In *Civil Society in the Middle East*, vol II, edited by Augustus Richard Norton, 17–44. New York: E.J. Brill, 1996.

Haddad, Yvonne Yazbeck. "The Challenge of Muslim Minoritiness: The American Experience." In *The Integration of Islam and Hinduism in Western Europe*, edited by W.A.R. Shahid and P.S. van Koningsveld, 134–51. Kampen: KOK Pharos, 1991.

———, ed. *The Muslims of America*. New York: Oxford University Press, 1993.

———. "Towards the Caving of Islamic Space in the West." *ISIM Newsletter.* October, 1998. <http://www.isim.nl/newsletter/1/regional/01AC08.html >.

Haddad, Yvonne Yazbeck and Adair T. Lummis. *Islamic Values in the United States: A Comparative Study.* New York Oxford University Press, 1987.

Haider, Gulzar. "Muslim Space and the Practice of Architecture: A Personal Odyssey." In *Making Muslim Space in North America and Europe,* edited by Barbara Metcalf, 31–45. Berkeley: University of California Press, 1996.

Haines, Byron L. "Perspectives of the American Churches on Islam and the Muslim Community in North America." In *The Muslims of America,* edited by Yvonne Yazbeck Haddad, 40–48. New York: Oxford University Press, 1991.

Haley, Alex. *The Autobiography of Malcolm X.* New York: Ballantine Books, 1964.

Haut Conseil à l'intégration. *L'intégration à la française.* Paris: Robert Laffont, 1993.

Helm, Jutta A. "No Laughing Matter: Joking about Turks." *German Politics and Society* 31 (1994): 47–62.

Hess, Stephen. "What Gets Covered and Where?" *International News and Foreign Correspondents.* Washington, D.C.: Brookings Institution Press, 1996, 28–46.

Hoefte, Rosemarijn. *In Place of Slavery: A Social History of British Indian and Javanese Laborers in Suriname.* Gainesville: University Press of Florida, 1998.

Holm, Svein. *Innvandrere og bokonsentrasjon i Oslo.* (*Immigrants and housing concentration in Oslo.*) Foreløpig rapport fra prosjekt for Kommunal-og arbeidsdepartement, Statistisk sentralbyrå. Oslo. April, 1995.

Houghton, Walter R., ed. *Neely's History of the Parliament of the World's Religions Compiled from Original Manuscripts and Stenographic Reports.* Chicago: F.T. Neely, 1893.

Humphage, Louise. "Refuge and Turmoil, Somali Refugee Adolescents in Christchurch Schools." M.A. Thesis, University of Canterbury, 1998.

Huntington, Samuel. "Clash of Civilizations." *Foreign Affairs* 72, no. 3 (1993): 22–49.

Islam in North America. Muslim Community Center: Accomplishments and Aspirations. MCC 25th Anniversary Commemoration. Chicago: Muslim Community Center, 1995.

Jelen, Christian. "Jeunes Africains: la dérive des enfants perdus." *Le Point* 1125 (9 April 1994): 44–47.

———. "La polygamie en France." *Le Point* 1098 (2 October 1993): 42–51.

Jeppie, Shamil. "Commemorations and Identities: The 1994 Tercentenary of Islam in South Africa." In *Islam and the Question of Minorities,* edited by Tamara Sonn, 73–92. Atlanta: Scholars Press, 1996.

Jones, Mary Lucille. "The Years of Decline, Australian Muslims 1900–40." In *An Australian Pilgrimage: Muslims in Australia from the Seventeenth Century to the Present,* edited by Mary Lucille Jones, 63–86. Melbourne: Victoria Press, 1993.

Kale, Madhavi. "Projecting Identities: Empire and Indentured Labor Migration from India to Trinidad and British Guiana." In *Nation and Migration, The Politics of Space in the South Asian Diaspora,* edited by Peter van der Veer, 73–92. Philadelphia: University of Pennsylvania Press, 1995.

Kaplan, Robert D. *The Arabists.* New York: The Free Press, 1993.

Karaksaglu, Yasemin. "Turkish Cultural Orientations in Germany and the Role of Islam," in *Turkish Culture in German Society Today,* edited by David Horrocks and Eva Kolinsky, 157–80. Providence, R.I.: Berghahn Books, 1996.

Karpat, Kemal H. "The Ottoman Emigration to America, 1860–1914." *International Journal of Middle East Studies* 17, no. 2 (1985): 175–209.

Kayal, Philip M. "Religion and Assimilation: Catholic 'Syrians' in America." *International Migration Review* 4 (1973): 409–25.

King, Michael, ed. *God's Law Versus State Law: The Construction of an Islamic Identity in Western Europe.* London: Grey Seal, 1995.

Kolan, Tufan. "International Labor Migration and Turkish Economic Development." In *Manpower Mobility Across Cultural Boundaries: Social, Economic, and Legal Aspects: The Case of Turkey and West Germany*, edited by R.E. Krane, 138–160. Leiden: E.J. Brill, 1975.

Kolinsky, Eva. "Non-German Minorities in Contemporary German Society." In *Turkish Culture in German Society Today*, edited by David Horrocks and Eva Kolinsky, 71–112. Providence, R.I.: Berghahn Books, 1996.

Korom, Frank J. "Memory, Innovation, and Emergent Ethnicity: The Creolization of an Indo-Trinidadian Performance." *Diaspora* 3, no. 2 (1994): 135–55.

Kursat-Ahlers, Elcin. "The Turkish Minority in German Society." In *Turkish Culture in German Society Today*, edited by David Horrocks and Eva Kolinsky, 113–36. Providence, R.I.: Berghahn Books, 1996.

Kwong, Julia. "Ethnic Organizations and Community Transformation: The Chinese in Winnipeg." *Ethnic and Racial Studies* 7 (1984): 374–86.

Kymlicka, Will. *Multicultural Citizenship*. Oxford and New York: Oxford University Press, 1995.

Kymlicka, Will and Wayne Norman, eds. *Citizenship in Diverse Societies*. Oxford and New York: Oxford University Press, 2000.

Kymicka, Will and Ian Shapiro. *Ethnicity and Group Rights*. New York and London: New York University Press, 1997.

Lake, Anthony. "Confronting Backlash States." *Foreign Affairs* 73, no. 2 (March–April 1994): 45–55.

Laurence, K.O. *A Question of Labour: Indentured Immigration into Trinidad and British Guiana 1875–1917*. New York: St. Martin's Press, 1994.

Leckie, J.V. *They Sleep Standing Up: Gujaratis in New Zealand to 1945*, Ph.D. Thesis, Dunedin: University of Otago, 1981.

Ledgister, F.S.J. *Class Alliances and the Liberal Authoritarian State: The Roots of Post-colonial Democracy in Jamaica, Trinidad and Tobago, and Surinam*. Trenton, N.J.: Africa World Press, 1998.

Leirvik, Oddbjørn. *Islam i Norge. Oversikt med bibliografi*. (Islam in Norway. Overview with bibliography. Private publication, 1997).

Lewis, Bernard. *The Emergence of Modern Turkey*. London: Oxford University Press, 1961.

———. *Islam and the West*. New York: Oxford University Press, 1993.

———. "Legal and Historical Reflections on the Position of Muslim Populations under Non-Muslim Rule." In *Islamic Britain: Religion, Politics, and Identity among British Muslims*, edited by Bernard Lewis and Dominique Schnapper. London: I. B. Tauris, 1994.

———. "The Roots of Muslim Rage." *The Atlantic Monthly* 266 (September 1990): 47–60.

Lewis, Bernard and Dominique Schnapper, eds. *Muslims in Europe: Social Change in Western Europe*. London: Pinter Publishers, 1994.

Lincoln, C. Eric. *The Black Muslims in America*. Boston: Beacon Press, 1961.

Lobe, Jim. "Rights: U.S. Chides China, Arab States on Religious Freedom." *Inter Press Service*, 5 September 2000.

Luxner, Larry. "Muslims in the Caribbean." *Aramco World* 38, no. 6 (1987): 2–11.

Mandel, Ruth. "A Place of Their Own: Contesting Spaces and Defining Places in Berlin's Migrant Community." In *Making Muslim Space in North America and Europe*, edited by Barbara Metcalf, 147–166. University of California Press, 1996.

———. "Shifting Centres and Emergent Identities: Turkey and Germany in the Lives of Turkish *Gastarbeiter*." In *Muslim Travelers: Pilgrimage, Migration, and the Religious Imagination*, edited by Dale F. Eickelman and James Piscatori, 153–171. London: Routledge, 1990.

Masud, Muhammad Khalil. "The Obligation to Migrate: The Doctrine of *Hijra* in Islamic law." In *Muslim Travelers*, edited by Dale Eickelman and James Piscatori, 29–49. Berkeley: University of California Press, 1990.

McAfee, Noelle. *Habermas, Kristeva and Citizenship*. Ithaca, N.Y.: Cornell University Press, 2000.

McLuhan, Marshall. *Understanding Media: The Extension of Man.* Cambridge, Mass.: MIT Press, 1964, 1994.

Meer, Fatima. *Portrait of Indian South Africans.* Durban: Avon House, 1969.

Migrations Société. Special issue "L'Afrique noire en France," 8, no. 44 (1996).

Min, Pyong Gap. *Caught in the Middle: Korean Communities in New York and Los Angeles.* Berkeley: University of California Press, 1996.

Minkenberg, Michael. "Civil Religion and German Unification." *German Studies Review* 20, no. 1 (1997): 63–82.

Moen, Bjørg. *Eldre innvandrere i Gamle Oslo.* Norsk gerontologisk institutt, rapport n. 4. (Elderly immigrants in Oslo), 1993.

Monson, Terry D. "Differences in Industrial Learning Behavior of Turkish Workers at Home and Abroad: Causes and Consequences." In *Manpower Mobility Across Cultural Boundaries: Social, Economic, and Legal Aspects, The Case of Turkey and West Germany,* edited by R.E. Krane, 95–123. Leiden: E.J. Brill, 1975.

Moore, Kathleen. *Al-Mughtaribun, American Law and the Transformation of Muslim Life in the United States.* Albany: State University of New York Press, 1996.

———. *The Unfamiliar Abode: The Construction of a Diasporic Islamic Jurisprudence.* Ann Arbor: University of Michigan Press, forthcoming.

Mumtaz Ali, Mohammad. "Reconstruction of Islamic Thought and Civilization." *Islamic Quarterly* 43, no. 1 (1999): 21–36.

"Muslim Brotherhood Statement Condemns US Delegation's Visit," *Al-Wafd,* 20 March 2001, 1; BBC Summary of World Broadcasts, 22 March 2001, Pt. 4, "The Middle East."

"Muslim Military Chaplains Gather for 1st Annual Professional Conference." *The Muslim Journal* 26, no. 6 (17 November 2000): 1–9.

Naff, Alixa. *The Arab Americans.* New York: Chelsea House, 1983.

Nagata, Judith. *The Reflowering of Malaysian Islam.* Vancouver: University of British Columbia Press, 1984.

Naguib, Saphinaz-Amal. "The Era of Martyrs: Texts and Contexts of Religious Memory." In *Between Desert and City: The Coptic Orthodox Church Today,* edited by Nelly van Doorn-Harder and Kari Vogt, 121–141. Institute for Comparative Research in Human Culture, Series B: Skrifter XCVII, Oslo: Novus Forlag, 1997.

———. "Kulturbrytning, tradisjonsendring og innovasjon." In *Kulturstudier: Kulturforståing, kulturbrytning, kulturpolitikk,* edited by Bjarne Hodne, 95–109. Kulturstudier 1: Norges forskningsråd, 1998.

———. "Religion og etikk i islamsk lys," (Religion and ethics in Islam) in *Mange religioner-en etikk?* Edited by L. Østnor. Oslo: Universitetsforlaget, 1995, 78–96.

———. Forthcoming. *The Temporalities of Cultural Memory,* (to be published in: Proceedings of the conference on Moving Matters, held in Cairo, December 1998).

Natvig, Richard. "Les musulmans de Norvège," in *L'islam et les musulmans dans le monde,* edited by Mohammed Arkoun, Rémy Leveau, and Bassem El-Jisr, 421–47. T. 1, L'Europe occidentale. Beirout: Centre Culturel Harari, 1993.

Nicholls, David G. "East Indians and Black Power in Trinidad." *Race* 12, no. 4 (1971): 443–59.

———. "Lebanese of the Antilles: Haiti, Dominican Republic, Jamaica, and Trinidad." In *The Lebanese in the World: A Century of Emigration,* edited by Albert Hourani and Nadim Shehadi, 339–60. London: I.B.Tauris, 1992.

Nicollet, Albert. *Femmes d'Afrique noire en France.* Paris: L'Harmattan, 1992.

Nielsen, Jørgen S. "Muslims in Europe in the Late Twentieth Century." In *Christian Muslim Encounters,* edited by Yvonne Yazbeck Haddad and Wadi Zaidan Haddad. Gainesville: University Press of Florida, 1995.

———. *Muslims in Western Europe.* Edinburgh: Edinburgh University Press, 1995.

Nojaim, Gregory T. "Memorandum: Omnibus Terrorism Act of 1995." American Civil Liberties Union, 2 March 1995.

Northrup, David. *Indentured Labor in the Age of Imperialism, 1834–1922.* Cambridge: Cambridge University Press, 1995.

Nyang, Sulayman *Islam in the United States of America.* Chicago: ABC, 1999.

O'Brien, Peter. "Continuity and Change in Germany's Treatment of Non-Germans." *International Migration Review* 22, no. 3 (1988): 109–34.

Oriental and Occidental Northern and Southern Portrait Types of Midway Plaisance. St. Louis: N.D. Thompson Publishing Company, 1894.

Oschinsky, Lawrence. *Islam in Chicago: Being a Study of the Acculturatio of a Muslim-Palestinian Community in that City.* M.A. Thesis, University of Chicago, 1947.

Park, Kyeyong. *The Korean American Dream: Immigrants and Small Business in New York City.* Ithaca, N.Y.: Cornell University Press, 1997.

The People of Chicago: Who We are and Who We Have Been: Census Data on Foreign Stock and Race: 1837–1970. (Mother Tongue Addendum 1910–1970). Chicago: City of Chicago, Department of Development and Planning, 1976.

Poiret, Christian. *Familles africaines en France.* Paris: CIEMI/L'Harmattan, 1996.

Portes, Alejandro and Ruben G. Rimbaut. *Immigrant America: A Portrait.* Berkeley: University of California, 1996.

Poston, Larry. *Islamic Da'wah in the West. Muslim Missionary Activity and the Dynamics of Conversion to Islam.* New York: Oxford Press, 1992.

Power, Carla. "The New Islam." *Newsweek,* 16 March 1998, 34–37.

Quiminal, Catherine. "Les jeunes filles d'origine africaine en France: Parcours scolaires, accès au travail et destin social." *Migrations Etudes* 78 (December 1997): 1–12.

———. "Qui sont ces 'jeunes Africains noirs'?" *Migrants-formation* 91 (1992): 113–20.

Quiminal, Catherine. et al. "Mobilisation associative et dynamiques d'intégration des femmes d'Afrique subsaharienne en France." *Migrations Etudes* 61 (1995): 1–12.

Rahman, Qamer. "Muslim Women in New Zealand: Problems and Prospects." *al-Nahda* 16, nos. 1–2 (1996): 34–35.

Rawls, John. *Political Liberalism.* New York: Columbia University Press, 1993.

Reis, Joao Jose. "Brazil." In *The Oxford Encyclopedia of the Modern Islamic World,* edited by John L. Esposito, vol. 1: 231–32. New York: Oxford University Press, 1995.

Reneard, John, ed. *Windows on the House of Islam.* Berkeley: University of California Press, 1995.

Representatives, House of. *Omnibus Counter-Terrorism Act.* [103rd Congress (February 10) H.R. 896.] 1995.

Richards, Alan and John Waterbury. *A Political Economy of the Middle East: State Class, and Economic Development.* Boulder, Colo.: Westview, 1990.

Rigaldiès, François and Jacques Barou. "Modes de vie et intégration des enfants et adolescents issus de familles africaines sub-sahariennes." *Migrations Etudes,* 88 (June 1999): 1–8.

Rist, Ray C. *Guestworkers in Germany.* New York: Praeger Publishers, 1978.

Rives, Maurice and Robert Dietrich. *Héros méconnus 1914–1918 1939–1945.* Paris: Frères d'armes, 1993.

———. "L'apport de l'Afrique Noire et de Madagascar pendant la Seconde Guerre Mondiale." *Frères d'armes* 188 (1995): 18–39.

Roosens, Eugen E. *Creating Ethnicity. The Process of Ethnogenesis.* Frontiers of Anthropology 5, London: Sage Publications, 1989.

Rosenblatt, Gary. "Monitoring the Muslim Threat." *The Jewish Week,* 24 March 2000, 7.

Rude-Antoine, Edwige. "Trajectoires familiales, transformations des rôles et des statuts." In *Immigration et Intégration: l'état des savoirs,* edited by Philippe Dewitte, 196–204. Paris: Editions La Découverte, 1999.

Saeed, Abdullah. "Islamic Banking Moving Towards a Pragmatic Approach." *ISIM (International Institute for the Study of Islam) Newsletter* 3 (July 1999): 7

Said, Edward W. *Covering Islam: How the Media and the Experts Determine How We See the Rest of the World.* New York: Random House, 1996.

———. *Culture and Imperialism.* New York: Alfred A. Knopf, 1993.

———. W. *Orientalism.* New York: Pantheon Books, 1978.

Saint-Blancat, Chantal. "Hypothèses sur l'évolution de l'Islam transplanté en Europe." *Social Compass* 40, no. 2 (1993): 323–41.

———. *L'islam de la diaspora.* Paris: Bayard Éditions, 1997.

Schmidt, Garbi. *American Medina: A Study of the Sunni Muslim Immigrant Communities in Chicago.* Lund Series in the Study of Religion, vol. 8. Stockholm: Almqvist and Wiksell International, 1998.

Schmidt di Friedberg, Ottavia and Reynald Blion. "Du Sénégal à New York, quel avenir pour la confrérie mouride?" *Hommes & Migrations* 1224 (March–April 2000): 36–45.

Scott, Gertrude M. *Village Performances: Villages at the Chicago World's Colombian Exposition.* Ph. D. dissertation. New York University, 1991.

Sen, Faruk. "Turkish Communities in Western Europe." In *Turkey Between East and West: New Challenges for a Rising Regional Power,* edited by Vojtech Mastny and R. Craig Nation, 233–66. Boulder, Colo.: Westview, 1996.

Shafiq, Muhammad. *Growth of Islamic Thought in America: Focus on Isma'il Raji al Faruqi.* Brentwood, Md.: Amana Publications, 1994.

Shahid, W.A.R. and P.S. van Koningsveld, eds. *The Integration of Islam and Hinduism in Western Europe.* Kampen: Kok Pharos Publishing House, 1991.

Sharif, Malik A. "All Roads Lead to Washington, D.C., for 'Faith Communities Together.'" *Muslim Journal* 26, 1 (13 October 2000): 1–3.

Sheffer, Gabriel, ed. *Modern Diasporas in International Politics.* London: Croom Helm, 1986.

Shepard, William. "Australia and New Zealand," with Michael Humphrey. In *Islam Outside the Arab World,* edited by David Westerlund and Ingvar Svanberg, 278–94. Surrey: Curzon Press, 1999.

———. "Muslims in New Zealand." *The Journal of the Institute of Muslim Minority Affairs* 16, no. 2 (1996): 211–32.

Siddiqui, Dilnawaz A. "Evolution of Bernard Lewis' Style of Covering Islam and Muslims." Paper presented at "Islam in America" Conference of the Islamic Society of North America, 4 July 1998.

Smith, Houston. *The World's Religions.* San Francisco: Harper, 1991.

Smith, Tom W. "Taking America's Pulse II: A Survey of Intergroup Relations." Preliminary Report prepared for the National Conference on Community and Justice: Survey conducted by Princeton Survey Research Associates, May 2000.

Sonn, Tamara. "Islamic Studies in South Africa." *American Journal of Islamic Social Sciences* 11, no. 2 (1994): 273–81.

Soysal, Yasemin. "Workers in Europe: Interactions with the Host Society." In *Turkey and the West: Changing Political and Cultural Identities.* Edited by Metin Heper, Ayse Öncü, and Heinz Kramer, 219–36. London: Tauris, 1993.

Sprang, Philippe. "Addi Ba, résistant, noir et musulman." *L'Evènement du Jeudi* 12–18 (November 1992): 90–98.

Stein, Edith M. *Some Near Eastern Immigrant Groups in Chicago.* M.A. Thesis. University of Chicago, 1922.

Stevens, Christine. "Afghan Camel Drivers: Founders of Islam in Australia." In *An Australian Pilgrimage: Muslims in Australia from the Seventeenth Century to the Present,* edited by Mary Lucille Jones, 50–62. Melbourne: Victoria Press, 1993.

———. *Tin Mosques and Ghantowns: A History of Afghan Camel Drivers in Australia.* Melbourne: OUP, 1989.

Stolcke, V. "Talking Culture, New Boundaries, New Rhetorics of Exclusion in Europe." *Current Anthropology* 36 (1995): 1–24.

Al-Tahrir, Abdul-Jadil. *The Arab Community in the Chicago Area: A Comparative Study of the Christian-Syrians and the Muslim-Palestinians.* Ph.D. Dissertation. University of Chicago, 1952.

Timera, Mahamet. "Identité, langue et religion dans l'immigration soninké en France." *Journal des anthropologues* 59 (Winter 1995): 73–76.

———. "Les jeunes issus de l'immigration soninké face aux identités familiales et communautaires." *Migrants-formation* 91 (December 1992): 90–112.

Todd, Emmanuel. *Le destin des immigrés: Assimilation et ségrégation dans les démocraties occidentales.* Paris: Seuil, 1994.

Tribalat, Michèle. *Faire France: une enquête sur les immigrés et leurs enfants.* Paris: Editions La Découverte, 1995.

Turkish Industrialists' and Businessmen's Association. *Perspectives on Democratisation in Turkey.* Istanbul, 1997.

Turner, Bryan S. *Orientalism, Postmodernism, and Globalism.* London: Routledge, 1994.

Turner, Richard B. *Islam in the African-American Experience.* Indianapolis: Indiana University Press, 1997.

Vassenden, Kåre. *Innvandrere i Norge. Hvem er de, hva gjør de og hvordan lever de?* Statistical Analyses 20. Oslo: Statistics Norway, 1997.

van der Veer, Peter, ed. *Nation and Migration. The Politics of Space in the South Asian Diaspora.* Philadelphia: University of Pennsylvania Press, 1995.

Vertovec, Steven and Alisdair Rogers, eds. *Muslim European Youth: Reproducing Ethnicity, Religion, Culture.* Aldershot: Ashgate, 1998.

Vogelaar, Harold and Asad Husain. "Activities of the Immigrant Muslim Communities in Chicago." In *Muslim Communities in North America,* edited by Yvonne Yazbeck Haddad and Jane Idleman Smith, 231–58. Albany: State Univeristy of New York Press, 1994.

Vogt, Kari. *Kommet for å bli. (Came to stay.)* Oslo: J. W. Cappelens forlag A.S., 1995.

Waardenburg, Jacques. "The Institutionalization of Islam in the Netherlands, 1961–1986." In *The New Islamic Presence in Western Europe,* edited by T. Gerholm and Y.G. Lithman, 8–31. London: Mansell, 1988.

Wadud-Muhsin, Amina. *Qur'an and Woman.* Kuala Lumpur: Fajar Bakti, 1992.

Werbner, Phina. *The Migration Process. Capital, Gifts and Offerings among British Pakistanis.* New York: Berg, 1990.

Westerlund, David and Eva Evers Rosander, eds. *African Islam and Islam in Malaysian Islam.* Vancouver: University of British Columbia Press, 1984.

Williams, Charles F. "FBI Overstepped Consent Decree, ACLU Charges." *Chicago Daily Law Bulletin.* 14 June 1994. Lexis-Nexis Database.

Williams, Patricia J. *The Alchemy of Race and Rights: Diary of a Law Professor.* Cambridge: Harvard University Press, 1991.

Wilson, William Julius. *The Declining Significance of Race.* Chicago: University of Chicago Press, 1980.

Yapp, M.E. "Europe in the Turkish Mirror," *Past and Present* (November 1992): 134–55.

Yelvington, Kevin A. "Introduction: Trinidad Ethnicity. " In *Trinidad Ethnicity,* edited by Kevin A. Yelvington, 1–32. Knoxville: University of Tennessee Press, 1993.

Younis, Adele L. *The Coming of the Arabic-Speaking People of the United States.* New York: Center for Migration Studies, 1995.

Zaleski, Jeff. *The Soul of Cyberspace: How New technology is Changing Our Lives.* New York: Harper Collins, 1997.

Index

About the Contributors

Kenneth K. Ayouby is adjunct lecturer in Arabic studies at the University of Michigan-Dearborn. Mr. Ayouby's areas of interest are in cross-cultural communication, Arabic pedagogy, second language/culture acquisition and Arab American studies. He received his M.A. in Near Eastern language and culture from Wayne State University in Detroit, Michigan, and is a doctoral degree candidate in education and cultural studies. Mr. Ayouby is the lead student services liaison and hearing officer in the Dearborn schools' central administration.

Robert M. Dannin is adjunct professor of metropolitan studies at New York University. He received his Ph.D. in anthropology and linguistics in 1981 from the *École des hautes études en sciences sociales* (Paris). In 1988 he began to study the ethnohistory of African American Muslims, conducting fieldwork with photographer, Jolie Stahl, in dozens of indigenous Muslim communities in North America and West Africa. He has written and lectured extensively on the development of Islam in the U.S. prison system. His articles and Ms. Stahl's photos have appeared in many newspapers, journals, and edited collections. He is the author of *Black Pilgrimage to Islam*, Oxford University Press, forthcoming in 2002.

Gary David is an assistant professor of sociology at Bentley College (Waltham, Mass.). A native of Detroit, he has done research on its Arab American community, ethnic organizations, ethnic identity, and immigrant entrepreneurship. He has published papers on Arab convenience store owners in Detroit, Arab immigrant work experiences, and has presented on intercultural communication, third-generation ethnic identity, and Arab American studies. He is engaged in research on the nature of intercultural communication and information technology in global decision making and collaboration, especially as it pertains to the Middle East.

Sylviane A. Diouf is a research associate at Rutgers University. She is the author of *Servants of Allah: African Muslims Enslaved in the Americas* (1998), a *Choice* Outstanding Academic Title 1999. She has also published numerous articles and chapters on African Muslims during slavery, contemporary West Africans in the North, race relations, and migration issues. She is the author of five history books for young readers, and is currently working on African strategies against the slave trade.

Khalid Fattah Griggs is a graduate of Howard University. He is a former member of the Islamic Party in North America and the former editor-in-chief of *The Message*, published by the Islamic Circle of North America. He is the imam of the Community Mosque of Winston-Salem, North Carolina, serves as a member of National Shura of MANA (Muslim Alliance of North America), and as the director of Re-Entry Academy (Winston-Salem/Forsyth County Schools). He is also a co-convenor Black Leadership Roundtable of W-S/Forsyth Co.

Yvonne Yazbeck Haddad is professor of history of Islam and Christian-Muslim Relations at the Center for Muslim-Christian Understanding, Edmund B. Walsh School of Foreign Service at Georgetown University. She is past president of the Middle East Studies Association and a former editor of *Muslim World*. Her published works include *Contemporary Islam and the Challenge of History; Islam, Gender and Social Change; Islamic Values in the United States* (with A. Lummis); *The Contemporary Islamic Revival* (with J. Voll and J. Esposito); *The Islamic Understanding of Death and Resurrection* (with J. Smith); *The Muslims of America; Mission to America* (with J. Smith); *Muslim Communities in North America* (with J. Smith); and *Christian-Muslim Encounters* (with W. Haddad). She is an associate editor of the *Oxford Encyclopedia of the Modern Islamic World*.

James Helicke completed his undergraduate studies at Georgetown University, Washington, D.C., and holds an M.A. in international relations from Bilkent University, Ankara, Turkey. His academic interests include interreligious relations and secularism. He is currently conducting research on Christian missionaries and civil society in modern Turkey.

Anthony H. Johns is a graduate of the School of Oriental and African Studies of the University of London. He taught Arabic and Islamic Studies at the Faculty of Asian Studies at the Australian National University (ANU). Currently, he is Visiting Fellow in the Division of Pacific and Asian History of the Research School of Asian and Pacific Studies at the ANU. He has published a number of major papers and chapters in books on the Qur'an and Qur'anic exegesis, and on the vernacularization of the basic texts of Islam in Malay and Javanese in Indonesia. He has written papers and given lectures designed to contribute to Muslim-Christian understanding.

Abdul Hamid Lotfi is professor of American civilization and culture at Mohammed V University in Rabat, Morocco. His scholarly interests include Islam in America and traditional Islamic education. He has published a number of articles on both topics in Moroccan and American scholarly publications. He is currently finishing a book manuscript, *Muslims on the Block: Five Centuries of Islam in America*.

Kathleen Moore is associate professor of political science at the University of Connecticut. She is author of *Al-Mughtaribun: American Law and the Transformation of Muslim Life in the United States*, and is currently studying the intersection of the processes of globalization with local practices of Islamic legal interpretation in British and American settings. She has published articles on topics ranging from questions of legal orientalism in American courts, to the legal mobilization of Muslim advocacy groups to defend the right of women to wear Islamic headscarves in the workplace, to British Muslims' rights-conscious demands on legal structures after the Rushdie Affair.

Saphinaz-Amal Naguib is professor of Culture History/Culture Analysis at the University of Oslo, Faculty of Arts. Her main fields of research are Ancient Egyptian religion and Coptic and Copto-Arabic hagiographies, with special focus on the role of the clergy, the concept of the person, gender, iconography, cultural contacts, and religious memory. Her other research interests include, Islamic iconography, museology, and Mediterranean studies. She is currently engaged in an interdisciplinary project on international migration and ethnic relations. Her recent publications include two books: *Le clergé féminin d'Amon thébain à la 21e dynastie* and *Miroirs du Passé*. She is also the author of the forthcoming volume: *Mosques in Norway. The Creation and Iconography of Sacred Space.*

Abdullah Saeed is head of the Arabic Islamic Studies program at the University of Melbourne. He has a B.A. in Arabic and Islamic Studies from Saudi Arabia, a Ph.D. in Islamic Studies and a Masters degree in Applied Linguistics, both from the University of Melbourne. His research interests include: modern Islamic thought, Islamic hermeneutics, and Arabic language teaching methods.

Agha Saeed is the Pakistani-American chairman of the American Muslim Alliance and professor of political science and speech communication at California State University, Hayward. His publications include the forthcoming book, *Pakistan in Its Own Mirror: Elite Autobiographies and National Consciousness.*

Garbi Schmidt holds a Ph.D. in Islamic studies from the University of Lund, Sweden. Her dissertational work was on the Muslim community in Chicago. She now works as a researcher in the ethnic minorities program at the Danish National Institute of Social Research, Denmark. Her current research project deals with Muslim youth activism in Denmark, Sweden and the United States.

William Shepard is associate professor of religious studies, retired, at the University of Canterbury in Christchurch, New Zealand, where he taught from 1978 to 1999. He received his Ph.D. in the Comparative Study of Religion from Harvard University in 1973 and taught at Cornell College in Mount Vernon, Iowa, from 1971 to 1978. He has written several articles on Muslims in New Zealand. His main area of research interest is modern Islamic thought, in which area he has published a number of articles and two books, *The Faith of a Modern Muslim Intellectual: The Religious Aspects and Implications of the Writings of Ahmad Amin,* (1982) and *Sayyid Qutb and Islamic Activism: A translation and critical analysis of 'Social Justice in Islam'* (1996).

Jane I. Smith is professor of Islamic Studies and co-director of the Macdonald Center for Christian-Muslim Relations at Hartford Seminary. She has done extensive work on Muslim communities in America, Christian theology in relation to Islam, historical relations between Christians and Muslims, Islamic conceptions of death and afterlife, and the role and status of women in Islam. She also is co-editor of *The Muslim World*, editor of the *Encyclopedia of Women in Islamic Cultures*, convener of the North American Regional Research Team for the Pew Program on Christian Theological Education in Muslim Contexts, and associate editor of the *Encyclopedia of Women and Religion in North America*. Her publications include: *Islam in America*; *Muslim Communities in North America* (with Yvonne Haddad); *Mission to America: Five Islamic Sectarian Communities in the United States* (with Yvonne Haddad).

Tamara Sonn is the William R. Kenan Distinguished Professor of Humanities in the Department of Religion at the College of William and Mary. Her books include *Interpreting Islam: Bandali Jawzi's Islamic Intellectual History*; *Islam and the Question of Minorities*; *Comparing Religions through Law: Judaism and Islam*; and *Between Qur'an and Crown: The Challenge of Political Legitimacy in the Arab World*. She has contributed chapters and articles to numerous books and journals, as well as *The Oxford Encyclopedia of the Modern Islamic World*, the *Oxford Dictionary of Islam*, the *Encyclopedia of Women and Religion*, and *Colliers Encyclopedia*. Her areas of specialization are Islamic intellectual history and Islam in the contemporary world.

John O. Voll is professor of Islamic history and associate director of the Center for Muslim-Christian Understanding of Georgetown University. He received his doctorate from Harvard University and taught for thirty years at the University of New Hampshire. He is a past president of the Middle East Studies Association and the author of *Islam: Continuity and Change in the Modern World*, and, with John L. Esposito, of *Islam and Democracy* and *Makers of Contemporary Islam*.

Samina Yasmeen is a senior lecturer in international politics in the Department of Political Science, the University of Western Australia (UWA), Perth. She has conducted research on U.S. military relations with Pakistan at the Strategic and Defense Studies Centre, the Australian National University, Canberra, and has worked as executive director of the Indian Ocean Centre for Peace Studies at UWA and Curtin Universities (1995), as well as a research specialist in defense at the Legislative Research Service of the Australian Parliament (1985). She is a specialist in political and strategic developments in South Asia, and the role of Islam in world politics. She coordinated a detailed sociological survey of the settlement needs of Muslims living in Perth Metropolitan Area in 1993–1994 and recently directed a large Australian Research Council grant project on women and citizenship. She has published articles on strategic developments in South Asia, as well as the needs of Muslim immigrants in Australia.